Books by Morton M. Hunt

The Natural History of Love

*Her Infinite Variety: The American Woman
as Lover, Mate and Rival*

Mental Hospital

The Talking Cure
(with Rena Corman and Louis R. Ormont)

*The Thinking Animal: A Report on the
Rational and Emotional Life of Modern Man*

The Thinking Animal

*A Report on the Rational and
Emotional Life of Modern Man*

The Thinking Animal

A Report on the Rational and Emotional Life of Modern Man

MORTON M. HUNT

LITTLE, BROWN AND COMPANY · BOSTON · TORONTO

ACKNOWLEDGMENTS

All the articles in this book appeared originally in leading American
periodicals, though many of them did so in somewhat shorter form than
I would have wished possible. Not being governed here by space limitations as stringent as those which affect magazines, I have chosen in a
number of cases to publish my manuscripts in their complete form. I am
more than grateful to the magazine publishers involved, every one of
whom unhesitatingly granted me permission to use either the previously
published or the longer form, according to my own wishes, and to retitle
the articles if I chose. I am delighted to publicly thank them for permission to reprint the following copyrighted material (in this listing I use
article titles as they appear in this book rather than in the magazines):

The Curtis Publishing Company, "The Killers Who Never Go to
Jail," Copyright 1954 by The Curtis Publishing Company; "Dr.
Kallmann's Seven Thousand Twins," Copyright 1954 by The
Curtis Publishing Company; "The Truant Officer Learns to Smile,"
Copyright © 1956 by The Curtis Publishing Company; "The De-
cline and Fall of Friendship," Copyright © 1962 by The Curtis
Publishing Company; "Our Tormented College Kids," Copyright ©
1963 by The Curtis Publishing Company; each of the articles ap-
peared originally in *The Saturday Evening Post*, the last appeared
in a somewhat different form than in this book.

Esquire, Inc., "Neurosis Factory," Copyright 1952 by Esquire, Inc., originally appeared in *Esquire*.

Harper & Row, Publishers, "The Wellesley Experiment," originally appeared in *Harper's Magazine*, July 1953.

The Hearst Corporation, "What Is a Husband? What Is a Wife?" Copyright © 1960 by The Hearst Corporation, originally appeared in *Good Housekeeping*. "Why They Fight About Money," Copyright © 1955 by The Hearst Corporation; "Our Manly Men," Copyright © 1959 by The Hearst Corporation; both articles appeared originally in slightly different form in *Cosmopolitan*.

Los Angeles State College of Applied Arts and Sciences, "New Bottles for New Wine," a speech delivered at the symposium "New Patterns in the Lives of Women," June 13, 1963, and reprinted in *Redbook* as "An Answer to Some Foolish Theories About Women."

McCall Corporation, "Why Husbands Are — or Are Not — Faithful," Copyright © 1957 by McCall Corporation; "Guilt Feelings — Our Most Confusing Emotions," Copyright © 1957 by McCall Corporation; "The Other Adults in Your Child's Life," Copyright © 1958 by McCall Corporation; "How Husbands Really Feel About Pregnancy," Copyright © 1959 by McCall Corporation; "An Answer to Some Foolish Theories About Women," Copyright © 1963 by McCall Corporation; "Major and Minor Emotional Problems: Treatment, Cost, and Cure," Copyright © 1963 by McCall Corporation; all of the articles appeared originally in *Redbook* virtually as they do in this book.

The New Yorker Magazine, Inc., "Five Who Broke Down" and "Revolution in the Mental Hospital" appeared originally as part of a series of two articles entitled "Pilgrim's Progress" in the September 30 and October 7, 1961, issues of *The New Yorker*; thereafter, Pyramid Publications, Inc. published this series from *The New Yorker* in expanded form as a book entitled MENTAL HOSPITAL in 1962.

The New York Times Company, "How the Analyst Stays Sane — Despite His Patients," Copyright © 1957 by The New York Times Company; "In Defense of Romantic Love," Copyright © 1959 by The New York Times Company; "Does Psychotherapy Really Work?" Copyright © 1962 by The New York Times Company; each of the articles appeared originally in *The New York Times Magazine* in slightly different form.

Pageant, "What Your Memory Reveals About You," Copyright © 1963 by *Pageant*, originally appeared in somewhat different form in *Pageant*.

Popular Medicine Publishing Company, Inc., "The Meaning of

Your Sense of Humor," Copyright © 1955 by Popular Medicine Publishing Company, Inc., originally appeared in *Popular Medicine*.

The Reader's Digest Association, Inc., "The Army Learns About First-Aid Psychiatry," Copyright © 1955 by The Reader's Digest Association, Inc.; "The Wisdom of Tears," Copyright © 1955 by The Reader's Digest Association, Inc.; "There's No Substitute for Parents," Copyright © 1956 by The Reader's Digest Association, Inc.; "Short-Circuits in the Brain and How to Repair Them," Copyright © 1957 by The Reader's Digest Association, Inc.; "How Do We Choose a Mate?" Copyright © 1959 by The Reader's Digest Association, Inc.; "Should You Keep Your Fears a Secret?" Copyright © 1960 by The Reader's Digest Association, Inc.; "Get Involved" Copyright © 1961 by The Reader's Digest Association, Inc.; "The Self-Healing Powers of the Mind," Copyright © 1964 by The Reader's Digest Association, Inc.; "The Limits of Intimacy," Copyright © 1964 by The Reader's Digest Association, Inc.; these articles appeared originally in somewhat different form in *The Reader's Digest*.

I also gratefully acknowledge permission given me by Rena Corman, a fellow writer, to reprint here two articles on which we collaborated, namely, "Does Psychotherapy Really Work?" and "Our Tormented College Kids."

Finally, I wish to acknowledge with thanks permission to reprint four lines from the song "I Whistle a Happy Tune," Copyright © 1951 by Richard Rodgers and Oscar Hammerstein II, by Williamson Music, Inc., New York, N.Y., owner of all publication and allied rights.

To my sister, Vivian

Man, with all his noble qualities . . .
his godlike intellect . . . still bears in
his bodily frame the indelible stamp
of his lowly origin.

CHARLES DARWIN

Author's Note

Now and again someone will ask me how, though I am not a trained psychologist, I came to write so frequently about psychology and psychiatry. It always reminds me of the question traditionally asked of the *demi-mondaine* by the young man, as he puts his clothes back on: "How did a nice girl like you ever get into this sort of thing?" Like her, I plead seduction, but of a different variety.

During World War II, I was a pilot, flying Mosquito Mark XVI's from East Anglia on unarmed intelligence flights deep over hostile Europe. The strain of this type of duty, plus the trauma of two take-off crashes, brought me to the very brink of breakdown; luckily for me, V-E Day arrived before I collapsed, and with the immediate threat of death removed, I slowly but spontaneously got better. (I have described this in more detail in "The Self-Healing Powers of the Mind," page 136.)

Six years later, as a free-lance writer, I was assigned by a major magazine to report on the studies of neurotic-like traits induced in animals by Pavlovian techniques at the Behavior Farm, a special laboratory at Cornell University.* Part of the background reading to which I was directed by Dr. Howard Liddell, director of the Behavior Farm, was *Men Under Stress* (Blakiston, 1945), written by two Air Force psychiatrists, Dr. Roy Grinker and Dr. John Spiegel. It dealt with the reactions of flying personnel in World War II who suffered combat neuroses of one sort or another, and with the therapy administered to them. Like

* See "Neurosis Factory," page 266.

one who unexpectedly comes upon a mirror and is startled by the sight of his own unguarded face, I was astonished to find my own feelings on virtually every page of the book. In one case history after another, I could recognize and relive my own fears, panic, and appalling sense of guilt. For a while, as the dreadful feelings came out of hiding once again, I palpitated and sweated; gradually, however, I began to get flashes of insight into the personality traits that predispose a man to combat breakdown, and so began to understand why I had felt the way I did. *Tout comprendre, c'est tout pardonner:* the saying, wonderfully enough, is true even of one's self — the more I understood, the more I forgave myself, and was freed at last from long-buried guilt and self-detestation for having been afraid to die. It was as though fresh air and sunlight had been let into a room long shuttered, musty, and infected.

Such was my seduction, over a dozen years ago. Though I have continued to write on many subjects, psychology and psychiatry have been my particular interest ever since then. Every investigation I have been assigned to has been not only intriguing in itself, but an additional small step toward better understanding both of myself and of the people around me. To judge from the letters I have received over the years, the articles have had a similar function for many a reader, and this, of course, rather than any personal benefit to me, is their real justification.

But how good is it for anyone to understand the inner workings of the self, whether his own or that of another person? A strong tide of obscurantism is running these days which holds that modern man is ill-advised to analyze, investigate, and dissect his feelings. Irrationalists, mystics, some existentialists, and certain literati cry out, like Keats, that philosophy will clip an angel's wings and unweave the rainbow. They seem to fear that the scientific study of man's mind and heart will make him incapable of feeling strong emotions, or will rob those emotions of their beauty, or will substitute self-consciousness and excuse-making for commitment and conscience.

Keats notwithstanding, though, you cannot spoil the rainbow by studying the physics of refraction unless you are a dull fellow to begin with; you can only become better capable of handling light to suit your own fancy, and will enjoy rainbows as much as ever, though in a different and perhaps even richer way. Men once feared to understand the workings of the solar system, lest it destroy their image of God and mankind; yet understanding came anyhow, and with it a new conception of the universe that liberated man even while humbling him — a conception, moreover, which allowed him to see beauties in the heavens and their movement which he had never seen before. Similarly, men have variously feared to learn about evolution, genetics, and atomic structure; each time, however, they have risen to larger conceptions of reality on the wreckage of their simplistic thoughts. And it will be likewise, I think, with the science of human psychology.

One must admit, however, that enlarged understandings do not bring unmixed good to man; all have their costs. Copernicus, Darwin, and Einstein all made the universe less reassuring in some ways, contributing to the dissolution first of the medieval synthesis and then of the Victorian order. But through the more complex and demanding view of reality that men have gradually accepted, they have been enabled to move about the world, oberve its phenomena, and shape it to their hands in a way they never could have while they were Aristotelian, scholastic, or primitive in their thinking. Man is not a worm, but a thinking animal, and his salvation is not to draw an arbitrary line and deny himself knowledge that lies beyond it, but to seek knowledge without limit, and to integrate it into his actions in time to save himself from destruction. It is not folly to look within ourselves, but the only road to the salvation of modern man and his social order; Icarus fell into the sea not because he dared to fly so high, but because his technology was defective.

As we become more familiar with the workings of our own personalities, we shall not become less capable of loving, but wiser in recognizing when we love ill and when well, and thus able to act so as to love better. We shall not lose all morality or sense of commitment, but gain new morals and commitments to replace those that were unsoundly built upon unconscious fears and guilt. We shall not destroy our emotions, but learn to enhance the healthful ones and to control the harmful ones. We shall not wreck the family and society, but find ways to rebuild them so that they may survive in an age of technology.

It is out of this stubborn optimism concerning the value of human rationality that I have enjoyed learning about, and communicating, a number of the recent trips made into the dark jungle of the heart and mind by explorers in psychology and psychiatry. Though this book is not an all-inclusive or encyclopedic guide to the subject, it will give the reader, I trust, some idea of the lay of the land, and some feeling for the topography of the human personality, including his own. If he gains even a tiny fraction as much from reading these articles as I have from writing them, I will feel both gratified and justified for having republished them in book form.*

* References to time in the articles (e.g., "last year"), and to the locations or academic connections of persons, have not been changed. But where it is important, I have added notes after certain articles to bring them up to date in important respects.

Foreword

by ROBERT H. FELIX, M.D.
Director, National Institute of Mental Health

IN THE FIELD of psychiatry today more and more physicians feel that the public needs a better understanding of what they, as practitioners and theoreticians, are doing and thinking.

With this I concur wholeheartedly, but how best is knowledge of the efforts of specialists such as psychiatrists and psychologists to be brought to the public? Specialists themselves are rarely popularizers of their own endeavors; the nature of their calling is such that they could not be expected to be skilled in the field of popular communications, and they cannot possess the perspectives of the outsider.

New ideas — and this is particularly true concerning matters of the mind — often are greeted with skepticism and criticism, but eventually, if those ideas are sound, they are digested and absorbed into the body of culture and of common knowledge. For example, Freud's theory of the nature of neuroses, which has helped bring about greater understanding of and freedom for the emotionally disturbed, has now been widely accepted, despite the furor and alarm raised by his early formulations.

The need for transmitting this type of information to the public in an understandable form is one reason that knowledgeable lay writers, acting as interpreters, explainers and teachers, have become so important. Without them, the gap between scientists and the general public would tend to widen. "Popularization" is not — or should not be — a pejorative term. Rather, it should signify a species of education without which specialists would be cut off from much of the broad-based understanding, sympathy and support their work needs.

The articles in this book, which represent Morton Hunt's work in popularizing various aspects of psychiatry and psychology over the past dozen years, are excellent examples of what I mean. Mr. Hunt, one of the leading interpreters of psychiatry to the public today, has taken many of the most important aspects of human psychology and made them understandable, intriguing and helpful to persons who have no previous knowledge of the subject.

But aside from personal benefits to the reader, articles such as those in this book have a larger and more important social value. They have helped provide the acceptance our science is now receiving from the American people. In hundreds of communities, mental health centers and psychiatric services are being used more widely than ever before. Growing outpatient services and the hiring of former mental hospital patients testify to the gradual but increasing assimilation and acceptance of mental health knowledge.

And, of course, one of the most significant indications of the value of public education is the fact that the program of community mental health centers proposed by the late President Kennedy has been so rapidly accepted by the American people. This impressive program, only now getting fully under way, owes much to the work of popularizers like Morton Hunt who have helped create an understanding of its value and support for it — without which it could not have come into existence.

Contents

I

The Normal — and Wonderful — Mind of Man

Laughter and Tears

The Meaning of Your Sense of Humor

WHAT ARE your six favorite jokes? Stop for a moment and recall the half-dozen jokes that have seemed funniest to you, and if you feel in an experimental mood, jot them down, or at least jot down the gag lines of each. If you make those notes before you go any further, and if the conclusions to be drawn from the current research projects of several psychologists and psychiatrists are correct, you may be privileged to peek momentarily into a dark and quite mysterious place — your own unconscious.

For humor, the modern mental scientists believe, is not at all what it seems. Far from being a trivial and shallow human activity, it is a most profound one. It isn't superficial, unimportant, and easy to understand; instead it is the result of forces that stir deep within us, and often expresses powerful hidden hates and fears. The funniest jokes amuse us the most for reasons we are not consciously aware of.

All this was originally the guess of the good Dr. Sigmund Freud, some years ago. On the basis of his pioneer experiences in psychoanalysis, Freud decided that humor was one of several ways in which we get momentary release for certain forbidden wishes or needs — wishes or needs we may not even know of, because we have managed to "forget" them or to shove them down into the unconscious. When you laugh at a bit of pie-in-the-face comedy, you never ask yourself why it is funny; but that part of you which was forbidden to make a sloppy mess and throw things at people when you were a child, and which would still enjoy going out and making a mess somewhere, gets a brief but delightful fulfillment.

In a way, it is comparable to the "letting off steam" process a man experiences when he has had a hard time with his boss all day and goes home to his cellar to beat the punching bag around for a while. With every punch, he unconsciously bloodies the boss's nose, and feels much better for it. In somewhat the same fashion, according to psychiatric theory, humor serves as a healthful and socially acceptable release for desires which are not, in themselves, socially acceptable at all.

Thousands of psychiatrists and clinical psychologists have found that their everyday work with patients confirms the Freudian idea about humor. And in just the past few years, two different groups — one composed of several psychologists formerly at Duke, and another composed of psychiatrists connected with Yale University — have finally perfected two quite different "sense of humor" tests. Neither test finds out whether you have a "good sense of humor," but both do reveal what it means about you when you find certain jokes funny and others quite unfunny. The humor test, says psychologist Dr. Raymond B. Cattell, now of the University of Illinois, "assays personality without the subject's being aware of what is revealed." And psychiatrist Dr. Frederick Redlich of Yale says, "We may depend upon what a person laughs at and how he laughs for significantly revealing clues about him."

Dr. Cattell's test uses written jokes, which the test-taker reads and scores as "funny" or "dull"; the personality clues are revealed by an intricate scoring process. The test itself is published and available to professional psychologists through the Institute for Personality and Ability Testing, of Champaign, Illinois, and hundreds of clinicians and researchers have been using it in recent years in their everyday work.

Dr. Redlich's test, in contrast, consists of a batch of cartoons which the test-taker looks at. A psychiatrist observes his responses and later discusses the cartoons with him in detail. The job of evaluating this kind of test is complex and takes much technical skill, but Dr. Redlich and several colleagues have been using it at the Yale Medical School and West Haven Veterans Administration Hospital since 1950, and find it has helped greatly in the diagnosis and treatment of several hundred mentally and emotionally ill patients.

Although the giving and the scoring of each test is quite complicated, the basic principles aren't too hard to explain. Let's look at a couple of extreme examples from the studies made by Dr. Redlich and his co-workers. A Charles Addams cartoon from *The New Yorker* shows a man talking on the phone and doodling; he has casually drawn a dagger, a noose, an ax, a coffin and a gun. His wife is calling to him through the doorway, "Is that mother, dear?"

To most of us, that joke is worth a chuckle. To a few people (as Dr. Redlich found when he tested this cartoon on both normal and mentally ill patients), it is outrageously funny, and produces howls of laughter. To some, however, it isn't funny at all; it's mean, disgusting and excessive. And to a few, the cartoon is completely obscure. They just don't get it.

Afterwards, Dr. Redlich went on to perform classical psychiatric studies of the tested people, and found that those who laughed most loudly had a lot of anger and resentment towards a mother or mother-in-law, but kept it under control most of the time. Some others with similar feelings were horribly ashamed of feeling that way; their upbringing made them feel that any hatred or resentment towards a mother-like person is utterly sinful, and hence they buried that hate in the deepest parts of their souls. Seeing the Addams cartoon did not release an old tension for them; instead, it stirred up the complex mixture of repressed hate-plus-guilt. Such people either thought the joke disgusting or completely failed to see the point of it.

The fundamental reason a person fails to "get" a joke (excluding cases of simple unfamiliarity with words or facts used in it), Dr. Redlich says, is due to "the press of inner needs which forces the individual to deny or distort what he sees." Most of us have occasionally resented the powers and attitudes of a mother or mother-in-law, but we have mastered these feelings without any frightening sensations of guilt; we do see the point of the cartoon, and we do enjoy it — but not excessively.

Another of Addams' quietly ghoulish cartoons shows a calm-looking fellow happily raking leaves around his wife, who is tied to a tree, as though he were about to burn her at the stake. Again, it's worth a chuckle — maybe more so to men than to women, since after all it's men who have to put up with women, and who occasionally long to do them in. Consider, though, the reaction of one male patient of Redlich's, who thoroughly detested and despised women, suffered the most painful guilt feelings about it, and had therefore banished his emotions about women from his conscious mind. When he saw the cartoon, he studied it closely and said: "I don't see any particular point to this cartoon. He is raking leaves and she is tied to a tree. He probably just wanted to get her out of the way while he was raking the leaves. I can't see any-thing particularly funny about it." The psychiatrist asked if perhaps the man was planning to burn his wife at the stake. The patient was annoyed and very emphatic. "Oh no!" he almost shouted. "Definitely *not!*"

A cartoon by Peter Arno shows a naked woman being examined by a doctor; the nipples of her breasts point sharply inwards, and the per-plexed doctor is saying, "Have you tried going to an oculist?" Dr. Jacob Levine, one of Redlich's collaborators, explains: "This cartoon seemed to us to be making fun of — that is, *being hostile towards* — the body of the woman. That's a normal enough way for the average man to feel, oc-casionally, towards self-admiring womanhood. But the cartoon also ought to bother a great many women, since most of them aren't ever too sure of the attractiveness or appeal of their own bodies, and they should emotionally recognize this as an attack." And in tests, he adds, the re-search team did actually find that most men laughed at the cartoon, while most women frowned at it and failed to find it funny.

The same principles hold true even in areas quite remote from the sex-charged subjects of these cartoons, according to studies conducted by Dr. Cattell, and a colleague, Dr. Lester Luborsky. They winnowed out one hundred jokes from an immense number gathered from books, TV, radio, and other sources, and gave them to one hundred Duke stu-dents who served as guinea pigs. Later, re-examining those students by known and validated personality testing methods, they found that the enjoyment of various clearly defined types of jokes could be connected with personality traits such as playfulness, self-composure, general hos-tility, resignation, impudence, realism, and so on.

Here's a sample from their test: "How do you get your kid sister to find so many fishing worms for you?" asked Bobby. "Oh, it's easy," said Tommy. "Out of every ten she digs up, I let her have one to eat."

I admit it isn't a screamer, but partly that's because few jokes seem funniest in printed form. Let this one be told by some skilled comedian like Bob Hope or Red Buttons, with the best timing and mimicry, and it would get a good laugh — yet as every comedian knows, the material has to be intrinsically funny before he can do anything with it.

And this one *is* intrinsically amusing. Why? One major reason, says Dr. Luborsky, is that "every one of us was a messy child at one time, who not only played with dirt but put the wrong things in his mouth. Parents forbade this, and taught us that such actions are 'wrong.' As we grew up, and conscience replaced the role of the parents, we learned to avoid such actions because they're 'wrong' and are disapproved of. But let a joke release that old suppressed urge — and we laugh. Unless, of course, cleanliness and squeamishness have become excessively painful emotional problems to us — then the joke may seem unfunny or disgusting."

A fundamental need in most people is to feel superior to others, to prove one's greater strength, or intelligence, or beauty, or maybe just virtue. We are all more or less aggressive towards others, and those of us who are the most unsure of themselves may be the most aggressive. In his book *The Origins of Wit and Humor*, Professor Albert Rapp of the University of Tennessee says that this is probably why a pun is usually a painful kind of joke to the hearer, though not to the punster. The pun thinly conceals an attack by punster upon listener. The listener feels — and rightly so — that he has been taken advantage of and caught with his guard down. A sudden trick has been played upon him, and though he may be amused by the cleverness of the pun, he may also be irritated by having been tricked. But the punster loves it; he feels superior, he has won the game.

If you don't like this theory, watch what happens. Pun: Do you know why they call them the Dark Ages? Because there were so many knights. You groan. But let's take the onus off yourself as the punned-upon, and put it on someone else. For instance: Edgar Bergen: "Mortimer, you know why they called them the Dark Ages, don't you?" Mortimer

Snerd: "Gawsh — I dunno — I guess on account of there was so many knights." That doesn't make it exactly immortal, but it does improve it a bit, because a well-known dolt made the pun, presumably out of ignorance, and Bergen took the jab, not you.

There may even be confirmation of this explanation of punning in the fact that in the old burlesque routines, where comics ask each other one punning conundrum after another, they also swat each other with slap-boards and inflated bags, kick each other in the pants, and take numerous pratfalls. Here is humor, both verbal and physical, of a simple aggressive sort. For the many people who have a thinly controlled desire to conquer or show their superiority to others, such humor gives a definite vicarious satisfaction.

Some years ago an experimenter surveyed school children to see what kinds of jokes they enjoyed most. To eight-year-olds, the funniest things involved other people being pinched, frightened, knocked over, and so on. A simple need was responded to simply by these children. But in each older age group from there on up, children enjoyed more and more "humane" kinds of humor, and laughed less at simple physical discomfort. Society was putting the pressure on them to become more civilized, and gradually their delight in straightforward aggressive humor was being repressed as naughty and nasty.

Yet just the other night I watched Lucille Ball on TV getting plastered over the head and face by ice cream, honey, coffee, and custard pie *seriatim,* while an adult audience shrieked with naive pleasure. Partly, this kind of thing fulfills the old desire to be messy of which I spoke earlier; but since all these substances were being poured or flung upon a tearful and screaming Miss Ball, I suspect the loudest laughers in the audience were releasing a basic, but repressed, urge to personally heave things at other people. (The corollary would be that people who find slapstick unfunny are either too neurotic to be able to blow off their aggressions in laughter, or so free of any need to feel superior that they experience no particular relief from this kind of humor.)

Nor is this mere guesswork. In their cross-checking experiments, psychologists Cattell and Luborsky proved that the people who enjoy reading simple uncomplicated puns are, in general, unaggressive, happy-go-lucky, and easygoing. Such people are too quietly certain of themselves to be bothered or made to feel inferior when a verbal trick is played upon them. The principle becomes still clearer in the case of punning riddles. Questioner: "I'm a little animal with lots of fur — and a great big heart. What am I?" The listener thinks, then gives up. "Okay — I'm a skunk." "A skunk? Where's the great big heart come in?" "Because I'd give you my last scent!" Ouch. Some people playfully swing at the guy who tells one like that — for deep inside they recognize that he has defeated them in an unfair contest: he loaded the dice by making a riddle which, due to the pun in it, was practically unguessable.

Yet many people enjoy such conundrums because they like getting the point of the play on words, and thus in a sense defeat or equal the joke-teller. They win a round and lose a round simultaneously. If they aren't personally insecure, the net result is pleasant; but if they hate to "have one put over on them," they groan and take that playful poke at the teller.

Another need that humor can fulfill is the drive or desire to get back at the people who have authority over us. Every child loves his parents, yet inevitably resents the rules they make him live by. Similarly, each of us admires or loves leading persons in the church, in school, in politics, and in business who partly run our lives, but at the same time resents those persons to some degree. A joke which momentarily humbles one of those commanding figures satisfies these thinly concealed dislikes that are all mixed up with our love or admiration of them.

Here's an example:

> A young priest asked an older one to listen in on the first confession he heard, to see if he was doing it right. The penitent was a pretty and very sexy young girl. Afterwards the young priest asked, "How did I do, Father? Was it all right?"
>
> "Very fine," said the older priest. "Very good indeed, except . . . well . . . to be frank, I think you ought to use a few more tsk, tsk's and a few less wow's."

In a perfectly harmless way, that enables the listener to find the young priest human and imperfect after all — a statement the listener might not make baldly and openly, but which he finds permissible in the form of humor.

But some jokes of this general type are far more savage and crude. Take this one, for instance, from the Cattell-Luborsky humor test:

PARSON: "Why don't you ever come to hear me preach?"
FRIEND: "I'd like to, but I make it a rule never to go to places of amusement on Sunday."

Some persons prove to take a consistent and strong delight in jokes of this type, which bluntly and unpleasantly tear down or deflate people of reputation such as ministers, college professors, senators, and psychiatrists. And that kind of sense of humor seems to belong to personalities in which there is either an excess of untamed hostility, or a great deal of shyness and social awkwardness. But to those who have no particular fear or envy of these possibly superior kinds of people, such jokes are not very amusing.

Nearly every boy alive is scolded, washed and spanked by his mother or some adult female, and hence has a certain amount of anti-female feeling wrapped up inside of his over-all love for mother. As he grows up, he is attracted to and eventually marries a girl of his own years, and transfers to her in altered form some of the old love — and some of the old resentments — he had for mother. Thus a certain amount of anti-feminism is, for most men, a normal and thinly repressed feeling. And that's why men love jokes that make the female out to be a bird-brain, a lousy driver, a nag and a vain thing. Women, too, see the point of these jokes, but they may not find them as amusing. The jokes don't fill the same inner needs.

During prohibition, liquor and drinking were forbidden activities. Professor Rapp points out that in those years, almost any reference to liquor promptly drew gales of laughter from an audience, while the words "dry," "wet," and "hootch" were automatic boffs. Came repeal: the funniness of all such jokes evaporated. Once again, the evidence indicates that humor offers a kind of symbolic striking back at outside forces.

In the last war, when Bob Hope was making his selfless rounds of the camps, he used to say to audiences of officer candidates in training: "You know what an officers' candidate school is — it's a concentration camp on our side." Today we still understand the joke, though few of

us find it funny enough to laugh at; but the officer candidates themselves — rigidly disciplined, full of gripes and unexpressed aggravations,
and fearful of their officers and their senior classmen — used to shout
and bellow in unabashed delight at the line.

A cartoon from *American Legion Magazine* shows a little girl saying
to her father, as he hangs up his hat, "If you didn't bring anything, why
did you come home?" Did you chuckle, and if so, why? Maybe, you
say, because that's just the way a little child is. But so what? A lot of
other things are the way a little child is, too, but we don't laugh at all
of them. Can it be that each of us, no matter how much he loves his
children, also resents and dislikes them from time to time for constantly
demanding all? That's an uncomfortable thought, one you wouldn't
often say or even admit to yourself. But the joke permits you to express
that feeling without hurting anyone.

Both groups of investigators have been intrigued by that kind of
humor which deals in sheer nonsense, absurdity, and impossibility. The
famous cartoon (again by Addams) showing a pair of ski tracks going
around a tree — one on each side — is a good example. So are the dear
old limericks of Edward Lear, with his Jumblies who go to sea in a
sieve, his Quangle Wangle in the Crumpetty Tree, and his Old Man
with a bird-infested beard. So, too, are most forms of pure word play
and double talk. Dr. Redlich feels that this humor of pure unalloyed
nonsense also fills a "need" — for it is enjoyed by those who would like
to go back, momentarily, to the childhood world where everything was
possible, where ski tracks could be wherever you wanted them to be,
where you were the center of the universe and obeyed no laws but your
own. On the other hand, people who don't get the point of such jokes
and cartoons tend, he finds, to have dangerously strong worries and in-
adequacies — people with, for instance, unresolved fears about their
own cleverness, or good looks, or ability to get along with others. They
are too concerned about the job of facing this world to be able lightly
to scoff at it all, or to enjoy the absurdity of denying the facts. You and
I might call them "too down-to-earth," but the psychiatrist sees them
as people with severe inner tensions.

Of all the basic drives which are subject to social repression, probably
none is stronger, yet more profoundly repressed than sex. Not alone our

actions and our conversation, but an immense amount of our private thoughts are subject to the censoring influences that have been brought to bear on us from childhood on. It is hardly any wonder, then, that the most explosive laughter comedians produce is generally the result of jokes which come perilously close to the border of the forbidden.

An innocent-looking cartoon in the *Saturday Evening Post* shows two Moslems standing at a street corner in some Near Eastern city, watching the heavily veiled and robed women passing by. With a leer, one man says to the other: "On a good windy day their veils blow up and you can see their mouths and chins."

If Professor Redlich's research is valid, there's more to such a gentle jest than mere amusement in the fact that a mouth and chin could be exciting and secret to anyone. For there's the unwritten implication that we, as readers of the cartoon, are thinking of the other things that might be seen in America on a windy day, but about which we don't speak in public. And of course, the kind of jokes which are told only after the third round of drinks, or in the locker room, get a lot closer to even more deeply tabooed thoughts and desires.

In any case, for the great majority of us humor is a blessed momentary relief from inner tensions we hardly know exist. The Greek historian Herodotus tells of an ancient king of Egypt, one Amasis, who used to work hard half the day, and then relax and swap jokes the other half. To critical counselors, he explained his habits by saying that if the archer did not unstring his bow after the battle, it would lose its snap, and it would be no good to him when he needed it again. Laughter unstrings the emotional bow, and permits it to keep its elasticity. That is why men have liked jokes ever since they began to talk, and will go on liking them as long as they continue to be born with impulses which have to be suppressed and repressed — and that, I suspect, will be rather a long time.

The Wisdom of Tears

"TEARS, IDLE TEARS, I know not what they mean," wrote Tennyson. If we thought about it, most of us would have to echo his sentiment. Although we take weeping for granted as a simple, unsubtle act, it is actually one of the most mysterious and little-understood areas of human behavior. As familiar as tears may be, most of us do not know what they mean — or how very much they *can* mean — to our happiness and well-being. Why should the human body react to sorrow by having mildly salty water gush from the eyes, overflowing the tear ducts and coursing down the cheeks? What conceivable good can there be in a mechanism that produces convulsive choking, absurd facial distortions, and makes us red of eye, sore of throat, stuffy of nose, and puffy of face? These effects seem like an extra burden of physical discomfort added onto our emotional distress, yet strangely enough they yield genuine relief from the agony of dry-eyed misery.

But even if one assumes we must undergo these indignities to ease our sadness, it seems all the more confounding that we do the very same things in times of great joy. The burial of a father and the wedding of a daughter call forth illogically identical physical reactions, and tears are even enjoyable in themselves to the many people who "love to have a good cry" over a sentimental novel or movie. In such situations, they seem puzzling, unreasonable, and inappropriate. Yet a significant lesson of contemporary psychology is that the most puzzling, unreasonable, and inappropriate things we do are those that stem from the most powerful but best-hidden needs and secrets of our own hearts. Such unaccountable tears can therefore be a means to self-revelation, personal wisdom, and deeper happiness.

Recently, a friend told me that his wife was leafing through their photo album and remembering their life nine years earlier when they were a poor young couple living in a tiny apartment, cooking dinner out of tin cans, and clinging to each other in the big city, full of fears, hopes, desires for a little success, and the wish to move on to better things. When he came into the living-room a little while later, he found her sitting there, the album on her lap, quietly and brokenheartedly crying for the lean and frightening days that were no more. He and she are happier and better off today in every way than they were then; yet she cried for those days all the same.

How strange, how illogical — and yet not illogical, after all. For behind her tears there lurked an important truth: she wept because a part of life and a part of youth were gone, and because no one lives as intensely and as warmly as he would, if he were only aware of the dreadful finality of the past, the pathetic shortness of our years. If you stopped for a moment to wonder how you might remember this day wistfully a decade from now, would you not live the day differently? Would you not be more tender to those you love, more amiable to those you pass on the street, more thirstily aware of the sights, the sounds, the passing shadows of the day? Are you not, instead, in such a rush to get on toward your future that you have forgotten how precious each day is in itself?

And so I suspect that my friend's wife was crying for the days and years — no matter that they were lean and anxious — in which they were in such a hurry to get on with life that they neglected to suck the full sweetness out of each blessed hour. And to realize this, it seems to me, is a very high form of wisdom. The unreasonable tears of nostalgia can teach each of us that truth.

So too with other kinds of tears. A cousin of mine recently began working as a volunteer in an old folks' home. One afternoon during her first week there, the aged people were given ice cream cones. A palsied old man in a wheel chair, shaking with his infirmities, dropped his ice cream on the floor; his smile of anticipation faded, and big soundless tears rolled down his cheeks. My cousin stared at him for a moment, and then fled to the anteroom, where she bawled like a baby. I asked her why, when she told me the story.

"Because he was so old," she said, "so pathetic — oh, you *know!*" But I think there was more to her tears, if she could only have found words for it. Man is a fragile thing, she might have said, and death hovers over him; let us have compassion for one another. But alas, most of the time we fear our own impulse towards sympathy, and clear our throats gruffly and laugh at what we call "sentimentality." Only when tears burst forth in spite of ourselves do we realize the universal need of all human beings to pity and sympathize with each other, and their pathetic failure to do so adequately most of the time.

An Army colonel I once knew was riding through southern Germany in a staff car shortly after V-E Day. Along the sides of the dusty road he saw long lines of ragged German soldiers who had just been released by our own forces, plodding homeward across the land with their packs on their shoulders and occasionally waving to sunburned peasant women and farmers in the fields. "I hated their guts," the colonel told me some years afterwards. "A few weeks earlier they had been shooting at us, and I knew that many of them were thorough Nazis who condoned all their leaders' war crimes. Yet suddenly I saw them there in the sunshine and the dust as human beings, hopefully hurrying back after long years of absence to the job of mating, rearing children, tilling the soil, running their businesses, living out their own joys and sorrows. And right there in my command car I found myself crying before I could help it." In one astonishing moment, he had glimpsed the universality of human desires and feelings, and the resultant tears had begun to wipe out in his own heart the bitterness of war.

Insights like this lie waiting for us behind the tears that mysteriously catch us by surprise at the unlikeliest times and in the unlikeliest places. What possible connection could there be, for instance, between freed German P.O.W.'s and a medieval cathedral? More than appears on the surface. Many a sensitive traveler has visited some great cathedral, famous in literature and painting, and in its echoing vaulted interior has found himself astonishingly moist-eyed and choked with unnamed emotion. Yet why should its majesty and rich detail call forth tears? Why not simply smiles of pleasure and appreciation?

The answer, I would venture to guess, lies in a dazzling vision of the kinship of all human beings, a momentary revelation of the labors, the hopes, and the achievements of unknown men who lived so long ago, but whom the traveler would like to have known and befriended. He looks at the incredibly detailed and artistic figures of the mighty carved façade, or gazes up at the soaring buttresses with their superbly ugly gargoyle heads glowering against the sky; and he thinks of the millions of careful blows of hammer upon chisel, the calloused and aching human hands that held the tools, the weary muscles and tired backs, the satisfied, proud faces of the craftsmen and the designers, all of them dead long ago, all gone centuries before he, the traveler, could ever know them, clasp their hands in fellowship, and smile into their eyes in unspoken appreciation. And so he weeps, because if man is often little and mean, he is also occasionally lofty and noble.

Like these tears of sympathy or identification, tears of joy can teach us much about our hidden selves. Tears of joy are no simple reflex of the lachrymal gland, no accidental secretion. They involve real weeping. The mother who has just watched her only daughter get married, the young wife who has just welcomed home her soldier-husband, can testify that the tears of joy are accompanied by all the physical accouterments of sorrow — the tight feeling in the throat, the heavy weight upon the chest, the deep unlocated sense of misery. Can this be joy? Can such weeping come from pure happiness?

Psychiatrists think not. In a recent study, Dr. Sandor Feldman, professor of psychiatry at the University of Rochester, concluded that no one ever weeps for unalloyed joy; such tears always tell of a hidden element of sadness. At the wedding, the bride is purely happy, even if nervous; she does not cry. But her mother, who is also happy, finds the future worrisome. Until this moment, the bride was her child, safe and protected; from now on she will face dangers and problems on her own. Her mother weeps for fear and for the sorrows that may come — and also, perhaps, because she, the mother, has lost part of her function in life now, and so has died a little. If the mother let her tears lead her to discovery of these inner feelings, she might more easily "let go" of her daughter and no longer try vainly to influence her; she might also more intelligently cast about for alternate interests in life that would help her be a happier and more fulfilled person.

The tears we experience — and seek — through literary tragedy are another matter altogether. Why should any of us pay money to experience anguish? Why should we willingly suffer and grieve for people we never knew — people who are, indeed, only make-believe? Yet a good cry has always seemed more precious than a good laugh, and tragic drama has always been more highly valued than comedy. One of the most astute analysts of the theater explained it by saying that tragedy produces an "alleviating discharge" of our unpleasant emotions, giving us "a kind of purgation and relief." In our daily lives we build up a reserve of unexpressed weeping over repressed sorrows and fears, but as members of an audience we find an acceptable way to release this accumulation in the name of someone else. The delight of the ensuing relief must be the reason for our paradoxical liking for something so painful. Though this explanation accords perfectly well with the grief theory of contemporary physiology and psychiatry, it is far from modern; it comes from wise old Aristotle, who thought it through some twenty-four hundred years ago.

In addition to crying at the bittersweet or the tragic, some people cry at the purely beautiful. Some years ago when Charles Laughton visited the University of North Carolina to do a reading, he went walking through the Chapel Hill flower gardens. Coming suddenly upon a bank of massed daffodils and narcissuses, he promptly burst into tears. Other people have likewise wept, or at least grown weepy, at the first sight of the Rocky Mountains, or a blue lake nestled in the hills, or the perfection of a Mozart quartet.

Once again, this reaction is not one of simple, unalloyed pleasure. Studies of the physiology of weeping show that it occurs neither during a state of complete tension of the sympathetic nervous system nor one of complete relaxation, but during the *transition* from the tense towards the pleasant. The principal reason beauty can bring forth tears may therefore lie within the nature of the one who so weeps and not within the beautiful object itself. He may be one who is more easily hurt than most of us, or more bottled up, or more tense. In the course of everyday living he is bound to gather many a minor wound and unexpressed sadness. Then the sudden sight of beauty brings pleasure, release, and the flooding forth of gentle emotions — and with the barriers down, there spill forth the accumulated tears of mingled joy and sadness. If this be a result of beauty, it can have little finer purpose.

This is no mere fanciful conceit. It rests upon facts about our own nervous structure and endocrine output which have recently come to light through medical research. Anger, fear, or the shock of sudden sorrow causes the adrenergic nerves (a part of the sympathetic nervous system) to send out messages gearing our bodies for "fight or flight." The digestion is shut down, the blood pressure is raised, the heart speeds up, the skin becomes cold. In an animal such a condition lasts a short while, and then the emergency is over. We human beings, however, often remain in a condition of anger or tension for weeks or even years, and this state makes the body tight, dry, and rigid — and the personality likewise. In people who are afraid to let themselves weep or pour forth their painful emotions, doctors find that the bottled-up tears — that is, the prolonged emergency state of the nervous system and the concomitant derangement of our digestive organs, our endocrine glands, and our very skins — can trigger off such ailments as asthma, arthritis, migraine headache, ulcerative colitis, urticaria, and many others.

Weeping, on the other hand, comes as part of the returning influence of the pleasure nerves — that other half of the sympathetic nervous system which takes over in times of peace, recuperation, and happiness. The pleasure nerves relax the body, return the vital juices and warmth to digestive and sex organs and skin, and reverse the conditions of alarm, shock, and anger. Tears do not, therefore, mark a breakdown or low point, but a return of warmth and hope and health.

Unfortunately, we twentieth-century Americans systematically deny ourselves the use of this built-in healing and protective device. We tolerate weeping in infants, but discourage it in toddlers and energetically inhibit it in older children. In grown men we consider it ridiculous and totally improper, and in women complacently view it as a sign of their weaker character — all this in spite of the abundant evidence that stifling the need to weep often makes us sicker and more wretched than we have to be. It is indeed a baffling case of human perversity.

We explain it by saying that weeping is not grownup, not the act of a strong personality. But history and anthropology testify against us, for many another people have known the value and dignity of unashamed weeping. The warlike ancient Greeks knew no qualms about it: Homer told how the mighty Achilles wailed openly and threw himself on the ground when his friend Patroclus was killed. King David was as manly a hero as there is in the Bible, yet he wept freely for

Absalom, and Jesus was not ashamed to weep for Lazarus. Ferocious Maori tribesmen cry in front of each other, and John Frémont and other American explorers found that even the most bloodthirsty Indian braves considered open sobbing a perfectly virile way to express regret and grief.

These and many other peoples have had a kind of folk wisdom modern Americans lack. They somehow sensed that tears can heal, but that dry sorrow corrodes the soul and body from within. "To weep," said Shakespeare's Richard, Duke of York, "is to make less the depth of grief."

All this is clearest in the case of bereavement. Here one can clearly see, today, that in weeping there is a fundamental wisdom of our bodies which our brains often try to deny. Dr. Erich Lindemann, psychiatrist-in-chief of the Massachusetts General Hospital and a pioneering investigator of human grief reactions, tells of a young nursing student who represents an extreme case. She tended her father, to whom she was deeply devoted, through the long months of his inoperable cancer, always fighting back the tears to maintain a cheerful face for his sake. When he died and she began to cry, the family pastor sternly forbade her to show any grief, so as to spare her mother's feelings and weak heart. "I froze up like a zombie," the girl said of this command. "I died right then."

Within a few hours she began suffering from intestinal distress, and after twelve days had a raging case of ulcerative colitis. In a modern hospital, doctors did everything for her known to medical science, but she lay in bed, dull and glazed of eye, her sorrow thrust so deeply into her unconscious that she could feel nothing. Her body, denied its native access to relief, was slowly corroded away from within by the disordered impulses of the adrenergic nerves. Day by day she withered away, apathetic, ulcer-ridden, unable to digest or absorb food; neither psychotherapy, penicillin, intravenous feeding nor an operation helped. On the thirtieth day in the hospital she died, a beautiful but shriveled girl of twenty-one, killed by an emotion she would not permit herself to express, destroyed by tears that would not flow.

Part of the treatment of persons who have not been able to recover from the loss of someone dear therefore lies in inducing them to do

what Dr. Lindemann calls "grief work." "This," he says, "is the necessary process by which a person extricates himself from bondage to the deceased and readjusts to his environment." The key step in grief work is weeping — actually permitting one's self to admit the horrible fact of sorrow — and often it produces a startling improvement in the patient.*
Many patients with complaints as dissimilar as a painful shoulder or recurrent nightmares have been dramatically relieved of them by the beginning of real weeping.

Although many animals have tears, true weeping is exclusively human. Scores of nature-fakers have written about the weeping of sad animals, and even the great Darwin spoke of tears streaming down the leathery cheeks of captured elephants. Almost all pet lovers, similarly, believe their animals capable of the tender and sorrowful act of weeping. But no modern zoologist will back them up. Even the apes do not weep, according to psychologist Robert Yerkes of Yale, who studied them intimately for many years.

For apparently, human beings — and only they — can send impulses to the tear glands over more than one set of nerves. In reflex tearing, the glands are set into activity by pain, or winking, or contortions of the face, operating through the fifth cranial nerve. Some human beings who have had the sensory root of this nerve cut by accident or in operations can no longer produce tears when grit or painful substances enter the eye — but they *can* still weep plentifully under the stimulus of emotion.

The howling of a newborn baby is not emotional crying, but chiefly a method of releasing excess energy. Economical Nature does not even provide the brand-new baby with tears; his glands are too immature to produce them. Within a couple of months, however, he is becoming aware enough of the world outside to react emotionally to it — and by that time his tear glands can, and do, function.

As the child grows older, he learns gradually that the world is often cruel, that cherished toys break, that loved parents can be unkind. Little by little, he discovers that weeping will relieve his feelings when he cannot bend the world to his own will, or when his emotions are simply too painful. And just as he is making this discovery, grownups begin telling him not to be a cry-baby, and to act like a man, not a sissy.

* The relation of weeping to recovery from grief is more fully exploded in "The Self-Healing Powers of the Mind," page 136.

Little girls are luckier. Our leftover double standard still permits them — and even full-grown females — to weep when they need to. Women thereby have a potent weapon in their body's defenses which is forbidden to men; it is a rare and lucky male in our world who is able to weep away his overwhelming feelings without a sense of disgrace and guilt. Perhaps this makes it less strange that, year in and year out, over three times as many men commit suicide as women. Tears might have saved some of them from themselves.

And thus there *is* a genuine wisdom in tears, based both in our chemistry and our psychology. And not just tears of grief or rage, for those of remembrance, of sympathy, of aesthetic pleasure, of the appreciation of grandeur, of poignant joy can likewise bring us health and understanding. For they all express deep-seated needs — the need to love and be loved, the need to cast out anger and hate, the need to wash away trouble and tension. In permitting ourselves to weep instead of manfully repressing the impulse, we help ourselves to health. And to wisdom — for in the state of physical release which tears bring, our thoughts can flow as freely as they, and bring us insights and understandings we never knew were within our grasp.

When we have had a sharp quarrel with a dear friend, for instance, and then found that our friend still loves and forgives, we are apt to feel tears arising, and in our surprise and discomfiture we change the subject, make a feeble joke, fight back the urge to let the tears come. More is the pity; there would be physical and spiritual health in letting go and in using the occasion to reflect upon the reasons behind it. Why do tears try to come in such a case, after the sorrow is past? Partly as a result of the release from tension; but what is more important, the tears are an atonement for our bad feelings toward our friend, an admission that we have wished him ill and are now cleansing ourselves of guilt. We pay off an emotional debt so that we may return to friendship; the tears of reconciliation wash away enmity as no amount of intelligent adult reasoning could do alone.

In the eighteenth century, the era of pure Rationalism, philosophers thought our emotions interfered with our ability to think, and that one had to discipline and eliminate his emotions before he could attain understanding. Modern medical science has brought us closer to more ancient truths: the *repression* of our feelings may be more damaging to our ability to think clearly than anything else. He who can weep can love; and he who can freely love touches upon the most valuable understanding a human being is capable of. "Heaven knows we need never be ashamed of our tears," wrote Charles Dickens, "for they are rain upon the blinding dust of earth, overlying our hard hearts."

Masculinity and Femininity

Our Manly Men

MEN HAVE always complained that times are changing, but oh, my brothers, how they have been changing recently! Not many years ago, a man would simply notify his wife he was going out for the evening to play poker with the boys. He would leave her to mind the kids, and would play hard and long with the boys, drink beer, belch out loud, use foul words, and lie about his winnings or losings. The other night I was invited to a poker game by the wife of a dear friend — yes, you read it right, the *wife* — and instructed to bring my own wife along. Seems the girls had been studying while we weren't looking. And so we played: four men, three women; ginger ale instead of beer; talk of drapes and children instead of dirty jokes and curses; not one audible belch all evening. Oh, the desecration of a hallowed male sanctuary! The infamous invasion of masculine privacy! Yet had it rested there, I still should not complain. But the sordid truth will out: the girls — all of whom have careers — played pretty well, and while I was losing five bucks during the evening, my wife was winning eleven, which made it pretty awkward for me, while my wife and I were driving home, to justify the way I had played certain hands.

Our grandfathers and even many of our fathers would have been horrified and aghast at the implications of such an evening. Indeed, in recent years there has been a rash of writings bearing such foreboding titles as "The Crisis of American Masculinity" and *The Decline of the American Male*. Their general message is that the American man has suffered so great a loss of prestige and importance lately that his very masculinity is threatened; in fact, it is in danger of extinction.

Psychiatrists like Dr. Edward Strecker and social commentators like Philip Wylie speak darkly of the American male as blighted by the possessive "Mom" whose excessive mothering turns him into a sissy or a muscular bully — either alternative being equally juvenile. From puberty on, American youths chase girls, but anthropologist Geoffrey Gorer finds this no affirmation of masculinity, but an admission of doubt about it: the young male continually reassures himself of his manhood by trying to "make a score" and prefers double-dating so that other young males will see him playing the manly part. Sociologists like Kingsley Davis are deeply concerned about the American youth's need to "prove himself" by going steady at fifteen, and about his eagerness to get safely married by twenty; the only alternative proof of manliness seems to consist of the leather-jacketed, sweaty uncouthness of the "beatnik" and the motorcycle bum.

The statisticians add their touch to the portrait of the dethroned male. According to government figures, 30 per cent of American wives — more than ever before — work today; man can hardly be boss in his own home under such circumstances. Even wives who are not working control the modern male financially; advertising men — quislings to their own sex — have treasonably revealed that women spend three-quarters or more of all retail dollars. A flood of articles and books has shown the modern man to be, in fact, little more than an economic slave bonded to his wife, children, and mortgage, and manumitted only by old age or heart failure. The best status he can achieve in his household is that of a mere satellite. Recently anthropologist Otto von Mering of the University of Pittsburgh informed a convention of family counselors that the modern male has become the "odd man out" of the family — a third party who, at best, can peacefully coexist with it by accepting the role of money-provider and noninterfering onlooker.

Some experts on family life want to drag this pitiful outcast into the nursery and kitchen, put an apron on him, and give him a sense of belonging; just as many others warn direly of the confusion that results when men try to play the role of substitute women. The popular opinion on the matter is expressed by the prevailing cliché of television and films, which shows the average young father as a bumbling, loud-mouthed incompetent who always makes a mess of things at home but is saved in the nick of time by his seemingly silly (but really shrewd) little wife.

Something, in short, has taken the starch out of the American male. It is no coincidence that two recent plays by Tennessee Williams, one of the country's most successful playwrights, deal with young men with potency problems, while his Broadway smash hit, *Sweet Bird of Youth*, displays for our edification a worthless young hero who, in despair at his own failure in life, passively allows a group of roughnecks to castrate him. In Greenwich Village — not exactly a typical American community, but sometimes a kind of frontier outpost — the *Village Voice*, a weekly newspaper, recently printed a long dialogue between a "straight guy" (normal man) and a homosexual. The latter got the best of the argument and concluded by sneering that the straight guy's dominance over society and morals is ending. "We will force our way into open society," he warned, "and you will have to acknowledge us. From four to seven million American adults — at least — are not going to be treated like criminals or freaks. . . . Baby, remember my words!"

All this ominous talk is more than a mere literary or psychiatric fad. For several generations the nature of the male role in life has been undergoing a major change, and the process has caught up with modern man with a vengeance. During most of history, man has been woman's superior according to law, religion, and custom. From Aristotle to Aquinas to Tennyson there was an unbroken literary tradition that Nature, having designed woman to bear children and provide man with comfort, had wisely limited her brain power, independence of spirit, and moral fiber. It made perfect sense, therefore, to keep her from the complexities of schools, courts of law, the professions, and the business and political world.

Only several generations ago, in England and in much of this country, a woman could not legally make a contract, incur debts, sue someone at law, or hold property in her own name. Until 1857, in England, everything she owned or earned was legally her husband's, even if he had deserted her. Queens and high-ranking women were exceptions, but a proper Victorian man could put even a queen in her place. Albert, the prince consort of Queen Victoria, once had a tiff with her and angrily retired to the bed chamber, locking the door. The Queen knocked imperiously. "Who is there?" growled Albert. "It is the Queen," she replied in her most majestic fashion. "*Who?*" asked Albert, as though he had never heard of her. She repeated it, and he simply ignored her; her knocking and calling, even her pleading, were of no avail. At last she got the idea and said, tearfully, "Albert, it is I, your wife," whereupon he unlocked the door and let her in, a chastened and penitent woman.

In the past century, however, this ancient order of things has completely fallen apart. Beginning with financial victories, the feminists went on to victories in the area of divorce and support, and finally in the area of the vote, which they obtained in this country in 1920. According to a recent survey by the Women's Bureau of the United States Government, women in this country now possess practically every legal right that men do — and any man who has tangled with his wife in alimony court will swear she seems to have a good many *more* rights than he.

As for her mental powers, the American female now gets one-third of all the college degrees granted each year. All the evidence of the classroom and of psychological studies proves there is no real difference between the male and female IQ, but because man has, for twenty-four or more centuries, assumed that braininess was exclusively a male attribute, he still is genuinely upset by the spectacle of a clever woman. College boys shun bright girls as though they had Dishpan Hands or Denture Breath. On two different campuses, recent surveys showed that four out of ten college girls deliberately "play dumb" in order not to drive away interesting men. Girls who are more honest are apt to become dateless schoolteachers, paying for their candor with spinsterhood.

When woman was confined to the home, man's business life was another attribute of masculinity, and business success a proof of virility. Femininity, on the other hand, consisted of staying home and accepting the husband's protection while rearing the children, growing vegetables, canning fruit, churning butter, mending clothes, preparing medicines, tending house, and, after fourteen hours or so of this, climbing into bed to render to her husband what Victorians called her "conjugal duty."

This division of labor, so agreeable to man, was wrecked by the industrial revolution, which gradually took many of woman's chores from her and gave them to factory workers and household machinery. After suffering from too much leisure for a few generations, women have forced their way, in the past half century, into one-third of all United States jobs and into practically every occupational specialty listed by the Bureau of the Census. The process has been going on for decades, but modern man has not gotten used to it. He still regards the career woman with fear or scorn and thinks her either mannish or misguided, and he is newly pleased every time he reads a story that shows her coming to her senses, renouncing her job, and taking to the nursery, dewy-eyed and maternally soft.

The head psychiatrist of a well-known Eastern mental hospital described a case that nicely illustrates the point. A recent patient — Arthur King, I'll call him — owns a small factory which makes desk barometers and novelty clocks. His bright young wife left her job in an advertising agency to play homemaker, but when no children arrived after several years, she got bored. She talked Arthur into letting her work with him in the factory, and proved uncommonly gifted at designing good sales literature, dealing with customers, and even improving his over-all management of production. Time after time she showed him shortcomings in his methods or patiently cleared up some minor tangle he had made of things. Though he was only in his mid-thirties, Arthur mysteriously began to find his sexual desire waning and his potency becoming embarrassingly unreliable. This, along with other problems, brought him to the edge of breakdown, and, after a nightmarish, drunken weekend, he committed himself to the hospital.

After he had been there about a month, his wife discovered that she was pregnant. She suffered severe morning sickness, and almost at the same time got into a labor dispute at the plant and a serious financial snarl over the purchase of new machinery. While visiting Arthur one day, she blurted out the whole situation in a storm of tears and sobs. No drug could have had a more startling effect: within four days Arthur, straight, vigorous, and firm of handshake, was visiting his plant every afternoon on special leave from the hospital, and taking hold of things, and a month later he was discharged as cured. He has gone on no more weekend benders, and, according to his psychiatrist, his potency has returned as mysteriously as it left him.

Most men do not face the challenge in so direct a form as did Arthur King, but the modern wife, even if she does not threaten her husband's male superiority through business success, sometimes seems to challenge it on every other front — the decisions concerning where they should live, what kind of house they should own, whom they should invite to dinner, how the children should be reared, where to spend their vacation, and so on.

All this is reflected in the final challenge to man's ancient rights — the challenge he faces nightly. For the concept of "conjugal duty" and the belief that the male has a right to his sexual enjoyment have all but vanished. A famous survey by psychologist Lewis Terman shows that, among educated people, wives often reject their husbands' advances: 10 per cent do so "frequently," 25 per cent "sometimes," and still more "on rare occasions" — a situation our grandmothers would have found unthinkable.

For the past thirty years, feminists and marriage advisers have sternly forbidden the male to enjoy his wife sexually without arousing her and completely fulfilling her. The impact of this campaign has led modern woman to expect a more superior performance than the average man can regularly put on. The requirement that he woo her carefully and long each time assumes the appearance of an onerous duty and a threat to manliness. I once knew a man who, warned by a doctor that he was giving his wife insufficient preparatory wooing, put a luminous clock by the bedside and faithfully tried to provide twenty minutes of arousal before obeying his own impulses. In less than half a year, he had taken up with a beer-joint doxy, with whom he was able to be riotous, selfish, and crudely masculine.

Little wonder that Kinsey found roughly half of all American husbands being unfaithful to their wives at some point or other during marriage. In the role of wolf chasing prey, the disgruntled husband feels manly once again, as he did during his bachelor days when his impetuous advances, whether met with warmth or resistance, were never opposed by technical criticisms. Unfortunately, the American male makes a poor cheat: by tradition, religion, and general sentiment, he tends to be ashamed of what he is doing. In any case, in the United States neither society nor wives will tolerate the husband's having open liaisons outside of marriage; infidelity is, therefore, a poor prop to his sense of masculinity, being always a worrisome and rather graceless thing. No hasty romp with a call girl or pick-up in a motel can begin to compare, in ego-building effect, with the gracious and elegant mood enjoyed by, say, a Portuguese man of substance when, with admiring smiles and nods to greet him, he escorts his acknowledged mistress of many years' standing into a fine restaurant for Sunday dinner, while his wife remains firmly shut up at home with the children.

The alleged crisis of American masculinity and decline of the male is, all in all, the result of a grand confusion between a particular conception of his *social role* (protector, money-earner, sage, lord and master) and the universal truth of his *biological role* (lover of woman, inseminator of the fertile womb, father of the family). The biological role cannot change (as yet) without extinguishing the human race, but the social role is hardly more fundamental than the form and style of a suit of clothes. The particular cut of the suit in this case is the ancient Western model, especially as adapted to the Victorian era, but many a man regards any attack on the clothing as an attack on the man inside.

Yet almost none of the social traits in question can be shown to be essentially masculine. Is it genuinely masculine to be successful in business, and unmasculine not to be? In some primitive societies, and even among the upper-caste Indians and orthodox Jews, many educated men busy themselves in study, talk, and contemplation of lofty matters, leaving their women to worry about the family finances. Similarly, upper-class Englishmen long thought it a disgrace to soil their hands with "trade" and avoided all useful work except the Army or the Church; no one, however, thought them unmanly.

Is it inherently masculine to possess intellectual power and to acquire learning? It has not always seemed so: on the American frontier, intellect and learning were both long suspect and seemed to connote effeminacy rather than manliness. Conversely, some women have been exceedingly bright and learned, and yet lost none of their femininity: one need only recall such women as Elizabeth Barrett, Marie Curie, Madame Pandit, and Margaret Mead.

Does a real man prefer simple, unaffected clothing and hearty, down-to-earth manners? George Washington, the Marquis de Lafayette, and a number of other eighteenth-century gentlemen of undeniable masculinity wore powdered wigs, fancy waistcoats, bunches of scented lace at the cuff and throat, and used such bows, smiles, flourishes, and delicate airs as would today stamp a man a member of the "gay society."

Is it feminine, rather than masculine, to handle babies, prepare delicious food, or ply the needle with skill? Hardly. In our very time, most pediatricians, chefs, and fine tailors are men. But they, of course, are well paid; when the same skills are ill-paid or unpaid, as they are in the wife's case, one regards them as inherently feminine activities. The logic is no better than that of the medieval knights who scorned learning to read and write because those were accomplishments of low-paid scribes and servants.

The fact is, according to most contemporary anthropologists and sociologists, that social masculinity does not consist of one unalterable cluster of traits and abilities. It has been defined and constructed in many different ways among the hundreds of human societies and even has shown wide variations within our own society. The present decline and fall of the male is actually not so much a descent from some past greatness as a transition from one social definition of masculinity to another which is at least equally good and, possibly, a lot better.

The changing nature of daily life and the rise in the status of woman have made it impossible for man to continue being a kind of tribal chieftain, defending his home with the loaded shotgun, ruling his wife and children by edict and wallop, assigning chores to each like Pharaoh's overseer, and making all his decisions in lonely splendor. In today's world, man and woman are no longer held together by economic necessity and self-preservation, nor, to any large extent, by religion. Modern men and women expect marriage to provide not goods and services, but love, companionship, and happiness, and if it does not, it has no other cement to keep it from falling apart. Such being the case, today's male has had to become friend, lover, and constant companion to his wife; if he tries to be instead what his grandfather was, he either forfeits her love, wrecks his home, or — possibly worst of all — gets laughed at for his pretensions.

As I have tried to show in *The Natural History of Love*, this new, equalitarian relationship between man and woman yields a closeness and an intimacy rarely known in previous centuries. But in the process of adjusting to it, modern man often finds himself stripped of his former sturdy independence, and dragged into a sharing of "womanly" activities until he no longer knows what constitutes his own identity and maleness. He suffers from what sociologists have come to call "sexual ambiguity," or a lack of sexual identity. A patient of a Boston psychoanalyst was unusually listless and depressed during his visit one Monday morning, and without apparent cause, until he recounted his weekend. It had consisted chiefly of helping his wife hang new curtains, tending the babies, assisting with the cooking and the dishes, and finally babysitting alone while she went to a Sunday evening committee meeting of the League of Women Voters. "Sometimes," he sighed, "I feel like the best wife a woman ever had. Doctor, do you think I'm abnormal, or something?"

Nevertheless, many facets of masculinity — those which are under the guidance of our biology — are not so easily made ambiguous. Man is, on the average, taller and stronger than woman; this not only makes him more fit for certain occupations, but in general predisposes the growing boy to seek, by analogy, attitudes of moral and spiritual strength. The man knows no monthly menstrual cycles, and, therefore, being unaccustomed to mood swings, he perhaps expects of himself more reliability and steadiness than most women do of themselves.

Man is more easily aroused to sexual excitement than woman, partly because of the location and nature of his organs; he is, also, more easily satisfied — and more easily depleted. All of these differences affect his personality structure. He can never know, with all the tissues and organs of his body, the meaning of motherhood or the love that springs from it; he must learn brotherly and fatherly love by example, by words, and by thought, rather than by the use of his viscera and nerves. Anthropologist Weston La Barre holds that this is what inclines the male to be the philosopher, the lawgiver, and the ruler: love and cooperation must, in him, involve the head, while for woman they come right from the womb and the breast.

But if there are some innately masculine characteristics, the new, emerging *social* definition of the male role is by no means innate or clear.

It is precisely the uncertainty we feel about the new definition that makes so many people think masculinity is dying. What, then, will be the definition of masculinity in the future?

To a large extent, it will depend on the continuing, and far more radical, redefinition of femininity. Twenty years ago many observers expected woman to become even more masculinized, career-minded, and uninterested in Home, Sweet Home. Marriages would be delayed, children would be fewer, adultery and divorce would increase, until, as sociologist Pitirim Sorokin flatly predicted, the home would become "a mere overnight parking place mainly for sex-relationship." Practically all these dismal forecasts were wonderfully incorrect. For the past fifteen years American women — despite their greater interest in working — have shown a growing inclination to marry early, have more children, seek houses in the suburbs, put great value on their home life, and treat work not as a career with values of its own, but merely as a way to increase the family income. Having gotten themselves thoroughly confused with men in the flat-chested 1920's and the childless 1930's, women seem to be working out a middle course in which they combine their new-found social freedoms with some of their unalterable feminine functions.

Men, likewise, will probably work out their new definition of masculinity in terms of synthesis and compromise. One cannot draw precisely the outlines of the new male without the risk of looking as ridiculous later on as did Professor Sorokin. But it would seem clear that man will not be able to appropriate to himself again the exclusive rights to learning, business ability, legal dominance over the family, or those other characteristics our Victorian grandfathers thought essential to masculinity. The new definition will probably be subtler — not a division between what is done by one sex and the other, but between the way each thing is done by one sex and the other. A man can pursue a scientific career doggedly and singlemindedly; a woman, with the major interruption of motherhood ahead, is likely to pursue the same career less earnestly, and place less value on her success. A man may swim energetically, walk vigorously, build and repair things, enjoy himself *hard*, all by way of living up to the promise of his body; a woman, no longer intent on proving herself as good as he (since she knows she is as good in a larger sense), will do similar things, but on a different scale. (I *will* make one foolish prediction: lady shot-putters and lady wrestlers will never conquer the heart of Western man; lady tennis players in lace pants, however, stand a good chance.) Men slightly exceed women in mechanical, mathematical and logical abilities, while women possess greater powers than men of intuition and empathy, and slightly greater language abilities; perhaps male doctors will always make the better diagnosticians and surgeons, while women doctors — equally excellent, but along somewhat different lines — may prove better general practitioners and psychiatrists.

When modern man recognizes how firmly the essential aspects of masculinity are built into his glands, bones, and nerves, he will cease worrying about the present changes in external manners and customs, knowing that genuine manhood will manifest itself in any case. The greatest affirmation of confidence in the male sex will be man's own admission that his ancient privileges and rights are as dated and as unimportant to true manliness as sleeve garters, handlebar mustaches, or celluloid collars.

But it has always been difficult to avoid being misled by externals. In the great days of Rome, there lived a mincing, perfumed, dandified young politician of whom Cicero publicly said, in scorn, "When I see his hair so carefully arranged and observe him adjusting it with one finger, I cannot imagine that it should enter into such a man's thoughts to subvert the Roman state." Cicero was monumentally wrong: the dandy proved to be the greatest lover, general, and subverter of the state that Rome had ever known — Gaius Julius Caesar.

An Answer to Some Foolish Theories About Women

No METAPHOR more aptly symbolizes the quest of modern woman than that which appears in the well-known words of Matthew ix, 17: "Neither do men put new wine into old bottles: else the bottles break, and the wine runneth out, and the bottles perish: but they put new wine into new bottles, and both are preserved." For American woman is indeed new wine, and her search is for the new roles and patterns of life into which to pour and preserve her heady modern womanhood. Taken as a genus, she is something new under the sun — and the old bottles of womanhood, as conceived and lived in the past, serve ill to contain her. Let us see how, though excellent in their own times, they are grossly unsuited to modern life.

1. First there is the *matriarch* — that half-mythical, half-historical woman who, according to nineteenth-century anthropologists, was the controlling, almighty ruler of earliest primitive societies in some forgotten golden age. Latter-day anthropologists say that this is nonsense, and that there never was a genuine matriarchy; the legend of the Amazons reflects men's fears, rather than history. Still, there have been many primitive cultures in which men worshiped female deities as well as male ones, in which woman was respected and important, and in which — because people had no idea how conception occurred — woman was regarded with awe as the magic source of human renewal, and solely responsible for the creation of new life.

But how does this pattern work today? Not well. The equivalent of the matriarch is regarded with dread and revulsion, rather than respect and awe; men call her a "Mom," and critics such as Philip Wylie, Geoffrey Gorer, Margaret Mead, and the late Edward Strecker have blamed matriarchal women for psychologically castrating their sons and husbands. The anti-Mom critics ought to add that the modern matriarch herself isn't happy in the role; she does not so much seek it as find in it a wretched compensation for other things that are lacking in her life.

2. In certain other times and places, woman has been the virtual *slave* of man. One theory as to how this came about was that when men ceased to be hunters, and began to plant seeds and grow their own food, they realized by analogy that they were also the possessors and planters of human seed; accordingly, they came to think much better of themselves and worse of woman, who became in effect a mere piece of fertile territory. A man who could afford more than one woman bought more — not, as we modern men licentiously imagine, for purposes of unbridled carnal pleasure, but to beget more young, and at the same time to hoe

more potatoes, weave more fabric, fetch more water, chop more wood, and thatch more roofs. For as one historian of marriage tartly observed, woman was man's "first domestic animal."

Oddly enough, you will find people, even today, who think that woman is happiest in this condition, and thrives best when she accepts total subordination, masochistically giving up all her own wishes in favor of those of her husband; the authorities I have seen making this claim range from psychoanalyst Helene Deutsch to Marlene Dietrich. Well, perhaps enslavement at hard labor made woman happy long ago, but I doubt that it would do so today. History can't be turned backwards: many a Great Reformer has, like Augustus Caesar, or Robert Owen, or Mahatma Gandhi, tried to get people to give up machinery, or comfort, or civilized sophistication, in order to recapture some olden golden purity, but it never works. Marie Antoinette would milk cows for fun, but only now and then; labor that isn't really necessary is amusing only when you don't have to do it. An unnecessary and anachronistic subjugation of modern woman is fun for her only if she plays the part on occasional evenings; force it on her as a regular thing, and you lose her altogether. In modern America, the patriarchal male and the subjugated female are found far more often among lower socio-economic groups than among the middle class — and by no mere coincidence, divorce rates are far higher among the lower class than among the middle class. The subjugated version of mother was the invention of necessity; but without that necessity the invention doesn't work.

3. The *cloistered wife* was another type. She was the product of wealthier times, or wealthier classes; she had plenty of help with her work, but was secluded, protected, and deprived of almost all civil and social rights. You find her type again and again, from Athens of the fifth century B.C. to modern Spain and Latin America. In some ways, it seems her pattern might be viable in modern life — but the essential precondition is her complete social and civil inferiority to man, a precondition which our schools and our laws rule out.

Still, tradition dies hard. Consider the Athenian *symposium* in which gentlemen sat or lay about the dining hall, and regaled themselves with food, wine, music, and philosophic talk; the inferior ladies, meanwhile, were all at home, confined to their own quarters. Gone and forgotten?

Not quite. Only a few weeks ago I dined at the town house of a distinguished publisher, and after dinner found myself being gently shunted off into the library for cognac, cigars, and male talk, while the ladies withdrew to the parlor. But after only half an hour we prudently rejoined them; we were permitted the gesture of defiance, but not the reality. I daresay that by the time my son is grown, he will never have the chance to see this ancient custom for himself; and if I say I did, he will be all the more sure that I am an old fogy.

4. Another, and considerably tastier, variety of woman was the *hetaira*, or courtesan. She appears in numerous guises throughout history, wherever men of money and good taste were unable to fall in love with their wives — or their friends' wives. She was no mere prostitute, but a well-educated conversationalist, and a seductive, amusing companion, who inspired something like love in her clients, and who, often as not, refused her favors to any man she did not care for. Men not only enjoyed her, but thought well of her and of her way of life; the great Saint-Évremond, writing to Ninon de l'Enclos in her later years, congratulated her on having lived a rich, wise, and happiest possible life, while King Louis XIV so respected her intellectual influence that he was wont to ask his advisers rather apprehensively, "What is Ninon saying now?"

The type, unfortunately, doesn't go over well in the United States today. Our Puritan traditions are all against it; what is worse, the would-be courtesan faces the toughest possible competitor: the modern wife, who today is just as well-educated and as willing to enjoy passion — but is a great deal more convenient. Besides, modern life affords a man almost no concealment; you cannot hide the expenses of a mistress in the glaring light of contemporary tax reports. Nor can you hide the mistress herself in the midst of a suburban housing development.

5. Enough of such disgraceful conjectures; let me pass on now to a more admirable type of woman — the *Lady*: that pure, uplifting, well-mannered, gracious creature, sweetly cruel and cruelly sweet, desirable and inaccessible, with whom the medieval knights fell in love, and who inspired them to feats of chivalry and deeds of derring-do. To win her kiss a man might serve her valiantly for years, risking his life in the lists; to win still greater rewards he might serve her thus for years. The best existing autobiographical account of such a courtship, in the thirteenth

century, indicates that it took the gentleman fifteen years to bed the lady. This wouldn't have been at all practical except that every such knight, while loving someone else's wife, had one of his own for more mundane purposes, who seemed to him not in the least marvelous, inspiring, or inaccessible. The very tenets of courtly love expressly state that love cannot exist between husband and wife; distance, difficulty, and deprivation were of the essence.

The modern girl still likes to think of herself as something of the inspiring lady — but most of those thoughts fade early in marriage, or even before it, as she ceases being distant, difficult, or depriving. Nor can she play the role, after marriage, to an outside lover; we have become too psychologically sophisticated to tolerate the platonic passion that yearns but remains unfulfilled for years. The modern adulterer expects either a rejection or a complete acceptance; anything else seems neurotic. "Listen," he says, "I can understand waiting a couple of weeks, but why do you want to frustrate yourself and me longer than that? It's sick. Ask your analyst if I'm not right."

6. From pre-Athenian times to the present, we also find woman often portrayed as the *shrew*, tyrant, nag, or battle-ax. This is not quite the same as the matriarch, who supposedly ruled by right; the shrew or nag uses venom and argument to get even with her husband for having a better deal in life than she. In the past, this may have yielded the shrew a certain kind of inverted satisfaction; today, with divorce being as widely accepted as it is, her ill temper or sharp tongue is more apt to drive the man out of her life, or at least drive him and her into marriage counseling — where her conduct will be appraised as misdirected or unsublimated aggression. Socrates, when asked why he endured Xantippe's scolding, said that if he could learn to endure her, he would be all the better able to bear the society of other people; modern man still admires the philosopher, but diagnoses his humility as masochism — and sees no reason to emulate it.

7. The Romantics and Victorians had their own preferred image of woman — the *clinging vine*, the sensitive plant, the pure maiden. She was short on brains, but long on sensibility; virtuously cool as marble, yet mightily inflaming to men's passions; patient as Griselda, but elusive as a butterfly. This, too, has come down to us today, though woman is

hard pressed to make it believable; willy-nilly, she displays her brains in school, her character on the job, and her passions in bed. Yet one version of the clinging vine *is* still current among us: the "angel in the house," as the poet Coventry Patmore once called her — the tender, pliant, good mother and wife who never exerts pressure, but rules her family through purity and gentleness. The home is her place; children and wifeliness are her business; all else is of no consequence.

But this pattern has become the greatest single source of discontent among American women today — even though they themselves continue to elect it. Today's woman, having chosen to abandon all outside interests in favor of homemaking and child rearing, all too often finds in about two or three years that she is feeling stifled, crushed, suffocated. The butterfly has metamorphosed backwards into a grub; the angel in the house has become a trapped housewife.

8. The final specimen in my collection is the *feminist* — or perhaps I should say the *old-style feminist:* the saloon smasher, the parading suffragette, the spinster intellectual wearing man-tailored suits and a bare face, the tooth-and-claw female careerist of whom men are afraid. The type was more to be seen a generation or so ago than now, yet you will still find some of them — even though man-tailored suits and bare faces are out of fashion. The old-style feminist never *was* a very adaptive pattern of womanhood; whether she preferred to be a virgin or to live in free love, her career drive made normal family life and motherhood impossible, and thus afflicted her with loneliness and emotional poverty. Nuns and priests, though they deny themselves sexuality and parenthood, do have a complicated emotional life, and a sense of higher purpose; the lady department-store president has neither — which may be why, in place of husband or child, she usually gets an ulcer.

So much for our array of old bottles. In looking them over, we have, perhaps, done more than see their inadequacy as models for modern femininity — for whatever their current shortcomings, they do prove that there has been a great variety of meanings of femininity in the past, and a wide range of possible ways in which to be a woman. If there is any one lesson to this little hop-skip-and-jump through history, it is that over the centuries women have shown almost as great a variety of faces as men have, and each in its time has seemed the right, the appropriate, the moral, and the healthful way for a woman to be.

The same lesson is taught — for those who will listen — by the abundant evidence of anthropology. Are women really feeble and frail, physically? Although they average only 60 per cent as much muscle power as men, in many parts of the world — central Africa for one — they and their men are convinced that females are better suited to hard work, and that it is hurtful for males. Are women mentally unsuited to business and logic? In many places — including modern Iran — it is men who are thought to be emotional, sensitive, and intuitive, while women are thought to be cool and calculating. Are women basically gossipy? — perhaps, but among certain Philippine tribes it is men who, it is agreed by all hands, are the natural gossips. Are girls timid, nervous, and afraid of initiation into the rites of love? Of course — but then again, among some peoples, including the Zuni Indians, it was the bridegroom who was overcome by fear on the wedding night, and might refuse to consummate the marriage for many days. Are women the better cooks, artists, and healers? Certainly — except that in some cultures men are. Are women sexually passive, yielding, and basically monogamous? Yes — at least often; but the Human Relations Area Files at Yale, and other cross-cultural surveys, show that in some societies women are as predatory, passionate, and polygamous as men.

The same message is told by modern psychology. Despite centuries of assertions that woman's mind and talents are vastly different from those of men, the concrete evidence of scientific testing is otherwise. There *are* some minor differences between boys and girls in innate abilities — girls are a little better at verbal performance, and boys at analytic thinking; girls are a trifle better at social or interpersonal problems, boys at arithmetical ones. Yet these are only minor differences — and only averages. By far the largest part of each sex lies in exactly the same range of excellence as the largest part of the other, with only a minority of each creating the slight differences in the averages.

Moreover, the well-known differences in masculine and feminine personality, as measured by the Terman-Miles M-F tests, are to a great extent acquired rather than innate. Education, for instance, decreases the difference: better-educated girls score less feminine, better-educated

boys less masculine, than less-educated girls and boys. Social background, religion, and occupation similarly are related to this synthetic
femininity and masculinity. As the clincher, even one's conscious inten-
tion affects the score drastically: girls who are told to answer the test
as if they were boys can out-perform normal boys with ease, and vice
versa.

Thus we see that history, anthropology, and psychology all offer
abundant proof that woman *can* successfully be any one of many things
— according to the time and place in which she lives. What thing, then,
should she be today? Let me at once reword my own question: not what
thing, but what things? For our society is changing more rapidly than
any other has ever changed in all of history; there is no single set of
agreed-upon goals, norms, and customs among us — and therefore no
single specific answer to the meaning of womanhood.

More than half of all American women (if one may judge from a
wide variety of surveys) are basically satisfied with the conservative answer — the domestic, home-oriented, patriarchal conception of womanhood. And for many of them, it may indeed be the best answer. But for
possibly a quarter to a third of American women it is *not* the best answer. Many of these women are perplexed, troubled, or even deeply
disturbed by their discontent with the home-oriented role, and guilt-
ridden by their longing for others; partly as a result, 600,000 housewives
are alcoholic, half of all women visiting doctors' offices have psychosomatic or hypochondriacal ills rather than organic ones, one out of four
wives sooner or later tries adultery, and 400,000 women end their marriages via divorce each year.

Others express their discontent in more constructive ways: 5 million
belong to women's clubs, 10 to 15 million do volunteer work for community organizations, over 24 million women, more than half of whom
are married, work part-time or full-time; and on a small but growing
scale, thousands of married women are going back to college to complete
their degrees, or take advanced or refresher courses, in order to expand
their activities as their children need them less.

This wide range of possible answers makes sense in America: we are
not one people but many, and though we live at one point in time, the

past centuries are very differently blended in us. The answer to womanhood that would work for a thirty-year-old agnostic Manhattan Demo-
crat, with an M.A. in European history, one child, and a husband in
the publishing world, would hardly serve for a devout forty-five-year-old
Republican in Rapid City, S.D., with a high-school education, five children, and a husband who is a Methodist minister. As far as woman is
concerned, our national motto needs to be inverted: Out of one, many.

Still, we want to discern the general direction in which the tide of
change is carrying women from the present toward the future, and to
see how they may best stay afloat during that voyage. Despite the diversity of answers suitable to American women, there *is* a definite, an in-
escapable shift in the balance of those answers. The emerging pattern
appears more clearly among college-educated middle-class women, but
already it is spreading to the high-school-educated middle-class women,
and eventually may be the dominant cultural mode. And I think one
can characterize that pattern in three words — *complexity, combination,* and *compromise.* Let me explain.

By *complexity* I mean that there is a clearly evident trend for more
and more women to play a multiplicity of roles in the course of their
lives — to be, in one person, several of those kinds of women I have
already described, plus others never dreamed of before. The modern
woman is girl friend, mother, and homemaker, and her husband's lover,
companion, and friend; she is also part-time intellectual, woman of the
world, community mover and shaker, property owner, and intermittent
or partial careerist. The conservatives cry that this complexity is what
ails her; I think the evidence proves exactly the contrary, and that complexity is the functional, satisfying answer in the modern milieu. And
I mean functional and satisfying not only for the woman, but for her
children, husband, and society.

Consider, for instance, the fact that technology has freed her of much
of the work she used to have to do — which, though it was exhausting,
made her valuable. Men and children would formerly have starved or
gone cold without her labors; today, all the goods and services she contributes to the home can be bought or hired for $4,000 or less. Home-
making today is a series of chores without prestige or importance, de-

spite the glamour treatment our magazines and advertisers continually strive to give it. Consider, further, how our society praises mothers and motherhood, but grants no real importance or recognition to the woman who is only a mother; perhaps the reason is that having children, though once a vital necessity, is today basically a luxury — a thing people do for their own pleasure. This being the case, it is through complexity — through adding new roles to her life — that modern woman can regain pride and self-esteem, can recapture her lost prestige and importance, and can have the fulfillments and pleasures of family life as well as a socially valuable outlet for her aggressive energies and ambitions.

And this is why her complexity works out better for her children. The woman who seeks all the meaning of life in motherhood places upon her children a burden their slim shoulders were never meant to bear — that of providing her with all her happiness. She is around them, under them, over them, in them, omniscient, devouring; she gives them not mother love, but what is often unkindly called "smother love"; she sucks joy out of them like juice out of an orange — and you know what that does to the orange. Many psychiatrists and social workers now feel that a number of women make better mothers and produce healthier children if they do not mother them full time.

The marital relationship, too, can benefit from complexity in woman. For one thing, ours is a fluid, mobile society in which men and women alike find it very hard to maintain the deep, loving friendships that once sustained people in earlier eras. That need for enduring, profound friendship can be met, and is being met, within modern "companionship marriage," even though in the long history of marriage you will find almost nothing about man and wife being friends of each other. Again, ours is the age of the Lonely Crowd, when each of us lacks the wide web of interpersonal links with a stable small community that used to involve people in multiple interactions with each other. Short of a radical change in society, we can best fill that need by creating more and stronger interactions between man and wife, rather than limiting marriage to a partnership for procreation and consumption. Again, for better or worse we have completed the long historical process of amalgamating sex with affection, and both of these to family life; sex has become thoroughly entwined with a whole set of major human emotions, and cannot very well be separated from them. The wife who is a good mistress to her husband therefore preserves her own happiness, while she who is so excessively maternal or housewifely as to be a poor mistress drives her husband outside for what begins only as sexual sport — and ends as new love and marriage.

Above all, complexity is well suited to the life-cycle of modern woman. In most of the past, she hardly outlived her fertile years; today she is virtually out of the child-rearing business before forty, with thirty-five or more years left which can be meaningful only if her being has other aspects than maternalism. But to wait till the crisis is upon her to start thinking of what to do with the second half of her life is folly. If an artist loses his sight at forty, we admire the heroism of his struggle to find another activity for himself; but in the needless suffering and heroism of the woman who has not prepared for the middle of life, there is something not so much admirable as deplorable.

This brings me to the second part of my alliterative trilogy — *combination* — by which I mean the skillful fitting together of various roles, in varying proportions, at different times of life. It is all very well for me to praise complexity, but women often find it difficult or impossible to be all things at one and the same time. To some extent, there are realistic external reasons for this: help is hard to find in the suburbs, and if our woman cannot get free part of the time, some roles must be dropped. But who said she had to pick a suburb? Who said she had to run a *House Beautiful* type of home? Who said the baby needs her twenty-four hours out of every twenty-four, and won't thrive on having other adults care for him part of the time? Why does she find fault with, or make excuses for not using, co-op sitting pools, nurseries, or day-care centers, when she thinks them perfectly acceptable for other women's children?

I am suggesting that behind many a woman's avoidance of solutions of these types there lies not a concrete external difficulty, but a more serious one — one which is both unconscious and internalized. And that difficulty is her deep-seated conflict about her roles, which makes her think of them as *alternatives*, mutually exclusive and not to be exercised at the same time. As a little girl, she was always being pulled to and fro by seemingly incommensurable meanings of femininity: career versus marriage, lovableness versus sensuality, achievement versus charm, brains versus beauty. As a result of having such dichotomies drilled into her, she may live her life as a series of discontinuous stages, in each of which she abruptly drops some roles and adopts others, usually with strain and difficulty. She goes suddenly from college girl who can neither cook nor soothe a crying infant, to young mother who never opens a book, to middle-aging woman distractedly busying herself in the stores and beauty parlors. She has been victimized by "either-or" upbringing; she sees herself as either A *or* B, but not A + B, and not even the alternatives, for different periods of her life, of $A + \frac{B}{2}$ or $\frac{A}{2} + B$.

The ability to combine roles successfully takes not only an internal self-image free of role conflicts, but even more fundamentally, a belief that one can do certain things not traditionally thought within the realm of female ability. A woman who has been sold on her inabilities acts accordingly, no matter what science says about her. It is not just a joke, but a fact attested by bankers, that women more often overdraw, or create errors in, their bank accounts than men do. It is a cliché — based on truth — that most businesswomen lack the dominance and decisiveness that would take them to the top. It is a tedious truth — but a true truth — that there have been almost no great women architects, physicists, or jurists, although there is insufficient difference in men's and women's innate abilities to explain it.

The usual *apologia,* naturally, is that women bear a double burden; in actual fact, a recent study of four hundred Radcliffe Ph.D.'s showed that unmarried female scholars published no more papers than married ones — and that both published far less than men, married or single. The difference probably lies not in ability or personal burdens, but, according to psychologist Eleanor Maccoby, in the anxiety women feel when they try to violate the childhood training in which they were overprotected, treated as more dependent than boys, and inhibited from developing self-confidence.

To overcome this is no easy task. But even when a woman does overcome it, to combine new roles successfully with old ones requires the further ability to tolerate intermittency — that is, to interpret a hiatus in a role as a temporary thing, rather than as an irrevocable change in her being. A recent report by Eva Hansl in the *Journal of the National Association of Women Deans and Counselors* abstracts a study of a hundred college-educated women who have combined family life with vocations. Mrs. Hansl scrupulously charted each subject's activities by type and by year, and discovered that few of her women followed the statistical average of pre-maternal employment, fifteen years or so of retirement, and a return to work. Instead, these successfully complex women combined their roles with great flexibility and variety, often reporting several periods of work interrupted by childbearing, study, travel, and the like. They achieved complexity by being ready to add or subtract roles as the exigencies of the moment required, without dropping those roles from their personal repertoire for good. It sounds like a simple discovery, but it has the simplicity of great profundity.

The third part of the trilogy is *compromise;* and by this I mean the readiness of modern woman to scale down her aspirations and settle for limited achievement, in order not to damage her love relationships and family life. This is quite a different thing from completely giving up her vocational or outside activities — but it is also very different from pursuing them in the same way a man does. The entire dilemma of career versus work, which plagued women of the earlier part of this century, hardly exists in that form today. Few young women now burn with ambition to reach the top in a career; few speak of putting off marriage or of not marrying at all; but still fewer envision themselves as being only homemakers. A vocation or a job before marriage is the almost universal rule, and among middle-class housewives who have had time to try out total domesticity, a majority — in survey after survey — are planning on, or thinking about, getting back into money-earning activities at some time in the near future, and more are actually doing so every year.

To subordinate her vocational aspirations, however, seems to be the answer modern woman is finding to the career-or-marriage dilemma. So it is that we now see women barely holding their own or even losing ground in the serious and demanding professions. One in ten Ph.D.'s is now granted to a woman, but forty years ago it was one in every six;

one-fifth of college faculty members are women today, but thirty years ago nearly a third of them were; 6 per cent of United States physicians today are women, which is no greater a proportion than half a century ago. But in contrast, in less demanding professions — those which require less time to prepare for, or those which can be quitted for a few years without irreparable loss of position — the proportion of women is rapidly growing: there has, for instance, been notable growth of the percentages of women in accounting, auditing, chemistry, drafting, and statistics — all of them, by the way, nontraditional fields for women.

Women who make a habit of being indignant about the remaining bastions of male privilege often point out that not one female holds a seat on the New York Stock Exchange, and that they are almost as rigorously barred from executive jobs in steel, automobiles, and other heavy industries. This is all absolutely true: the men in those businesses *do* consider women unsuitable as partners. Yet the more important question is: Why have women failed to exert sufficient pressure in these areas, as they did in certain others, to force their way in? At least one reason may be that the remaining masculine enclaves are those in which intermittent, or part-time, or gentle efforts produce not moderate success, but failure; in much of American life, as in Wonderland, one must run as fast as one can merely to stay in the same place.

There is, of course, another alternative in the form of volunteer or community work, which can be taken in measured doses, not interfering with family life or wifely duties. But volunteer work seems to be on the decline. One area after another of volunteer work is succumbing to "professionalization," which sounds as though the quality of work is being improved, but which quite often means only that women will gladly work all week, for too little money, at a job they will not do once a week for free. For it isn't the cash value of the job that counts; it is the fact that the work carries the title, prestige, and above all the *demands* of employment rather than of voluntary effort. The volunteer is in that most difficult of all human positions — she must do good, on her own, day after day, without being required to do so; she is like that pathetic little girl in the permissive modern school who asked the teacher one day, "Miss Smith, do I *have* to do whatever I *want* to do all day long?"

American women, in sum, are now inventing new forms of femininity geared to the conditions of modern society and to the needs of modern marriage. To hark back to my original biblical metaphor, they are designing new bottles into which to decant and preserve the wine of their own lives. I am encouraged to think that this is a real and growing trend by much of what I see going on around me:

— I think, for instance, of the new emphasis on excellence in both high school and college — an emphasis which seems now to affect girls as well as boys;

— I think of the early but perceptible signs of waning in the teen-age marriage fad, and the increasing efforts being made to prevent drop-outs;

— I think of the changing emphasis on female vocations, which is now minimizing the marriage-career conflict and yet not requiring total domesticity of women;

— I think of the women at Temple University, Sarah Lawrence, Radcliffe, Minnesota, and many other schools, who in their vital, vibrant thirties or forties have returned to college to renew aspects of themselves which they are about ready to use again;

— I think of the statistics of the Women's Bureau which, in their dispassionate impersonal fashion, tell of millions of women who lay aside their vocations or outside activities for only the busiest mothering years, or even shift from full-time to part-time participation and have no break whatever in the continuity of their lives;

— I think of inventive housewives who simplify their housekeeping, or form cooperative nurseries, or find any of a dozen other ways of winning some time away from domestic chores and mothering, so as in the end to be better mothers, wives, and housekeepers by being, first of all, more nearly whole and fulfilled human beings.

I find all this good and cheering. The ethical man — and I hope I am one — can wish no less for his fellow man than wholeness, completion, and the fulfillment of each person's potentialities. And by my fellow man I mean mankind — and therefore I mean woman.

Love and Marriage

The first of the following pair of articles praises romantic love; the second analyzes love clinically and mathematically. Yet there is no conflict between the two viewpoints; they are really only different aspects of the same highly complex reality. Love's meaning can be spelled out historically and culturally, as in the first article; its psychological meaning can be dissected by the scientific methods outlined in the second article. I have put the two pieces together here precisely because I find it so intriguing to see how different a human emotion looks when studied from such different angles.

In Defense of Romantic Love

IN THE NATION'S institutions of higher learning, some thousands of sociologists and professors of family life are currently waging a campaign against an insidious and malign philosophy to which youth is perennially attracted — romantic love. Well over seven hundred universities and colleges are now offering courses in courtship, marriage, and the family, and the instructors who teach them are, almost to a man, hostile to romantic love, and hold it to be a deception, a danger, and even a disease.

In rare moments of jocularity, some of them sneeringly refer to it as "cardiac-respiratory love," but most of the time they soberly harry it with case histories, belabor it with statistics, and lay siege to it with random samples. Their avowed aim is to convince their students that it is a sickly fantasy, best abandoned as soon as possible in favor of "mature love" or "conjugal love," a sensible, realistic emotion. They speak and write of romantic love in terms like these:

> Only those people who do not know each other intimately can feel romantic. — MAGOUN, *Love and Marriage*.

> [Romantic love] is like a drug. . . . Fortunately, its power can be more easily broken than that of drugs. Time and common sense . . . frequently restore even the violent afflicted to sanity — and happiness. — BABER, *Marriage and the Family*.

There have, of course, always been people who spoke ill of romantic love. Francis Bacon acidly maintained that of all the really great persons in history "not one . . . hath been transported to the mad degree of love"; Jonathan Swift termed it "a ridiculous passion which hath no being but in play-books and romances"; and H. L. Mencken dismissed it airily as a "state of perceptual anesthesia." But all this was only philosophic rodomontade; it waited upon modern sociology and anthropology to dignify the attack with the name of science.

Margaret Mead lived with the Arapesh of New Guinea in the 1920's, and with the Samoans somewhat later; her writings clearly implied that these peoples, who possessed nothing akin to Western romantic love, were happier and healthier without it. Similar reports came in from fieldworkers in Tahiti, Rhodesia, and a score of other areas. Finally, in 1936 anthropologist Ralph Linton summarized the feelings of the social-science *avant-garde* in these classically sarcastic words:

> All societies recognize that there are occasional violent attachments between persons of opposite sex, but our present American culture is practically the only one which has attempted to capitalize on these and make them the basis for marriage. . . . Their rarity in most societies suggests that they are psychological abnormalities to which our culture has attached an extraordinary value just as other cultures have attached extreme values to other abnormalities. The hero of the modern Ameri-

can movie is always a romantic lover just as the hero of the old Arab epic is always an epileptic.

Ever since, this has been the prevailing view of most social scientists, a considerable number of whom have earned their Ph.D.'s by attacking some tenet or practice of romantic love. And just what *is* this psychological abnormality from which they would cure us with the psychotherapy of cross-cultural studies and statistics? There is no satisfactorily rigorous definition of it, but as one sociologist writes, "In sociology it has been customary to apply the term 'romantic' to a kind of love characterized by idealization of the love-object and by its inaccessibility." From these fundamental characteristics stem the other qualities — its power and intensity, its bittersweet joy, its picturesque, poetic, or strange circumstances, its overvaluation of physical appeal, to which the lover ascribes all manner of spiritual and mental values.

Typically, the romantic lover has only to see the right girl the first time, and something deep within him vibrates, or perhaps melts, or even perhaps rings like a bell. She may be a stranger across a crowded room, but somehow he *knows*. It does not matter that he is, say, a middle-aged French exile with half-breed children, and she an ignorant young girl from Arkansas, for love not only ignores such obstacles but thrives upon them.

The course of romantic love, however, does not run smoothly; there are always obstacles, separations, and conflicts. The lovers yearn, despair, toss on their beds sleepless, walk alone in the moonlight, write notes and tear them up, and think vaguely about renouncing everything or committing suicide. For the value of the world now depends upon the beloved: he (or she) is perfect, wonderful, and unique, and without him (or her) the world and life are worthless.

In this condition of wretched happiness and miserable joy, the romantic lovers want only one thing — to link their lives forever. They expect that when they marry, all problems will be solved, all wants and needs fulfilled. They will require no others, being sufficient unto themselves; they will be perennially entranced, continuously happy, their life an endless succession of mountain-top picnics, candle-lit dinners, love-filled nights. But the love is always tender, rather than lusty: as seen in the advertisements in magazines for young women, the handsome husband, faultlessly dressed, hovers adoringly over his wife after dinner, gallantly lighting her cigarette while she smiles prettily up at him. Every day is a date for two; there are no dirty dishes, cranky children, or unpaid bills.

Such is the general picture of romantic love, perpetuated in movies, fiction, and advertising, against which the antiromantics have been waging armed combat with their surveys and chi-square analyses. They accuse it of misdirecting young people in their choice of mates, of leading them to expect of marriage something unreal and nonexistent, of creating desires that can never be fulfilled, of blocking the development of satisfactory married love. They therefore term it a major cause of divorce, and have even turned their masses of statistics into marriage prediction tests which show, to the second decimal place, that every difference between the cultural background of the lovers, or their education, religion, or social status, decreases the chances of happy marriage and lasting love. Indeed, by a logical extension of their arguments — though they never make it — the ideal mate for each man would be his sister, were it not for a certain regrettable narrow-mindedness people have about such arrangements.

The sociologists are not alone in condemning romantic love and viewing its consequences with alarm. Some psychoanalysts side with them; Lawrence Kubie, for instance, declares that "being in love is an obsessional state which, like all obsessions, is in part driven by unconscious anger"; and Theodore Reik calls love "a reaction-formation to envy, possessiveness, and hostility." Many marriage counselors consider any love affair between people of dissimilar background a form of retribution against one's parents. The Swiss religionist Denis de Rougemont argues learnedly that romantic love, being an outgrowth of the Manichean heresy, is irreconcilable with marriage and social health. In sum, the antiromantics feel that romantic love is an antiquated, nonfunctional, and immature (or perhaps neurotic) pattern which poisons the minds of the young and prevents them from experiencing that richer and healthier variety, mature or conjugal love.

And now, one wants to know, what *is* this marvelous thing, conjugal love? Here begins a mystery. It is easy to piece together the picture of romantic love, and to describe the actions and fancies of lovers of that stripe; but of conjugal love and lovers there is hardly a scrap of description to be found. Search as you will in the writings of the antiromantics, you cannot find any clear portrait of the thing. Some of the advocates of conjugal love speak of it in terms of "adjustment," and tabulate the average months or years needed to adjust to each other in religious matters, sexual matters, and so on; so treated, conjugal love sounds like a truce reached after battlefield exhaustion. Others equate it with companionship, though this quite fails to distinguish the love of people of different sexes from the friendship of men for each other; there is, happily, a difference. Still others discuss conjugal love in terms of "habit formation" and "accommodation to a standardized pattern of living, working, and playing together"; this sounds unpleasantly like basic military training.

Psychologist A. H. Maslow of Brandeis University, lauding the intimacy and freedom of self-expression possible in mature conjugal love, says that in it "there is much less tendency to put the best foot forward . . . [or hide] physical defects. . . . There is much less maintenance of distance, mystery, and glamour." Like much of the writing on the subject, this tells us what conjugal love is not, rather than what it is; one might even be pardoned for wondering if anything recognizable as love exists within the state of so-called conjugal love. And it is no surprise, therefore, to find some of the critics of romantic love admitting plainly that love really has nothing to do with marriage, or should not have. Simone de Beauvoir and Denis de Rougemont both take that point of view, albeit from different assumptions, and right here in New York City Dr. Ernest van den Haag of New York University recently told a *New York Times* reporter, "Love is a passion, and the literal meaning of passion is 'suffering.' It is the tension between desire and fulfillment. As love becomes fulfilled, it ceases to exist. . . . Marriage, on the other hand, is a very serious matter. It is rational, very legal, and quite public. It is, in fact, based on the temporary nature of love, and was designed by society to compel people to continue to live together long after their ardor has cooled."

Clearly, the opponents of romantic love would like to rid us of a disease most of us have found enjoyable and important, and are offering us instead a condition of health that will be good for us, and no pleasure whatever. But how valid, how fruitful, how meaningful have their teachings been? Does it, for instance, really help marriage to eliminate romantic attitudes from it? In magazine articles and in the files of family counselors, no complaint is more common than that concerning the way even articulate and sensitive men, tender and expressive in courtship, become lumpish brutes after marriage. Marriage counselors like the late Dr. Abraham Stone were forever trying to teach both husbands and wives the value of preserving certain romantic attitudes and practices in order to satisfy their partners' continuing emotional needs.

Is it helpful to cultivate adjustment, rather than love, within marriage? Curiously enough, it is among the educated and intelligent stratum of Americans who strive for adjustment hardest that the incidence of infidelity grows with each year of marriage, reaching a peak in the late thirties just when conjugal love should have become totally mature and satisfying. Although the libido slowly diminishes in intensity, the emotional hungers would seem to increase, or to be increasingly unsatisfied.

But by far the gravest defect in contemporary antiromanticism is its internal inconsistency, which makes its advice and its directives conflicting and unworkable. Most of the antiromantic marriage analysts admit that romantic love is, in our society, the only functioning method of mate selection; they further admit that it holds bride and groom together long enough to permit them to build permanent ties. Yet at the same time they counsel young people *against* choosing a mate on the basis of romantic ideas, and even urge them to expel these feelings and ideas from their marriages as rapidly as they can. The late Willard Waller, a sociologist of considerable influence, actively advocated measured doses of quarreling early in marriage "to liquidate the effects of the romantic complex." Neither he nor any of his followers ever had the scientific good grace to follow up this suggestion and see what results it yielded.

What has been passed off as a theory based on scientific method is, therefore, so tangled in its own contradictions that one may suspect the method has been used wrongly. But where and how? Maybe in the use made of cross-cultural comparisons. Romantic love is absent from Samoan life, and the Samoans are the better off thereby, but how does that prove that urbanized Americans, with no tribal and intimate community life, can likewise thrive without it? Quite possibly we would be as badly off without it as they would be without the outrigger canoe.

Or perhaps the scientific method has come unglued because it has rated kinds of love in terms of adjustment, assuming that to be good without first proving it so. Americans have a rich cultural heritage that shapes their thinking and feeling, and that has stressed achievement, success, independence, freedom, and other so-called Puritan values rather than adjustment. There are no scientific grounds for believing that adjustment is better in any absolute sense than our native values — or if there are, the antiromantics have never bothered to demonstrate them.

Even this is but a trifling bobble compared to the major error of the antiromantics — the mistaking of the part for the whole. Romantic love is a rich, complicated, cultural tradition with an eight-century history. Sociologists are not always the best cultural historians, however, and it suits them to marshal under the label "romantic love" only the foolish and unrealistic aspects of the total complex; meanwhile they ignore those other elements of romantic love which are among the most important constituents of modern marriage.

Romantic love originated in the medieval code of *l'amour courtois* or courtly love. Undeniably, part of that code was silly and full of make-believe. A mature lordling would ignore his lands, retainers, and family to moon over the divine perfections he imagined in another knight's wife. He might spend years secretly serving her to gain a smile, risk his life in combat for a single kiss, and think himself blessed to be granted a minute alone in her sacred presence. This side of courtly love has descended clear to the present, existing in the form of puppy love, adolescent crushes, and the amorous daydreams of the young. The sociologists stoutly attack this concept of love as being unsuited to the needs of marriage and the facts of everyday intimacy — but the lords and ladies of the Middle Ages made that criticism eight hundred years ago. "We declare and we hold it as firmly established," proclaimed the leading propagandist for courtly love, Countess Marie of Champagne, in 1174, "that love cannot exert its powers between two people who are married to each other." The extremes of unrealistic romance have always remained outside of marriage; in our own young people they are outgrown along with acne and awkwardness. Not only do the intimacy of going steady and the practical side of planning for marriage wear away illusion, but maturing young men and women neither require make-believe love nor are satisfied by it as they were a few years earlier. The dangers of romantic love are thus marvelously exaggerated, as are all the peculiarities of adolescence.

Still, Countess Marie was wrong; she could not know or see in her time that the middle classes would hanker for the new form of love, but, being unable to afford it, would borrow from it many of its values and incorporate them in marriage. For courtly love was a larger and far more important thing than its superficially gamelike appearance would indicate. Despite its unreality and its foolishness, it introduced into the relationship between man and woman qualities which are hardly to be found in earlier history.

For nearly a millennium the Catholic-Teutonic tradition had given the husband patriarchal power over his wife's money, body, and even mind. Romantic love reversed the roles; the man prostrated himself, quivering, at the feet of the beautiful cruel lady and begged her to be kind. The end result, after much evolution, was a rough balance. Man and wife became approximate equals, each trying to serve and please the other. This, the very core of modern marriage, is a direct, if long-term, result of the elevation of woman in the game of *l'amour courtois*.

Sexual expression, too, was greatly changed by romantic love, becoming much more tender and aesthetic. The unfortunate and unavoidable concomitant was that it also became much more subject to neurosis and functional failure; the near-impotence of that ultraromantic, Rousseau, is a perfect case in point. Yet it is just because of our inhibitions and complications about sex that we have entangled it in our deepest emotions and allied it to concepts of friendship and lasting loyalty. Sex was far simpler for the Greek of classic times than for us, but he regarded his wife as a housekeeper, and sought love in the arms of whores or boys. The difference between his way and ours is due in large part to romanticism.

The most striking innovation of romantic love, however, was its notion that love improved one's character and therefore had ethical value.

"Oh, what a wonderful thing is love," wrote Andreas Capellanus in 1175 or so, "which makes a man shine with so many virtues and teaches everyone, no matter who he is, so many good traits of character!" Before the appearance of courtly love that note had almost never been sounded; afterwards it was never silenced. Renaissance courtiers considered love a stairway to spiritual excellence, Romanticists of the late eighteenth century sought in love an answer to the meaning of life, and Victorians praised love as the redeeming experience that saved them from brutalization in the market place.

Modern men and women, similarly, make love an ethical good. Without it, they believe, life is barren, selfish, and worthless, and until one has loved his character is incomplete and imperfect. Even the antiromantics believe this, though they hide the ethical content behind scientific language: they term the inability to love conjugally a sign of immaturity (which is the equivalent of *bad*) and the opposite as a sign of maturity (which is the equivalent of *good*). Who can quarrel with this? Yet it exposes the weakness of antiromanticism as nothing else: the very people who identify romantic love as the *opposite* of conjugal love also describe conjugal love in terms borrowed from the romantic tradition.

Granted that the more unrealistic and foolish aspects of romantic love can be hurtful, if carried over beyond adolescence; still the over-all attack on romantic love may be even more hurtful. The antiromantics are salesmen of the humdrum in place of the wonderful, and advocates of pain-reducing adjustment rather than emotional satisfaction. To "liquidate the effects of the romantic complex" is to rob marriage of much of its major function in the present era.

For what is that function? Not the breeding of warriors or farmhands. Not the maintenance of a dynastic name. Not the establishment of a food- and clothing-making economic unit. Modern man can buy all the goods and services he needs for cash, and he has no compelling urge to continue a clear-cut family line. But the more our society becomes urban, mobile, fluid, and subject to rapid change, the more he needs warmth, reassurance, belongingness, enduring friendship, and certainty of affection. All these, combined with sex and expressed in part through it, are what he seeks in marriage. A studied liquidation of romantic values can only weaken it, blunt its purposes, and make it dull and un-satisfying. It is not so dreadful of us to continue hungering for romantic love after we marry; it is only dreadful if the marriage itself cannot appease that hunger.

So it is the larger forces of history and industrialism that have increased the need of the individual for those more basic and important components of romantic love that we have just spelled out. Yet even the more superficial and seemingly foolish side of romantic love has a certain value in modern marriage, and ought not wholly to be abandoned to the teen-agers. Perhaps it seems immature to the psychologist for anyone to maintain illusions of physical attractiveness before his mate, but is it loving and generous to cease doing so? Each of us needs to feel capable of winning the love of someone desirable and attractive; the maturity that scorns this is the maturity of the saint or the corpse. To make the effort to seem attractive in the eyes of one's love partner is not just vanity and immaturity, but a form of thoughtfulness and generosity towards him or her.

Perhaps excessive idealization of a scarcely known person is ridiculous, and even harmful. But a small dollop of idealization of one's mate — seeing him or her as a little handsomer, kinder, or more gifted than he really is — contributes to the satisfaction of both parties, and makes each a little more satisfied than he ought, in hardheaded realism, to be.

Perhaps the jousting, the silent sufferings, and the self-abasement of the knight were a worthless sort of service to the lady. But in modern marriage the effort of each partner to meet the other's emotional needs and to do services for the other is unquestionably gratifying to both, and important to the maintenance of the union.

Perhaps it is both undesirable and impossible to maintain a romantic aura throughout all the days and years of marriage. But those married people who can create it for themselves at appropriate times will find their married love-making continually satisfying. It becomes dull only for those who discard, as unnecessary, the aesthetic and mood-inducing circumstances, and who wonder afterwards, as the pathetic cliché has it, why the magic has gone out of their marriages.

No reasonable person will deny that the adolescent and fictional variety of romantic love is unsuited to adult life, and that a heavy diet of it may misguide and harm some young people. But there is an even greater danger in condemning all romantic values and trying to root them out of marriage — the danger that we may weaken its structural ties and render it unrewarding. It may be virtuous to strive for maturity, but because one is virtuous, shall there be no more cakes and ale?

How Do We Choose a Mate?

FOR EVEN LONGER than they have wondered about such things as gravity and light, men have wondered what it is that makes us love. Unlike gravity and light, however, love has remained a matter for poetic, philosophic, and psychological speculation rather than scientific theory, experimental data, and mathematical proof. Or at least such was the case until the recent publication (almost unnoticed by the world of lovers) of a profound little volume entitled *Mate-Selection,* written by sociologist Robert F. Winch of Northwestern University.

Professor Winch, a tanned, athletic, genial man of forty-eight, uses the insights of psychology, the data of sociology, and the rigorous proofs of statistical analysis in arriving at his "complementary" theory of love. And that theory firmly contradicts all those poets and philosophers who have long described love as a mystical union of similar spirits, or a noble desire to protect and serve someone, or an unselfish and altruistic impulse akin to the feeling God has towards all His creatures. According to Winch's evidence, the love of man for woman and woman for man is basically self-serving, and perhaps plain selfish. Its primary purpose is to benefit the lover, not his beloved.

Each of us tends to fall in love with someone whose personality is the complement of his own, and through whom he can therefore relieve his own frustrations and substitutively live out his impossible wishes. A tough, brusque, hard-driving man may long — in some secret chamber of the psyche — to be a cared-for child again. He cannot, but

instead he falls in love with a timid, frail girl whom he can enjoy sheltering — and through whom, by proxy, he enjoys that would-be other
self. She, meanwhile, has always yearned to be more aggressive and
competent, and because she identifies her life with his, she achieves it
at last, even though only vicariously. So each benefits and fulfills the
other — and thus love, though selfish in its origin, succeeds in being
a mutual blessing and in seeming noble.

Professor Winch calls this dovetailing of psychological needs "com-
plementariness," and conceives it to be the essential reason for love (or,
at least, the kind of love known to middle-class Americans in our time).
Sexual desire, beauty, and similarity of likes and dislikes are all minor
forces compared to the pull of complementary psychological needs, according to the eight-year study Winch made of fifty young husbands
and wives upon which *Mate-Selection* is based. In a way, of course,
the theory is very old. The common man has long said that "opposites
attract" (though he also says that "like marries like"), and as far back
as the fourth century B.C., Plato had likened lovers to two halves of
an original creature, needful to make one whole person. But this was
only one of scores of equally plausible viewpoints about love until 1958,
when *Mate-Selection* appeared and made it the first and only validated
theory. Hailing Winch for this contribution, the *American Journal of
Sociology* commented, "The idea [of complementary needs] is not new;
indeed it is very old, but Winch is the first person to prove that it is
true."

The book is based upon a study of twelve psychological needs and
three general traits, all of them familiar to everyone. They include, for
instance, the need to dominate, the need for achievement, the need to
be deferent (admiring of someone else), the need to express hostility, the
need to abase one's self (or take blame for things), the need to be recognized or approved by others, the need to take care of someone, the need
to be taken care of by someone, and so on. Out of these raw materials
— none of which sounds at all amorous — love itself is fashioned, almost as a rare drug may be synthesized out of common and lowly
chemicals.

For the traits of any one person, though not lovable in the abstract,
seem lovable when viewed through the eyes of the person whose needs

they meet. Among Winch's cases, for instance, was an easy-going, overly "nice" man who married a girl with a quick, flashing temper — and found it delicious to watch. A bright egotistical chap was married to an ignorant farm girl who admired his egotism as "manliness" and his self-ishness as a sign of importance. Indeed, the theory of complementary needs answers the most-asked question in the realm of love — "What on earth does he see in her?" A sharp tongue in a woman will look like shrewishness to one man, but like delightful vivacity to another; a pre-occupation with homemaking may seem wonderfully feminine to one man and merely insipid to another.

What she sees in him is likewise explained by her needs. Outsiders might regard Adam, a would-be writer, as a soft, lumbering, Saint Bernard of a man, a veritable Mr. Milquetoast who eats whatever his wife, Alice, suggests, goes wherever she wants to go, listens while she talks. Alice interprets these qualities in a quite different way: "He's like Dad," she says. "He's kind and understanding, and he has a great capacity for loving and being affectionate." (All names in Winch's book are altered, but the words he quotes are taken from verbatim transcripts of inter-views, and are in no way fictionalized.)

The need theory also explains the mystifying way in which so many men and women fall in love with people almost the opposite of what they were looking for. Herb always conceived of his ideal girl as "blonde and real sweet and quiet" — and married Harriet, who is dark, bouncy, and incredibly talkative. Jonathan always expected to fall in love with a girl who was intelligent, ambitious, and energetic — and chose Jean, a beautiful well-groomed bird-brain who lies in bed all morning, and who often falls into moods of depression because of her own incom-petence.

Why this should be so is no mystery to Winch. Many a young person expects he will fall in love with someone emotionally like himself, but such a person will only duplicate, rather than complete, his personality and fulfill his needs. Hence, even if he finds her, he either fails to fall in love, or the love fails to prosper. When the psychological opposite of one's self comes along, although she contradicts the ideal image, a mightier and more satisfying love springs up in the breast. No wonder love has traditionally been associated with sensations of surprise, dismay, and bewilderment.

Yet it sometimes happens that a person who falls in love with the opposite of what he wanted soon sets about trying to change her and remake her into the original image. This is a curious paradox, for if he succeeds, she may no longer be the person he fell in love with. The man who tries to make his childish wife more competent about running things, the woman who tries to make her easygoing husband more ambitious, may only succeed in creating a partner who no longer satisfies his or her emotional needs. Happily for all concerned, says Professor Winch, the reformer generally picks a partner who cannot really change as radically as he desires. He thus can play educator and teacher year after year without loss, since his beloved never becomes what he *thinks* he wants, but remains what he *truly* wants.

Such analyses may offend those who feel that "true love" or "mature love" cannot have so mundane and selfish a basis, but must be benevolent, unselfish, and noble. With this Professor Winch disagrees completely. "My data make it clear," he says, "that the person who is benevolent and giving has a psychological need to be that way. The overfull breast hurts and needs a hungry infant. The overfull personality likewise needs someone who requires cherishing and nurturing. I have never found any instance of a nurturant person falling in love with another nurturant person; such people are drawn instead towards those who need them — and whom they themselves need. I see no reason for us to be apologetic about it; we are, after all, men, not gods."

Whether or not one finds Winch's theory disturbing, it should really be judged as are all scientific theories — by the number of different phenomena it explains, and by the simplicity of the principles it uses. So judged, it does well, indeed. With a single major principle, it is capable of making sense out of the crushes of the bobby-soxer, the romances of high-school youth, the love that blossoms into marriage, and the love that exists within marriages of many years' duration; the magic concept "need" is the key to all of them.

The adolescent has no achievements as yet, and no sense of importance as a person, in our society. His needs for recognition and identity are overwhelming, and the easiest way to meet them is to be in love with someone famous, such as a movie star (thus gaining a vicarious sense of fame himself), or to be involved in a crush with a girl of his own age and so show his peers that he is worth considering.

As boys and girls finish high school and start earning money or going to college, their needs change. More sure of their status and their personal value, they are less impelled to love merely for the sake of being in love. They gradually cease to ascribe marvelous properties to mere physical attributes, and begin to respond to deep-lying traits of character that meet their own emerging needs; typically, this is the kind of love that actually produces marriage.

Successful marriages tend to grow closer and better adjusted as the years pass, yet it is undeniable that some of the magical honeymoon qualities inevitably disappear. This, too, is the result of changing needs; the insecurities and emotional hungers of young married people make their new intimacy an intense and wonderful thing, but after years together they become far surer of themselves and require less repeated and less exuberant assurances of love, even though their ability to supply each other with fundamental satisfactions may be increasing.

Everyone has heard, nonetheless, of some solid, stoutly built marriage which endured through years of financial struggle, only to disintegrate mysteriously when finally the husband achieved real success. The theory makes sense even of this. Once he may have loved (because he needed) a wife who gave him reassurance, support, and comfort; but when his good fortune reduces his need for these things, he finds his marriage suddenly gone stale, and is unaccountably captivated by a giddy and childish minx whom he never before would have found appealing.

These are but a few of the insights and understandings yielded by the theory of complementary needs. In recent decades, something akin to this had been advanced in a general way by a few Freudian psychoanalysts, and Winch found that it appeared to explain the many aspects of dating, courtship, and marriage better than any other available theory. Yet it lacked what he calls "hard" evidence — detailed data, careful surveys, precise statistical analysis.

Hoping to put the theory on a scientific basis, he got a small grant from Northwestern University in 1948, and later won a considerably larger one from the National Institute of Mental Health. With a small staff of psychologically trained sociologists and graduate students, he began preliminary studies, and in 1950 was ready to capture his specimens. He compiled a list of all married students at Northwestern University, struck off those who belonged to minority groups (so as to eliminate confusing side issues), and from the final list picked names at random. He then had an assistant telephone the students and offer them a tiny fee ($7.50) to cooperate. When he had twenty-five willing couples, he was ready to begin.

Over a five-month period in 1950 the fifty young husbands and wives came in, by appointment, to the interview rooms in Fisk Hall on the Evanston campus. They were a real grab-bag assortment — tall young men and short young men; pretty girls and homely ones; country-bred types and city-bred ones; would-be writers, fledgling accountants, and embryo lawyers; working wives, teaching wives, and plain housewives. All of them were young; all were still childless; all had been married under two years and therefore could still vividly remember their meeting, courtship, and first months of marital adjustment. Some spoke of these things haltingly and shyly, but most "opened up" in the first half hour and talked freely. Each spoke for a total of nearly five hours, and also took two psychological tests; the result was a dossier, on each person, of anywhere from seventy to two hundred pages of raw material.

The interviewing and testing was designed to ferret out clues as to the psychological needs of each subject. As one of their investigative tools, Winch and his assistants had designed a set of questions for this specific purpose. The question, "What do you do if someone steps in front of you in line in a crowded restaurant?" may sound provocative and amusing, but to a trained observer it provides very revealing answers. (Overtly hostile persons push back or speak up; average persons seethe quietly but say nothing; persons in whom anger was sternly forbidden during childhood shrug and say, "It takes all kinds to make a world.") A question that evokes hidden sexual attitudes read: "With what kind of man (woman) would you like to be shipwrecked, if you knew it was just for a day?" (One aggressive, seemingly self-confident woman revealed much about her inner fearfulness by answering, "A man who would comfort me because I was scared but stay away from me; preferably one who had a wife he loved.") The question, "If you and your spouse were both nominated for president of a club, would you run?" seems harmless enough, but women who quickly insisted

they would not run against their husbands revealed something profoundly different in their attitudes toward dominance in marriage from
those who brightly asserted that they saw no reason why they shouldn't.

For the next two years, Winch and his staff were busily occupied
with the detailed analysis of every case. From the dossiers they made
six complete and separate estimates of each subject's needs, and then,
cross-comparing them, finally assigned each case a set of numerical
values. (A "1" in "achievement" meant, for example, that the individual
had a very low need to be successful or to create something; a "5" in
achievement meant the extreme opposite.) When a whole series of final
values had thus been worked out for each of the fifty people, the staff
was able to consider their fifty people as so much statistical information,
and by the use of equations could test whether the husbands' scores
were really correlated (arithmetically linked) with their wives' scores
in complementary traits. Anyone could *see* the correlations, but only
statistical computation could show whether the correlations were large
enough to be meaningful.

In some cases, the correlations came out very high. A strong need
for recognition in one spouse was, for instance, highly correlated with
a small need for recognition in the other spouse, and a need to dominate
in one was usually linked with a need to be deferent in the other. Some
computations, however, showed certain complementary linkages to exist
only weakly, if at all; sociability in one spouse, for instance, seemed
not to be tied up at all with reserve in the other. But in general, people
who liked to dominate, teach, or direct — whether male or female —
fell in love with persons of the opposite sex who liked to be steered,
have decisions made for them, or be instructed and criticized.

The ultimate test, however, was purely statistical, and consisted of
taking a reckoning of the whole sample of correlations and measuring
what proportion of them favored the theory and what proportion went
against it. Winch's group used mathematical methods on a total of 388
pairs of traits; in the end, 256 of them showed correlations favoring his
theory. This was something less than a perfect score, but man is a complicated creature and not easy to measure accurately. Nevertheless,
when this score is tested by the formulas of probability theory, it proves
to be a result that would occur by accident only once in a thousand

times; put another way, Winch's imperfect result is a 99.9 per cent proof that the theory of complementary needs is correct.

Winch's own work ended when he completed writing up his results and published them in the form of the book (which, incidentally, pares the dry statistics to the bone, but fleshes out the theory with vivid case histories), but he fervently hopes that the theory will yield many practical applications. American divorce, for instance, has been studied from many an angle — money, women's careers, the effect of education, children, and so on — but perhaps the need theory will yield more helpful information than any of these. Marriages that end in divorce may prove to be less the result of any of these other factors than of the failure by one or both partners to recognize their own important needs.

A typical case is that of a gifted, but rather conceited biochemist who thought that he wanted a brilliant well-educated wife. He met such a girl, fell in love, and married her, only to find their life one unending wrangle for supremacy. Neither could tolerate the other's abilities and efforts at dominance, and after five years they split up amidst bitter denunciations. Each, however, had learned something about himself; the man then married a frequently tearful clinging vine of a girl, while his ex-wife married a moody bohemian novelist, and now each has a warmer, sounder marriage than before.

If the need theory does cast new light on divorce, it may eventually lead to preventive action. Young people — at least as many of them as attend courses on marriage in colleges and high schools — might be made sharply aware that enduring and satisfying love is based on more than pride of ownership of a popular partner with the "right kind" of looks, a good dance-floor technique, or other such qualities. Through teachers, counselors, ministers, and other sources, still other young people might gain similar self-knowledge early enough to help them avoid impulsive or quixotic teen-age marriages.

Indeed, one of the most important implications of the need theory is that the present trend towards early courtship and early marriage is robbing many young people of the opportunity to experience lasting love. The need patterns of the adolescent are radically different from those of the young adult; it must follow that juvenile love, however delicious, is a hopelessly inadequate basis on which to choose a lifelong partner. The proof is that girls who marry under the age of twenty have three times as great a chance of winding up in divorce court as girls who wait to marry between the ages of twenty-two and twenty-four; the data for boys tell a similar story.

What implications does the need theory have for married people? Professor Winch is extremely reluctant to predict that it will yield increased marital happiness, but he does maintain that it can give both husband and wife a clearer and more fruitful way of thinking about each other, about what each of them wants in marriage, and about the way in which they can satisfy each other and themselves simultaneously. To give but one example, consider the man or woman who is always discontented with his mate, who always complains, feels put-upon, and tries to reform and change the spouse. Such a person, through clearer understanding of the nature of love, might recognize that his own deep-lying needs made him choose as he did, and might lead him to slacken his pressures, lose some of his perennial discontent, and so make his marriage happier.

Marriages which are in more serious difficulties may benefit from the new tools that the need theory puts into the hands of professional counselors. By a happy coincidence, Winch's wife, Martha Winch, is executive director of the Family Service of Highland Park, Illinois, where she has counseled couples in trouble for many years, and has been able to evaluate the practical uses of need theory. She feels that it gives a marriage counselor a way to do more than search for the sources of frustration and friction in a marriage — it enables him to look for those complementary and cohesive factors which originally produced love, which can be strengthened in order to repair the marriage, and which might disintegrate altogether if the counselor too energetically set about changing the personalities of the troubled people.

But it is much too early to guess at more than a few of the ways in which the need theory may prove useful. One thing, however, is clear: it will help all who love, or who hope to love, by bringing them keener and clearer understandings of what it is that produces and sustains that most marvelous and desired of all emotions. Try it yourself, if you are not one of those who fear to put love under thoughtful scrutiny. Stop and recall the loves in your own life: the bittersweet romance of youth;

the strong imperious love that drew you and your mate together in marriage; the love you know after years of marriage. Ask yourself *why* you once loved or why you love now, trying to see what needs were at work, and why they either sustained love or failed to keep it going.

Never fear that you will harm anything by so doing; you can only strengthen love by gaining some insight. For through such reflection you may become newly aware of how vital the love is which we tend to take for granted. "Look at each other!" cries the spirit of Emily in *Our Town*, as she returns and sees the scenes of her youth. She means, of course, "Love each other! Hold your love precious; never take it for granted." Better advice was never given to mortal man.

Child-Rearing

An odd paradox exists in the area of modern parenthood. On the one hand, many contemporary parents doubt their own capacity or right to shape and develop the important traits of character in their children, and try to delegate this responsibility to schools, camps, and other outside agencies. On the other hand, these selfsame parents are virtually the only adults whose private responses and personalities their children ever see at close range; despite their poor opinion of their own capacity to affect their children, they therefore have an exceedingly great influence on them. Both halves of the paradox are examined in the following pair of articles, the first of which advises parents not to hopefully delegate authority to outside institutions concerning their children's character development, and the second of which urges them to seek out additional intimate parentlike contacts to enhance and enrich their children's perception of the adult world. For a paradox is not necessarily a conflict, but merely a truth held up to light and examined on both sides.

There's No Substitute for Parents

WAS THERE EVER so poor a bargain hunter as the modern parent? The more he spends on his children, studies books about child-rearing, and rearranges his life to benefit them, the more he doubts his own ability or right to shape their characters and teach them the virtues he thinks valuable.

All around him he sees more experts and outside agencies than ever before, actively trying to teach moral values, develop the character, and mold the personality of his children. Most schools today make "character training" or "life adjustment" more important than academic studies. Day camps and play groups conceive of "socialization" as their prime function. Family guidance workers, ministers, camp counselors, playground directors and child psychologists are all far more active and better recognized than ever. Many contemporary parents, seeing all this, are half convinced that these specialists are better able than they to teach their children the major values in life.

In the past year I have discussed this tendency with dozens of people who specialize in youth and family problems, ranging from lawyers to psychoanalysts. Most of them are deeply concerned by it, and feel that although the family is changing today, it is *not* becoming any less important in the area of character formation. There still is no substitute for parents. Most of the human qualities we think valuable can still best be taught by parents — and sometimes only by them. Even those parents who try to hand over their function to outsiders don't succeed in doing so; for good or for bad, their influence or neglect remains the paramount factor.

"The family," sociologist Leonard Cottrell of the Russell Sage Foundation told me, "is still the matrix of social experience in which the most persistent and pervasive personality patterns are formed." And Dr. Gunnar Dybwad, director of the Child Study Association of America said, "According to all the recent studies I've seen, the influence of the home remains far stronger than all the important outside forces that exist today."

Most experts agree. If, for instance, a child is always late, never does his homework, and loses his valuables, people are apt to say he should be sent to camp, where "they" will teach him a sense of responsibility. But parents who think so underrate their own power over the child. As one Scout executive put it, "All the training in the world at camp is of no avail if, when the child gets home, he is again allowed to be completely dependent on members of his family."

It may seem like the act of a loving mother to pick up after Junior, to brush and feed his dog when he forgets, and to buy him another wrist watch to replace the one he has lost. Certainly it's quicker and simpler than working out ways to get him to do these things for himself. But the gift of a new watch is cheap and tinselly next to the gift of an inner guide to conduct. The parent who would give the finer gift cannot buy it cheaply, or expect to have it given the child by outsiders.

It is the same with honesty. Schools cannot teach it successfully when there are conflicting values at home. Dr. Howard Lane of New York University, specialist in early childhood education, studied classroom cheating in a Midwestern community some years ago. He let the children grade their own papers, but checked to see how many answers they changed. A group of good middle-class children proved, shockingly enough, to cheat far more than a group of reform-school kids. Why? Because in the "good" homes honesty was given lip service — but success was the goal more sincerely sought. The children had seen their success-driven parents lie to their employers, welcome those they disliked, and do a hundred other similar things. Under such circumstances, honesty doesn't "take" on the children any more than a skin graft from one person to another; for a while, there is the appearance of success, but antagonistic chemicals in the cells of the body kill off the graft, and it is lost.

It is in the network of a thousand tiny and unimportant experiences in the home that a quality such as honesty can be caught. Yet one cannot teach a child honesty unless he teaches something else along with it. A confidence shark who fleeces an elderly woman of her savings is not just dishonest; he is callous to human suffering. A husband who runs off with the family bank account and deserts his wife and children is not just dishonest; he is emotionally frigid. Such people don't care enough about other human beings for honesty to matter to them; without love for humanity, it is only an empty name of a virtue.

What can make a child grow up to be callous, frigid or cruel? Many things, most of them within the home. Child psychologists preparing a report for the Midcentury White House Conference on Children and Youth agreed that a basic liking for the human race can be created or prevented *during the child's first year of life*. If an infant is always handled gently, fed when hungry, and comforted when miserable, if he knows the same friendly faces will appear whenever he needs them, he begins to get a fundamental trust in others and an unshakable liking for human beings. Parents who are impatient, nervous or easily angered, or who are too busy being successful to spend freely of their time and attention on their children, are building characters with sand. Outsiders will later try to patch them up, but they will never be solid and fine inside. It is a child's love of his parents that makes him want to adopt their traits of character, and learn the qualities they urge upon him. Without that love — and no outside agency or expert can adequately supply it — the qualities he is taught are like clothes, put on to conform to convention, but easy to take off, and easy to exchange. Instead, they should be like his very flesh — able to be cast aside only when life is over.

During World War II thousands of English children were sent out of London to avoid the bombings, and lived under the guidance of a few adults in carefully supervised children's communities. Psychiatrist Anna Freud studied a number of them, and found that they did indeed learn such aspects of behavior as how to defend themselves or attack others, how to be ingratiating, how to yield to authority, and how to get along with each other. But Dr. Freud learned that such qualities were adopted only to suit the needs of the moment, and were in no way comparable to the deep and permanent traits of courage, generosity, pity and self-sacrifice we admire. For the latter, she says, "are rooted exclusively in the love for the parents, and *in the child's identification with them.*" Without the power of love to make them sincerely emulate their parents, the children were turning out to be moral zombies — animated bodies with no souls, no consciences, guiding them from within.

Parents likewise play the major role in teaching their children courage — even when they least realize it. For courage comes to a child by indirection; it sneaks in by the back door of a quiet, secure belief that he can face up to problems and new situations. It isn't something that can be beaten, lectured, or exhorted into him. It comes from somewhere inside — from his glands and the juices they pour into his bloodstream, in response to the unconscious, rather than the thinking mind.

"Real courage has its roots," says Dr. M. Robert Gomberg, executive director of the Jewish Family Service, "in the child's feeling about himself, in his sense of worth and self-respect. The child who is made to feel too little, too young, too immature, too stupid to think his own thoughts, feel his own emotions, or make his own decisions, will not develop courage."

That's why the sink-or-swim method is a fraud. It succeeds with those who don't need it. It fails with those who lack the inner resources from which courage comes. The child who, from the time he learns to button his clothes to the time he goes away to college, is always given encouragement, and recognition of his own developing powers, will develop that kind of healthful self-esteem that will not fail him in a crisis. He may even be realistic enough to be frightened by the danger he faces — but he will find the courage to face it rather than collapse or blindly run from it.

Self-confidence is closely related to courage. "But surely," you may be thinking, "*there* is a trait the child has to develop outside the home." You may be recalling how, as an adolescent, you were embarrassed and shy at parties or on dates, and how by gaining experience in meeting, talking to, and socializing with other young people, you gradually learned to be at ease. Yet this is far from the whole story.

Several years ago a psychologist at the University of Michigan had a group of students write down their estimates of two short distances. He collected their papers and then announced the group average — deliberately giving false figures twice the real size. Then he asked them all to judge again. Some changed their guesses in the direction of the bogus group average, others didn't. Afterwards he studied them all intensively by means of personality tests to find out why some were influenced by a group opinion, even when it looked all wrong.

The suggestible students, he discovered, had grown up in homes where the parents were domineering and punitive, where childish efforts to gain independence were suppressed or scorned. As these children had grown up and mingled in the world, they never developed adequate belief in themselves or in their own opinions. Even when their eyes told them the group was wrong, they lacked confidence to stick with their own judgment.

Self-confidence, in other words, also has its origins in the home. Your children may mingle with outsiders and equals for years without ever gaining more than a kind of cover-up self-confidence — the kind that leaves them always unsure whether other people really like them or find them truly worthwhile. It is basic self-esteem on which a child builds social self-confidence. "A good home," someone once said, "is the place where you don't have to deserve what you get." It's a charming thought, but an even truer one would be: "A good home is the place where what you get makes you feel deserving."

It is the same with most of the other traits we deem worthy and good. Repeatedly, youth specialists told me that they are basically formed — or blocked — by the relationships and experiences of home life. Spiritual faith, the ability to work with other people, a sense of humor, tenderness — you can write your own list — are chiefly learned from, or at least grounded in, contacts with the parents. Later experiences and outside influences can build upon them or somewhat modify them; they can almost never entirely replace them or offer adequate substitutes.

Why then do many modern parents doubt their own importance and willingly give away to others the most precious right they own — that of creating their children in their own image and passing along to them the family's spiritual and ethical heritage?

Probably it is because this is a time of abrupt change in the patterns of family life. During most of the 10,000 years since the family came into being, it had many life-supporting functions that bound its members close together and kept them in each other's presence most of the time. Girls learned from their mothers how to cook, fashion clothing, and bring forth babies. Boys learned from their fathers how to plant, hunt, build, and defend the home. Along with these skills, they learned work habits, a set of goals in life, and a whole concept of morality.

But we have moved into the cities and the suburbs, as we have become an industrial nation. Fathers work far from their sons, and see them only under leisure-time circumstances. Mothers buy pre-cooked foods, ready-made clothing, and bear their babies in hospitals. The results include a far higher standard of living, a life that is cleaner and more comfortable and certainly more interesting. But they also include a sense of bewilderment on the part of the parents, who have lost the chance to use the old techniques of child-rearing, and have not yet found the new ones with which they can pass on to their children those truths they have found in life.

This doesn't mean that the job is beyond the abilities of modern parents. It *does* mean that they have to replace the old patterns with new ones, and that they must consciously lavish time and ingenuity on the job of child-rearing. One doesn't expect a garden to grow beautiful merely because he waters it routinely. There is a whole series of careful tasks to be done in making a garden grow — and in making a child's personality grow.

Take the condition sometimes called "technological unemployment of the young." Children were once an economic asset to the household. They helped produce the food, tend the animals, and make things for the home; they were of value, and they knew it. Today's children are freed from chores and can spend their out-of-school time in play and social activities. But they lack the chance to experience the unique satisfaction of being important to the family's well-being. They aren't necessary, and they sense this with a dim, nagging discontent.

Yet this can be overcome, and by surprisingly little acts. "You have to deliberately seek out and think up ways to *make* your children feel necessary," says Mrs. Sidonie Gruenberg, editor of the *Encyclopedia of Child Care and Guidance.* "It isn't easy to do under modern home conditions; it takes constant thought and planning. But even in an apartment you can send a child on an important errand for food. You can train him to take telephone messages. You can teach him to help out with a smaller brother or sister. You can call him the 'official mechanic' and put him in charge of changing light bulbs and making little repairs. Of course, it's much simpler and quicker to do everything yourself, but that deprives the child of the chance to feel needed, and to learn responsibility." The size of the job you allot the child is not important, either; even small jobs, if he is really responsible for them, serve the purpose.

Similarly, Dr. Ray Baber, a sociologist who has intensively studied the family, urges modern parents to deliberately encourage the children to participate in various family decisions, and be responsible for them at least to some degree. In important matters, he says reassuringly, parents can use suggestion and hints to ensure a choice within a reasonable range. But the child who feels as though she actually picked the new wallpaper for her room, or the boy who took some part in deciding where the family should spend its vacation, not only achieves a sense of importance, but recognizes that his wishes — and his reasons for them — may have a real effect on the rest of the family. And from this too comes a sense of responsibility.

A parent can't expect his tastes and enthusiasms to be naturally catching, like the measles. An enthusiasm for good literature, for instance, or for fine music, or for history, has to be communicated artfully, and made to seem like fun rather than something one *ought* to share. Cornelia Otis Skinner, the handsome actress who both writes and acts her wonderful evocative monologues, re-creating typical characters of other eras, says she gained much of her unique combination of acting talent and feeling for history from her father. He was Otis Skinner, the most celebrated actor in America a generation or two ago. But he didn't expect his daughter to acquire his tastes and interests without effort on his part.

"Father carefully taught me my awareness of period and of historical flavor," she says. "He was able to make history seem like delicious fun. On a rainy day, for instance, he might say that if I'd been a very good girl and would wash my hands very well, I could leaf through his costume books — the great volumes of colored prints of the clothing of other times. The way he granted this favor made it seem like a special treat, not an obligation, to roam around in the past and pick up the 'feel' of different periods." Even in the full flush of his triumphs on Broadway, Otis Skinner fought off the celebrity seekers and devoted his leisure time and energy to his family. Though he would be performing eight times a week, he always had time to read aloud to his wife and daughter great intoxicating draughts of Shakespeare and Dickens. And he read them just as wonderful stories; the culture was smuggled in, unnoticed.

"But best of all," says Miss Skinner, "was when we used to play historical charades. Someone — usually Father — would act out a famous historical event and I'd have to figure out what it was. Mother and I would scream with laughter to watch Father teetering on a chair with his arm in his coat, crossing the Delaware. It was just a game — but I got to love both history and acting through it." Not many of us could read Shakespeare or act out charades to compare with Otis Skinner, but that isn't the point; the point is that this is how one man devoted his creative talents to rearing a child just as he did to making a career. Each of us, in his own way, can do likewise.

It is much easier, for instance, to answer a child's questions with flat pronouncements than to discuss them with him creatively and listen patiently to his fanciful or confused ideas. Yet it is just through such painstaking discussion that children and parents may become wonderfully close to each other in spirit, according to Dr. Reuben Hill, research professor in family life at the University of North Carolina.

Dr. Hill ought to know: he's been using the technique in his own home. He stumbled upon a routine known to his children as the "What do you think?" game. One night as his two elder children were climbing into bed, four-year-old David asked him why the moon and stars don't fall down, like the snow. Hill couldn't think for the moment of the appropriate law of physics, so he passed the buck by asking seven-year-old Judy, "What do you think?" She excitedly guessed that maybe they were too far away to fall; David chimed in that maybe God held them up; and both children bubbled over with ideas. Hill was astonished at their eagerness to think and project fancies, the moment he offered them such bait.

From then on it was a nightly game that he or his wife played with them. But it was a good deal more than a game. For among the subjects they talked about were sex differences, conception, digestion, death, heaven, and poverty. The children acquired a wealth of new understanding — yet quite obliquely. For the Hills found that the most productive technique was to listen, pass the question around, and only offer answers when the children finally asked for them. "With us," says Dr. Hill, "and with many of our friends who have tried it, it became a short cut to issues which were most pressing . . . It established a chummy 'we' feeling between us. And strangest of all, there was a keenness in the questions and in the answers we had not anticipated. We were frankly dismayed to discover how badly we had underestimated the shrewdness of our youngsters."

Dr. Dybwad of the Child Study Association says that because the modern father works far from home, his children may find it hard to appreciate the importance and the satisfactions of what he is doing. Dybwad suggests that fathers should arrange to have their children visit them occasionally at the office or shop, or take them on Saturday visits to the factory. "The purpose isn't vocational instruction," says Dr. Dybwad, "but to give the child a positive feeling toward the job which deprives him so often of his father's company."

A child whose father lets him in on what it means to work also discovers that it is more than something you *have* to do; it is very often something you *want* to do. And a man at his work is often a man demonstrating his most deeply felt principles of conduct, principles that may never show up in the routine of the household. The late Will Bankhead, when he was campaigning for his seat in the House of Representatives, often took his little daughter with him around the countryside. From being with him and watching him in action, she acquired a love of public appearance — plus a concept of what integrity meant.

In her autobiography she recalls how they went to a small schoolhouse where Bankhead was to address a crowd of farmers. Only five showed up. Thinly concealing his annoyance, he said, "I'll speak to you only a few minutes, since I have so long a schedule —" Yet even as he said it, he realized it was unfair of him. Each of the five had gone to as much personal trouble to hear him as each of a crowd would. Bankhead spoke to them for three solid hours, and made five of his staunchest supporters that day. "I'm pleased to think," says Tallulah Bankhead, "that I soaked up Daddy's campaigning integrity. I try to give as good a performance to an empty house as to a first-night throng."

But each person must find his own pattern of parenthood. If a man has a hobby of woodworking, for instance, it may take him away from his children just when he should be with them, but a man who cares can solve the problem one way or another. Allen Funt, the creator of *Candid Camera*, equipped his cellar with a splendid workshop, but it kept him from his two small children, Pete and Patty. Yet if he let them visit him in the workshop, they got underfoot, were bored, and kept getting dangerously close to the big power tools. Funt turned the whole situation around advantageously. Near his own workbench, he built each child a small, individually tailored workbench, complete with an assortment of pintsize (and safe) tools. All three thereupon worked assiduously and happily together, each on whatever he wanted to make. The products of the children's workbenches are something less than triumphs of cabinet-making, but they've been making other and more permanent things down there — patience, comradely sharing, a respect for safety-first rules, and much else.

That is why there are no hard-and-fast rules about passing on the important values to your children; the best ways to pass them on will come out of your own imagination, if you exercise it.

How should you teach a child the value of money? Can you communicate to him what your own spiritual faith means to you? What approach will best give him strength of character to stick to what he believes and likes even when he finds it is unpopular among his peers? Can you make him kind, diligent, able to stand up for his own rights?

There is no set technique or gimmick that will make you expert in each of these areas. "Each man and woman who approaches the job of raising a child with love and intelligence," says Mrs. Gruenberg, "can learn much from reading about proven child-care principles — but in the end, the parent must always find his own ways to express his own personality. There are no rules or technical tricks that will work for everybody. There are a hundred ways to be a good parent."

In modern living, none of these ways is liable to be automatic. The parent cannot expect it to be an effortless and unconscious process; he must give some of the best part of himself to the task, as he would to any important piece of creative work. The rewards, however, are unlike any other we experience in life, for we can win a kind of immortality that we see and enjoy while we are still alive, by giving to our children the best aspects of our character, our beliefs, and our wisdom. To see these things being perpetuated in other human beings makes us know that even after death, that which was most valuable about us will still be here on earth.

The Other Adults in Your Child's Life

PARENTS TODAY spend a good deal of time trying to see to it that their children come in contact with the right kind of classmates and playmates. It is traditional for them to do so but, according to many childcare experts, they should also concern themselves with the *adults* in their children's lives. For a new problem has been created as a byproduct of the modern family.

The last two or three generations have evolved a kind of home life that is intimate, mobile — and limited to parents and their growing children. This kind of living has helped solve such ancient problems as lack of privacy, lack of individual attention to children, and the struggle for control between in-laws and young parents. But the modern family has also cut off children from all but superficial contact with most adults.

The child has little idea how people other than Mother and Father think and feel, how they react in anger or in pleasure, what they do when they are tired, energetic, moody or gay. He has little chance to study other grown-ups close at hand. The result is that the child grows up with a one-dimensional view of the world of human beings in which he must someday lead an independent life.

Recently a friend of mine was reminiscing about his early years. "My folks were much older than most," he told me. "They were warm, kindly people, but from my earliest days I recall them as being gray, weary, and unenthusiastic. For many years I thought that was what happened to all people when they became parents. Then when I was fifteen I spent a weekend at a friend's house. I'll never forget seeing his parents getting ready to go to a party. They practically floated down the stairs in high spirits. They mixed a cocktail and admired each other's looks. Then they waved a gay good night, and bounced out like two kids off to a senior prom.

"It seemed marvelous to me, and yet shocking and improper. Parents weren't *supposed* to be full of youth and zest and silliness. I liked it, but it confused and upset me. And it came too late to have any real influence on the pattern of my life. To this day I'm a stick-in-the-mud, like my parents."

In hundreds of similar ways, the children of today are limited in their personal growth by restricted views of human nature in early life. "Early" is the key word. Psychiatrists and child-care experts agree that a process they call "identification" begins in about the fifth or sixth year. It is the effort the child makes, consciously and unconsciously, to pattern himself upon adults he admires. "The child," says sociologist Clifford Kirkpatrick of Indiana University, "struts, threatens, scolds, slaps, pleads, argues, and reasons in accordance with the examples provided by his parents. As with some plastic substance, his growing nature is molded — and sets in the mold. Later changes are difficult, and often impossible."

Parents, with such great power to affect the character and ideas of their children, face not only a challenge but a responsibility. Until relatively recently, parents had the help of grandparents, aunts and uncles, boarders and servants. For until modern times the family consisted of large clans of blood relatives with several generations living together or close by and having continual contact. Today, of course, this is no longer true.

The present form of family life is something new under the sun. Sociologists say that we have been changing over from the "kinship group family" to the "immediate" or "nuclear" family, which is very different: in it there is room only for parents, plus their offspring — and even those are impelled by many motives to desert the nest as soon as possible after finishing schooling. In our time it is embarrassing, almost shameful, for a young couple not to set up their own home the moment they are married. Just as urgently as they seek this privacy, so do they later guard it against the needs of their aging parents, whom they shunt off to doze in the Florida sunshine, or inter in nursing homes. The same is true of all other classes of adults. Even those families who can afford live-in help often refuse to have it, because they want no other adults in their household after dark.

The nuclear family results in an intensified relationship between parents and children, and most experts agree this is a considerable gain. But many of them admit that the nuclear family also robs the child of *breadth* of experience — and his many school contacts, his busier child social life, his many modern group activities, teach him only how to get along with other children, not how to train his sights upon the adult world he will eventually live in.

Census figures reveal how quick and sharp the change has been. The average American family now consists of only 3.4 persons, as compared to nearly six in 1790. A little over half this shrinkage is due to the smaller average number of children per family; the rest is caused by the expulsion of all adults, except parents, from the home. Just before World War II, for instance, four out of every ten families with children under eighteen had at least one other adult living with them. Thirteen years later this was true of only three out of ten families — and the downward trend is continuing all the time.

There is a simple mathematical way, easy enough for any high-school child to use, to see in numerical terms the effect of the reduction in family size. It's called the Law of Family Interaction, and it is expressed by a simple equation: $x = \dfrac{n^2 - n}{2}$. This yields the number of relationships existing in a family of any given size (in the equation, x = relationships, n = size of family). In a family of only two members, for instance, there is only one relationship (that which exists between husband and wife). But in a family of one more person, the number of relationships triples (husband-wife, father-child, mother-child). In a family of four, there are six relationships, and in the typical completed family of a century ago, with a dozen persons, there were sixty-six!

Let's pin that down to what a child sees and experiences of adults. In today's family he *has two* relationships with adults, and *observes one* between adults. The same child, if a pair of grandparents are living in his home, *has four* relationships with adults, and *observes six* among them. In the family of a century ago he might have *had six*, and *observed fifteen*. That is a dramatically different learning experience, a startlingly different training ground for life, from the nuclear family.

Most family and child-care specialists believe that such advantages of the smaller family as privacy and a closer relationship between parents and children offset the drawbacks, but they stress the need for bringing a variety of adults into the early life of children. But doesn't a child normally come in contact with many adults, even in his earliest years? What of teachers, ministers, playground directors, scoutmasters? Isn't a child's character shaped by these contacts?

Some years ago two investigators made a study of the places from which children get their ideas of right and wrong. The results showed that what the children thought corresponded in great degree with the ideas of their parents, but very little with those of their day-school teachers, and almost not at all with their Sunday-school teachers. Evidently the relationships that really influence character are the ones with intimacy, personal involvement and emotional content.

A child learns much more than just a sense of right and wrong from grown-ups. Through them he becomes involved with the whole fabric of living — the ability to understand an expression, a tone of voice, a phrase; the power to sympathize and to care for those who are different; the use of words and gestures and the self-control that enables one to deal with the thousand delicate nuances of everyday relationships with other people. The child needs more than two adults as a model for these characteristics; his parents alone are too small a sample of the human race.

This is why a friend of mine, a sensitive and thoughtful novelist, told me not long ago, "When I find any worth-while adult who takes an interest in one of my kids, I tend and water the relationship as if it were a tree on which pearls grew." For several years my friend has kept an eye out for such grown-ups, and he is willing to invest energy, time, and money to nurture these child-adult friendships.

He invites a widowed aunt, who lives in New England, to come to Baltimore for a two-week stay twice a year, and pays her fare and all expenses. He arranges small picnics with the wife of a neighbor, and does the necessary driving, because the neighbor enjoys taking her own two sons and his daughters on all-day outings. And he hires a former baby-sitter who is now in college to take the girls on visits to museums and historic places.

That is one man's thoughtful, diligent approach to the problem. He, of course, does all the things with his children that these outsiders do. "But I'm a quiet, bookish fellow," he says, "and that's okay. I have a right to be, and my children love me for it — or despite it. But I think it's good for them to love and be close to people unlike me, and to have to get along with them in any way they can."

A number of child-rearing specialists have given serious thought to the same matter, and offered other suggestions for ways to accomplish the same ends. Mrs. Rhoda Bacmeister, child-care author and director of the Manhattanville Day Nursery, urges that parents thoughtfully and deliberately invite many kinds of people to their homes at times when the children can join in conversations with them. Visitors who seem to enjoy these contacts can be encouraged to spend additional time with the children. "Give your children every chance," she urges, "to develop that good feeling of *belonging* in a wide range of relationships. There is real nourishment in it."

Sociologist James Bossard of the University of Pennsylvania studied the role house guests play in the formation of a child's character. In *The Sociology of Child Development*, he reports that a survey of 200 published autobiographies revealed that 117 of the authors described guests as being of real consequence in their early lives. In 200 interviews with young people he verified the same finding. Sometimes the guest, because of his profession or some character trait, inspired or motivated the child. Sometimes the guest personified likes or dislikes about clothes, food or manners, and broadened the child's attitude. Sometimes he was mainly a "practice person" on whom the child tried out his social skills and his ideas. Sometimes he caused the child's parents to appear in a different light — gracious and generous, false and brittle, ill-at-ease or charming.

Dr. Gunnar Dybwad, former director of the Child Study Association, says that some vague awareness of the modern family's limitations may be the reason that family visiting is becoming popular. An entire family will spend the afternoon and stay for dinner with another family. "If the children are permitted to participate with the adults," he says, "they get what is, in effect, a brief period of enriched family life, and a variety of new interrelations with adults."

An engineer who lives in a suburb of Newark told me of his family's experience along these lines. About a year ago his wife was on the phone inviting two of their friends to come for cocktails and dinner. Suddenly he had an impulse. "Say," he broke in, taking the phone from her, "why not bring your boys along and let them stay for dinner, too? We'll make a big thing of it. We'll make it family day."

And it was a big thing — not what one might call restful, but a rich, enjoyable day all around. "Ever since," he told me, "we've had an unspoken deal with Bill and Lucille, swapping home-style dinners. I think it's been excellent for our kids. They put on their good manners, they suddenly get responsible for things and careful of what they're doing, and they've come to be very fond of Bill and Lucille."

Dr. Dybwad and others also believe that trips away from home, for a child who is old enough to undertake them alone, can be immensely useful. A musician I know, whose only son leads a confined life in a city apartment, sent the nine-year-old off alone this past summer for a month in a cabin in a forest far north of Toronto. His hosts were the parents of one of his schoolmates, and about as unlike his own parents as people could be: they were orderly, disciplined, teacherish, and rather demanding. The two boys had duties to perform — gathering wood for the stove, hauling the water, and cleaning their own room — and all this had to be done right on schedule.

"But Johnny enjoyed it all," his mother told me. "He thrived on having things expected of him — something we've never tried, or succeeded with, at home. He also had lots of fun canoeing and hiking and all that; but the real difference I found in him was that he came home happy, with a new sense of his own capabilities and usefulness."

These are only a few of the ways in which modern parents can expand the adult content of their children's lives. The one underlying factor is that all of them are personal, intimate, familylike contacts, as opposed to the more formal relationships of the classroom.

Undoubtedly there are many more ways, but they need not be listed. It is up to each parent, knowing himself, his family, and his surroundings, to devise and discover his own best ways. For we cannot be all things to our children, try as we may; and as wonderful as we may seem to someone else's children, just so valuable may their parents seem to our children.

My wife recently got a long letter from a childhood friend she has not seen in many years, reminiscing about many things. At one point, she wrote:

"I'm sure you know of the many intangibles I was exposed to in my childhood through your wonderful mother. Exactly what she did for me it is difficult to remember concretely, but I know that emotionally and spiritually I shall never forget her. In fact — as she must have told you — I recently traveled a good part of one day with my two little daughters just so they could be exposed to her."

The young woman who wrote that letter had a perfectly normal home life, but the existence of a meaningful relationship with an outside grown-up was something she has remembered for twenty years with gratitude. I think no more eloquent argument can be made in favor of the other adults in your child's life.

Memory

What Your Memory Reveals About You

ARE YOU THE kind of person who, twenty or thirty years after leaving school, still remembers his classmates and teachers by name, but hasn't the faintest idea what Pythagoras proved — or are you unable to summon to mind any of the old faces and names, but still feel on very good terms with the square of the hypotenuse? In thinking back on a novel you read a while ago, do you recall only the general outline of the plot, or do you remember instead a score of incidents and snatches of dialogue? When you think or talk about your life thus far, do your successes and the praise you've received come most easily to mind, or do you tend to recall the times you have fallen short or been criticized?

These and other differences in our memories were long supposed to be the result of exercising the mind or letting it go flabby, of a higher or lower I.Q., or of good or poor education and habits of thought. But in recent years a number of psychologists and psychiatrists have been doing experimental studies of memory which take a very different tack, the gist of their investigations being that most of the variations in our memory patterns are due to personality factors and to each person's basic outlook on life.

They find that the effects of mental exercise such as memory drills are only minor, and that although I.Q. and education do play a part in memory, what is far more significant is that among people of the same general educational and intelligence level, there are very great differences in memory, related to each person's character and emotional make-up. What you remember and what you forget, it now appears, are largely determined by your interests, your attitudes towards other people, and your feelings about yourself. Thus memory now appears to be a new way for scientists to explore personality, mental health, and the hidden machinery of the mind.

Most of us are already aware — in a general, unscientific way — of the connection between personality and the kind of memory an individual has, for we have all seen examples of two people with shared experiences but differing recollections of them. Let any husband and wife start to reminisce about their courtship or honeymoon, and it is astonishing the discrepancies that pop up, or the differences in which details each recalls. Likewise, nearly every pair of old friends, or brothers and sisters, will recall different things from their common childhood or will have widely divergent recollections of the same events.

I became sharply aware of this a few years ago when, for the first time in a long while, I spent an evening reminiscing with my former navigator who flew with me on a number of reconnaissance missions over Germany during World War II. He is a genial, hearty, easily amused man, while I am rather the converse. As we talked about the old days, what came to his mind were such things as the time someone landed safely, but so low on gas that his engines died just as he turned off the runway, or the wild party during which someone fired a flare gun in the officers' bar and had to put out the fire with seltzer water. To my mind came things like the endless poker games with which I tried to deaden my fears, or the crashes I witnessed in which men I knew were turned into jelly or ashes, or the exact look of flak bursts homing in on my plane over Leipzig on a clear winter's day — memories which, however, I have rehashed so many times that they no longer hurt or have any feeling about them. According to psychologists I talked to while visiting the National Institute of Mental Health, my navigator's choice of memories indicates that he is the type of personality who handles painful experiences and fears by forgetting them; I, in contrast, evidently handle them by thinking them over analytically again and again until the hurtful feelings have been stripped away, leaving only the facts themselves.

Current research is casting sharp new light of this sort on many of our everyday observations about memory. We all know of people, for example, who recall only the bare factual bones of their experiences, and repeat them with no interpretation or embellishment; we also know people who invariably add to and enlarge upon their experiences, but hotly deny any accusation of exaggerating. Just this sort of difference has been closely studied at New York University's Research Center for Mental Health by a young psychologist named I. H. Paul. Dr. Paul uses several techniques, one of which consists of asking his volunteers to memorize seven brief statements which make up the plot outline of a story; then he reads to them an actual story based on the seven statements; and finally he asks them to restate the original seven sentences as accurately as they can.

At this point, a genuine difference shows up: some people can recall the original wording exactly, adding nothing to it (Dr. Paul calls them "skeletonizers"), while others are unable to avoid enlarging or fattening the originals with details from the complete story (Dr. Paul calls them "importers"). Here is a sample original statement: "Indian boys are playing at testing their strength." And here is how an importer recalls it a short while later, after hearing the full story: "A group of Indian boys were playing games by a river, testing their strength." The differences seem trifling — but to a doctor, even a degree or two of fever is a meaningful symptom.

"The difference between skeletonizers and importers," Dr. Paul says, "is a real characteristic of personality. I did thorough work-ups of each volunteer, using reliable psychological tests and interview methods, and found a definite link between the tendency to skeletonize or import, and traits of personality. Most of the skeletonizers tend to be somewhat quiet, withdrawn, cautious, thoughtful persons — the kind who prefer thinking rather than acting, and who try to be as correct as possible even when it means leaving out things that would fill in gaps in memory.

"The importer, on the other hand, turns out to be a more outgoing, active, impulsive type. He isn't interested in accuracy, but he does care about completeness; a gap in his information bothers him, and in remembering something he is likely to fill in the holes without realizing he is doing so. He doesn't knowingly falsify or exaggerate; it's just the style of thinking that makes him feel better."

At the Menninger Foundation in Topeka, a number of researchers, backed by a grant from the National Institute of Mental Health, have likewise been studying differences in how people perceive, think, and remember. Dr. Philip Holzman, Dr. Riley Gardner, and others have been particularly intrigued by the tendency of some people to be "sharpeners" — that is, to preserve new experiences sharply and in detail, not adding them to, or pigeonholing them with, previous experiences; and by the tendency of others to be "levelers" — that is, to forget the individual specifics of their experiences, but to classify and amalgamate them with general ideas gained from past experience.

One of their research methods involves reading to their subjects a primitive folk tale told in a somewhat jerky manner, and full of odd details (a boy turns himself into a peanut in order to hide from his father, and is swallowed by a fowl, which is swallowed by a cat, and so on — and in the end he is found by his father anyhow). Then they ask their subjects to repeat the story to the best of their ability. The levelers tend to simplify it, or omit many details, or distort the narrative until it is more generalized and similar to familiar stories and clichés of thought already stored in simple form in their memories. Sharpeners, however, cling strongly to the odd and puzzling details, not only retelling the story but sometimes expanding it as much as 20 or 30 per cent in order to explain cryptic passages; they do not, however, distort the story to make it fit more general and acceptable lines.

Once again, these tendencies — which are rather different from skeletonizing and importing — are familiar to all of us from everyday life: we all know people who talk only in generalities and tend to oversimplify, never being able to think of a concrete instance of any point they are discussing, and we also know people who have virtually total recall, but can rarely give a brief abstract statement of what they want to say.

Dr. Holzman and Dr. Gardner also wanted to try a folk tale more familiar to Americans, and not so odd and primitive as the previous example, so they asked a number of people who were already classified as sharpeners or levelers to retell the story of the Pied Piper of Hamelin. The story tells, of course, of the Pied Piper who offered to rid the German town of its rats for a certain sum; how he played his pipes and led the rats into water, drowning them; was refused his money, by the mayor;

and in revenge played his pipes again, luring all the town children (except one lame boy) away and into a mountain, where they disappeared forever. Sharpeners remembered, on the average, half the important elements of the story; levelers remembered only a third. More importantly, 58 per cent of the sharpeners remembered the revenge theme, but only 26 per cent of the levelers did so. Here, for instance, is a typical leveler's version:

"Well, there was once a man in this village who played a very wonderful, I guess it was a magic, flute, and he could walk through the town and all the children would be so entranced that they would follow him along to listen to him play. And so he, I guess, went through the village collecting all the children — I — let's see — Oh, I think *this* is the Pied Piper [story]: This village was full of mice and rats, and there was this man that could play a flute, and so he went through the village and played the flute and out of the houses came the mice and rats and they followed him and he led them into the ocean and in that way the town got rid of all the rodents."

Notice how this leveler remembered both major parts of the story, but failed to connect them, and how the details of time, place, and persons have been blurred (no mayor, no lame boy).

The Menninger Foundation researchers relate the memory differences to differences in an overall "cognitive style" (style of knowing). For instance, when they flash squares of light on a screen, changing the size of the squares slightly but continually, levelers are much slower than sharpeners to notice the change. When a leveler puts on special distorting eyeglasses that cause an apparent tilt in the room around him, he is less sensitive or aware of this new experience than the sharpener, and accepts the tilt, feeling it to be truly vertical or horizontal. In still other well-known psychological tests such as the familiar Rorschach (ink-blot) test, the leveler shows up as a person who involuntarily fails to see, or forgets, things that alarm or displease him, while the sharpener sees and remembers them clearly.

The leveler, in short, is more likely to be a person not keenly aware of many things around him because he blanks them out, or levels them into the mass of his past experiences; he also is likely to forget personally painful experiences altogether, along with things related to them. The sharpener is very different: he is more clearly alert to new experiences, less likely to add them to, or confuse them with, past experiences, and more willing to remember and mentally "play" with unpleasant or personally painful ideas.

Yet these generalizations are a little unfair, for not all levelers are given to extensive repressing (forgetting), nor is leveling necessarily a poor use of the mind. "There may be important advantages to leveling as a memory style," says Dr. Holzman. "It is true enough that in the anxious or repressive person, leveling may cause inefficient thinking and remembering, but in the emotionally healthy person it may well be related to the capacity for making useful abstractions and summaries of experience." The theoretician or high-level thinker who omits a thousand interesting details but achieves a single principle that covers them all may be the leveler putting his style of memory to its best use. The dramatist with a "perfect ear" for individual speech patterns, or the ideal executive secretary who never forgets anything about her boss's business affairs, may be specimens of the sharpener putting the opposite style of memory to best use.

Yet in general, though leveling may have important potentialities, it is true that most levelers are people who repress a great deal — that is, involuntarily forget many important experiences for emotional reasons. (This is a distinctly different kind of forgetting from the normal "fading" away of such things as unused dates, chemical formulae, and old telephone numbers.)

Back in the early years of psychoanalysis, when Freud was trying to discover what hurtful events in childhood had made his patients become neurotic, he was greatly puzzled to discover that his patients almost always had forgotten some of the most important parts of their life stories. During psychoanalysis, however, they slowly and painfully retrieved these memories from the dungeon of the unconscious, and Freud gradually recognized that almost always these were thoughts which would conflict with the individual's moral standards and would cause intolerable guilt or shame if kept in the conscious part of the mind (unless, as in treatment, they were rethought and dealt with constructively).

A child learns, for instance, that his sexual interest in his parents, or his hatred for his brothers or sisters, is absolutely impermissible and sinful; in order not to suffer terrible guilt about having such feelings, he buries them in the underground vaults of the unconscious where they remain unseen, though not nonexistent. This kind of purposeful forgetting is what psychologists mean by repression, and it serves as a defense of the self — though in some ways an expensive one — against harmful ideas and memories. "Remembrances embellish life," someone has said, "but only forgetfulness makes it endurable."

Childhood experiences of this sort are not the only ideas on which repression may work. Anything related to unwelcome aspects of our personalities — traits we wish we did not possess, or desires that cause conflicts in us — may be banished from awareness without our willing it to be so. This is why so many of our disturbing emotions and the events that caused them become blurred and faded after only a few years. Many a person, for instance, has suffered through the lingering and costly final illness of a parent, and been tormented by the terrible wish, again and again, that it might all be over with and done; accordingly, in a fairly short time, much of the experience drops from view.

Sometimes, indeed, we can recall very little from our worst periods of despair or wretchedness — nothing, perhaps, but incidental and harmless details. Dante Gabriel Rossetti, the Victorian artist and poet, once described this beautifully in a little poem which tells of a day on which its narrator was suffering from overwhelming grief (we are never told the cause, but that does not matter). He wandered into the fields, and sank down to meditate, with his head sunk between his knees:

> My eyes, wide open, had the run
> Of some ten weeds to fix upon;
> Among those few, out of the sun,
> The woodspurge flowered, three cups in one.
>
> From perfect grief there need not be
> Wisdom or even memory;
> One thing then learned remains to me —
> The woodspurge has a cup of three.

Repression also works on less intense experiences, erasing even minor everyday displeasures and hurts, particularly if they are linked with things we do not like about ourselves. In one typical study, a psychologist asked 132 college students to rate their Christmas vacations as pleasant or unpleasant, shortly after they returned to school. Six weeks later he asked them to do so again — and found a considerable shift towards the pleasant end of the scale. Apparently, in the interim they had begun forgetting some of the tensions or unpleasantnesses of their visits home — after all, one is supposed to feel happy and delighted at being with one's family — and concentrating on the pleasant and positive aspects.

Sociologist Robert O. Blood of the University of Michigan recently queried a large number of wives about their lives, and found that while women are rearing their offspring, they can name plenty of dissatisfactions and problems their children cause. But women whose children have grown up and left home view the whole process in rosy retrospect and can think of very little that was bad about it. This is not the better judgment of age so much as a result of women's disapproving of any negative feelings in themselves about motherhood or children, and proceeding to forget such feelings, once the children are grown.

All of us, therefore, tend to forget certain general classes of experiences. But the most interesting question is *who* it is that forgets *more* — and which things he forgets, and how his patterns of forgetting or remembering are anchored in personality. "It is most instructive," Dr. Lawrence Stross, psychiatrist at the Menninger Foundation, told me, "to compare the different sets of memories people have of similar past experiences — and to see how these vary according to each person's pattern of psychological defenses." The kind of man who remembers the subjects he studied in school but not the names or faces of his classmates, Dr. Stross suggests, has not really lost the latter totally, but repressed them (such people can often bring forth the names under hypnosis). But why should anyone repress the names and faces of classmates? Very likely because in his school years he was ill at ease in social relationships and considered himself rather a flop at that side of life; he therefore forgot about it, remembering instead his studies, from which he got a sense of success and worth. Yet a classmate of his may recall all the personalities and none of the things he studied because he, in contrast, felt unsure of his mental abilities, but confident about his personal charm and his relationships with other people.

Concrete knowledge about who forgets what kinds of things to protect his ego was recently increased by a kind of accident. For some years, experimental psychologists have wanted to find out whether people are better able to remember tasks they finished successfully, or tasks they have not been able to complete. Dozens of psychologists have inflicted on their volunteers jigsaw puzzles, scrambled phrases, figure-matching tests, and the like, arranging things so that some of the jobs could be done in the time allotted while others simply could not. At first, the answer seemed clear: unfinished jobs left a residue of tension, and were thus better remembered. But as other experimenters did similar studies, the picture grew cloudy; it turned out that sometimes the volunteers remembered incompleted tasks better, and sometimes the completed ones. The whole issue became a running argument among various groups of psychologists.

Finally, however, it began to appear that the results were being greatly influenced by the way in which each researcher introduced the experimental tasks to his volunteers. If he made the people feel that it was immaterial whether they finished or not, they were better able to remember the unfinished tasks; if he made them feel that not to finish was a personal failure and sign of lesser intelligence, they were likely, on the average, to forget more of the incompleted tasks. In other words, if their egos were threatened, they tended to forget whatever posed the threat.

Yet this was only true on the average, for some of the volunteers, even in a threatening situation, could remember more of their failures than could others. Why? Here was the very crux of one connection between personality and memory, and many a useful experiment has been done on this point in recent years. Most psychologists have described the people who can remember "failures" in such terms as proud, ambitious, mature, self-confident, and sure of their personal value. Such people can tolerate failure — and hence remember it — because they have strong egos; people with weak egos forget their failures for their own good.

"Where self-esteem is firmly established," writes psychologist Stanley Coopersmith of Wesleyan University, "failures are more readily recalled and perceived, while insecure or lowered self-esteem results in denial." And this only confirms a suspicion many of us have long had — that the braggart or the perennial optimist who always speaks of his successes, and never admits to any flaw in himself or failure in his life, is something of a fraud. Underneath he is full of self-doubt — and refuses to remember his failures not so much to deceive us as to reassure himself.

Most of the new studies about the connection between memory and personality have not yet resulted in specifically useful applications, but in one area memory has for years been serving as a diagnostic tool for psychologists and psychiatrists. This is the use of what are called "earliest memories" — those tiny odds and ends of our first recollections which usually date back as far as our fourth years, and sometimes even much earlier.

If you are an average person, you probably do not recall more than a very few tiny moments or scenes from these early years, and usually they are quite fragmentary and unimportant. Or so it seems. Yet in your first four or five years you had a vast number of experiences; why should you remember so few of them — and why those particular unimpressive bits? For it is an axiom of psychology, as of all science, that nothing happens by "pure accident"; there must, therefore, be reasons why you kept those few special little scraps out of your large potential fund of things to remember.

This very question attracted the attention both of Freud and of his one-time follower, Alfred Adler, decades ago; independently, each concluded that a person's earliest memories were no chance selection, but bore a significant relation to his whole pattern of personality. Adler felt that these brief, vague, trifling memories actually revealed and epitomized a person's "style of life" in a rather direct way. A whining, dependent weakling of an adult, for instance, might recall a little episode of being spoonfed while sick, or of running into his parents' room in some childish fright.

Freud, however, felt that earliest memories were more often bland substitutions for childish ideas that had been too frightening to remember directly; he therefore called them "screen memories," and held that they had a connection — which could be discovered — with the real hidden memories. A man whose life has been shaped by driving competitiveness with other men, for instance, might recall a peaceful scene of playing with his brother as a screen to hide the truth of his early and lifelong bitter rivalry with his brother.

In recent years, psychologists working in this area have gathered a great deal of firsthand evidence on the question, and many of them now think that both men were right: early memories are sometimes directly revealing, sometimes concealing — but are always significantly related to the inner workings of the psyche. No matter how commonplace your own early memories seem, therefore, they have either a fairly plain, or else a darkly symbolic, link to your over-all conception of yourself, or to your major problems in life.

One researcher reports, for instance, that self-assured or secure people more often tend to have early memories involving group activity than do insecure people, whose memories feature aloneness; the insecure people, moreover, more often have memories involving someone's getting hurt than do the secure people.

Two psychologists, working independently, have found two extreme opposite types of people especially likely to have early memories involving punishment and discipline — one, the very strict, controlled, self-regulating type; the other, the overly emotional, impulsive, and immature type.

Still other psychologists and psychiatrists have reported that people with psychosomatic ailments often (but not always) remember some childhood incident involving the part of the body through which they later came to express adult nervousness. The late Dr. Victor Eisenstein, a psychiatrist affiliated with Lenox Hill Hospital in New York, once cited as an example the case of a young man admitted to the hospital with a bleeding stomach ulcer. His earliest memory, dating from age three and a half, was of being in the street and suddenly missing his mother, at which point he became frightened and vomited. In the course of treatment for his ulcer, it became clear that he had always been overprotected by his mother, who plied him with food and worried about his eating and digestion. Moreover, the immediate cause for his ulcer was the conflict between his wish to stay in his mother's house, and his opposed wish to set up a separate home with his young wife. Seen in this light, his earliest memory proves to have been not only an excellent clue to the heart of his problem but, Dr. Eisenstein observed, it even foretold the very area of the body in which he would suffer neurotic symptoms.

For such reasons, a number of psychiatrists now regard earliest memories as an excellent keyhole through which to peep into the secret troubles of their patients. A study of early memories written by Dr. Leon

Saul, psychiatrist at the University of Pennsylvania School of Medicine, and several of his colleagues, unhesitatingly asserts that earliest memories reveal better than any other single psychological fact a person's inner motives, workings, and hidden problems. Dr. Saul cites the case of a man who sought psychiatric help because of difficulties in both his business and personal life. His earliest memory dated from about age two: he was in his mother's arms and his father reached out to take him, but he felt that his mother was warm and smooth, his father hard and rough, and clung to her rather than go to him. The incident is but a speck, and could hardly have affected his later development, but to Dr. Saul and associates it was virtually a psychological fingerprint of the man — for his difficulties turned out to be a fear of competition with other men which gave him a continuing sense of uneasiness and babyishness in their presence and, as a result, a compensating exaggerated drive to succeed with women and to win their affections away from other men.

The current effort among students of this phenomenon is to make the analysis of early memories more exact, and even statistical, so as to increase their diagnostic reliability. Psychiatrist Robert J. Langs and several co-workers at New York's Albert Einstein College of Medicine have recently developed a formidable procedure for evaluating earliest memories, assigning numerical weights to such factors as the persons appearing in the memory, the content (punishment, holidays, a trip, etc.), the self-image of the person having the memory, and many other items. Dr. Langs expects that it will soon become a useful tool for appraising the mental health of an individual. Independently, Dr. Martin Mayman, director of psychological training at the Menninger Foundation, has developed an early-memories test and used it on some five hundred people in the past half-dozen years. His approach is less statistical and more freely interpretive; he asks such things as whether the person *sees himself* in the memory or *feels himself* in it (the former would indicate that it was not a real memory, but a reconstruction from hearsay), which details stand out most clearly, and so on. He is enthusiastic about the diagnostic value of early memories. "I keep rediscovering, time and again," he says, "how much can be learned from them, and to what an extent they reveal a person's view of himself, the world, and his place in it."

He offers the example of a young engineer who seemed to be a hard-working, cheerful, self-assured young man, with a great readiness to help other people and do favors for them, but who paradoxically seemed very weak, suffering from spells of vomiting whenever his wife was away for a few days to visit her parents, and falling into a serious depression when, after four years of marriage, she left him and asked for a divorce. His early memories cast a good deal of light on this, the earliest of them all (dating from about age two) being particularly illuminating:

"My mother turned the hot water on instead of cold water in the sink. She used to bathe me in the sink and she got the wrong water faucet. I seem to remember telling her she turned the wrong faucet on, but I don't know whether I was able to talk or not. Just an honest mistake. It burned, of course."

"He pictures himself," comments Dr. Mayman, "as someone who even in infancy was not a defenseless trusting child, but someone who needed to look after himself. Along with other memories, this helped us recognize that he had two conflicting images of himself — that of a lonely, unhappy, uncared-for person, and that of a self-sufficient, competent, happy person. Even his readiness to help other people and do them favors turned out to be not real strength, but a neurotic effort to win their friendship and so make them stay with him and be kind to him."

All the preceding research findings are only tentative groping efforts to identify the connections between the kinds of things we remember and the structural secrets of our personalities. Along with speech, memory is perhaps the most human thing about us, and the efforts are surely bound to be rewarding, if the present discoveries are any indication. Long ago that elegant wit, the Duc de la Rochefoucauld, jested that "everyone complains of his memory, but no one of his judgment," but today science has stood his witticism on its head: we now know that our memories *are* our judgment, and that the way we remember — and what we remember — is itself our considered appraisal of life and of ourselves.

II

The World of
Psychological
Illness

The first article in this section — by far the longest piece in the book — is a comprehensive survey of the various emotional and mental illnesses, the treatments available, the specialists who administer those treatments, the costs of getting help, the chances that therapy will do some good, and the places to go for referrals or reliable therapists. The idea for such a piece was given me by Robert Stein, editor of Redbook, who deserves praise for his willingness to commission and print a study so long and so demanding of the reader's attention. Virtually all the major concepts treated in the rest of the book are touched on and defined in this article, which I consider the backbone of the volume.

The second article tries to balance the picture of the process of mental healing by discussing the much-neglected topic of the mind's own self-reparative processes. As pointed out, however, there is no conflict between the existence of self-repairing mechanisms and the practice of psychiatry and psychotherapy: therapists merely take advantage of the natural self-healing tendency of the mind in their work, assisting and speeding up the process, or tipping the balance in favor of the self-healing mechanisms when they have been overcome by the forces making for sickness.

The third article is an effort to evaluate the effectiveness of psychotherapies; as is made clear, the evidence is far from rigorous. Yet there are good grounds for believing in the therapies; were it otherwise, I could not have written most of the articles in this book. Still, honesty compels us to look clearly at the defects in the present evaluation of results, and to hope for more definitive studies in the near future.

Major and Minor Emotional Problems:
Treatment, Cost, and Cure

THE SUBJECT of mental illness fascinates most Americans — and bewilders them. We avidly consume unprecedented quantities of fiction and nonfiction about psychological ailments, yet the whole field is so new and fast-changing that conflicting points of view are everywhere to be seen; what is more serious, much of what passes for information is either distortion or outright error or a mixture of truth and falsehood.

The movie *Psycho*, for instance, firmly linked the image of insanity to the idea of murder, perpetuating the old idea of the "mad killer"; in actual fact, the great majority of insane people are confused or depressed or fearful or excited or abusive, but not homicidal. The movie *Freud* repeats the old cliché that the psychiatrist produces a sudden, magical cure by getting the patient to remember a childhood hurt which "explains" everything; in everyday treatment, however, such a recollection is usually only one small step on the long road to a cure.

What can one believe? Not fiction, evidently; its authors are under no obligation to offer textbook lessons in abnormal psychology. Then how about nonfiction? Scores of magazine articles and books describe in faithful detail how marital problems are solved and emotional disorders cured through counseling, psychotherapy or psychoanalysis; others, however, attack these treatments, belabor the tendency to seek help for problems as a sign of moral weakness and cite statistics to show that untreated neurotics are just as likely to get well as those who receive therapy.

The reading and thinking public uses the words of psychology ever more freely and seems to understand them. But a researcher at the University of Chicago tested 3500 people on their ability to recognize mental illness, as demonstrated in six short case histories, and found that the majority of people offered "natural" explanations for the behavior of five out of the six instead of recognizing them as mentally ill. Most of us have only to try to distinguish between "psychiatrist," "psychoanalyst," "psychologist" and "psychotherapist" to see how uncertain a grasp we have of the subject. And even assuming that we can identify these four classes of professionals, do we know which of them is the right one to go to or the most trustworthy? What of the people we hear about who have spent months or years in treatment and seem no better, or even seem worse; but what, too, of others who seem healthier, happier in marriage, and more successful in their careers as a result of treatment? What can one believe?

To answer questions like these is the aim of this report on the who, what, and where of psychological illness and treatment in the United States today.*

WHO IS SICK?

In past centuries only the real "madman" or "maniac" was recognized as being psychologically ill, but in recent decades we have been shifting the boundary between illness and health; much conduct that once was thought simply unwise or due to weakness of character is now viewed as a sign of psychological disorder. Many people feel, for instance, that a person who has been divorced three or four times is not just unwise or weak, but has unresolved problems that prevent him from choosing well, or keep him from making a good adjustment once he has chosen.

Far from limiting their attention to those with severe mental illness, practitioners of mental healing today are interested also in the nearly 800,000 people each year who get divorced, the 700,000 children annually haled into court as delinquents, the 200,000 women in any one year who bear illegitimate babies, the 5 million or more alcoholics, and the many other millions whose symptoms of emotional tension range

* In this survey I have aimed at reflecting broad, nonpartisan views, like those expressed in *Action for Mental Health,* the final report of the Joint Commission on Mental Illness and Health, which contributed so importantly to President Kennedy's proposals to Congress for a national mental health program. Among the organizations that provided information for the following article were the American Psychiatric Association, the American Psychoanalytic Association, the Family Service Association of America, the National Association of Social Workers, and the National Association for Mental Health.

from colitis to friendlessness, from migraine to unhappy spinsterhood. Adding them all together, *Action for Mental Health* states that nearly 20 million Americans, or one out of ten people, are emotionally or mentally ill.

It is not only the professional surveyors who report such large numbers of people to be "sick" in some degree. One out of five adults queried for the Joint Commission survey, *Americans View Their Mental Health,* said that at one time or another they had felt themselves to be on the verge of a nervous breakdown. One out of seven adults has sought the help at some point of a clergyman, doctor or professional mental-health worker for his personal problems.

The figures are huge, but that should not necessarily cause dismay. They mean in large part that much of what man has accepted in the past as his lot he now considers to be needless and correctable. About a quarter of the mentally and emotionally ill are sick enough to be seriously hampered in daily living and in the pursuit of happiness, but the majority have symptoms that, like dandruff, are troublesome but do not necessarily require professional treatment.

Noncritical emotional illnesses. Many of us feel that mental illness of any sort, serious or not, is strange, alien and unreasonable; we find it hard to understand how people with these ailments can feel or act the way they do.

Yet each of us at one time or another has experienced some of the common symptoms of mental or emotional illness. Think back, for instance, to the feelings you had during your teens when you fell out of love the first time, and in deep dismay wondered how you had become involved with the wrong person and how to get out of it. Or think of the agonizing indecision and worry you knew in high school or in college as to what career to pursue. These same states of mind persist in some people into adulthood, and even become intensified. The worry and indecision may cause serious dissatisfaction with work, no matter what work is chosen; or make it unusually difficult to know whether one is enough in love to marry; or create an unhappy marriage; or result in the constant inability to handle one's money intelligently.

Persistent difficulties with work, marriage or money sometimes are symptoms of serious mental disorders. But more often recurrent troubles like these, while upsetting and disrupting, are expressions of what we may call simply the *noncritical emotional illnesses*. Anyone with such an illness may be sleepless, angry, deeply discouraged or suffering real pain in any one of a number of other ways, but his disorder is "noncritical" in the sense that despite his real discomfort, he is able to get along. He doesn't develop crippling psychosomatic illnesses or find it impossible to distinguish between the real world and his fantasies, but he does live with pain and frustration, and usually cannot achieve a more satisfying life through his own efforts alone.

Formerly, people with such disorders aired their problems, if they did so at all, to a minister, doctor or old friend. Today they are more likely to tell such troubles to a person with psychological training and technique.

Character disorders. Persons with noncritical emotional illnesses are, of course, sane. So are a high percentage of the individuals with *character disorders* or *behavior disorders* (these terms mean roughly the same thing), but their illnesses are more harmful — sometimes to themselves and sometimes to society. Indeed, they behave very much as if they did not care about the standards of conduct or achievement that are important to most people in our society.

At the least serious level, a person with a character disorder may flunk out of college because he can't make himself care about doing good work. Although this may trouble his family and friends a great deal, his problem is not always considered "serious" because it affects only him and because many such youngsters outgrow their immature behavior. A person with a more serious character disorder acts in ways that adversely affect other people. He may lie, cheat or steal, even though there is no realistic need for his actions, or he may become an alcoholic, a drug addict or a sexual deviate.

The thing that people with character disorders have in common is that they usually do not feel great anxiety or guilt about their behavior, whereas most other emotionally ill persons with the same symptoms (those who drink too much or steal or violate sexual taboos) do. The individual with a character disorder who lacks a normal sense of anxiety or guilt about socially destructive acts is sometimes called a *psychopath*. No one is quite sure why the psychopath rejects social norms, but there are several likely reasons. Sometimes he is a person who has not yet developed an adequate conscience; like a child he is impulsive, selfish and shortsighted. Or he may have grown up in a subculture (an immigrant minority group, for instance) that did not have the same values as the large part of American society. This is the case with some juvenile delinquents, who believe that engaging in violence is a legitimate aspect of manhood. It is often very difficult to know whether an individual with a character disorder is emotionally ill, or healthy but merely antisocial; in fact, some experts use the term *sociopath* rather than psychopath.

Psychosomatic diseases. This type of emotional illness should be understandable enough to anyone who has ever had diarrhea before taking an important examination, suffered from a splitting headache after fighting with his employer or wife, or broken out in a rash during a time of financial worries. These symptoms are passing versions of such longer-lasting physical ailments as asthma, peptic ulcer and urticaria — disorders that may have organic causes but may also be the product of emotional stress. Regardless of the cause, the illness is very real. The person suffering from an emotionally induced physical ailment needs psychological treatment — but he also is as much in need of medical treatment as the individual whose disease has an organic cause. He is very different from the hypochondriac who, though convinced that he is ill, actually has nothing organically wrong.

Psychosomatic illnesses often reflect symbolically the underlying emotional trouble. A child who is improperly fed by his mother may grow up to be a man with chronic stomach trouble and a perpetual craving to be pampered with special foods; a swaggering but insecure actor may develop mouth ulcers, which prevent him from having to perform; a woman whose husband threatens to leave her may develop crippling arthritis.

Neuroses. Unlike people with psychosomatic illnesses, neurotics for the most part do not develop clear-cut, tangible physical symptoms. Their troubles are more a matter of how they feel — and most of them feel pretty bad. Each of us at times has started off from home and suddenly had a sinking feeling that we have left the door unlocked or the gas on or the water running; intellectually we feel certain we did not, yet are so uncomfortable and so bothered by the idea that we have to go back and doublecheck. Neurotics may be continually plagued by that kind of alarmed or sinking feeling. It uses up their energies, fills them with nameless dread, and hinders their efforts to work, love and lead a normal life.

The fanatically neat person who gets upset if anything is out of place or dusty may be neurotic; so may the inveterate worrier, whose nerves are always on edge and who is always dwelling on the worst that might happen, the uncontrollable overeater (or undereater), the hypochondriac, the sleepwalker, the amnesiac. Neurotics are very similar in some ways to the people with noncritical emotional ailments, but they are more severely handicapped; their anxieties can be so great that at times some of them even have to be hospitalized for a while. Most neurotics, however, earn a living — even a good one (but painfully and with effort) — have a home life (but often a wretched one), and seemingly are normal in some activities (while grossly abnormal in others).

A full-blown neurosis is extremely painful, but in a curious way it often protects the victim from something he unconsciously feels will be even more painful. A mother who worries excessively about her children may actually resent them, but the feeling may be so loathsome to her that she unconsciously hides it from herself by being overattentive. A frigid woman may have been taught as a child that sexual intercourse is sinful and now holds herself back from enjoyment, since if she did let go and find satisfaction, she might be engulfed in feelings of wickedness.

Psychoses. The most serious cases of mental illness are those persons who cannot get along in the world, even in the limping, suffering fashion of the neurotics. If you have ever awakened in a sweat from a nightmare, trembling and momentarily unsure whether the horror of it was real or imagined, you can grasp very faintly how some seriously ill people feel — they live in the uncertainty and agony of the nightmare all the time. Others feel all day long the confusion you might have felt fleetingly when, on some occasion, you thought you saw an old friend down the street and greeted him, only to find out it was a stranger, or when you tried to think of a word or a name you knew very well but could not grasp it, or when you had the feeling that you were being followed or secretly watched. These are among the typical feelings that plague persons who suffer from illnesses called *psychoses*.

Psychotics make up the greatest number of the 717,000 persons who are in state, federal and private mental hospitals. There are a number of types of psychosis, but among hospitalized patients *schizophrenia* is the most common type; other fairly common ailments are *manic-depressive* and *involutional psychoses*.

People suffering from neuroses or from the noncritical emotional or mental illnesses usually have a grasp of reality; they know who is who and what is what. The psychotic, however, may think himself somebody he isn't; he may mistake his neighbor for a college classmate or for a secret agent; he may be convinced that everyone around him is plotting against him and trying to poison him; he may hear voices or see apparitions; he may fly into wild rages or laugh uncontrollably, or merely huddle in a ball, silent, sad, unhearing and uncomprehending; he may even lose bowel and bladder control, as if he were an infant again. He often needs hospitalization — because he can no longer perform even the simplest everyday tasks, or because he has become a danger to himself, or because he performs grossly antisocial acts, such as running naked into the street.

Sometimes psychotic symptoms appear quite suddenly and with little warning; this is what people often mean by the ill-defined term "nervous breakdown" (though sometimes the term also refers to acute symptoms of neurosis rather than psychosis). Formerly most psychotics required long-term or lifetime care, but in modern hospitals, under good treatment, psychotic symptoms sometimes recede rapidly and apparently disappear — particularly when the psychosis has an emotional cause. There is still no agreement about what these emotional causes are, but most psychiatrists now believe that in the largest number of sufferers both external pressures and internal psychological weakness play a part.

Among another large group of psychotics, however, the symptoms have organic sources — that is, they have such physical causes as tumors of the brain, hardening of brain arteries because of age, damage to brain tissue from alcohol or drugs. Curiously, although the causes in these cases are so tangible, the behavior they produce is often quite similar to that of psychologically caused psychoses, and may include anger, suspicion, confusion, excitement, disconnected thinking, depression and infantile actions. For some of the organic psychoses there are medical treatments that will help; for others, little can be done except to calm the patient, make him comfortable, and try to keep him interested in something.

The major mental-health problem in the country is, in one way, the psychotics, since they cannot get along on their own. But the other categories of mentally or emotionally ill people are a far larger problem numerically.

The sickest people are the most likely to get at least some kind of treatment; the National Association for Mental Health estimates that about half the nation's seriously psychotic people are either hospitalized or receiving outpatient treatment from a hospital. Among people with the less severe forms of psychological illness, however, only about one in ten (roughly 1.5 million to 2 million people) is receiving treatment. Whether all mentally and emotionally ill people really *need* help is another question; some seem to cope with their emotional troubles and live with them adequately. But it is generally felt that even those who do not need help could often benefit from it.

HOW PROBLEMS ARE TREATED

There are three major ways of treating mental and emotional illness today — the psychological, the physical and the social.

Psychological treatments. The overall term for psychological forms of treatment is *psychotherapy*. Among professionals there are scores of different definitions, but most of them agree that, broadly speaking, it means treatment through the medium of words exchanged by patient and therapist in the form of discussions, probing, evaluation, advice, and so on. Psychotherapy per se does not include the use of drugs, operations, shock treatments, rest or other physical treatments of mental illness, though any of these may be used in conjunction with it.

In most forms of psychotherapy the patient and the therapist sit facing each other in a quiet, restful room, although sometimes the patient may lie on a couch with the therapist out of sight behind him. In their dialogues the therapist encourages the patient to speak of himself and his feelings freely and honestly. Often the combination of open communication by the patient and sensitive interpretations and suggestions by the therapist helps the patient come to see himself more clearly, acquire new knowledge, and become less afraid of certain feelings or situations. Sometimes he is even "reconditioned" to feel different about old, familiar problems in his life. The goal of psychotherapy may range anywhere from the mere relief of a temporary gloomy spell, achieved in half an hour's time, to a fairly fundamental remaking of the personality, achieved over a period of years in hundreds of hours of self-searching sessions.

The least ambitious and briefest forms of psychotherapy are mere mental first aid, undertaking no major repairs but rather patching up an immediate damage or easing a hurt. Probably the simplest therapy of all is that performed by a sympathetic doctor or minister who lets a distraught person blow off steam or talk out his worries — a process sometimes technically called *ventilation*. For best results the listener should withhold criticism and disapproval, something often difficult to do without special training. When it is handled in the proper way, ventilation alone may enable a relatively healthy person in a minor crisis to shake off his panic, gloom or immobility and regain his accustomed self-control.

For any emotional problem of real magnitude, however, ventilation by itself seldom is enough. The therapist then tries to help the patient with additional techniques. Often ventilation is coupled with *reassurance* based on *information*. Most soldiers suffering from acute combat nerves during the Korean conflict, for example, were restored to duty by a few talks with a psychiatrist or aide who not only encouraged them to express fear and guilt feelings, but explained in detail that nearly every soldier is secretly afraid and feels guilty if he collapses in battle.

Because the psychotherapist has special knowledge of emotional problems and is free of personal involvement with his patient's troubles, the patient can often accept *direct advice* from him — advice he would ignore or rebut if it came from friends or family. Specific suggestions as to how to handle a child's tantrums or how to resolve persistent husband-wife disagreements are cases in point.

The therapist also may use the method of *support and encouragement*. This sounds deceptively simple — don't we all try to encourage friends in trouble? But often our efforts do not help, for the success of support depends on many factors. When it is skillfully given, in a proper setting, it can be highly effective. Alcoholics Anonymous, which claims a 75 per cent success ratio, depends heavily on this technique. The members encourage, exhort and advise one another; what keeps them sober is the support of the group — a kind of therapy that makes no basic change in personality, even though it makes a great change in habits.

None of the preceding techniques digs deep into hidden chambers of the mind. Rather, they seek to help a patient get a clearer perspective on problems of which he is already consciously aware. Such forms of psychotherapy (sometimes referred to as *surface, simple, shallow* or *supportive psychotherapy*) are practiced by certain ministers, doctors and lawyers (though not all of them realize that that is what they are doing), by social workers (who *do* realize what they are doing and do it professionally, although they may refer to it as *casework* or *counseling*), and by clinical psychologists and psychiatrists.

In contrast to these methods of surface psychotherapy, there are a number of techniques that try to make some internal repairs to and corrections of the personality — treatments that some specialists refer to as *reparative psychotherapy*. Instead of merely helping the patient gain a better perspective on problems of which he is already aware, these forms of psychotherapy turn their attention to internal problems of which he is not aware but which exert powerful influences on his life — struggles about whether to love or to hate, for instance, or whether to be cooperative or to be rebellious, and so on. People whose emotional distress is caused by serious external stress — the death of a wife, the loss of a good job — may not need these deeper-probing kinds of treatment, but those who are easily upset by mild, daily stresses, such as the give-and-take of married life or the responsibility of parenthood, may require such treatment.

As the patient speaks of his problems and voices his feelings the therapist, using his special psychological training, tries to get some idea of the implied, unspoken and often unconscious motives that lie beneath the actual words and that are causing the patient so much distress. The patient may never need to understand the hidden feelings completely; instead, the therapist often will use his knowledge of the patient's inner thoughts to guide the discussions, to ask leading questions, or to offer guarded but pointed interpretations, like a skilled teacher who knows his subject and knows how much his pupil can digest profitably.

Moreover, the therapist will often seek to bring about changes in the patient's external situation without fully exposing the patient to his own inner need for the change. A bossy, domineering woman, for example, may be steered into taking a job that will gratify her need to dominate. She and the therapist may openly discuss how this move will ease the pressures on her husband and children, but they need not acknowledge or discuss the fact that her bossiness may be related to a deeply hidden resentment about being a woman. This mixture of partial insight and partial direction has proved to be an effective prescription for many a fairly complex emotional ailment.

A good deal of the counseling done by social workers consists of psychotherapy of this sort. It is appropriate for many marital problems, child-rearing problems or emotional difficulties associated with work, but when there is psychosomatic illness, deep-seated neurosis or severe emotional and mental illness, still deeper psychotherapy is usually required. Then the person is referred by the therapist to a clinical psychologist or to a psychiatrist.

One rapidly growing method of treating patients is known as *group psychotherapy*. Half a dozen or more people meet simultaneously with one therapist and discuss together their problems and feelings. For some patients the group method is better than the individual method because of its similarity to social interaction in the real world; for others, particularly those who need a good deal of reassurance and support, it is not as helpful as individual treatment.

Psychoanalysis or *reconstructive psychotherapy* has the most ambitious goals of any form of psychological treatment of emotional or mental illness. Classic Freudian psychoanalysis is the archetype, but there are many other forms, including "analytically oriented psychotherapy," "ego analysis," "existential analysis" and the kinds of psychoanalysis subscribed to by followers of such noted therapists as Harry Stack Sullivan, Karen Horney, Carl Jung, Otto Rank and Alfred Adler. Although there are considerable differences among these schools both as to theory and treatment, they all strive to help the patient examine his patterns of thought and behavior, to uncover concealed wounds and hidden distortions of thought and to rebuild the patient's personality structure along more healthful and productive lines.

Almost all schools of psychoanalysis believe that to achieve these goals neither conscious thinking about one's emotional illness nor insight alone is enough. What is needed is a virtual reliving of certain formative periods or a reconditioning of one's reactions to crucial persons and experiences in order to reshape the inner psychological patterns and responses. The man who must touch every tree as he walks down the street will agree with you that it is ridiculous of him to do so, but the panic he feels if he misses one tree is none the weaker for his admitting this. The man who flies into a rage over trivia may be fully aware that his anger is out of proportion to the situation, but no matter how hard he tries, he cannot control himself. Irrational responses, in other words, do not disappear only because they are acknowledged. It takes not only awareness of underlying fears, confusions and frustrations, but also a long process of changing troublesome inner attitudes.

In pursuit of these goals, most practitioners of psychoanalysis use several major technical tools. One is *free association*. The patient, while he is with the analyst, tries to speak freely and without concealing or modifying his thoughts, no matter how irrelevant or shameful they may seem. The sequence in which his thoughts appear reveals to the therapist a great deal about the unconscious connections of the patient's ideas and is thus useful in explaining the sources of his disorder.

Another tool used by followers of almost all schools of analysis is the *analysis of transference*. The patient tends to react to all people by transferring to them the emotions and responses he has had toward important people in his early life, although often the responses are not appropriate. In the doctor-patient relationship, for instance, the patient may come late, fail to pay his bills, refuse to talk, use foul language or do any one of many other things similar to acts that used to get him into trouble when he was a naughty small boy defying his parents. The analyst, instead of scolding him or getting angry, helps the patient to understand the irrationality of his behavior and points the way toward more adult responses.

Day after day, month after month, as the patient acts or speaks in neurotic or immature ways, the analyst helps him to examine his feelings and responses. And bit by bit the patient becomes aware of what is appropriate and inappropriate, rational and irrational — and why he thinks and acts in these ways. As he does he begins to think and speak in a more mature and healthier fashion, and strengthened by his own success, he becomes increasingly able, over a period of time, to function in a mature and independent fashion.

Psychoanalysis is expensive, often exhausting and sometimes tormenting. But when it works well, which unfortunately is not always the case, it can bring a generous measure of fulfillment and satisfaction into the life of the patient. It is at the present time the only widely used treatment that is likely to achieve such ambitious goals for the neurotic.

Physical therapy. Though men have talked, pleaded and reasoned with the mentally ill since the dawn of history, they also have tried physical treatments, on the theory that the disorders of the mind result from disorders of the body. Primitive medicine men sometimes discovered herbal infusions and brews that seemed to calm the mad. Greek and Roman physicians had a fairly wide knowledge of sedative drugs that helped somewhat, and medieval doctors sometimes tried to cure maniacs by trepanning (cutting out a small portion of the skull). In recent decades there have been experiments with other kinds of *somatic* (physical) *therapy.* They have included such direct approaches to the body as prolonged warm tubbing, "wet packs" (restraint under a heavy, wet, laced-up sheet), alternating hot and cold sprays, insulin shock, electric shock, and lobotomy (a brain operation that relieves anxieties but often has other, undesirable effects). For reasons never clearly understood, some of these procedures have helped certain psychotics to calm down or shake off depression or lay aside wild delusions.

In 1955 the first two tranquilizers — drugs called chlorpromazine and reserpine — were introduced into American mental hospitals and immediately began to cause revolutionary changes. With many patients, they reduced wild, reckless, abusive or confused behavior so remarkably that the patients could be given considerable liberty and responsibility and could take part in beneficial hospital activities, which further accelerated their improvement. Some psychotics, especially new cases, improved with such amazing speed on little more than drug therapy that they were able to leave the hospital in a matter of weeks. As time went on it became apparent that a brief course of tranquilizer therapy is seldom enough for a permanent cure, but there is no question that the drugs often cause dramatic improvement when the possibility of change had previously been either nil or very slight.

Many guesses have been made as to how the drugs work chemically in the body, but doctors are not agreed on any explanation as yet. From the broader psychological viewpoint, however, it is somewhat easier to explain why they are helpful. When the body is injured it tends to heal itself, unless the wound or infection is overwhelming; then the doctor's antibiotics or dressings help, not by curing the disease or hurt but by tipping the balance and allowing natural healing processes to get to work. With mental illness the situation may be much the same. The tranquilizing drugs probably do not of themselves cure the patient of psychosis, but by damping down the intensity of his fears, hallucinations and wild ideas they may give his mind a chance to repair itself. The same process may explain the success of other physical attacks on psychosis. Shock treatment, for instance, causes a kind of temporary forgetfulness of one's troubles during which some self-healing can take place.

Somatic therapy, in short, does not uproot and destroy the internal problems that brought about collapse; it merely offers a breathing spell to help the patient get things back under control. He may remain in control the rest of his life or break down again in a matter of months or years, depending on his circumstances. A more certain cure usually requires psychological treatment as well as somatic treatment. Unfortunately, very few psychotic patients receive intense psychotherapy, because there simply aren't many trained therapists available in most mental hospitals. Moreover, psychotherapy is painfully slow and inefficient with most psychotics; it deals in words, and some psychotics don't talk at all, others talk in strange and distorted fashion, and still others fail to understand what is being said to them. At small, private mental hospitals where there is an ample staff, the combination of psychotherapy and physical therapy is used and has generally good results.

Despite the ability of tranquilizers to make many psychoses recede and even disappear, the drugs are of only limited value in the treatment of neuroses. With tranquilizers the neurotic remains what he is, but he doesn't feel quite as bad about it all — until the drug wears off.

Social treatment. A third general approach to treating the patient consists of putting him in a sheltered environment, such as a mental hospital, and there consciously and deliberately arranging for him to have a multitude of friendly, reassuring, useful experiences with staff members and other patients, involving eating, dressing, games, work and other daily activities. This social treatment is designed, through the many human contacts, to bring the patient back from his private nightmare, bit by bit, into a world of reality — a friendly, well-meaning and interesting world that is not as alarming as the one from which he fled, but one in which he relearns his own value and abilities. Like the tranquilizing drugs, social treatment helps him to rebuild his self and to lay aside the harmful thoughts that have been ruling him. More than that, however, it enables him to see himself again as a person connected to other people, rather than withdrawn into the privacy of his own disorder.

To accomplish this, the better state and federal hospitals, and most private hospitals, surround the patient with trained persons who talk, play and work with him. Activities are prescribed for him in kind and amount by the psychiatrist almost as if they were medicines. Thanks to tranquilizers, most severely ill patients can be permitted to move about on their own from ward to library, to snack bar, theater workshop, laundry or auto-repair depot. In this setting the whole hospital environment becomes the therapeutic milieu, and all the patient's interactions with other people help him rediscover himself as a useful member of society.

Social treatment is also used in some institutions that treat primarily nonpsychotic patients. The small private mental hospitals, for instance, which sometimes have more neurotics than psychotics, often utilize *milieu therapy.* So do "residential treatment centers," which are a mixture of mental hospital, recreational camp and detention home for emotionally disturbed or problem children. To a lesser extent it is also used by reform schools, where juvenile delinquents are treated. Even the wards or parts of wards allocated to psychiatry in many general hospitals employ a certain amount of social treatment. It is, after all, nothing but wholesome contact between people, applied in as nearly scientific a fashion as present knowledge permits.

THE THERAPISTS

A wide variety of therapies is available to treat the mental and emotional illnesses to which we are subject. But who are the people who offer these services and what kind of training have they had? It is a confusing subject. Those who deal professionally with the mentally ill run the gamut from the hospital attendant with virtually no training to the psychoanalyst who has prepared for his work for a dozen years. In between there is a wide range of specialists, both medical and nonmedical, who are qualified to handle certain kinds of cases or certain aspects of diagnosis and therapy.

Psychiatrists and psychoanalysts. The most broadly trained practitioners are the psychiatrists. They are physicians (M.D.s) who, after completing medical school, go on to specialize in the illnesses of the mind. They receive their training primarily in mental hospitals, where they learn to diagnose and treat severely disturbed patients. They also receive training in handling the less crippling disorders, such as neuroses and character disorders. They can prescribe and use a wide variety of both physical and psychological therapy. A psychiatrist's patients may range from a hospitalized menopausal woman who attempted suicide (and whom he may treat with electroshock therapy and a program of recreation and work) to a driving, successful businessman with ulcers (whom he may treat with medication and several months of psychotherapy) to an intelligent but rebellious college student who is flunking a couple of courses (whom he may treat adequately in half a dozen hours with surface psychotherapy).

There are only about 13,000 psychiatrists in the United States, and these few are unevenly distributed, a disproportionate number being in the East and in large cities. The maldistribution is not only geographic but economic; the poor get far less than their share. Because the income from private practice is much better than that from hospital or clinic work, nearly two-thirds of all psychiatrists spend part or all of their time seeing patients privately. Less than a fifth of the country's psychiatrists devote themselves exclusively to clinics, social agencies or hospitals — which is precisely where the caseload is greatest. Ironically, therefore, the most severely disabled people, the institutionalized psychotics, are the very ones who get the least amount of direct contact with psychiatrists.

Although the majority of psychiatrists use psychotherapy with most of their patients, they are not automatically equipped to practice psychoanalysis and similar "depth" therapy. To practice these forms of treatment psychiatrists must have still further training. In fact, to be accepted as a member of the American Psychoanalytic Association (the principal organization of analysts with medical degrees), a psychiatrist must enroll in one of 19 recognized training institutes, take special courses and seminars for an average of six years, analyze no fewer than two patients under the supervision of an experienced psychoanalyst, and undergo analysis himself.

The American Psychoanalytic Association will not accept anyone for membership unless he is a physician, although it does allow some laymen to study at its institutes in order to prepare for a research or teaching career. Nevertheless, there are nonmedical practitioners (lay analysts) who have had this same sort of stringent psychoanalytic training in institutes that require not an M.D. for admission but a Ph.D. in clinical psychology or in a related science such as anthropology or sociology.

Despite the impression given by cartoons and TV, there are actually very few psychoanalysts in this country. Only about 1000 physicians are engaged in psychoanalytic practice, each of whom, in the nature of the therapy, can analyze only a few hundred patients in his entire working lifetime. In addition, there are at least a thousand and perhaps several thousand practicing lay analysts. Nobody knows the exact number or how many lay analysts have studied at reputable analytic schools. This lack of information occurs partly because there are few states with licensing laws that cover lay therapists and partly because there is no agency responsible for accrediting lay institutes. The American Psychoanalytic Association, which would seem to be the logical organization to assume this role, claims that it has no authority to concern itself with nonmedical practitioners. It and other medical organizations, however, *do* concern themselves with fighting against lay therapists.

Certain words — "illness," "diagnosis," "therapy," "prescription," and the like — seem to the medical profession to be its own personal property and its sacred trust. Many physicians feel that, at the very least, all activities connected with these words should be under their supervision and control. Yet most psychological illnesses have no primary physical causes or cures. The diagnosis and treatment of some psychological disorders is a medical matter; the diagnosis and treatment of many others is *not*, even though doctors may learn to do it as well as anyone else. *Action for Mental Health* expressly recommended to Congress that psychoanalysis and shorter-term psychotherapy be practiced not only by physicians but by nonmedical persons with suitable professional training.

Because of the conflict among professionals themselves about who is and who is not qualified to practice psychoanalysis, it is particularly important for people who are contemplating this kind of treatment to follow the advice given below in "How to Find the Proper Help."

Clinical psychologists. Psychologists deal with all areas of human behavior, but only those who are clinical psychologists — and not even all of these — have received extensive training in psychotherapy. They hold at least a master's degree, and often a Ph.D., in psychology, and have had training in diagnostic testing or in psychotherapy or in both disciplines. Many lay analysts are clinical psychologists who have gone on to study psychoanalysis at special institutes.

About one-third of the 18,000 psychologists in the United States are clinical psychologists. They cannot prescribe medicines or other physical treatments, but they can use any form of psychotherapy for which they have been trained. Working in mental hospitals, family service organizations, mental-health clinics and other organizations, as well as in private practice, most of these therapists offer guidance, support, counseling and deeper-reaching forms of psychotherapy to persons whose troubles range across the whole spectrum of psychological disorder. Often they work under the supervision of psychiatrists. They must do so when treating an emotional or mental disorder that has physical causes or physical results.

Clinical psychologists also administer and interpret diagnostic devices like the Rorschach ink-blot test or various word-completion tests, which seek to reveal hidden traits and conflicts of the individual.

Social workers. About 20,000 of the nation's 105,000 social workers are trained to do surface psychotherapy and even some deeper-probing therapy. These 20,000 have received a master's degree from an accredited school of social work, where they chose to take special courses in counseling. Though only some of them have the background or experience to do more than brief supportive psychotherapy, they all are trained to recognize and diagnose serious emotional problems and to make referrals to proper sources of help. They are most likely to work in organizations that have other kinds of trained personnel available, such as hospitals, mental-health clinics, family service organizations, courts, child-welfare agencies and the like. Social workers used to see many clients whose problems were basically economic and external — poverty, unemployment, illegitimacy, and the like — but in the last few decades their practice has shifted toward middle-class and psychological problems. Today social-work counseling is more likely to be psychotherapy — with extra attention to the realistic and economic problems that may contribute to the client's difficulty.

Sometimes social workers work in schools, where they deal with the transient emotional problems so many children have at one time or another, but most school systems do not have funds for such specialized help; nor do most child-welfare or public-welfare departments, even though emotional complications are almost always a part of the problems brought to these public agencies.

About 2000 social workers offer psychotherapy and other social-work services in part-time or full-time private practice.

Pastoral counselors. Although professional therapists are scattered across the land, the majority of Americans who seek help for emotional disturbances go to persons with little or no specific psychological training. According to *Americans View Their Mental Health,* 42 per cent of people seeking help consult their clergymen, but only about 9000 clergymen (one out of every 25) have taken special training in pastoral counseling. Furthermore, according to *Action for Mental Health,* more than one-third of the counseling problems taken to clergymen are of serious psychiatric dimensions, but only one-tenth of them are referred by the clergymen to psychiatric resources. For these reasons, if you seek help, it is wise to follow the procedures described in "How to Find the Proper Help" — unless you are sure your clergyman is qualified to recognize psychological disorders and will know what to do about them.

WHERE THERAPISTS PRACTICE

Mental-health workers are found both in private practice and in institutions of various sorts. Nearly all the psychoanalysts, two-thirds of the psychiatrists, and minorities of the clinical psychologists and social workers are in part-time or full-time private practice. Agencies, clinics and hospitals, however, serve far more Americans than do private practitioners.

Family service agencies. Family service agencies are usually directed and staffed by trained social workers; in these agencies interviews are conducted in a setting similar in privacy and atmosphere to a doctor's or lawyer's office. Family agencies are mostly voluntary and receive about 90 per cent of their income from the United Fund and Community Chest. They are equipped to handle practical problems, such as the placement of children in foster homes, as well as many emotional disorders. When necessary, family counselors consult with psychiatrists and other specialists or arrange for referrals.

Over 300 family service agencies, mostly nonsectarian, are affiliated with the Family Service Association of America. These are scattered irregularly across the country, more of them being in the East than in other sections and more in urban than rural areas. Within these agencies some 2600 social workers see about 700,000 people a year. In addition to the F.S.A.A. affiliates there are other agencies that provide family casework and auxiliary services; among them are the family service bureaus of the Salvation Army and the family service departments of Catholic Charities.

Mental-health clinics. Only about half the people in the United States are within easy traveling distance of a family service agency. Many more are near one of the 1600 mental-health clinics in the United States, which already serve an estimated 450,000 people yearly and are growing rapidly in number. These outpatient clinics or psychiatric clinics (to use two other names for them), whether under state, federal, community or private control, all are directed by psychiatrists. Unlike the family service agencies, therefore, they can deal with serious neuroses and even with some psychoses. The bulk of their work, nevertheless, concerns the less severe ailments, and most of the treatment is carried out by social workers or clinical psychologists. The mental-health clinics do not maintain beds or wards and do not generally administer shock treatments, but they may prescribe and dispense drugs.

Pastoral counseling centers. The clergy, particularly of Protestant denominations, is beginning to assume an important role in the mental-health field. The limitations of the individual clergyman's knowledge of psychiatry are being overcome by a new development — the creation of pastoral counseling centers. They have much the same sort of facilities and personnel as family service agencies, plus psychologically knowledgeable clergymen. More than 100 such centers have appeared within the last decade. Unfortunately, like the family service agencies most of them are located in the large urban regions, but they portend a spreading of mental-health services into areas at present without them.

Mental hospitals. Small, private mental hospitals — of which there are about 220 in the United States — often are well staffed with highly qualified personnel and offer a wide range of treatment. But these hospitals take care of less than 14 per cent of the people who are admitted to mental hospitals each year. Moreover, the private hospitals are prohibitively expensive for most people.

For several years there has been a trend toward the creation of psychiatric facilities within general hospitals. Well over 600 nonprofit, voluntary community hospitals now have anywhere from a few beds to a whole wing reserved for mental patients, and over 40 per cent of the nation's yearly mental-patient admissions go first to these institutions. The great majority of these facilities are accredited and are comparatively well staffed.

But most of the 717,000 mental patients who are hospitalized at any given time are still lodged in some 300 state hospitals. These are for the most part overlarge — some so vast as to be veritable towns of many thousands of insane people. They are often impersonal, cold, and concerned more with keeping their patients under control than trying to cure them. This is not completely the fault of the hospitals or their administrators. Many patients are senile and cannot improve greatly with any treatment. Furthermore, public ignorance of the nature of mental illness forced state officials in the past to build huge, economical hospitals far from populated areas and to maintain prisonlike control over the patients. Even today, changes in policy are hard to make in the face of public outcries over each highly publicized brush of an escaped patient with the outside world.

A major part of the problem is manpower, although this is only part of the larger problem of insufficient funds. By the minimum standards for adequate care set by the American Psychiatric Association, state and county hospitals on the average are staffed with only 63 per cent of the adequate number of physicians, 40 per cent of the adequate number of social workers and 25 per cent of the adequate number of nurses.

There are other kinds of workers in these hospitals. Almost 6000 *occupational therapists,* whose qualifications are a college education plus nine months of resident training in an occupational-therapy program, play a useful role in treatment and rehabilitation. And there are between 80,000 and 90,000 *attendants* — or *psychiatric aides,* as they may be called — ranging from unskilled persons, sometimes with serious personality problems of their own, to well-qualified and devoted individuals. These attendants are the primary and often almost the only contact the patient has with hospital authority, but they are rarely qualified to offer any formal psychotherapy.

It is evident that there are grave lacks in the present treatment of emotional and mental disorders. There are not nearly enough trained people or sufficient funds to pay their wages or to house the ill. Even where modern therapeutic techniques and personnel are available, outmoded viewpoints often prevent their use. But serious attempts are being made to attract the needed manpower, and salaries are being raised. Public interest is greater than ever, and municipal and state governments are increasingly aware of their responsibilities. Finally, President Kennedy's proposals for the establishment of comprehensive mental-health centers *within* the communities they are to serve point the way to a future in which adequate treatment will be within the reach of everyone. In the meantime, it is encouraging to note that even the poorest state hosptials discharge 40 per cent of their patients within one year after admission.

WHAT DOES THERAPY COST?

The treatment of mental or emotional illness is often expensive, particularly when the illness is severe and the treatment is prolonged. But so is the cost of major surgery or the treatment of any chronic disease; even orthodontia can run into thousands of dollars. Bear these comparisons in mind when you read of the costs of treatment for a psychological illness.

Some people are fortunate enough not to have to worry about costs. For such persons the small private mental hospital offers the optimum solution to severe mental illness, at a cost of up to $2000 a month. All the better private hospitals run close to that top; at that level the patient gets a rich diet of personal attention and treatment, ranging from drugs and electroshock, if needed, to intensive psychotherapy, plus the comfort and services of a good hotel.

Most patients, of course, cannot afford such prices. For them the psychiatric section of a general hospital is more feasible. The average cost per day in these hospitals is $35, or about $1000 a month, but most patients pay only part of that amount, depending on the hospital and the patient's circumstances; the balance is made up from hospital contributions, trust funds and government allotments. Because of space and staffing problems, these general hospitals limit admissions to acute cases that are expected to improve rapidly. About a quarter of the patients must be transferred to private or state hospitals after a few weeks. But the majority are well enough to be discharged in a month or so — at a cost to them, on the average, of between several hundred and a thousand dollars.

The least expensive hospital care throughout the nation is provided by the state hospitals. Some people go to them out of choice; most do so because of financial need or because there are no other available facilities. The fees at state hospitals are usually based on the family's ability to pay, and vary from nothing to about $200 a month. This means taxes pay most of the bill. In New York State, as in many other states, only about one-tenth of the cost is paid by the hospitals' patients.

The hospitals of New York State are among the few state mental institutions giving modern therapy; treatment in four-fifths of the state hospitals ranges down to the merest custodial care. One can judge the type of care from the amount of money spent per patient. A recently published survey contrasts Veterans Administration mental hospitals, which have federal funds and spend up to $20 a day for each patient, with state hospitals, the best of which spend under $9 a day and the worst of which spend under $3 a day. Low-cost custodial care, as knowing observers have long pointed out, is no real bargain. A good state hospital, which may charge a middle-income patient about $50 a month, will in most cases be able to release him on convalescent status after six months, at a cost to him of about $300. A poor state hospital, which may charge him only $10 to $20 per month, may have to keep him, unimproved, for years (eleven years being the average stay for schizophrenics in such hospitals) for a total cost on the order of $2000 — plus, of course, ten and a half years of his life.

The treatment of serious mental illness, even when it is adjusted to income, often creates a personal financial burden. Unfortunately, although three-quarters of the American people now have some form of health insurance, the coverage of psychological disorders has lagged far behind the coverage of physical diseases. Few Blue Cross plans offer as much hospital care for mental illnesses as for physical ones, and some offer none whatever. The situation is changing rapidly, however, in the direction of fuller coverage. Already, all Blue Shield plans pay for part of the costs of the patient's own psychiatrist while in the hospital, and some private insurance companies cover a variety of other psychological and psychiatric services, including group therapy, psychological tests and visits to private offices of psychiatrists.

But this is only a beginning. Although strides are being made in providing insurance coverage for people with severe mental illnesses, treatment of the neuroses and lesser disorders is rarely covered by Blue Shield or other insurance programs — and it can be costly.

The least expensive resources for treating the less severe disorders are the family service agencies and the mental-health clinics, since for the most part these organizations base their charges on the client's ability to pay. The fees (which vary somewhat from agency to agency and tend to be higher in the big cities) range from nothing to a maximum of $25 an hour. But few people pay the top fee. At most of the agencies affiliated with the Family Service Association of America, a family of four with a take-home pay of from $7500 to $9000 would be charged $7 to $10 an hour. Similarly, the clinic of New York City's American Foundation of Religion and Psychiatry charges from $3 to $12.50 an hour, plus a $5 fee for a psychiatric evaluation and graded charges for psychological tests. And at a typical mental-health clinic the average charge is considerably less than its high of $10 a visit.

The per-hour cost, to be sure, is only part of the matter; what the patient wants to know is the prospective *total* cost — that is, the per-hour cost multiplied by the number of visits likely to be needed. How long, then, is it likely to take? A single interview with a social case-worker, at $10, may be enough to help a husbandless mother by informing her of the financial assistance available to her through the Aid to Families with Dependent Children. On the other hand, irrational feelings of anxiety and immobilizing panic may keep a young business-man going to a psychiatrist at a mental-health clinic for close to a year, at a total cost of $500. Again, six months of once-a-week visits may be necessary to settle a marital maladjustment and enable a husband and wife to find a satisfactory way of living together peacefully and lovingly; at $10 an hour, the cost for this problem would be $250 — no more than it would cost to improve the shape of a nose by plastic surgery.

Mental-health clinics and social-work agencies thus offer bargain rates in psychotherapy — but those who desire a private practitioner don't always pay a great deal either. Social caseworkers in private practice charge from $5 to $15 an hour. Psychiatrists, psychoanalysts, clinical psychologists and other practitioners of deeper forms of psychotherapy set their own fees, which range from under $15 (rarely) to as much as $50 (very rarely) per visit. Most psychiatrists vary their fees according to the financial circumstances of the patient.

But again, what of the *total* cost? How often and how long does the patient pay these fees? Reparative psychotherapy usually takes from three to six months, and the patient is generally seen once or twice a week. At $15 a visit for five months, this would cost him $300 to $600. More intensive and deeper-probing treatment consists of several visits a week, and positive results are rarely achieved in less than eight months. A client paying $20 a visit and going three times a week for eight months would spend about $2000. The most profound treatment, psychoanalysis, may last for four or five years and involve almost daily visits. If a patient went five times a week for 46 weeks of the year (treatment being suspended during the analyst's vacation) for five years and paid $25 a visit, it would cost him over $28,000.

Such long-term analysis obviously is not for everyone. Most people will be helped adequately by shorter-term, more widely used forms of therapy. And those are not always as expensive as they may seem. Many a family might benefit a great deal more if a disturbed mother received psychotherapy than if the same amount of money were spent on a family vacation. The therapy in many cases is expensive only in the sense that it displaces a luxury; in itself it is far from being a luxury.

WHAT GOOD DOES THERAPY DO?

It is comparatively easy to judge the effectiveness of hospital treatment of severe mental illness. When the patient's behavior reaches a point at which his family or the public or he himself cannot stand it, he is hospitalized; when he is sufficiently recovered to get along once more in the world outside — even if there is a chance he may need to be readmitted — he is released. And this is the simple measure of success or failure. In good state hospitals between 70 and 85 per cent of the patients can be discharged within six months of the time they are admitted.

It is more difficult to measure improvement in the nonhospitalized person who simply feels wretched or who makes others unhappy or who violates the ordinary standards of decent behavior in our society.

Many factors confuse and becloud the issue. For one thing, nonhospitalized patients are subject to outside influences not under the therapist's control. A new job may encourage a patient and make him more amenable to treatment aimed at improving his domestic difficulties, but a new baby may cause him to be fatigued and irritable and thus worsen his home situation just as it was mending. It is almost impossible to appraise the effect of therapy in such a case — and most cases are just as confusing.

The confusing factors come not only from the patient; the therapist unfortunately is responsible for some of them, since he too is human. In his reporting of results, for example, he may so *want* his efforts to have helped his patient that he sees or imagines improvement where outsiders see little or none.

It is extremely difficult for the patient, too, to distinguish between the *actual* and the *imagined* effects of therapy, or, to be more exact, between the effects genuinely created by the treatment itself and those created by the patient's faith in the process. (A medical parallel is the distinction between the effects of a real drug and those of a placebo, or dummy pill.) On occasion, for instance, there can be major and lasting improvement from "faith cures" if the new faith leads to new forms of behavior more rewarding than the old.

Again, it is difficult to establish beyond question whether some of those who get better during psychotherapy wouldn't have improved just as much without it. Certain people recover from some emotional illnesses without help — and some get worse with the passage of time.* In any case, the chance of "spontaneous remission" — improvement without external cause — is not used by rational people as an excuse for avoiding treatment of physical diseases, and should not be in the case of psychological ones.

Difficult as it often is for the therapist or for the patient to judge improvement, it may be even more difficult for the patient's friends and relatives. A child who is docile, quiet and unhappy before therapy may be much more pleasing to a domineering teacher or parent than the more outspoken, self-assured child he may become with treatment. A cheerful life-of-the-party may win nothing but disapproval from his erstwhile friends when he finds inner resources to replace his constant need for companionship. The self-sacrificing son who refrains from marriage in order to have his mother live with him is not likely to win her approval if therapy brings him the independence to find a wife of his own.

* See "The Self-Healing Powers of the Mind," page 136.

These differing personal reactions all make it difficult to appraise the usefulness of psychotherapy to any one individual, but the greatest difficulty of all comes from the lack of any clear definition of the words "cure" and "improvement." Emotional illnesses in many ways are intangible and subjective. If only there were something we could *see* or *feel* — a broken bone, a tumor, a rash — the task would be easier; instead, we must deal with such things as "irrational fear," "a neurotic need for praise" or "inability to use one's talents to the full." There are no calipers, no scales, with which to measure these things precisely.

And even when therapists agree on the severity of a symptom and the amount of change in a given patient, they can't always agree about whether the change constitutes major improvement or only minor amelioration. The value of change usually depends on the therapist and his aims — and the patient and *his* aims. For the goals of various types of psychotherapy are dissimilar, and so, therefore, is the meaning of improvement.

Consider, for example, a man whose job is so irritating and who is under such pressure from his supervisor that he comes home each night tense and furious. He is so taut that the mildest hint of criticism or disagreement from his wife or little boy enrages him. If he goes to his minister to complain about his family he may get a sympathetic hearing, a reminder that man is born unto trouble, and an exhortation to be more tolerant. Having rid himself briefly of his pent-up anger, the husband leaves in better spirits — "improved," in the eyes of the clergyman and himself, though the effect may last only a few days.

If, however, he goes to a social worker to complain of his wife and child, and perhaps to express his deeper fear that his marriage may be in trouble, the social worker will probably consider mere ventilation insufficient. He may not be satisfied unless the husband becomes aware of his tendency to use his family as the target for hostile feelings that have been aroused by others, and perhaps agrees to find a job that does not cause so much stress.

If, finally, the young man goes to a psychoanalyst, wanting to get to the heart of what is going wrong, the analyst will probably consider the goal to be nothing less than self-awareness sufficient to change the patient's inner responses to external stress. Thus, to be improved in the analyst's view, the husband would have to get to the point where he no longer seethed with rage at his employer's manner, could deal with his employer comfortably, stay on the job — and go home nightly to his family without the need to blow off steam at them or anyone else.

How comforting it would be if we could slip each former patient into a super-machine from which he would emerge cellophane-wrapped and stamped "Cured — Prime" or "Improved — Choice" or simply "Rejected — Unimproved"! Alas, some doubts will have to remain with us until the means of truly scientific proof are available. Unfortunately, this is close to a Utopian dream. To be scientifically evaluated, treatment would have to be freely available to everyone, and teams of psychologists, psychiatrists, sociologists and statisticians would have to appraise the results according to standards that haven't yet been developed.

For the time being, even though the therapist may sometimes exaggerate his success, the measure of improvement must depend primarily on his ability to deduce the degree of change from the patient's own reports. Hundreds of papers that evaluate the results of psychotherapy indicate that this is reasonably reliable, for they show a rather striking unanimity of experience; *nearly all of them report improvement in about two-thirds of the patients treated.* The figure is the same whether the standard of improvement is the patient's own comfort or his effectiveness in social situations or a combination of the two. Some reports are based on the results of psychological tests taken before and after therapy, some on the therapist's impressions of change, some (in controlled situations such as in institutions) on evaluation by attendants, nurses and other workers — but no matter what the source, improvement ratios cluster around the two-thirds mark.*

There is, however, a fairly consistent tendency for the percentages of improvement reported to be higher for longer and deeper courses of treatment. One study of over 1000 psychoanalytic patients showed that while 66 per cent of all cases showed improvement, the figure for cases treated more than six months was 92 per cent. Not only in psychoanalysis does the length of therapy have an effect. For example, in 1961,

* For further discussion of this subject, see "Does Psychotherapy Really Work?" page 151.

one large-city affiliate of the Family Service Association of America reported on the results of family counseling for over 1600 families. The counselors felt that nearly all the clients who had had more than 25 interviews had been helped, but only two-thirds of those who had had fewer than six interviews were benefited.

To judge by this kind of evidence, a person with a mental or emotional disorder who goes to a qualified practitioner has a good chance of obtaining improvement, no matter how he defines it, if he undertakes the kind of therapy designed to achieve the goal he seeks. Whatever the goal — whether it be release from a hospital or amelioration of a constricting symptom or personality reconstruction — the chances of obtaining it today are close to two out of three. This is not the same as a sure thing — but it is pretty good, at that, and would seem to be well worth the gamble.

HOW TO FIND THE PROPER HELP

We have seen the kinds of treatment that are available for psychological ailments ranging from totally incapacitating psychoses to noncrippling emotional illnesses, and we have seen that these treatments are administered by several types of practitioner at fees ranging from the very cheap to the very dear. The range of skills and of costs is, in fact, so broad that the patient may unwittingly select a therapist who is grossly underqualified (or overqualified) to treat his disorder or whose fees are so high as to prohibit a long-enough course of treatment. Moreover, mental healing is so new and has so few legal controls that practitioners run the gamut from highly ethical, dedicated and qualified men to unscrupulous quacks and charlatans.

How, then, can you find the therapist best qualified to help you or the person for whom you seek aid?

The first step, of course, is to determine what kind of practitioner and therapy are called for. But this is definitely not a responsibility the layman should take upon himself. Every responsible source consulted in the preparation of this article offered the same warning: Don't try to diagnose the trouble yourself. Typically, Clark Blackburn, general director of the Family Service Association of America, says, "I cannot overemphasize the wisdom of going first for diagnostic help to a qualified, reputable family service agency, mental-health clinic or similar organization. Psychological symptoms, even more so than physical ones, are apt to be misleading and difficult to interpret — most of all to the patient himself."

Finding a mental-health service. To find the mental-health agency, clinic or center nearest you, do one of the following:

Call your local *mental-health association*; this will be listed in the telephone directory either as "Mental Health Association of [Your County]" or as "[Your County] Mental Health Association." There are 900 such chapters and divisions of the National Association for Mental Health throughout the country, nearly all of which maintain directories of approved local psychiatric and mental-health facilities. The one you find in the phone book will almost surely be able to offer the names of nearby agencies, clinics or centers in which diagnosis and therapy are available.

If there is no mental-health association in your area, call the *United Fund, Community Chest, Council of Social Agencies* or the *Department of Public Welfare* in your community; any of these ought to be able to supply the names of agencies, clinics and centers in the area.

Consult the *classified telephone directory* — but be careful. Names may be misleading; some clinics do not handle children's problems, for example, though this may not be apparent from the name. Nor is even the most respectable-sounding name a guarantee of reliability and professional standards; names like "Child Guidance Clinic," "Human Relations Center" or "Marriage Counseling Center" are not restricted by law, and they can be used by quacks as well as by the best-qualified groups. In consulting the classified directory, therefore, look for the phrase "Family Service Association of America — Accredited Agency," or look under "Mental Health Association of [Your County]." Under these headings you will find the actual name of the local organization affiliated with, and certified by, each of these national professional groups.

In an emergency — when there is a threat of suicide or violence, for instance — there is no time for a cautious approach. What to do in such situations is discussed at the end of this section.

Finding a private therapist or analyst. There may be no agency or clinic near you, or perhaps you simply prefer to consult a private psychotherapist. Although it is harder and riskier to find a reputable individual on your own, you can do so if you observe certain precautions.

First, if there is a *mental-health association* in or near your area, you may be able to get names of privately practicing therapists from it. About one-quarter of these associations run referral services; those that do usually require the applicant to come in for one interview. A *family service agency* or *mental-health clinic* will do the same thing for you, and even if none is near you, it will be worth the effort to travel to a nearby city to obtain such a referral before beginning therapy with a private practitioner.

Second, lacking these referral services, your own *doctor* ought to be able to refer you to a medical therapist. Your *local medical society* — look under "[Your County] Medical Society" in the phone book — will have a list of the names of psychiatrists and medical analysts in the region. For nonmedical psychotherapists and nonmedical analysts (lay analysts), you may start by telephoning or writing the *psychology department* of the nearest college or university; usually someone on the faculty will be able to give you names of individuals or the addresses of organizations of lay analysts. At the nearest library you may consult the *Directory of Medical Specialists* (in which you will find psychiatrists listed by geographical area) or the *membership directory of the American Psychological Association* (although this lists all member psychologists and not only those who do therapy).

Finding a private marriage counselor or social worker. Marriage counselors are often listed in the classified phone book, but this is the poorest possible way to choose one; the title "marriage counselor" may be used with impunity by anyone in most states, regardless of training or the lack of it. For the names of trained and qualified marriage counselors near you, write to American Association of Marriage Counselors, 27 Woodcliff Drive, Madison, New Jersey. All members of this organization have either a master's degree in social work, or an M.D., or a Ph.D. in psychology, sociology or a related field of study, or a three-year graduate degree from a theological seminary.

You may wish to consult a privately practicing social worker for diagnosis and perhaps for psychotherapy. If so, write to National Association of Social Workers, 2 Park Avenue, New York, New York. The NASW will send you its list of chapter chairmen. You select the one nearest to you and contact him; he in turn will supply you with the names and addresses of social workers in his chapter, all of whom have at least a master's degree in social work.

For more advanced qualifications in social workers you may prefer to ask the NASW, or the chapter chairman, for the names of private practitioners who belong to the Academy of Certified Social Workers. All these individuals have not only a master's degree, but also at least two additional years of supervised experience in counseling. You may also look in the classified phone directory for counselors listing the initials ACSW after their names.

Word-of-mouth recommendations. Many people, out of laziness, timidity or embarrassment, are reluctant to make formal requests for the names of practitioners and prefer to accept a friend's recommendation. This is a very common procedure — and a risky one. Many an untrained or partly trained therapist has been of real help to certain patients (your friend may be one), while being seriously damaging to others (*you* may be one). Emotionally disturbed people can be badly shaken, and even catapulted into severe mental illness, by ill-considered probing or other therapy administered by an unqualified practitioner.

If, therefore, you have heard glowing reports from a friend about a therapist, check up on his credentials before going to him yourself. Checking up involves going to the same sources of information already named — the local mental-health association, family service agency, United Fund, Community Chest, Council of Social Agencies, medical society, department of public welfare or library. In going to these sources, ask questions such as these: If he is an M.D., did he take special training in psychiatry, and was it at a good school or hospital? (Some M.D.s drift into the practice of psychotherapy without special training; they can be as dangerous to their patients as any other untrained, self-appointed psychotherapist.) If he is not an M.D., does he hold an advanced degree in social work or clinical psychology? Is he a member of the AAMC, NASW or ACSW? If he is a psychoanalyst, did he train at a recognized institute?

Beware of the quack! There are thousands of self-styled "psychoanalysts" and "psychotherapists" in the United States today who have had no formal training, or who possess degrees from diploma mills or nonexistent universities. Ask questions, inquire, write. You cannot afford not to.

Finding the right mental hospital. If, after diagnosis by a suitable mental-health facility, qualified private practitioner or physician, it becomes clear that a member of your family should enter a mental hospital, you will want to exercise as much care in choosing one as you would in choosing a private psychotherapist.

The major sources of information about private mental hospitals, or psychiatric wards in general hospitals, are those already mentioned — the local mental-health association, the local mental-health clinic, the nearest family service agency or the county medical society. Most family physicians also have a good idea where to refer you, or at least how to get the information if you yourself cannot get it. Since costs run high for some private mental hospitals, be sure to inquire exactly what they are when gathering data. If money is a serious problem, the same sources will be able to inform you if the state hospitals in your state have instituted modern therapeutic methods and are likely to be helpful.

Emergencies. All this talk about careful investigation becomes meaningless if someone in your family goes into an abrupt "psychotic episode," behaving hysterically, suicidally, violently or in some other radical and intolerable fashion. In such cases:

Call your doctor first. He will take necessary emergency actions, possibly including temporary tranquilizing of the patient through drugs. He will arrange for a psychiatric examination and, if necessary, for admission to a general or mental hospital.

If your doctor isn't available, call your local medical society. It will assist you in finding a physician who can see the patient in the emergency. The medical society will also advise you about the standards and admissions policies of nearby hospitals.

Don't call the police unless your life, or someone else's, is being threat-ened. All too often, policemen are ignorant of the proper methods of dealing with a psychotic person; moreover, in most jurisdictions they have no authority to do anything with an apparently violent person ex-cept put him in jail — an experience that may seriously aggravate his mental illness.

Don't call a general hospital yourself, even if it has a psychiatric sec-tion. Most of these hospitals cannot admit a person as mentally ill un-less a doctor has made the diagnosis and arranged for the admission.

The road to mental health is seldom easy to follow. It requires deter-mination, time, money and a good deal of personal effort. Yet the great philosopher Benedict Spinoza might have been speaking of this very thing in the closing words of "Of Human Liberty," the final section of his *Ethics:*

If the way which leads hither seem very difficult, it can nevertheless be found. It must indeed be very difficult since it is so seldom discovered; for if salvation lay ready to hand and could be discovered without great labor, how could it be neglected by almost everyone? But all noble things are as difficult as they are rare.

The Self-Healing Powers of the Mind

SOME 2,000,000 Americans are currently seeking and getting profes-sional help for their emotional and mental disorders — a striking in-dication of the growing acceptance of the value of psychiatry. Yet far more remarkable is the fact that although nearly ten times as many others never seek nor get any help for their emotional and mental ailments, the great majority of them muddle along fairly well anyhow, many of them actually getting well by themselves. "There are an infinite number of persons who at some time during their lives have suffered a major or minor mental illness and who have recovered without ever consulting a physician or psychiatrist," wrote Dr. Louis Wolberg, then psychiatrist at King's Park State Hospital, New York, in *Psychiatric Quarterly* in 1944.

He was keynoting what has become an important trend in the intervening years: the dawning recognition by psychologists and psychiatrists that the human mind is stronger, more resistant to emotional infection, and more inclined to heal its own ills, than was long thought. During the past sixty or seventy years, while psychiatrists have been making great strides in understanding and treating psychological disorders, many of them have naturally focused on the mind's frailties and imperfections, all but ignoring the fact that, like the body, it has a whole battery of weapons for combatting its own ailments. Now, however, a more balanced and hopeful view of the human mind is emerging.

Dr. Franz Alexander, the eminent psychoanalyst, says that even in involved psychoanalysis "the therapist only frees the natural maturational powers of his patients. Nature heals; the physician only helps the natural healing process." And one of America's most distinguished psychologists, Professor Gordon Allport of Harvard University, sums up his own view of the human personality in these simple words: "Although traces of neurotic traits and mechanisms may be found in many healthy people, these threads are minor as compared with the sturdier weave of wholesome growth."

That basic healthiness and wholesomeness is what accounts for the infinity of spontaneous recoveries from illness of which Dr. Wolberg spoke. Such recoveries seem to take place gradually and automatically, just as a cut or bruise heals by itself. A charming and good-humored woman I know suffered a severe emotional shock after the birth of a baby who only lived a few hours: she grew deeply depressed, weak, and fearful, and took to her bed, unable to set foot outside her own house. She and her husband, to their own discredit, were both unwilling to call in a psychiatrist, and she languished in a semi-invalid state for half a year; then, slowly but unmistakably, she began to gain strength, take an interest in life, and venture out of doors a little. In another half year she had become her former cheerful self again, almost no trace of her illness remaining.

During the Second World War, I was an Eighth Air Force pilot, flying lonely reconnaissance missions deep into Germany without so much as a pistol for defense. Under this stress I became strange and alien to myself: my handwriting grew crabbed and illegible, I drank and gambled night after night, I could read nothing more substantial than the scandal sheets, and music, one of the chief joys of my life, had become boring and meaningless to me. One pitch-black night, on my way to the briefing room, I even tried to break my ankle so as to be hospitalized and live longer. Three times I sought to wrench it sideways on a curb, three times I could not do it; then, almost crying in shame and bewilderment, I went on and flew my mission, wondering what had ever become of me, for I neither knew nor liked this person who lived inside my body.

Then the fighting ended and I was reassigned to the Army of Occupation. For weeks I slept, daydreamed, and drifted through my duties; meanwhile, deep inside where the wellsprings of joy and health had never run dry, a healing and regrowth was taking place. I began to read poetry and enjoy music again, my handwriting ceased to look like that of an old man, and one day, hearing a familiar, sweetly melancholy Mozart aria being sung on a nearby radio, I suddenly felt a flood of old good feelings wash through me. I had the eery feeling that all at once I was in the presence of a dear long-lost friend — myself. "It's me!" I thought in amazement and joy. "I'm back!"

Not everyone is lucky enough to have an emotional ailment disappear untreated like this; yet the occurrence is vastly more common than most people realize. Dr. Ian Stevenson reports in the *American Journal of Psychiatry* that according to several recent surveys, from 40 to 60 per cent of people who begin showing signs of neurosis, but who receive no treatment, recover unaided within a few years. A newly published report on an eight-year experiment in comprehensive family medical care, conducted at New York's Montefiore Hospital, found much the same thing: some families with psychological problems sought help, and others did not, but Dr. George A. Silver, author of the report, observes that most of those who did not seek help managed nonetheless to deal with their ailments successfully. "It makes no difference," he writes, "whether they were aware of the difficulties with which they struggled to cope; the fact is that they healed themselves without outside help."

The same is true in many cases of severe mental illness. In some of the worst state mental hospitals in this country, very little is done to treat psychotic patients; yet 40 per cent of those who enter such hospitals improve enough to be released within a year. Better-equipped and better-staffed mental hospitals greatly shorten the process, of course, by using such therapies as electroshock treatment and tranquilizing drugs; but many leading mental-hospital doctors feel that shock and drugs do not of themselves "cure" the illness — they merely reduce the pressure of painful thoughts, fears, or hallucinations, thus allowing the artificially calmed mind to patch up its own cracks, re-erect its barricades, make its own excuses, and rediscover its reasons for pride. This belief in the mind's innate drive toward health — even in psychotics — is rapidly gaining ground. Says Dr. Shepherd Kellam, research psychiatrist of the National Institute of Mental Health, "The major effort in psychiatry today is to reduce the degree to which the physician and the mental hospital stand in the way of the patient's own capacity to get better."

None of this is a valid argument for avoiding professional help when one is emotionally or mentally ill. A sensible man doesn't subject his body to a desperate month-long struggle with a raging streptococcic infection if penicillin will snap him out of it in a couple of days. Nor does a sensible person endure the prolonged pain and corrosion of emotional illness if some form of psychotherapy will rescue him from it. But there is no conflict between the body's self-healing tendencies and the doctor's ministrations; by and large he merely assists the body in its own work, or tips the balance in its favor when the enemy forces have been too strong. And so it is too with psychiatry; its practitioners use and assist the natural forces that make for mental health. Because our bodies fight disease, we do not shun medical help; and just because we learn to appreciate our own powers to resist emotional disease, we need not shun psychiatry.

Although these powers have been so largely ignored until lately, their existence should have been plain enough by analogy to our bodies, which, during millions of years of evolution, developed superb built-in mechanisms for maintaining health and combating most of the ills that flesh is heir to. Our blood has fibrin to clot it when the skin is broken; our white cells wage war against invading microbes; our nerves, bones, blood vessels and flesh skillfully reconnect themselves after a wound. Without such acquired devices, we would long ago have joined Tyrannosaurus Rex on the rubbish heap of evolution. And without comparable reparative mechanisms in the mental area, we would surely have joined Neanderthal Man in the annals of extinction.

Some of our self-healing mental mechanisms, indeed, are surprisingly parallel to those of the body. One of the body's basic principles, for instance, is that of homeostasis, or equilibrium: when we get too hot, we sweat in order to keep our temperature constant; when our blood sugar drops too low, we get hunger pangs in our stomach, driving us to eat and thus restore the proper blood sugar level. In a comparable way, our minds try to redress the emotional balance upset by various hurts. People plagued by feelings of inadequacy, unworthiness, guilt, or fear of death often unconsciously turn, for instance, to a kind of lifework which offsets these very feelings — a mental device known as "compensation." A Lutheran-sponsored conference on the psychology of the clergy last year heard a report that their profession has a particular appeal for psychologically ailing people — and that a number of neurotic and prepsychotic men get better when they begin to practice their ministry.

This is only one of many forms of compensation. Dr. Allport points out that many a homely person has restored his emotional equilibrium by developing great charm, or wit, or seeking and attaining power, and that many a weakling has fended off emotional illness by redoubling his efforts to find pleasure and success through intellectual work. Some people, however, make up for their defects by directly attacking them, conquering them, and turning them into exaggerated strengths: Demosthenes, with his dreadful stammer, might have become a neurotic recluse, but instead filled his mouth with pebbles, declaimed speeches against the roar of the surf, and became a great — and healthy-minded — orator.

An even more remarkable parallel exists between the body's ability to wall off an invading foreign object within a cyst and the mental mechanism of self-delusion, or "rationalization." For when we fool ourselves into thinking an agreeable thought about a disagreeable fact, we are encysting the hurt of it. A friend of mine lost money in a foolish investment, of which he now cheerfully says, "It was an expensive lesson, but it was worth it." A woman who always drove too fast, and finally had an accident, says, "It put me in the hospital and gave me time to think about my life. It was the best thing that ever happened to me."

In the past, many psychiatrists thought of compensation, rationalization, and other mental defenses as unhealthy; adult realistic thinking was the ideal of health they had in mind. Today, however, some of them boldly state that although mental defenses can be harmful — just as fevers can sometimes run too high to serve that purpose, or scar tissue can grow too thick and strong, interfering with movement — more often they are helpful and disease-limiting. In the authoritative *American Handbook of Psychiatry* Dr. Melitta Schmideberg expresses the new view: "In current psychiatric thinking," she writes, "the impression [still] prevails that defenses are something undesirable and pathological. On the contrary, they are as essential for mental functioning as is any vital organ of the body."

Even the seemingly childish act of making believe that a frightening thing simply doesn't exist — a device known as "denial" — has recently been found to be more often healthful than harmful. Psychiatrist Lester Grinspoon of Harvard Medical School recently studied the ways in which modern Americans adjust, without severe emotional disturbance, to the ever-present threat of nuclear war. He reported to last winter's meeting of the American Association for the Advancement of Science that we use a variety of defenses, including denial and rationalization, and thereby protect ourselves from anxiety and emotional illness arising from a truth too alarming to face, and too vast to deal with individually.

No doubt it would be more admirable and more healthful if we human beings were always able to face the truth squarely, accept it, and live with it. But in the nature of things most of us cannot, unaided, achieve that degree of personal development, and we are therefore fortunate to have defenses to bolster us. Without the ability to deny unpleasant realities, we would quake every time we boarded a plane, shudder every time we ate meat, and weep whenever we came to another birthday, for some truths are too much to bear continually.

It thus begins to appear that many of the sad, bad, foolish, or wild things that men do are Nature's ways of safeguarding the personality from major harm by combating it with a judicious dose of minor harm

— almost as a forester sets a backfire to check a larger impending destruction. "Blowing off steam" is the name folk wisdom gives to one such kind of preventive reaction. One man will get drunk, profane, and violent at the height of an emotional upset; the next morning, bruised, shaking, and headachy, he is practically stable. (He has not, of course, solved his problems, but he has at least weathered the crisis and remained able to live with them.) Another man may find relief in physical exhaustion. A friend of mine whose mother was dying while he was on duty in England during the war was denied his request for return to the States. He wept, cursed, paced his quarters like a madman for hours; finally, unable to endure it another moment, he put on a sweatsuit, ran cross-country for miles until he collapsed in a meadow, and later limped back to his room, sad but calm.

Even the act of revenge, so often ugly and detestable, has its place among the remedies of the aching soul. "Be comforted," says a friend to Macduff, whose wife and children have just been murdered by Macbeth's men. "Let's make us medicines of our great revenge / To cure this deadly grief." And today the scientific study of human nature proves the poet right. Dr. Thomas P. Hackett, a psychiatrist at the Massachusetts General Hospital, recently reported on the case of Nick, an elderly Greek produce dealer who, after twenty years of selling his fruit and vegetables at the same stall in the market place, was dispossessed from it by a young, strong bully. At first Nick was crushed; then he rallied by organizing his life around the effort to get revenge. For ten years he battled through friends, through lawyers, and even through God, to Whom he offered many prayers and candles. When his enemy died, Nick literally attributed it to God's response to his pleas; but now he had no motive to go on striving, and almost immediately developed a bleeding ulcer. He told the psychiatrist that he would die despite surgery, and did — not because of the operation, but because he had nothing left to live for.

Many of the useful counterirritants to anger or sorrow are not this ugly. In games, for instance, we often expend emotional energy that would hurt us — or others dear to us — if not used up in a healthful way. When a man with a harsh boss goes to the gym and whacks a handball around for an hour, he gets rid of more than calories and sweat.

Says Dr. Karl Menninger, "We are all subject and liable to the disease of disturbed morale — demoralization — and one of the best antidotes against this is to be found in recreation . . . Play can be [both] therapeutically useful and prophylactically useful."

An equally valuable antidote to emotional disorder, says Dr. Menninger, is work. Sometimes we sourly think of work as a painful necessity ("In the sweat of thy face shalt thou eat bread"), but we also recognize that it releases, fulfills, and satisfies us. As Thomas Carlyle extravagantly put it, "Work is the grand cure for all the maladies and miseries that ever beset mankind." The great American success stories are the result not only of economic opportunities, but of the inner forces that drove certain men to empire-building actions. In times and places when such success was not possible, a man with a blaze in his belly might have fled to the monastery, or gone to war, or become a cutthroat, to keep the inner fire from burning him into madness.

The new findings about the mind's self-healing powers are changing many a pessimistic notion about the human personality. Consider the theory, held by many psychoanalysts and embedded in orthodox psychoanalytic thought, that we stop growing after adolescence, and that the flaws built into a person's character in the early years are there to stay unless removed by intensive therapy. And not only psychoanalysts have thought so: popular tradition has long held that "as the twig is bent, the tree's inclined." But the latest data indicate that in many cases the personality is quite capable of straightening itself during maturity.

Many a college student who drops out, for instance, is diagnosed by clinicians as having a "character disorder" — that is, a type of psychiatric ailment that makes him impulsive, willful, irresponsible, lacking in conscience, and often somewhat "wild." But folk wisdom has sometimes been optimistic about the wild one. "Wait until he marries and gets a job," it says. "He'll settle down. He'll turn out all right." Pollyanna-ish? No; researchers at Yale University recently surveyed a number of men who had dropped out because of character disorders, and found that most of them, after a while, had either come back to Yale to finish, or gone to another college, or taken jobs. All in all, after some years the great majority of them had turned out surprisingly well.* Similarly, a

* For more detail on this, see "Our Tormented College Kids," page 290.

psychiatrist who deals with a great many drug addicts (most of whom have character disorders) told me last year that "most of these people, if they live into their thirties, just seem to get better."

But why do they? Because the forces of growth still exist within, long after childhood or adolescence; it often takes only the sunshine and rain of love, marriage, work, and parenthood to make the bent plant straighten up and start growing once again. When we fall in love, we gain a sudden new perspective on ourselves — we know how we want the beloved one to see us, and practically transform ourselves to match that image. As A. E. Housman so lyrically put it:

> Oh, when I was in love with you,
> Then I was clean and brave;
> And miles around the wonder grew,
> How well did I behave.

In a less poetic, but more precise, vein, sociologist Robert Winch of Northwestern University has analyzed and measured the character traits of couples in love to see what kind of matching of qualities love involves.* He found that for the most part we fall in love with someone whose personality is the complement of our own — the strong, driving person with the frail, timid one, for instance — and through whom we can therefore fulfill ourselves and end our frustrations. Behind all the rapture, the poetry, and the exhilaration, there is thus a built-in health-seeking force in love — a drive to complete ourselves and to release our pent-up unachieved desires.

Similarly, a few years ago researchers at the Dallas Child Guidance Clinic did a study of thirty-four adults who, in their childhood, had been uncommonly shy and withdrawn. Most of them, it was revealed, had turned out quite well as grown-ups — and significantly, three-quarters of these had married outgoing extroverts, unlike themselves, who completed their personalities and healed their old hurts.

This is only one of the self-healing devices which adulthood calls into being. Taking on adult duties is another one. Even a wild and dangerous youth has, buried in his mind, the fantasy of himself as a mature and responsible person; under the stimuli of the right circumstances, that dor-

* See "How Do We Choose a Mate?" page 58.

mant seed germinates and springs forth, often to the amazement of those who know the youth best. A distant relative of mine, whom I will call Charley, was a scandal to the family during his teens. He swore, drank, visited brothels, quit college, ran away from home, drove like a maniac, and beat up men twice his size. All the relatives thought him unredeemable. Charley went to war and came home meaner than ever, but after a while he got married and had a son. Sometime later I heard that he was taking night courses in college, while holding down a job as a tough private detective; still later, I heard he had won his degree and was slowly forcing himself through law school; and finally Charley became a lawyer, threatening, blustering, and fighting at the professional level — while at home he had become a steady, warm-hearted husband and father.

Psychological disorders like Charley's often reflect youth's lack of a sense of being *somebody* — somebody with a specific skill, a place in the world, a love, a family. All these things make up one's *identity* — his *who* and *what* — but until he knows his own identity, he can be bewildered, lost, angry, and even sick. Professor Erik Erikson, Harvard's noted student of child development, says that a great many young people go through a sharp "identity crisis" or period of maladjustment and actual neurosis, when they are trying to figure out who they are going to be.

But the eventual discovery and achievement of one's identity often permits a dramatic self-healing of the emotions — and even of the body. William James, the great nineteenth-century psychologist, was a neurotic semi-invalid in his twenties, at a time when he was trying to decide whether his life lay in art or science. After years of crippling melancholia and assorted physical ailments, he finally chose science, and within it even came to specialize in psychology, in which he had such a vested interest. He got over his youthful invalidism, developed a capacity to work harder and more productively than many a sturdier man, and rapidly became a leading psychologist and philosopher. His lectures, essays, and books stand as an impressive monument to a self-healed mind.

Such delayed growth or spontaneous healing, occurring in early or even middle adult life, is one of the things that have made wise men call Time "the best medicine" and "a healer of all ills." But it need not always require long years to bring health; many sorrows and disorders lose their power over us in months or even weeks. The "bad spell," the "trying time," the "personal crisis," very often comes and goes; half a year later, it is fading fast from view, and we hardly know how Time has worked the miracle.

Time itself, of course, did not, but certain healing mechanisms did — and required Time in which to do their beneficent work. The most important such mechanism is the mental activity known as repression,* a special kind of forgetting which takes place over a period of time, but which is quite different from the mere fading of unimportant details from memory. For in repression, we involuntarily forget very important but painful things such as embarrassments, personal failures, and vicious or forbidden wishes.

In some cases, we totally obliterate those emotions and ideas that would sicken us, and cannot remember ever having had them; a grown man may be quite unable to believe that as a child he used to wish his older brother were dead. In other cases, however, we forget only the hurtful part of an idea or experience. Bygone days that were wretched often begin to look good in fond retrospect, as we forget their painful aspects and remember only their pleasant ones; ancient sorrows seem sweetened by the passage of time, and assume a gentle bittersweet flavor. As a character in a Dumas novel says, "Oh, the good times when we were so unhappy!"

How wisely Nature has developed in us this capacity for forgetting! For the recollection of dread thoughts may lead to serious illness, while forgetting them may be necessary to health. Even in the centuries before the advent of modern psychiatric treatment, many madmen slowly recovered their wits in asylums, sometimes thanks to their repressing again things they had unhappily dug up from the depths of the mind. In *The Philosophy of Insanity,* published in 1860, a former inmate of a Scottish lunatic asylum tells how, during his worst period of madness, a "spirit in his stomach" used to read terrible things to him out of a book, including

* This is dealt with in more detail in "What Your Memory Reveals About You," page 86.

circumstances which could only have been seen or known by me in infancy, [but] mingled with the most horrible lies. . . . The truths must have lain forgotten and illegible in some dark corner of the brain till lighted up and rendered readable by the wild glare which madness throws.

At one point, when the spirit read him something particularly dreadful about his father, he demanded to know the name of the book.

"It is the text-book of hell, the bible of the damned," was the instant reply. After this, let him do as he liked, I would listen no more to him or his book; and by persevering in this, the entire delusion slowly faded away.

Modern psychological literature has no clearer example of the sickness resulting from the exposure of shocking ideas, and the return to health resulting from repressing them again.

Another healing device we possess, one which takes time in which to do its work, is a laborious process of mental work we might call reconditioning — a kind of rewiring of the brain, so to speak, in which our reactions to a variety of stimuli are changed, one by one. It happens in psychotherapy, and is sometimes spoken of as emotional re-education. But we do it for ourselves in such processes as grieving for a dead person. When we grieve for someone newly lost to us, the very process of going over the fond thoughts again and again, day after day, gradually conditions us to our new status and slowly reconnects the mental circuits; after a while, the knowledge of the loss is no longer shocking and sickening, but familiar and acceptable. Shelley was right that grief itself is mortal — or at least, so it is in the healthy person. The unhealthy one may mourn without end, while the healthy one slowly works a metamorphosis in his feelings, accepts the fact of death, begins to seek new sources of love and joy, and slowly arrives at the point where he can look back with a loving smile instead of tears.

The passage of time sooner or later brings new forces into our lives to which, if we are innately healthy, we respond with regrowth and a knitting-up of the wounds. "Time, the consoler," wrote Emerson, "Time, the rich carrier of all changes, dries the freshest tears by obtruding new figures, new costumes, new roads on our eye, new voices on our ear. . . . Nature will not sit still; the faculties will do somewhat; new hopes spring, new affections twine and the broken is whole again."

And more than mere repair is involved; the hurt, once healed, may leave us with a net gain in greater self-awareness, increased maturity. "Sadder and wiser" might often be reworded, "wiser and healthier." Studies of teen-age and college-age love affairs, for instance, have shown that the average person falls in love somewhere between three and seven times before marrying — with his later loves being increasingly realistic and better suited to his own emotional needs. Experience is thus not only a teacher, but a promoter of mental health.

To view it another way, many an experience that causes pain may also bring about health in the way that a mustard plaster or rubefacient ointment irritates the skin, bringing about a curative flow of blood to a congested chest or to aching muscles. A shocking event can set off a process of reorganization and growth in the whole personality. Sudden separation from home and family, such as going off to military service or to college, has a transforming effect on many a young man. Many a chronic bachelor, ne'er-do-well, or playboy has grown up only after his parents died. "The loss of supportive persons through death, defection, or other kinds of separation," writes Dr. Stevenson, "seems often to contribute to recovery from the psychoneuroses. Many persons have experienced a marked acceleration in their own maturation with the death of a parent which obliged them to live differently and more responsibly."

The stimulus of experience may trigger off growth and recovery even in seemingly hopeless cases. Many of the very sickest mental hospital patients, says Dr. Wolberg, attempt desperately to establish relationships with other human beings around them; let one such relationship work, and the reassured patient may suddenly begin to improve and to test out the possibility of getting along with many other people, rather than hiding in the retreat of his psychotic isolation.

Yet retreating is not always bad; in some of us, a certain moderate use of withdrawal can be a useful protective tactic, removing us temporarily from infectious surroundings or abrasive relationships. A man I know whose marriage had become intolerable used to become uncontrollably sleepy in his wife's presence, thus avoiding either arguments or stony silence. After his divorce his sleepiness vanished, to the amazement of friends who used to call him "the Dormouse." Others retreat not into sleep or psychosis, but physically remove themselves from an atmosphere they cannot tolerate, and seek one that is more healthful for them. Many a crank and dissident, ailing and sore in his own society, has gone to some frontier or New World and there found health and vigor as a pioneer.

In part, of course, it is not only the change of atmosphere that helps, but the fresh sense of purpose and the sense of challenge; these, too, stimulate the built-in powers of self-healing. Suicides fall off sharply in war years in part because the need of people for each other — and their sense of challenge and common purpose — transcends personal despair. Dr. E. Graham Howe, a British psychologist, says war can actually be a healing influence on some people. He writes of a former patient of his, an ailing, purposeless, neurotic woman, whom he met again during the London Blitz of 1940; she was laboring day and night as assistant to an overburdened physician, and had been transformed into a vigorous and healthy woman.

Some of history's greatest men have been saved from their own psychological ailments by such challenges. Several decades ago, a young lawyer from the Midwest suffered such depressions as to seem dangerously suicidal. In a note, he once wrote:

I am now the most miserable man living. If what I feel were equally distributed to the whole human family, there would not be one cheerful face on the earth. Whether I shall ever be better, I cannot tell; I awfully forebode I shall not.

But he was wrong. The challenges life offered him — and the longer he lived, the greater they became — brought him a health and a strength that saved both him and his country from dissolution; his name, of course, was Abraham Lincoln.

Finally, perhaps the most valuable and pervasive of all the mind's defenses against disease is a quality of belief in self and in life. It has been given many names and many explanations. William James himself spoke of it as the "religion of healthy-mindedness," and theologian Arnold Koestler calls it the "oceanic sense." Dr. Menninger speaks of an inner strength, which he feels all people have in varying degrees. Still other psychologists and students of man talk of "self-approval" or "self-acceptance," which enables us to see ourselves realistically, and to like what we see.

Where does such a basic force for health come from? Probably from parental love, which, when it is freely and warmly given, instills into us an early and undying feeling of being valuable, and hence is a basic source of courage and hope about how we and the world will get along together. Those who have this inner strength — and most normal people have it in some degree — come back from the defeats of life with continually renewed optimism, and not only resist the wear and tear of time but actually feel that they are making continual improvement and progress.

None of this means that we can sit back and smugly assume that all will be well with us, and that everything will automatically turn out for the best. We know today that many people live with chronic emotional disorders all their lives, never getting better, and that others who are healthy in youth tend to weaken and crumple into emotional and mental illness in middle or old age. We know that if modern therapies are introduced into an old-fashioned mental hospital, many patients who remained unable to improve by themselves abruptly do so, and even get completely well. We know that the sooner a person with a serious emotional problem seeks professional help, the more likely it is that his ailment will yield quickly to treatment.

Yet having looked closely at the self-healing powers of the human mind, I am encouraged to think that we are better made than I had realized; that our natural inclination is to mend ourselves rather than to destroy ourselves; and that within the human mind psychologists have a most potent array of correctives with which to heal its disorders. A thousand wise and gloomy philosophers have called man a frail, wretched, and miserable creature, but I prefer to side with Sophocles, who said, "Many wonders there be, but naught more wondrous than man"; and with the Psalmist, who sang, in simple eloquence, "I am fearfully and wonderfully made."

Does Psychotherapy Really Work?

(Coauthor: RENA CORMAN)

WHENEVER the subject of psychoanalysis crops up in company, the result almost always is a raging argument in which dear friends find themselves on opposite sides of a line as sharp and impassable as those that separated Blue from Gray, York from Lancaster, Guelph from Ghibelline. These days, in New York and certain other American cities, it seems that practically everybody who is anybody — plus quite a few who are nobody — has experienced some form of psychotherapeutic treatment, or intimately knows people who have. Nearly everyone, therefore, is ready to assert that it either works wonders, or does no good at all; improves the character and personality, or breaks them down; is a rational and admirable effort to improve oneself, or a purblind and contemptible effort to lean on someone else.

Arguments of this sort can thrive only because there is no indisputable evidence on one side or the other. And this is extraordinary: the psychotherapies (including psychoanalysis) have come to play an immense role in American intellectual and emotional life, yet in the sixty-odd years since Freud started the whole business, they have received no rigorous scientific proof of their effectiveness. And no disproof.

Freud himself, always a deeply thoughtful man, despaired of finding reliable evidence in the statistics collected by psychiatric clinics because of the extreme complexity and diversity of the neuroses. Rather than mass clinical data, he wrote, "it is better to examine one's own individual experience" — thereby providing psychoanalysts ever since with the excuse for writing subjective narratives of their cases — usually the successful ones — and calling them scientific contributions. One leading professor of medicine, hostile to psychiatry, puts it caustically:

"Surgeons and pathologists analyze their failures, and thus advance toward scientific understanding; psychotherapists and psychoanalysts write up their successes, and thus prove whatever they believed in the first place."

Even the eminent psychoanalyst Lawrence S. Kubie commented a few years ago that "the lack of critical and objective evaluation of psychotherapy is . . . an indication of where the greatest deficiencies of psychiatry as a medical and therapeutic science are to be found."

For several decades, to be sure, various therapists have been collecting and publishing data on the frequency with which treatment yields improvement or cure in their patients. But unfortunately the published results are either of dubious value or not useful for comparative purposes for many reasons — the most obvious being that there is no agreement yet on the meaning of "improvement" or "cure." On Broadway or television, the paralyzed patient suddenly understands why she is afraid to walk, and thereupon arises and takes a few shaky steps, but 99 and 44/100ths per cent of all cases are not so pure. The definitions of cure range from mere relief of symptoms to total reconstruction of the character. Homosexuality is the classic example: many a therapist considers treatment successful if an anxiety-ridden homosexual simply learns not to be uneasy about his ways, but other therapists consider it successful only if he abjures boys and switches to girls.

This is far from the only flaw in the published studies to date. Few therapists record treatment sessions in detail; few, therefore, are able to be accurate and objective after two or more years, when trying to recall and report what the patient was like at the outset. Nor does the psychotherapist have the money — or the ethical right — to put gumshoes on the trail of his patients to verify what they say about their behavior outside the office.

Again, since the therapist has an understandable bias in favor of the treatment he is providing, he is apt to interpret all the improvement in the patient as the result of therapy, minimizing the influence of such external events as the inheriting of money, promotion to a better job or the death of a domineering boss or parent. The technical difficulties of designing a research study that would surmount these shortcomings are staggering.

"I confess," said psychoanalyst Phyllis Greenacre to a symposium of therapists a few years ago, "that the question of methods of evaluating therapeutic results frightens me somewhat."

Lacking her timorousness — and perhaps her appreciation of the scientific difficulties involved — private psychotherapists, clinical psychologists, family counselors and others continue to publish little batches of "results" from time to time.

Despite the vast differences in what they do to their patients, and what they mean by cure, and how they attempt to judge their results, their reports are in astonishing agreement: the figures on "cure" and "improvement" cluster rather closely about the two-thirds mark — almost never being under 60 per cent, and going over 90 per cent in only one published study. Among the many therapists we have spoken to personally, nearly all estimate their success ratio in the same general range.

Encouraging as these data seem, a decade ago British psychologist H. J. Eysenck cast doubt on the value of psychotherapy by comparing these figures with data derived from two studies of untreated neurotics. One group had been hospitalized, while the other consisted of people cared for at home by general practitioners; neither was given formal psychotherapy.

According to Eysenck's calculations, the two groups showed a two-year collective rate of recovery from neurosis of 70 per cent. He uncompromisingly concluded that "roughly two-thirds of a group of neurotic patients will recover or improve to a marked extent within about two years of the onset of their illness, whether they are treated by means of psychotherapy or not."

This and a later similar attack on psychotherapy from an American source were, however, no better as research than the papers they relied on. The first defect in Eysenck's case — as must be obvious — is the very fact that there is no agreed meaning to "cured" or "improved" in the studies he sums up and compares. Adding results so differently defined is like adding peas, pears and potatoes; one gets only statistical pap. Second, the entire set of circumstances surrounding hospitalized neurotics is radically different from that of neurotics who live at home, continue to work, and see a therapist privately. Third, people who get better within two years of the onset of illness are certainly far less serious cases than those whose neuroses date back to childhood. Finally, in no instance were treated and untreated neurotics observed and evaluated by the same group of professionals. Eysenck's entire comparison of the two groups is therefore suspect, if not meaningless.

For all that, it is deeply disturbing. It can make everyone who believes in the value of psychotherapy long for something in the way of ineluctable proof, even though in the present state of psychiatry it seems impossible to meet the criteria of an objective, controlled, completely rigorous experiment.

A novel, and relatively simple, approach to the problem has, however, been employed in a significant new research study to be published shortly by the Bureau of Publications of Teachers College, Columbia University. Written by Arthur T. Jersild, a psychologist and professor at Teachers College, and two associates of his, Mrs. Eve Lazar and Mrs. Adele Brodkin, it avoids the difficult task of defining cure or improvement in objective terms, completely bypasses the therapists and their inevitable bias in favor of their own work, and sidesteps the complex, inordinately difficult job of observing and measuring improvement in actual behavior. It does all this by focusing directly on what the patients themselves feel therapy has done for them.

"There are a number of ways to test and evaluate people in the search for changes caused by therapy," says Dr. Jersild, "but all these ways involve great procedural problems, and at best have serious defects. Yet one thing is clear: if a person feels lousy before therapy, and much better after it, that is an indisputable fact, and one of supreme importance to him, no matter what other measurements may seem to show."

This seemingly simple idea, he explains, is part of the tendency in modern psychology to assign greater importance to "subjective reality." One may, for example, carefully and objectively ascertain that a given husband is kindly and tolerant toward his wife, but if she happens to feel that he is harsh and intolerant, her faulty perception of him is a reality of major significance for them both. Similarly, a child's feeling about his parents, even if he wrongly interprets their attitudes and actions, may have as much importance in his development as their actual words and deeds.

Accordingly, Jersild reasoned that until the complexities and difficulties of obtaining external proof of the results of psychotherapy are solved, a subjective appraisal by the patients themselves would not only be fairly easy to obtain, but would yield useful data on one major aspect of the reality of the treatment. For almost no one begins therapy unless he is in distress, and if his distress is relieved by it, that alone is significant proof that something desirable happened to him.

This approach sounds solipsistic and existential, to be sure, but Dr. Jersild does not maintain that inner good feeling is the only desideratum or product of psychotherapy. On the contrary, he maintains that people who feel comfortable about themselves and the persons around them are very likely to behave better and function more effectively. The inner feeling simply happens to be an accessible and measurable datum, but from it one can infer a good deal about actual behavior.

Dr. Jersild's study, which was four years in the making and was in part supported by the Horace Mann–Lincoln Institute of School Experimentation, is entitled, "The Meaning of Psychotherapy in the Teacher's Life and Work." This has a misleadingly parochial sound. Although Jersild was interested in learning whether psychotherapy makes better teachers, the implications of his study apply to psychotherapy in general.

For their basic data, Jersild and his associates collected information either by interview or questionnaire from 201 public-school and college teachers in the East, each of whom had had two or more years of intensive psychotherapy or psychoanalysis with therapists from any one of a score of schools of thought.

The teachers revealed that they had been driven into therapy by a variety of familiar neurotic difficulties — a lack of enjoyment of their work, an unhappy love affair (or no love affairs at all), a feeling of drifting aimlessly, a compulsion to do foolish and self-destructive things, unaccountable feelings of rage or depression, a sense of alienation and loneliness, and so on. Some of them also suffered from such physical symptoms as fatigue, colds, digestive disorders, skin trouble and sexual coldness.

And what do these patients say psychotherapy did for them? A great majority of them claim improvement — though not total cure — in nearly every area of major difficulty; 97 per cent feel that the money was well spent, and even the dissenting 3 per cent admit that therapy has helped them. More specifically, all the treated people have suffered from anxiety, but now, to varying degrees, nine-tenths of them feel they understand the inner sources of their anxiety and are much more capable of coping with it.

Nearly all of them maintain that they are now better able to handle their own anger and that of others, to understand and come close to their students, to accept themselves as they are, to assert themselves and hold onto their own beliefs, even if unpopular, and to express, give and receive love.

A majority said therapy had increased their earning power, their ability to enjoy food and drink, and their satisfaction in their work, and had made them feel less driven to please others at any cost. Somewhat smaller percentages said it had benefited their physical ailments anywhere from "somewhat" to "greatly." All in all, the data add up to a resounding affirmative to the question, "Does psychotherapy do any good?"

So far, so good. But since the response is entirely in terms of self-appraisal, Jersild felt it important to compare the feelings of these patients to those of a control group — 58 teachers, also from public schools and colleges, who had never received psychotherapy of any kind. These people were asked whether they had had problems in the same areas on which there was evidence from the therapy patients and whether in the past four years — a purely arbitrary figure — they had improved in respect to these problems.

The results are disconcerting: although only a minority of the control group felt they had had serious difficulties with anxiety, sex, anger and competitiveness, a good proportion of them state that within the past four years they have definitely improved in these areas.

Shades of Émile Coué . . . Can it be that his formula, "Every day, in every way, I am getting better and better," is a universal human fact? Or is it merely a delusion in which we imperfect creatures indulge ourselves, so as to avoid the torment of the truth? Does the passing of each of our numbered years really make us better, or do we only say so to console ourselves for time's pitiless erosion of youth, beauty and vitality?

The answer probably is that only part of the claimed improvement is illusory; many people do, after all, accumulate wisdom, experience and stature with the years. But let armchair philosophers argue the matter further; here we need ask only whether the existence of this general sense of improvement invalidates the testimony of the people who have had psychotherapy. Dr. Jersild thinks it does not. Even if some part of the improvement reported by therapy patients is due to human wishful thinking, the differences between their scores and those of the control group are consistent, positive and statistically impressive.

The treated people, in general, report much greater improvement, and in far more areas of their lives, than the control group; yet Jersild says that indirect clues in the questionnaire replies indicate that the untreated people have many of the same problems, but fail to recognize their existence. Regarding specific difficulties, the treated people report great improvement three to six times as often as the controls.

When these and other differences between the treated and untreated people are put to the test, they turn out to be "statistically significant" — that is, there is only a vanishingly small chance that they could be accidental or meaningless.

There are good reasons, nevertheless, why outside observers might not agree that therapy had helped these people. Before treatment, for instance, a considerable number of the patients used to stifle or deny legitimate feelings of anger against their mates, relatives or colleagues, and instead "took it out on themselves via headaches, colitis, fatigue and other ailments."

Therapy explores and frees up such stifled feelings, often to the dismay of people closest to the patient, who thereupon maintain, writes Dr. Jersild, "that the person undergoing analysis is getting worse rather than better. They are especially likely to make this judgment when a person who has allowed himself to be pushed around begins to assert himself, or when a person who has always seemed serene and courteous begins to show a temper."

Again, 79 per cent of the treated people had been troubled by loneliness, and nearly all of them said therapy had helped with this problem — not, however, by making them more gregarious, but by the seeming converse; that is, by making them more selective and intense in their friendships. Typically, one patient who was a great joiner dropped many of his activities during the course of therapy and many of his acquaintances thought it plain that therapy was harming him. But in fact he had recognized that his social activities were a compulsion and he was delighted to be rid of the need for boring, empty friendships and free to cultivate fewer, richer ones.

Friends, associates and relatives thus have a host of reasons of their own for liking or disliking traits of character in a person — often without real regard to that person's best interests; this is why it often turns out that therapy alters the patient in ways the people around him do not welcome. The heated parlor discussions as to who has been bettered or worsened by therapy may therefore tell more about the appraiser than the appraisee.

Sometimes, however, the patient seems virtually unchanged to outside observers; they wonder what on earth he got for his money. Yet if he achieved only a notable internal change, that may have been worth the price. One art teacher formerly had been suffused with feelings of rage at the messes her students made, though she stringently masked these feelings with an air of pleasantness and charm. After therapy, she still behaves the same outwardly, but within herself is comfortable and happy. Others, who did good scholarly work out of a desire to prove themselves to other people, now still do so — but out of a love of their work.

In contrast to such outwardly unchanged patients, or to those whose changes are apparent but not universally agreeable, many patients reported changes that can only be applauded on all sides. Four-fifths of the women and over two-thirds of the men said that therapy had made them feel better about, and care more about, their appearance. Jersild maintains that he personally saw many of these people — particularly women — becoming noticeably better looking as therapy progressed.

This was only the outward expression of certain valuable inner alterations. Most of the patients say, for instance, that because of therapy they more thoroughly accept their own masculinity or femininity, without rebelling or exaggerating it. Many, before therapy, had suffered guilt feelings about their sex desires and experiences. Some even worried about their responsiveness. After therapy, most of them reported lessened guilt feelings and diminished worry about impotence and frigidity — but, more importantly, their principal concern shifted to the receiving and giving of affection (with sex seen as part of this rather than a thing in itself); 89 per cent report that they are now more easily able to receive affection from the opposite sex, and 82 per cent are more easily able to feel it for the opposite sex.

Nearly all these claims are unverified and, perhaps, unverifiable.

Within the terms of Dr. Jersild's experiment, they are valuable and informative, but for the hard-bitten disbeliever or for the scientist who demands a totally objective, fully demonstrated, controlled experiment, the question of the value and results of psychotherapy remains imperfectly answered.

Nor can such proof exist today. As Dr. Kubie suggests, in order to carry out any systematic evaluation, the individual patient with his private therapist will have to be augmented by subsidized treatment and studies made in hospitals, medical schools and educational institutions, in social agencies and in industry. Instead of the occasional well-to-do patient, people from every social and economic background must have the opportunity to be treated.

Studies can then be made which will consider the relationships of the cultural mores and the socioeconomic forces to the various neuroses, and the outcome of therapy in each situation. On each patient a massive dossier of evidence — including various psychological tests, clinical observation and testimony from outside sources — will be collected and evaluated; but at the same time, an equally massive dossier will be compiled for at least two kinds of controls. Each patient will be matched with a person similar as to background and symptoms who gets no treatment, and with yet another person similar in background who was normal at the outset of the study.

From such a mass of data, and using a single objective set of criteria for "cure" or "improvement," the conclusions will be drawn by teams of professional people, including neuropsychologists, clinical psychologists, sociologists, social workers — and, of course, psychotherapists. But until that great day, those suffering from neurotic disorders have two choices: they may either disbelieve in therapy and hope for spontaneous recovery, or believe in it and commit themselves to a costly, painful — and non-guaranteed — course of treatment.

Yet, even without existence of proof or guarantees, there are many thousands of therapists, and hundreds of thousands of patients, who feel and believe with complete conviction that it does a great deal of good. They witness it, they experience it in their nerve endings and blood chemistry, they live by it. It is of no avail to tell them that as yet there is no irrefutable evidence on the books.

"Each of my patients and I," says one analyst, "see and feel the cause-and-effect of therapy in the office. Each of them knows, and I know, that after a certain dream was analyzed, or the reason for a given outburst found, or some long silence broken by admitting the resistance, he began to feel and act better in such-and-such ways.

"For him and me, there isn't any doubt; we have the evidence of our own senses. And until there's something better that will do very nicely."

The preceding article, which appeared originally in The New York Times Magazine, *drew many letters. Perhaps the most significant came from the highly regarded Dr. Jerome D. Frank, professor of psychiatry at the Henry Phipps Psychiatric Clinic, Johns Hopkins Hospital, who said, in part: "Morton Hunt and Rena Corman are to be warmly congratulated on [their article]. They have handled a difficult and thorny problem in an admirably lucid and objective fashion. The article may leave the misleading impression, however, that the neurotic sufferer has no choice but to rely on spontaneous recovery or on a costly, painful form of treatment. There may be other alternatives. . . . Long-term, intensive, individual psychotherapy can never reach more than a small fraction of persons seeking relief from neurotic distress. From the public-health standpoint, the task is to develop and use less time-consuming methods that may well be equally effective." To this I say, of course, Amen; the very point Dr. Frank is referring to is dealt with in some detail in the survey article, "Major and Minor Emotional Problems: Treatment, Cost, and Cure," page* 102.

III

Some Minor Emotional and Mental Problems

Alienation

One of the most prevalent psychosocial disorders of our time is alienation — an endemic sense of detachment, not-belonging, and loneliness. It is both symptom and disease — the former, because it is the byproduct of rapid social change and the consequent loss of agreed-upon goals and codes; the latter, because it is productive of psychological distress. The focus of this book being psychological, I do not here attempt to probe the ultimate causes of alienation or suggest ultimate cures; rather, I examine the phenomenon more personally, in terms of some of its hurtful results, and offer some suggestions as to ways in which the individual can modify or counteract alienation in his own life.

The first article discusses lack of involvement in general, while the second focuses specifically on the effects of alienation upon the classic values of friendship; both articles suggest ways in which to intensify and preserve interpersonal ties. The third article, however, is a qualification and refinement of this general plea, and attempts to show the boundaries beyond which intimacy and interpersonal involvement can be harmful rather than beneficial. The first two articles say, in effect: We need each other, we thrive on clinging together and belonging to each other. The third says, in effect: Yes, but in our clinging together, let us be sure we do no damage to each other by making each other bear burdens our own hearts should, alone, be responsible for.

Get Involved

EVERY CHILD is taught to despise the meaning of Cain's classic question, "Am I my brother's keeper?" — yet every day you can hear decent, well-meaning adults restating Cain's position in any one of a dozen different clichés. "It's not my affair," they may say, or, "Leave me out of it," or, "I don't want to get involved." Just as often, they give their closest friends what they think is good advice: "Don't get yourself mixed up in it," they will say, or, "Stay out of it — you can never tell about these things," or again, "Look out for Number One — don't get yourself involved."

How often we hear such statements — it almost seems that they tell us something special about the time we live in. Not that it is full of sinful people of Cain's type — rather, it is full of people who are too fearful of hurt to invite others into their lives, too afraid of rebuff to knock upon the doors of other souls and ask to be let in. The habit of hiding within ourselves and avoiding human complications seems more widespread today than in most previous eras. In a world too big and too fast-changing to make warm intimacy easy, we desperately need to get involved with each other; the cautious words about not getting involved are thus the worst advice possible. Ethically, they are no better than Cain's question, but, what is even more to the point, they lead us — in the name of privacy and precaution — to cheat ourselves out of living fully the only life that each of us has.

For involvement seems bad only when, through fear, we paint it with ugly colors — when, for instance, we think of it in negative terms such as "entanglement," "commitment," "complication," "intrusion," and the like. Through the will to live, and to enjoy being human, we can turn these very words around and see the positive — and truer — meanings in them. Does not romantic love grow upon, and thrive upon, an entanglement of two personalities? Do not business partnerships, scientific teamwork, and loyalty to one's country all rest upon commitments by men to other men? Is not the richness of the experiences of parenthood a real meaning of the word "complication"? And is not "intrusion" merely the pessimist's way of viewing what might also be called "human contact" — the blessed antidote for loneliness and emotional starvation?

Years ago, when I first moved to New York, I bought a small apartment in a cooperative building. Shortly thereafter, we co-op owners had our first general meeting, and because I spoke out on one or two matters, someone nominated me for president. I accepted and let myself be voted in. Friends laughed at me and told me I was foolish. "Why get involved?" they said. "You'll have plenty of headaches but no thanks for your trouble." True enough, I did have headaches and no thanks. As unpaid president for two years, I was plagued by budget problems, noisy wrangles at our business meetings, and irate fellow owners ringing my doorbell to complain about leaks or insufficient heat.

Yet the final balance showed a huge profit for me. I had learned a few facts about business and law which have been useful to me ever since. I had learned some things about human nature — that blusterers and loudmouths, for instance, often are merely insecure, lonely people who respond much better to a little attention and praise than to a withering reply. I also learned something about myself — that I am not a good administrator, being too inclined to get excited and rush off madly, and too little able to delegate responsibility; knowing my limitations, I have steered my course accordingly ever since. Yet far more valuable than any of these benefits was still another: among the tenants I had to deal with were two who gradually became dear friends, and with whom I have spent countless warm and enriching hours these past fourteen years. Any headaches I may have had as a result of getting involved were the cheapest of prices to pay for such a reward.

Yet such is the nature of contemporary life that it is always easy to forget this truth. Time and again I have been astonished at rediscovering it, after falling back into the pattern of aloofness and withdrawal. Time and again I find myself amazed at the importance to me — and to others — of getting involved. Some years ago I wrote an article on the psychology of suicide,* and got a flood of mail from readers, some

* See "The Killers Who Never Go to Jail," page 305.

of whom were plainly abnormal or emotionally disturbed. Most authors are wary of answering letters of this kind, and I was, too, using blank stationery and very brief replies so as to stay clear of complications. I was even about to discard altogether one very long letter from a woman in a mental hospital when, leafing through it, I saw that in the middle of a sentence she had broken off to write, in large, shaky block letters, the words HELP ME! and then continued her sentence. Something about that pathetic distress signal overcame my selfish tendency to be cautious. On my own stationery, bearing my name and address, I wrote her an impulsive reply in the tones I would have used to a dear friend; I told her that although I was not a psychiatrist and could not help her directly, I felt sure that anyone who would write to a stranger asking for help, as she had done, must be anxious to get better — must, indeed, be at the very point of accepting the help of her own hospital doctors. She was, I predicted, about to begin making real progress.

She never replied, but two years later, when I was away on business, the phone rang one day and a woman told my wife that she was the writer of that letter. Fully recovered for the past year and a half, she had a job not far from New York, and had suddenly felt like telling me that in her own mind she had always dated the beginning of improvement from the moment when she received my reply — an answer from a total stranger who cared about her anguish, and who wanted to give her courage and hope. Among the few acts I am genuinely proud of having done in my life, this one ranks high — yet even more important than my pride is my sense of awe that so small a deed, and one I might so easily have avoided, could have been so valuable to another human being.

And therein lies the marvelous paradox of involvement: it is when we are most spontaneous and most true to ourselves that we tend to do unselfish things for others — and it is when we unselfishly get involved with the men and the society around us that we enrich ourselves the most.

Not everyone can be a Florence Nightingale, an Albert Schweitzer, or a Saint Paul, yet in little daily deeds that add up impressively each of us can contribute to the world he lives in — and to his own life. A friend of mine was riding on a bus not long ago when a gang of noisy teen-agers started taunting a gray-haired woman who had asked them to stop shoving. "Everyone else in the bus looked out the windows, or straight ahead, as though he couldn't hear the kids saying fresh things about her out loud," he told me. "So did I. Then all at once — I don't know quite why — I thought, *How dare I keep out of this? This is part of the world I live in.* So I turned and snapped out at them, 'Haven't you young people any decent parents? Didn't anyone ever teach you at home how to act towards older people? How would you like other teen-agers to treat your own mother the way you're treating this lady?' To my astonishment, they looked sheepish and fell quiet, rather than telling me off. I found myself shaking all over, but for the rest of the day I felt warm inside because I had done a tiny bit of something useful for my world."

Why should involvement with others prove so valuable and enriching? What mechanism can explain the pride, the satisfaction, the feelings of warmth that come from getting involved? Biologists say that our nervous and glandular systems operate better under the stimuli of friendly contact with others. Social scientists say that a healthy society, beneficial to its members, is one in which people have many reliable relationships to each other. But involvement, it seems to me, means something deeper still. It is more than friendly contacts or reliable relationships; its vast power for good rests, in my opinion, on what psychologists call "ego interaction."

Each of us is a speck adrift in the universe, a living mote, ephemeral and afraid. To the extent that our minuscule self overlaps the selves of other persons, interpenetrates them, becomes identified with them, just so much do we feel enlarged, strengthened, increased in size, and relieved from fear. It is not simply being side by side that counts; it is being *inside.* When I genuinely care about you and your experiences, I have a little more than one short life, for I live a little in you; and when you care about me and my experiences, I become a little less afraid of man's well-known inhumanity to man, and even a little less terrified of the passing of time and the inevitability of death.

Is it not curious how the times of most intense interaction with other men stand out, in our memories, as the times when we were least frightened, least bored, least pessimistic about life itself? And this, even in the worst circumstances. In his book *Humanity and Happiness,* Georg Brochmann dwells on the strange fact that he was never so happy or so vibrantly alive as during the wretched years of the Nazi occupation of his beloved Norway. For that was a time when, despite sorrows, hardships, and constant danger, he and his fellow patriots in the underground were bound to each other by a sense of high purpose, by mutual trust, by intense human interaction. Many of us, likewise, remember our war years with curious longing; the memories of barracks, camp, and battlefield ought to be painful, but we find ourselves peculiarly nostalgic for those times when we were closer to our fellow men than ever before or since.

Stop and think, for a moment: which of your friends are your *real* friends — the ones you wouldn't hesitate to ask for help if you were in trouble, the ones you would *want* to come to you for help when they were in trouble? Aren't such friends almost always those you have known for many years? For it takes time to achieve that status — not merely of friendship, but of the interweaving and merging of your inner beings, the growth of each one's identity beyond the Me to the We. It is not possible, alas, to multiply at will the number of friends we possess of this order of closeness — but every little act of genuine involvement does somewhat the same thing for us, weaving us into many other selves a little, until the thread of our life is no longer a single strand but a part of the fabric of humankind.

But (you may ask) how can anyone deny the risks and dangers of freely involving one's self with other people? I do not deny them; it would be ridiculous to do so. Getting involved does mean taking a chance on your fellow man, and paying the penalty when you misjudge the situation. The girl you fall in love with may hurt you terribly by not caring, the drowning man you try to save may pull you under with him, the quarreling friends you try to reconcile may turn their joint anger upon you. Yet without taking such chances, how should you manage to win love, to save a life, or to salvage friendship? Because there are harmful insects above ground, should the seedling not venture to put forth leaves and roots, but lie dormant in the ground, ignorant of the sweetness of sunshine and rain and air?

The effort to avoid hurts and disappointments by remaining uninvolved is the greater danger; it makes us cold, inhuman, unloving, and even uninterested in our own lives. One of the most unpleasant, yet pathetic, characters in literature is Alexis Karenin in Tolstoy's *Anna Karenina*, who refused to become a father because, as he said, "A child will only make me vulnerable at another point." British author C. S. Lewis, in his book *The Four Loves*, says, "If you want to make sure of keeping your heart intact, you must give it to no one, not even to an animal. . . . Avoid all entanglements, lock it up safe in the coffin of your selfishness. But in that coffin — safe, dark, motionless, airless — it will change. It will not be broken; it will become unbreakable, impenetrable, irredeemable. The alternative to tragedy, or at least to the risk of tragedy, is damnation."

For specimens of the unbreakable, unredeemable heart, look at those philosophers of ancient times who tried to attain serenity by schooling themselves not to care deeply about mortal or perishable things. Anaxagoras is a case in point. When brought word of his son's death, he maintained an icy calm and said merely, "I never supposed I had begotten an immortal." Epictetus, the great Stoic, urged his followers to be as unperturbed by the deaths of their own wives and children as they would be by the deaths of someone else's, since the one event was just as natural and inevitable as the other.

Many people today, for less philosophic reasons, similarly try to lock away their hearts and keep them safe from ties to the rest of humanity. We regard some of the more extreme cases with amusement and pity — the recluse, for instance, who barricades himself in a house full of junk, or the little old lady who hasn't stepped outside her hotel room for fifteen years and won't even open her mail. But we recognize others as people who are emotionally or mentally ill — and part of whose sickness is their noninvolvement. Indeed, most of the 717,000 patients in this country's mental hospitals can be defined as people who have cut themselves off, or been cut off by their diseases, from normal human communication and involvement, from healthful sharing and caring. The psychiatrists in charge of them even regard a patient's degree of isolation or of involvement as a clear measurement of illness and recovery.

These extreme cases are easy enough to recognize. But we all too often fail to notice that many of us are the same sort of case, though in lesser degree. Every bachelor who avoids taking out eligible girls and concentrates on those he could never marry, every widow or widower who finds excuses for staying at home and avoiding the effort of seeking out new friends, every host or hostess who nervously steers company conversations away from religion or politics to safer trivia, every employee who sees his fellow employee cheating the boss but figures it's none of his business, every citizen who dislikes the way things are being run but shies away from writing letters or organizing protests — all these and scores of others are, to a minor degree, doing the same thing the hermit and the psychotic do to extremes. All deliberate noninvolvement is a limitation of growth and health, but we rarely realize this except when it has become a crippling malady.

That is why men who are wiser than Epictetus or Alexis Karenin have willingly faced the chance of pain in order to know the joy of involvement, and have manfully accepted hurt when it came their way. Tennyson, after long mourning the untimely death of his closest friend, Arthur Hallam, found comfort in the thought he wrote so nobly, though it has been so often quoted as to seem overly familiar:

> I hold it true, whate'er befall;
> I feel it, when I sorrow most —
> 'Tis better to have loved and lost
> Than never to have loved at all.

And there have even been some who have shut themselves away from human involvement only to have it thrust on them — and who, though wounded by it, have preferred the hurt to their former painless isolation. In the seventeenth century, a Portuguese nun named Marianna Alcoforado was wooed from her vows by a French aristocrat, the Marquis de Chamilly, who became her lover and later abandoned her and returned to France. Marianna lives in history because she wrote the Marquis five magnificent letters filled with such sentiments as these: "I would be freed from all of my troubles the moment I stopped loving you. But what a solution! No, I prefer suffering to forgetting you. . . . I thank you from the bottom of my heart for the desperation you cause me, and I detest the tranquillity in which I lived before I knew you."

The avoidance of such pain is at least a semirespectable motive for staying uninvolved; many people, however, are motivated to uninvolvement by far more prosaic considerations, namely, the desire to escape the bother of responsibilities. Oddly enough, these very same people, unaware of the contradiction in their thinking, are apt to join the rest of us in praising those who do take on responsibilities to mankind. Who today celebrates and venerates the hermits of early Christianity, who avoided all human contact and obligation by fleeing to the desert and living in caves? Not many of us. Instead we revere Jesus, Paul, and the many dedicated men who actually taught Christian ideals to men by mingling with them, arguing with them, loving them, and sometimes suffering for them.

But despite the suffering, the lives of such men often illustrate the paradox of involvement — that in doing for others, one does for himself. Saint Jerome wrote in his own words the story of his desert sojourn, when, parched, filthy, and emaciated, he tormented himself for seven years in the attempt to attain a state of perfect purity. They were vain and wasted years because his eyes remained fixed upon himself. At last, however, he returned to Rome and took up an active role in the life of church and city, teaching and converting wealthy Roman matrons to Christianity. In so doing, he finally became a valuable asset to his ailing world — and an infinitely more satisfied and fulfilled human being.

The same has been true of many of those whom we honor for having shouldered responsibilities, but whom we neglect to imitate. George Washington longed to remain in rural seclusion, yet gave up his precious retirement for his nation; in the end, he could only have regarded himself as lucky to have done so. Dorothea Dix was a spinster schoolteacher of thirty-nine who had just retired to repair her health and to enjoy peace and quiet, when she learned about the desperate condition of America's mentally ill. Abandoning her long-sought retirement, she spent the next thirty-six years vigorously campaigning to get the mentally ill out of chains and jails and into asylums, where they could be given humane medical treatment. Far from weighing upon her, this immense responsibility was the best thing that ever happened to her, giving her a measure of health, strength, and cheer she had never known.

For responsibilities are not just dead weight, but the most precious freight we can carry — a cargo that makes our journey through time a valuable expedition, and not just an idle passage towards death. Who is the more alive person — the middle-aged bachelor, undisturbed before his television set in his quiet hotel room, or the equally middle-aged father whose wife and children are clamoring for his attention and love in an anything-but-quiet living room? Who would you rather have been, if you could have your choice — Alexander Selkirk (the real-life Robinson Crusoe), alone on his Pacific island and indebted to no man, or Abraham Lincoln, bowed by the weight of his cares and duties?

It is not a simple choice between pleasure and pain, between comfort and cares. It is a choice between life and nonlife, between vitality and a kind of dessication of the body and spirit. For body and spirit both suffer from noninvolvement and the lack of interaction. Just as babies cared for in institutions, and getting no direct loving care or intimate relationship with adults, suffer from poor circulation and digestion, so uninvolved people seem to dry up and become lifeless personalities. Conversely, any family doctor can testify that many barren and rather juiceless women bloom and become pregnant shortly after actually adopting a child and experiencing maternal love and responsibility.

Interaction and deep commitment to other persons and outside interests seem not only to make people bloom, but to stave off the shrinkage and drying-up of age. The great senior citizens of our time — Bernard Baruch, Konrad Adenauer, Carl Sandburg, Eleanor Roosevelt, Pierre Monteux — have been people not only lucky enough to have inherited sturdy mechanisms but also able to remain vital through their unceasing involvement in the world around them. Lord Bertrand Russell, as hearty and alive as any man of eighty-eight on hand, says that in his youth he was melancholy and unhappy because he was given to brooding about himself, by himself. Then slowly he learned to fasten his attention on other objects and persons, outside himself — and found his personal answer to life. "The happy man," he has written, "is the man who has free affections and wide interests, who secures his happiness through these affections and interests and through the fact that they, in turn, make him an object of interest and affection to many others."

And thus for babies, young adults, and the aged alike, *the great secret about involvement is that, quite literally, it is life, and life is involvement.* Noninvolvement, if not actual death, is a limbo, a vacuum, a frozen and inanimate existence. Poets and philosophers have long been trying to tell us that in their own special ways. Andrew Marvell was ostensibly only wooing a reluctant lady when he wrote:

> The grave's a fine and private place,
> But none, I think, do there embrace,

— but he was also hinting at a deeper truth: that living and embracing are part of each other, while privacy (noninvolvement) and death go hand in hand. The eighteenth-century philosopher, Fichte, wrote massive impenetrable tracts to illustrate the thesis that man's real self exists only insofar as it acts and interacts with other selves; then, in a stroke of brilliance, he said the whole thing in nine little words: "The I," he wrote, "is not a fact, but an act." For we are living human beings only to the extent that we are actively aware of our dependence upon, and our interconnection with, the rest of mankind. All of which John Donne said, long ago, far more simply: "No man is an island, entire of itself."

If you would really know the difference involvement can make, look at the ways in which men face the ultimate challenge of death, in old age. Those who have been involved and have drunk deeply are not greedy or resentful; they are sated, and satisfied that they have spent their time on earth well. As Walter Savage Landor so beautifully said:

> I warmed both hands before the fire of life,
> It sinks, and I am ready to depart.

But those who have hesitated, who have held back, who have stood apart — they are the ones who feel frantic, who rage, who are unready and unwilling to go. They feel cheated, and they are right — but it is they who have cheated themselves. As Epicurus pointed out long ago, the fool does not so much live as always get ready to live. And then one day it is too late.

The Decline and Fall of Friendship

O N A RECENT plane trip to the Midwest I was talking to my seatmate, an electronics engineer of about forty, who told me that he was about to move his family to Chicago. It would be their fourth move from city to city in ten years, and he expected as many more in the next ten — all as part of his progress towards higher position. I began to offer my sympathy, but he shrugged it off. "The kids fuss a bit," he said, "and my wife hates the packing and unpacking, but it's part of the game."

"But your friends!" I protested. "Don't you find it terribly painful to uproot yourself and lose the people who mean something to you?"

He smiled condescendingly. "One bunch of suburbanites is pretty much like another at the same income level," he said. "My wife and I make new friends each time in a matter of weeks. But we never let it get so deep that it bothers us to leave. It's no problem at all."

For me, this incident typifies the growing tendency in modern relationships: all affability, neighborliness and friendliness — a very different thing from friendship. The bitter old adage is more valid than ever today: "A true friend is the greatest of all blessings and the one which we take the least thought to acquire." Friendly people are everywhere today — easy at introducing themselves, quick to invite you in for a drink, giving you the dubious gift of their first names within two minutes. But they never really invite you in behind their eyes and their smiles, where the real person dwells. Friendship is not, for them, a pearl of great price, but a useful commodity, to be shopped for and stocked up on locally, along with toothpaste and toilet paper.

This is a far cry from friendship as William Penn saw it — a "union of the spirits," a "marriage of hearts"; or as the philosopher Montaigne envisioned it — "one soul in bodies twain." And how far, how pathetically far, it is from those soaring words of Jesus, "Greater love hath no man than this, that a man lay down his life for his friends."

In ancient times, men never tired of thinking about and discussing friendship; to them it was no mere commodity but a sacred bond, linking man as closely as ties of blood. Indeed, as recently as the fifteenth century men still took mighty oaths of mutual loyalty and ritually mingled their blood and drank it, to insure lifelong brotherhood. Such friends would thenceforth share their fortunes and their dangers without a moment's hesitation. In immoral or lawless times, a man so armed could face the world unafraid and uplifted in heart.

But with the beginnings of modern society, four or five centuries ago, modern government began to emerge and to exercise greater control over men's actions. Poisonings no longer went unpunished, petty barons were not allowed to war on each other, men had to sue for fair treatment in court instead of obtaining it by the sword.

Thus the meaning of friendship changed. It became less a matter of mutual defense, and more a free and noble meeting of minds, a sharing of thoughts and emotions. This deepened and purified it — and yet made it rather fragile. Like early love, or love outside of marriage, it was sweet and intense, but lacked the structural bonds that once held it together.

This being the case, friendship easily became prey to the competitive, success-oriented, individualistic frame of mind. Each man pursues personal success above all else; if friendship becomes an extra weight, it is heaved overboard. Even the modern bulwarks against personal disaster — social security, unemployment insurance, health and retirement programs — mean that a man no longer faces troubles by himself; where he once needed warm, living friends, he now has cold, inhumanly efficient ones. Instead of mingling his blood with that of another man, he mingles it with institutional ink.

Deep friendships still exist, of course — a precious treasure for those who still care to dig — but the idealization of friendship and the extravagant practice of it seem old-fashioned to the modern eye. Where in real life or even in fiction is there anything like the friendships of David and Jonathan, Damon and Pythias, Luther and Melancthon, Goethe and Schiller? Where is Ruth, loyal to her Naomi? The modern Ruth says, "Whither thou goest, I would go, if it weren't for this new job in Baltimore. You understand, don't you?" Where are Roland and Oliver, fighting and dying together without a thought of self, but only of each other? The modern Roland says, "Golly, Oliver, old pal, I'd like to help you out, but my wife . . ."

When Tennyson's dear friend Arthur Hallam died in 1833, the poet devoted seventeen years to perfecting *In Memoriam* — probably the greatest elegy in the English language. Can one conceive of any writer doing the same today? More likely, he would act like a Kerouac character, getting hideously drunk, driving too fast, and winding up in the hospital, as his way of expressing his grief. Only two centuries ago Horace Walpole, gentleman and author, wrote eight hundred and forty-eight letters during forty-six years to his close friend Sir Horace Mann, discussing events of the day, sharing experiences he'd had and thoughts he was thinking. If he lived today, Walpole would very likely drop Sir Horace a Christmas card each year on which he'd add in a scrawl, "Long time no see — let's get together soon."

The pace and the circumstances of modern life, having greatly increased the fragility of friendships, make it discouraging to start new ones and difficult to preserve old ones. People now move about at an astonishing rate — one out of every five families changes its address each year — shuttling from one suburb to another in search of the ideal house and community, only to move back to the city after the children are grown up. Or else they uproot themselves periodically to follow opportunity, or to obey company policy of shifting people around. Some suffer keenly: "I am a modern nomad," writes a young woman to the editor of a women's magazine, "one of the new breed known as a company wife. Bits and pieces of my life are scattered all over the country." Others, like my companion on the airplane, refuse to let themselves make deep friendships, and thus avoid the hurt. Still others lose the power to recognize the real thing altogether, and accept the synthetic one in its place.

But we Americans move about socially as much as we do geographically, prizing nothing more about our society than the freedom it offers us to move upwards according to our ability and diligence. And this, too, separates friends, and makes uncomfortable and unbridgeable chasms between them. It used to be that people felt contempt for the social climber who shunned his old friends, fearful they would link him with his discarded past, but the practice is now achieving a certain amount of acceptance and recognition. William H. Whyte, writing recently in *Fortune,* said that in many large companies a rising young executive is now expected to entertain and befriend only those who are appropriate to his status, and to disengage himself from those above whom he has risen. His wife, too, must understand and help in this; if she stubbornly clings to old friends, she is considered an impediment to his rise. One corporation wife typically said to Whyte, "You have got to leave behind your old friends. You have to weigh the people you invite to parties. You have to be careful of who you send Christmas cards to and who you don't. It sounds like snobbery, but it's just something you have to do."

Even modern love and marriage tend to displace friendship. Teenagers go steady sooner and more assiduously than they used to, becoming too absorbed in love to take time for developing the habit of friendship. Marriage, similarly, all but preempts the whole of each person, leaving little of the self to give to any friend; as Ben Hecht has tartly observed, "Marriage can put an end to a dozen friendships without a word being said."

A man I know, discussing this with me a while ago, told me wistfully of the disintegration of an old friendship. "Back in college we were total pals," he says. "We studied together, dated together, roomed together. Every night we'd close our books at midnight and start to talk. We'd argue about a thousand things, rage at each other, laugh like loons, horse around, wax poetic, and fall into bed at last, hoarse but happy. But right after college Joe started going steady, and I felt him slipping away. When he got married, I could sense that much of him was inaccessible to me. On top of that, I can't seem to like his wife. Joe loves her, and that's all to the good — but it means there's a huge unmentionable barrier between us forever. There's no good answer, but only a bad one — I avoid him nowadays. And somehow I feel I've been robbed."

One could argue that the entire decline of friendship is inevitable, and doesn't much matter anyhow. With the government, the employer, and the insurance company standing behind a man, he doesn't face troubles and dangers alone; and with the present suburban custom of easy meeting and mingling, he needn't remain a stranger in any new neighborhood for long.

But friendship is something beyond mutual support or sociable getting-together. Whatever reasons man had for valuing it in the past, the terms of modern life make for one overwhelming truth about it: it is the only important emotional bond between ourselves and human beings outside our immediate families. We have no clan or tribal loyalties, no fixed community of life, to tie us to our fellow men. "The threads of friendship," André Maurois says, "are a weaker, more delicate weft than fleshly love, but without it society could not exist . . . [it is a] miraculous fabric of affection, trust, and loyalty which upholds a civilization."

Despite the changes of the centuries, friendship is not mere sociability and hobnobbing; it is a response to a need as important as the attraction that first brought single cells together to live in clusters, and thence to evolve into animals and finally into man himself. And it is a need of both soul and body: as Bhartrihari, a wise Hindu, said a thousand years ago, anticipating modern psychosomatic medicine, "If a man has a friend, what need has he of medicines?"

As a teen-ager, I was often moody; for reasons I no longer recall, during one particularly bad week I was filled with thoughts of suicide, found it hard to take a deep breath, and would have wept if I had not thought it unmanly. One night, when I was at my lowest ebb, thinking myself ugly, misunderstood, and unlikable, the phone rang for me. A high-school fraternity brother of mine, a good-looking, self-assured lad, was on the line. "What's wrong?" he said gently, when he heard my voice. "You sound as if you didn't have a friend in the world — and I'm not dead yet!" A glib, graceful phrase, perhaps — but in twenty-five years I have not forgotten it, nor how I sat up straighter, smiled, took a deep breath and felt alive again that night. And by more than coincidence, that friend went on to study medicine, and today is one of the finest psychiatrists practicing in Philadelphia.

This need for friends is not satisfied by mere conviviality, for man needs an *inner* nearness, not an outer one. The English scholar C. S. Lewis has perceptively pointed out in *The Four Loves* that companionship grows into friendship only when there is a mutual unveiling of secrets and a discovery by two people that they have tastes or feelings or beliefs in common which each had thought his private treasure — or burden. "The typical expression of opening friendship," writes Mr.

Lewis, "would be something like, 'What? You too? I thought I was the only one.'"

That is why trafficking in friendship is both obvious and ugly. But many who would never do it are equally guilty of degrading friendship by identifying it with simple sociability. They busy themselves with social activities, make pleasant conversation and avoid controversial subjects, exert themselves to be charming and act charmed. To equate this with friendship and seek for nothing more is to do one's self harm, to cheat one's self of a part of life.

Sagely, the Greeks and then the Romans referred to a friend as "another I" — the *alter ego*, the second self. And from that second self we draw strength to live. When I have a friend and he has me, each of us is a bit less alone in the vastness of time, less afraid of the dark, the cold, the unknown. We are still children in the woods at night — but we are holding hands.

If friendship is so precious and important, how can we cultivate and protect it, despite the many forces that nowadays weaken and destroy it? The first and most important thing, I suspect, is to remember to *exercise* it continually, for it is not an object, but a process. This means performing the acts of friendship, rather than regarding it as a product which will keep on the shelf until we happen to want it. Some may think it high-minded to insist that true friendship will endure, though time, distance, or silence intervene, and there may be cases to prove it — but usually this belief is only an excuse for the lazy failure to provide the necessary nourishment. "The only way to have a friend," said Emerson, "is to be one."

And that is not automatic for modern man; it takes some systematic planning. On our daily list of things to be done, for instance, we might well assign to the deeds of friendship a priority in keeping with their real importance. We ought to write it down as urgent business to visit, call, drop a note or send a gift to a friend, and make ourselves do it before the trivial, timewasting, mundane things. How easy it is to neglect friends just because they *are* friends, to answer their calls or letters after all the business calls and letters because they won't get angry, and to put their needs last because they'll "understand."

Several years ago, a well-known New York psychoanalyst, who is an old friend of mine, reconstructed his own daily and weekly schedule so as to insure time for long lunches with one friend at a time. He scrupulously refuses to allot this time to business conferences or to larger get-togethers, preserving these midday intervals for quiet, person-to-person association. "How often," he asks, "can you feel close to an old friend or exchange your innermost thoughts with him in a roomful of company — or even in front of a third friend?"

Often, distance prevents such meetings, but there is no way of visiting with a friend so private and warm as writing him a letter, and none so neglected in this age. The telephone is much easier — but a letter contains words that have been considered and set down in total privacy. It represents thought and effort — and thus says even more than the words it contains. My own closest friend lives ninety miles from me — too far to drop by of an evening, too near for letters. Last year he spent six months in Europe and we began to correspond at length. Suddenly we were talking and listening to each other in a most marvelous fashion about a hundred different things — his experiences in Europe, our thoughts about the Algerian war, feelings about cathedrals and religious art, ideas about rearing our children, impressions of the latest novels we'd read, our changing ambitions as we both reach our forties, and much, much more. We bridged four thousand miles better than ninety; we saw again qualities in each other we had forgotten or grown used to, and have prized each other the more ever since. In the slower, horse-drawn past, men knew this better than we do today; George Washington, for instance, regarded friendship as "a plant of slow growth," and faithfully watered and nurtured his own with some 20,000 letters. Teachers ought to tell that to their pupils instead of the cherry-tree story.

And why not also deliberately plan to invest some time and money on trips to visit friends who live too far off for frequent meeting? We expect lovers to travel hundreds of miles willingly for a few hours with each other, but how often does anyone drive two hours, or spend the price of a short plane ride, to pass an evening with a dear friend? During the war I was extremely close to a man who flew with me, and came close to dying with me, but for the past thirteen years he has lived a thousand miles away and I have seen him only briefly during his rare business trips to New York. I told myself sadly that he and I had very little in common any longer. Last spring I had reason to be in his area, and decided, though with misgivings, to spend some time with him. As it turned out, I spent a four-day vacation with him and his wife in an isolated seashore hideaway — and found my friend again.

There are many ways to preserve friendship — if we have something to be friends about. The circumstances of our private modern lives, however, keep us from having much to *do* together except to *get* together. We no longer fight our way across Europe side by side, or labor together in the West to clear the fields, hoist the ridgepoles, and serve as vigilantes to bring law and order into the community. Yet friendship prospers in proportion to the number of activities and interests we share, in proportion to the overlap of our lives.

Sociologist Nelson Foote therefore recommends that we carefully provide ourselves with "an ample supply of successive and concurrent common interests" to make our friendships strong, and to keep them so by replacing interests that become outworn. To entice a friend into sharing one of your own new enthusiasms is to give him a precious gift of your inner self, and to cement him to you a little more firmly. One of my own friends persuaded me, years ago, to let him teach me sailing; ever since, the delights of that sport have been not only an enrichment of my own life, but an additional link between him and me. So, too, should it be with many other things. Urge upon your friend a favorite book, drag him to a museum with you, talk him into joining your club or trying some outlandish delicacy you like or working with you in a local political rhubarb.

And having things to be friends about, don't weigh and measure the acts of friendship like a miser. There are certain people who chart each round of social entertaining: "Do they owe us an evening or do we owe them?" they ask themselves, and are offended if a debt is not soon paid off. Nothing could more plainly show the decline of friendship. In the past many a philosopher debated whether a true friend was one who willingly did you favors ("A friend in need is a friend indeed"), or one for whom you willingly did them ("Nothing is dearer to a man than a friend in need"). Either answer is better than the weighing of one dinner against another as a test of friendship.

But one can go further: the giving or receiving of favors is really irrelevant. *Of course* I will help my friend and he will help me; it goes without saying — and it ought never occur to us to count points. What difference does it make if a friend has not repaid my dinner invitation? I will invite him again simply because I want to have him near me; is that not reward enough? And if he comes again, is that not proof that he too wants to be with me? What matter that he has not repaid the dinners in kind? If he is my friend he repays me best by coming.

And don't squander your life, or any part of it, on people who don't matter to you; build your leisure around your friends, not around places or activities alone. How often we spend a weekend, a fortnight, a summer in a "nice place to be" — and care little for it in the end because no close friends were there. We form friendships of convenience — shipboard or summer friendships — in order not to be outcasts, but in our hearts we secretly know they are shams. When the ship docks or the summer season closes, we part with hearty promises to look each other up, but nothing comes of it, for the friendships were built on sand. Actors have a bitter little saying that tells it perfectly: "I love you, but the show closed."

In our society the nuptial tie remains the great bond between individuals. But surely a man or woman can preserve the one-to-one relationship with another man or woman that existed before marriage. Not all marriages, to be sure, sound the death knell of friendships; there is even a special joy in having one's beloved become the friend of his friend. Yet the meaning and power of friendship are best maintained when we meet again as individuals, and not as half of our marriages.

For it is only when we are two together that we confide and open our hearts to each other. Two men having a chat in the deserted office at the end of the day; two women sitting long in delicious, shadowed privacy at the back of a tea shop; two friends staying up late before the fire, far past their bedtimes, but unable to stop and let each other go — these are the times when friendship is kept in repair, and when souls are bound one to the other.

Nor does an independent and courageous man have to drop his old friends when he rises in the ranks. No industrial clique is more ingrown and conforming than that of the auto executives in Detroit, yet Robert

McNamara, now Secretary of Defense, won his way to the top of the Ford Motor Company without ever yielding to these pressures. He lived fifty-eight miles from Detroit in the university town of Ann Arbor, stuck to his own egghead tastes in books, and stubbornly kept his own friends. Lesser men would do well to heed his example.

The same is true of entertaining. No doubt there are times when it is proper to entertain business associates, but the giving of food, according to many psychiatrists, is a symbolic act of love — and acts of love should not be performed for gain. We only cheat ourselves when we do so. A celebrated baritone I know is an accomplished cook, and delights in preparing wonderful Italian specialties for his friends, spending hours in the kitchen cheerfully singing, talking, and joking at his work. But when he entertains people for business reasons, he usually takes them out to a restaurant. I daresay he has never even thought this out — but with instinctive wisdom reserves the gift of food made with his own hands for those he loves.

If, to keep friendship in flower, you must take some extra trouble, so much the better. Curious as it may at first seem, when you go to trouble for a friend it is very likely that he will love you the better for it — but it is beyond question that *you* will love *him* the better for it. For all the sad, cynical words about friends who flee when we need them, it was also very wisely said by Epicurus that "it is more pleasant to do good than to receive good."

It also works the other way: we draw a true friend even closer to us when we ask his help and make him trouble himself for us. Our life and our problems become his life and his problems, our success his. An acquaintance of mine recently was talking about a mutual friend. "You know, of course, that Josh and I have been friendly for years," he said, "but we were never really thick. Then one night three years ago, when he was on the verge of bankruptcy, he called me in a blind panic. He didn't want money from me, but advice and fresh ideas — and some comfort and encouragement. I gave him all those, as best I could, and even volunteered to talk to his major creditors and plead for a delay, trading on my reputation in the community as a civic do-gooder. I succeeded only in part, but it helped, and Josh pulled through. Ever since, we've been extremely dear friends — not because he feels indebted to me, but because I feel so involved in him. It's as though he were a son of mine, the very sight of whom — grown-up and a success — makes me feel good again and again."

Yet there is a second lesson in his story: friendship becomes sound when built not with the straw of trivia, but the brick of important things. How seldom we dare to thrust our way into the lives of our friends, when they are perplexed or grappling with serious problems; how seldom we are willing to admit to them that we are troubled or in difficulty. Even our conversation is often a thin veneer covering up the real persons underneath. In *The House of Intellect* Jacques Barzun scathingly points out that the contemporary fashion in conversation is to stick to safe, bland, neutral topics, skirting whatever is controversial or profound. Who will risk "spoiling" a sociable evening by broaching the subject of how to prevent a nuclear war, or whether capitalism can really survive, or whether science has made religion hollow and meaningless?

Yet when our hearts were younger and more vital, when we were readier to reach out to each other, we dared to say what we thought — and were willing to listen to that with which we violently disagreed. And we loved our friend the more because we were talking about important things, even though we sounded and looked passionately angry.

For that matter, may not friendship thrive on major differences — if each of us *cares* both to speak and to listen? It is safe and simple to be friends with those who think as we do — and with whom we rarely exchange a real thought. But it is exciting and deeply reassuring to become the friend of a man with whom we differ. The friendship that bridges a gap in religion, in politics, in race, is a friendship that allows us to drink deeply of humanity, and to sense the underlying brotherhood of man.

Only some vast unimaginable miracle could make modern society again favor stable, intimate relationships between men; everything about it tends to do the opposite. Yet in small ways and large, each man is capable of working a minor miracle in his own life. The sea animals who left the sheltering ocean environment and moved onto land survived in that unkindly milieu by developing their own body temperature controls and body fluid regulators — in a word, by managing to carry their own environment around with them. We likewise, leaving behind the sheltering environment of simpler days and more personal ways, can make around ourselves — in the midst of our complex, impersonal civilization — a small enclave of human warmth by repairing, preserving, and intensifying our true friendships.

The Limits of Intimacy

When I was in my teens, I had a favorite daydream of the ideal girl I would some day meet and love. Naturally, she would be beautiful, intelligent, warm, and gentle, but the essential thing about her was that she would *understand* me. She would listen to all my innermost thoughts, my darkest moods and memories, my sorrows and sins, and she would look deep into my eyes in brimming-over sympathy and adoration. And I in turn would adore her for her ability to listen and to love. At the time, I was perhaps unduly impressed by Othello's account of how he wooed Desdemona: he had poured out the long and agonizing narrative of his life, and then,

> My story being done,
> She gave me for my pains a world of sighs:
> She swore, in faith, 'twas strange, 'twas passing
>   strange,
> 'Twas pitiful, 'twas wondrous pitiful . . .
> She loved me for the dangers I had passed,
> And I loved her that she did pity them.
> This only is the witchcraft I have used.

Unlike Othello, I had passed few dangers, but the dream of being loved involved the telling of everything about myself. Somehow, though, I never envisioned myself as listening to her in return, or entering every nook and cranny of her secret soul. I would find her dear because she would listen, understand, and accept me; it did not occur to me, nor would I have found it appealing, to listen, understand, and accept her. For the desire for total intimacy and self-revelation is both immature and selfish. The wish to tell all about one's self and to be totally understood and accepted is felt most keenly in adolescence, when we are most insecure and self-centered — and least concerned about the feelings of the very people whose love we want.

Yet even in adulthood, many people suppose that they have a right and almost an obligation to expose everything to the people closest to them, including their doubts and fears, their ugliest or most pessimistic thoughts, their most shameful memories, as if to tell them to a lover, mate, or friend were the right way to ease the heart's discomfort.

I submit, however, that we have no such right and no such obligation. If anything, the obligation is in the other direction: it is incumbent on us *not* to indulge in total self-revelation to those we love and who love us. Intimacy between any two loving human beings should have certain limits, for the good of both persons; and when we ignore those limits, we do so selfishly and childishly, out of an immature desire to shift our burden onto the other person and free ourselves of the responsibility for our own thoughts. But as a wise rabbi, long forgotten, said fifteen centuries ago, "If thy secret oppress thine own heart, how canst thou expect the heart of another to endure it?"

And it was another and far greater rabbi of several centuries earlier who veiled many of his utterances in obscurity because the secret of his coming agony would be too much for his followers to bear. As Luke told it (9:43-45): "But while they wondered every one at all things which Jesus did, he said unto his disciples, Let these sayings sink down into your ears: for the Son of man shall be delivered into the hands of men. But they understood not this saying, and it was hid from them, that they perceived it not . . ."

Thoughtful men, and even merely witty ones, have always known that certain kinds of things cannot be told without danger or injury to the listener. Plutarch tells of a comic poet named Philippides, who lived in the fourth century B.C., and whose work greatly pleased King Lysimachus. The king, wishing to reward him, asked, "What is there of mine that I may share with you?" "Anything you like, sire," said Philippides, "except your secrets."

Would that other men were as wise! Consider, for instance, a young architect about whom a psychiatrist told me: though he was happily married, he carried with him the heavy secret that for about half a year, during his college days, he had had a homosexual relationship with his roommate. Ashamed and wretched, he broke away and moved out, successfully fought down his deviant desires, and after graduation got married. But the secret oppressed him, and several years later he finally told his wife all, and felt greatly relieved that at last she knew, understood, and forgave. Happy ending? Not exactly: she has never felt the same about their marriage since then. She often wonders whether their life together is really satisfying to him, whether he finds her somehow repulsive at times, and whether he is still secretly attracted to men he meets in business and social life. She, finally, had to seek out a psychiatrist because her husband had unloaded this burden upon her.

Consider, again, a woman with whom I had been friendly for years, who once wrote me a long and incredibly revealing letter when I was gathering data for a book on American women and their problems. Writing late at night when she was feeling sorry for herself and unusually communicative, she told me in scorching words that very often she bitterly regretted having children. They had brought her far less joy and far more emotional upset than she had ever expected, and while she often felt loving towards them, quite often she felt not just anger, but actual hatred toward them. A day or so later I got a telegram asking me to burn the letter, and though she and her husband were long-time friends of mine, I have never seen or heard from them since. Friendship, though it flourishes when fed the nutrients of sharing and intimacy, can be killed altogether by an overdose; it is impossible to feel close to someone before whom you have stripped yourself of all human dignity and decency.

Or consider a former photographer's model, now nearing forty, whose private anguish was her exceptionally strong revulsion at the thought of growing older and seeing her beauty fade. Once in a while she would say in passing, to her husband or to friends, that she had a basically pessimistic outlook on life, but would never elaborate on it. Recently, though, her older child died of leukemia, and in the course of her ensuing depression, she poured forth her private vision to her husband

and to several friends — a nightmarish collage of the terrible brevity of youth, the decay of beauty and strength, the absurdity of human hopes and efforts, the fragility of love, the inevitability of aging and death, and above all, her own sick despair at the minor year-by-year physical changes in herself and everyone else. Since then, she has recovered her equilibrium, but her personal inner hell, once opened to view, has not been forgotten by her husband and friends, who no longer feel cheerful and at ease in her presence: they are always aware of the invisible black wings hovering near, the grinning skull beneath the flesh, the slow rot and corruption in all living things.

But the secret which most often lies like a crushing stone inside the bosom of modern man, and which he wants to confess — to the very person it will hurt worst — concerns sexual infidelity. When a man or woman has an extramarital affair, even though it be shallow and brief, he or she is likely to be left with a nagging feeling of guilt. Many an adulterer, though he is glad he got away with it undetected, almost wishes that his wife would find out somehow, so that he might be forced to confess, explain it to her, ask forgiveness, and be rid of that stone inside himself. Yet when that happens, he frees himself of pain by transferring it to her; he is healed while she suffers a grievous wound. Of course, he does not think of it that way; rather, he thinks she will understand and forgive, as a saintly or godlike person should. But a wife is neither saint nor god, and it is terribly unjust to treat her as though she were.

A prominent marriage counselor told me a case in point, of a young woman married to a busy, brilliant real estate developer in his late thirties. Their marriage had been reasonably warm and rewarding for some years until one night, in a seeming burst of affection, he told her about a brief, torrid affair he'd had while he had been on a prolonged out-of-town negotiation some months earlier. He said that he realized how cheap it was compared to their marriage; it had been nothing but animal passion, unleashed by drinking, but there had been no emotional significance to it. Having been through it, he felt he'd be able to control such impulses in the future, and he said he felt far better for having told her, and believed it would bring them closer together than ever before.

But he was wrong, as any psychologist — and many an errant husband — could have told him. For since that night, two years ago, things have not been the same. Their love life, which previously seemed fine, has been blighted for her; she finds herself always wondering, "Am I as exciting as that other woman? — or was it really other *women?*" She feels suspicious about the women he meets in the line of business, and is in an agony of doubt whenever he goes out of town. Worst of all, she often feels herself to be pallid, unappealing, and insipid. And while she sometimes realizes that these are irrational feelings, she cannot will them out of existence; his secret, once shared, has thoroughly shattered her peace of mind.

Why do people make such revelations to those who love them? Why did the real estate developer confess to his wife, though the thing was safely in the past and had no real meaning? Was it a valid act of contrition and a genuine effort to become even closer to his wife? Her marriage counselor thinks not. The confession was not a mature and loving act, but the very opposite. "Let me see how real your love is," he was saying, in effect. "Let's see if you can love me even if I show you something ugly and sickening." Possibly there was something unconsciously self-destructive in this; possibly it was unconsciously intended to hurt; but more likely than either of these explanations, he did it out of a childish wish to be easily rid of his own guilt, and a childish expectation that she, like a good mommy, would forgive and forget. But real mature love on *his* part would have made him say to himself, "This was my wrongdoing, this is my cross to bear, and I have no right to free myself of it at her expense."

In Morris West's recent novel *Daughter of Silence,* a psychiatrist named Peter Landon has slept with the wife of a close friend, thereby wronging both the friend and his own fiancée. But though the thing torments him, he knows better than the average man how both his fiancée and his friend will suffer if he confesses the deed. "With a consummate irony," writes Mr. West, "he was forced back to the prescription which he imposed on all his patients: accept the guilt, know yourself for what you are, wear the knowledge like a Nessus shirt on your own back and bear the pricks and poison with as much dignity as you can muster."

The same is true of sexual wishes we never actually carry out. Lewis Terman, a psychologist, made a famous survey some years ago in which he found out that the great majority of husbands, and a considerable number of wives, feel longings for extramarital affairs anywhere from once in a while to nearly all the time, even when their marriages are happy ones. Total intimacy would call for them to confide such yearnings to their mates; happily, compassion and caution combine to keep most of their mouths shut. I say "happily" because the admission of such desires is tantamount to telling one's mate, "You are not enough for me; you leave me wanting something more. This is the way things are. But because I love you, I will deny myself — willingly — and yet, still, this is how it is with me." Yet why should anyone expect his mate to receive this kind of news without hurt? — would he himself like to hear the same thing from her? Would he not prefer to hear that she wants no one but him, that he makes all the other men in the world unnecessary?

In Arthur Miller's play *After the Fall*, Quentin and his wife have a quarrel during which she recalls how, early in their marriage, he came back from a trip and told her he'd met a woman he wanted to sleep with, but hadn't. She had been hurt and furious for months. "It was an idiotic thing to tell you," he admits, "but I still say I meant it as a compliment; that I did not touch her because I realized what you meant to me. And for damn near a year you looked at me as though I were some kind of monster who could never be trusted again." His wife tells him, bitterly, a simple truth: "You don't know how much to hide," and Quentin, later, musing alone about the desire to confess his urges, realizes that his belief that "the truth must save" is a selfish wish, since it takes no account of the other person's need to believe in an illusion.

"So the truth, after all, may be merely murderous," he says. "Maybe there is only one sin, to destroy your own credibility." Each of us, one might add, is a Garden of Eden to those who love us in ignorance and innocence; if we insist that they eat the fruit that brings knowledge of good and evil, we may only cast them out of paradise.

Like the love between a man and a woman, the love between two friends may be tarnished or even destroyed by telling too much, or by demanding to know too much of the other. We accept the obvious truth about friendship, that it involves a blessed freedom to be truthful about ourselves (Thackeray once wrote, in a letter, "If I mayn't tell you what I feel, what is the use of a friend?"); but we are loath to admit that like all freedoms, this one, too, must be exercised with restraint, lest it become license.

Intimacy, in other words, can be self-defeating when pushed beyond adult bounds. Indeed, it is typical of adolescents, not adults, to seek super-intimate friendships. The adolescent attitude can be paraphrased as follows: "I'll tell you everything if you tell me everything." According to psychiatrist Edmund Bergler, this attitude involves a combination of exhibitionism and Peeping Tomism; adults should grow beyond both, though many of us do not entirely do so.

"Friends generally expect too much of each other," writes Dr. Bergler. "The hunger to be understood is usually carried so far that they demand full inner acceptance, instead of realizing that they can meet on even terms only on a very specific and carefully delineated common ground. . . . When you tell your friend your secrets you exhibit [yourself] before him, but at the same time you are making him peep at you. In the long run, it is resented; both conscious and unconscious feelings of guilt are aroused when others know too much about one. Knowing too much is therefore the beginning of the end of a friendship."

As a case in point, a friend of mine, while going with a girl and verging on engagement, kept me up late one night telling me all the things he didn't like about her, and about all his misgivings. Finally, to give him peace of mind, I agreed with him that she was the wrong girl for him, and he went home, seemingly relieved and clear in his mind. A week later, however, he was engaged to her — and our friendship was on the rocks.

One similarly trespasses beyond the allowable borders of intimacy when he tells a friend the things he dislikes about him; at least it is so if those things are essential parts of his character. To tell a friend you are angry at him because of something he has done may be very helpful; to tell him his basic faults, rather than accepting them without comment, is a very different matter. With his customary elegance, the Duc de la Rochefoucauld said, "The proper sentiments we should feel for friends and those who have been kind to us cannot long be maintained if we consider ourselves free to discuss their defects at frequent intervals." Or as an old joke puts it succinctly:

FIRST WOMAN: Jane and I agreed to be frank with each other about our faults.
SECOND WOMAN: Was it helpful?
FIRST WOMAN: I don't know — we haven't spoken since.

Even Sigmund Freud, though he diligently delved into the minds of his patients for their secrets (which he needed to know in order to treat them), was quite secretive, with his own close friends, about his early years, his love life, and even about whatever he was currently writing on. Though his friend Fliess served as a veritable father-confessor to him, Freud felt compelled to quote, in a letter to Fliess, a line from Goethe's *Faust:* "The best of what one knows must not be told."

A gentle, sensitive man I know — I'll call him Gerald — went into business with his very dear friend Arnie, a strong, domineering, thick-skinned type. What had been a marvelous combination in friendship became often quite painful in partnership, with Gerald virtually reliving his many childhood defeats at the hands of his older brother and bigger kids. Not surprisingly, he found some of his hidden resentments of Arnie coming to the surface. Now, nearly all of us have at least a certain amount of repressed anger or even hatred towards the very people we love, though generally we are unaware of it except when it breaks through in the form of dreams. Even then, we either fail to recognize what the dream means, or are wise enough to keep it to ourselves. Gerald, however, was a dabbler in psychology, and one evening when he and Arnie worked late and then unwound over a few drinks, he felt the urge toward total intimacy, and said something about like this:

"Arnie, isn't it amazing how friends can love each other and still hate each other a little? Like the other night, guess what — I had a nightmare in which I found the office all torn up, the lights not working, and you lying dead on top of your desk." And he explained that the dream signified a death-wish against Arnie — but added that they were such good friends that Arnie could know about such a thing, and understand it, and not even mind it. Only Arnie didn't feel that way; he was stunned, deeply wounded, and bitterly resentful. Even after he got over this initial reaction, he was unable to feel comfortable in Gerald's friendship, and their partnership may not endure much longer. *Homo homini lupus,* said the Romans — man is a wolf to man; and even when he restrains his impulse to violence, he may use words to be wolflike, even to a friend.

To avoid being wolflike means to conceal those thoughts, secrets, and desires that would harm our friends, though the telling might make us feel better. And this is true even when the forbidden thoughts are not hostile, but are fears and worries of a contagious kind.* In *My Life in Court,* for instance, Louis Nizer speaks of the clammy hands, dry lips, and queasy feelings he and other trial lawyers suffer at the outset of a major trial. Yet this is just the time when he may not seek personal relief by showing or telling his emotions. "This is the time," he writes, "when the lawyer must bring confidence to his distressed army. I greet clients and witnesses with hearty cheerfulness. I engage them in light jests. They must be comforted by my easy serenity. They clutch at it and derive strength from it. At all times the lawyer must be the central tower of strength upon which all lean."

In far greater degree, this same need to keep one's secret anxiety and fear hidden is true of military leaders and the rulers of nations. Caesar himself, when he was ready to cross the Rubicon with his men still under arm — an act tantamount to declaring war upon the Roman Senate — stopped and thought, and argued it out with himself. "The nearer he came to his purpose," Plutarch tells us, "the more remorse he had in his conscience, to think what an enterprise he took in hand: and his thoughts also fell out more doubtful, when he entered into consideration of the desperateness of his attempt. So he fell into many thoughts with himself, and spake never a word, wavering sometime one way, sometime another way." But when he had made his decision at last, he cried to his officers, "A desperate man feareth no danger. Come on!", and led the way on the run, never faltering for an instant.

It is the particular affliction of a leader to have to bear his misgivings and qualms in silence. Machiavelli's *The Prince,* that amoral handbook

* For a more detailed discussion of the effects of revealing one's fears, see "Should You Keep Your Fears a Secret?" (page 245).

of deception and political cunning, frequently warns the would-be ruler to endure his worries and doubts in silence, the better to preserve confidence on the part of his subordinates as well as the multitude. Shakespeare's Henry the Fifth, walking around his camp at night, sleepless and apprehensive the night before the battle of Agincourt, looks upon his sleeping soldiers and reflects, "What infinite heart's ease/ Must kings neglect, that private men enjoy!" Never can the king, despite all his wealth and ceremony, "sleep so soundly as the wretched slave,/ Who with a body filled and vacant mind/ Gets him to rest, crammed with distressful bread/ . . . and all night sleeps in Elysium."

No sensible man, of course, is unafraid in the face of real danger; true courage lies in behaving bravely, despite one's fear — all the more so if one dare not confide in anyone, but must wear the mask of unconcern. Probably the reason Admiral Horatio Hornblower is so popular a fictional hero is that before each combat action he always doubts himself, quakes inwardly, curses his hands for trembling, but never allows himself to seek reassurance or sympathy among even his closest associates. Choking back his feelings, he plays his role nobly — that of the icy, imperturbable commander — and thus inspires his men, who draw courage from his sangfroid. He is thereby the more human, and yet the greater hero; his triumph is the more admirable for being a triumph over himself.

In the case of a commanding officer or ruler, it is easy to see the merits of setting limits to intimacy. For the rest of us, though, the notion of such a self-imposed limitation may seem to run counter to our fondest fantasies about closeness and understanding. But like most other fantasies, this one is unworkable because it originates in an infantile wish which we should have given up — and still feel to some degree. And it is the nature of that wish which accounts for the ironic fact that the very people we feel are the "right" ones to confide our secrets to are the most apt to be damaged by them.

For fundamentally, the desire to pour out our ugliest thoughts and to confess our misdeeds to the people closest to us originates in the child's conception of love. As one psychiatrist explains it, "To tell everything — one's past or present misdeeds, hostile feelings, impermissible wishes — is the infant's way of testing and demanding parental love. It is like being a baby who makes a mess, and expects mommy not to be angry, but to clean him up with a forgiving smile on her face. In the case of an infant, that's reasonable enough, but it's quite wrong in the case of an adult. When a grown man or woman tells his mate or close friends the worst things within himself, he is symbolically making a mess and asking to be loved despite it, just as if he were a baby." But only the baby, he adds, has the right to be completely selfish and demanding in the love relationship; the adult should seek love, and give it, on a quite different basis.

Still, isn't it well known that confession is good for the soul? Doesn't the whole practice of psychiatry prove that certain private sorrows, fears and secrets, if kept bottled up, will sometimes overwhelm and destroy us? Of course — but the crucial question is: If you must confide, to whom should you do so? In the case of secrets of the sort I have been discussing all along, the answer is: Not to the persons you are most intimate with, but to someone detached, uninvolved, unlikely to be personally wounded by what you reveal; someone you will not hate afterwards for knowing the worst about you; someone you confide in not in order to be uncritically loved, like an infant, but in order to be judiciously helped, like an adult.

For such reasons, ministers, rabbis, and priests are often an excellent choice as confidant and adviser. Quite apart from the spiritual or practical advice we may get from such a person, the mere act of telling what we feel — without hurtful aftereffects — brings relief that is at least briefly healing, and sometimes helps us permanently turn a corner in our time of crisis. To Catholics, of course, confession is sacramental, guilt being formally discharged through assigned penance; and even non-Catholics recognize that this is an effective, if limited, form of psychotherapy. Dr. Karl Menninger comments that although it is no cure-all, and is ineffective against most of the severe neuroses, for lesser emotional disturbances it is "an ancient form of relief . . . [which] accomplishes commendable psychotherapy." Family doctors and lawyers, though they lack the prerogatives of spiritual leadership, are often able to perform much the same function for the person needing to open up and tell his inner torment.

In the case of more severe emotional problems and disorders, it may be necessary to seek someone professionally trained to listen, understand, and provide actual emotional help — a social worker, a psychologist, or a psychiatrist. Such people can let us say the worst we have to tell — indeed, can encourage it — without being harmed by it themselves; moreover, they are trained to recognize the psychological processes at work, and to help us learn to live with our own feelings. The kind of intimacy achieved in such a relationship harms no one, but it is significant that such psychotherapists often warn their patients *not* to discuss the troubling emotions outside the office, and especially not with those they feel closest to.

Still another form of outlet (for less seriously distressing secrets), which hurts no one but relieves the surcharged heart, is the diary. Many a diarist has had his eye on later publication, and therefore bared only as much of his inner self as he thought would look good, but others have meant their pages for no eyes but their own, and therefore carried on a dialogue with themselves — a curious but very helpful form of intimacy with one's *alter ego*.

Gamaliel Bradford, in a book about Samuel Pepys, speculated about the motives of diarists. "What fundamentally holds him to his daily task," he wrote, "is the [need] . . . to find escape somehow, anyhow, from the close tormenting prison of our own microscopic, infinite selves. . . . Precisely because he shrinks from laying bare his spiritual secrets to the prying gaze of the flesh and blood about him, he is all the more disposed to reveal his heart in those private pages which he comes to love as if they represented the most intimate possibilities of friendship." And he points out that only once in his life did Pepys so much as mention to anyone that he was keeping a diary — and then regretted having told even that one man.

Contemporary psychology has made it clear that the desire for total intimacy and total self-revelation is usually juvenile, if not childish, and unwise, if not downright dangerous. But as is so often true, this modern insight is remarkably foreshadowed in Scripture. In Matthew (15:11, 18–19) Jesus defends his disciples for failing to ritually wash their hands before eating, and explains: "Not that which goeth into the mouth defileth a man; but that which cometh out of the mouth. . . . Those things which proceed out of the mouth come forth from the heart; and they defile the man. For out of the heart proceed evil thoughts, murders, adulteries, fornications, thefts, false witness, blasphemies . . ."

Which is about as good a case as anyone has ever made for living with one's own dark thoughts, and setting limits to intimacy, for the good of those we love.

Mental Blocks

Short Circuits in the Brain, and How To Repair Them

THE BRAIN is man's most remarkable possession — and the most remarkable thing about it is that he has never learned to make use of more than a tiny fraction of its powers. Each of us, in the fantastic tangle of electrical circuits within that three-pound lump of soft tissue, has millions of pieces of information stored away. Whenever we have a problem to solve — whether it be as simple as rewiring a broken lamp or as complex as writing a novel — we try to plug in on the right circuits and draw upon all our relevant knowledge. But what we often get is only a smattering of what is actually within us, for the brain, like a flood-damaged telephone exchange, is full of short circuits and crossed wires which prevent the bulk of the messages from getting through. Psychologists call them "mental blocks," and have been studying ways to avoid or repair them.

Most of the short-circuiting is psychological, rather than physical. It isn't surprising to find a mental block in someone who has had an actual brain injury. Accidents and strokes (blood clots in the brain) often cause some remarkable limitations in their victims. One man, after his recovery from a stroke, remained unable to read; his speech returned, his vision was normal, and he could even take dictation, translate it into any one of several languages he knew, and write it down clearly — but still be unable to comprehend his own writing. But most mental blocks occur in normal people without any physical injury to the brain, and these blocks are, in their own way, equally remarkable. If you have ever forgotten a friend's name when introducing him at a party, or found it all but impossible to make a simple decision on some everyday matter, or stared at some gadget in total bafflement until someone showed you its obvious use, you have felt the effect of an ordinary mental block. As with these trivial examples, so too with the larger efforts of the human being to be creative and imaginative in dealing with life: even the best minds can be rendered partially ineffective by these hindrances, but conversely even average minds, when free of them, have formidable powers.

Psychologists began to study the phenomenon of mental blocking about a generation ago, but intensive work on it has been done only since World War II. The actual information available thus far is still meager but so exciting that it is already being put to use. Such major firms as General Electric, General Motors, and U. S. Steel have inaugurated "creative thinking" sessions for designers and top executives. A number of universities have introduced special courses to help students surmount mental blocks in activities as varied as designing power shovels and writing poetry. And even the average person, equipped with a little knowledge of the mechanisms of blocking, can begin to apply some of the knowledge to himself and increase his own mental efficiency.

The largest category of mental blocks includes those with an emotional basis, for certain emotions are potent inhibitors of thinking. Fear, for one, can sometimes almost completely cancel out the power of intelligent thought. The terrible circus-tent fire in Hartford of some years ago, or the Coconut Grove nightclub fire in Boston, are both perfect examples: in each there was heavy and unnecessary loss of life because of senseless panic, which kept the forebrains of the people involved from sending the proper messages through to their legs.

The T.A.T. (Thematic Apperception Test) used by psychologists to evaluate personality often reveals the power of fear in preventing any clear perception of a problem — without which, of course, no solution is possible. The T.A.T. consists of a number of untitled and somewhat vague pictures, which the subject looks at and tries to interpret. One of the pictures shows a woman lying on a bed, her face turned away; standing nearby, his head bent forward or bowed, is a man. Some people, asked to explain the picture, say that the woman has just died and the man is grieving. Others think he has just made love to her and is leaving her. But fear can block out any solution by making the subject all but invisible: at the Menninger Clinic one young girl, who was terribly afraid of sex, looked at the picture and saw no woman at all, but only mussed bed-clothing. Her fear of the subject had prevented her conscious mind from admitting to itself the potentially frightening side of what her eyes were seeing.

This, to be sure, is an extreme case. But even mild apprehensions and worries can partially block mental functioning by making it difficult to pay attention to the problem at hand. In an experiment at Syracuse University, fifty students had to decipher a number of sentences in a simple code. Some of the sentences were neutral, or devoid of emotional content (e.g., "Some bushes were planted by the boys"), but other sentences contained ideas which might make the student nervous as the words began to appear in the clear. One such was: "My family do not respect my judgment," and another was, "Now on my date I belched quite loudly." The uneasiness these ideas caused had an immediate and measurable effect on the students' thinking power: the average student not only took longer to finish decoding the loaded sentences, but made 50 per cent more errors. Perhaps the lesson in this is that when we find an apparently simple problem perplexingly difficult to solve, we ought to ask ourselves whether some element in it is vaguely upsetting, or reminds us of something worrisome; the very recognition of the presence of such a component may help clear the lines of internal communication and restore our ability to think effectively about the matter at hand.

Worse than the mild fears engendered in these students by the loaded sentences was the blocking effect of pressure or overmotivation. For when the examiner stood in front of the students with a stop-watch in hand and said somewhat unpleasantly, "Can't you do it a little bit faster?" the error rate soared. In our society, we often think that people produce best under the stimulus of fierce competition. That may be true in business dealings, a footrace, or a stage performance — but not in problem-solving. Doing a familiar task under pressure is a far cry from seeking new ideas or trying to solve a knotty problem; in these situations, the increase in pressure seems to decrease efficiency.

Any college student can tell you how the things he has studied often seem to vanish from his mind when he's taking a final exam — and come back to him immediately afterward. Even a long-distance phone call does the same thing to many of us: conscious of the cost of the three minutes, we talk rapidly — and remember only after hanging up the things we had really wanted to say. Likewise, the unemployed man, desperately in need of a job, may stammer and mumble when being interviewed for a position he is quite competent to handle. This is something built into our basic animal nerve structure, for even as simple a creature as the rat loses much of his mental ability under excessive pressure. Dr. Jerome S. Bruner, psychologist of Harvard University, taught rats to solve a tricky maze to get to food. Rats that hadn't eaten for twelve hours caught on in about six tries — but rats that had been starved for thirty-six hours were frantic to get to food, and took more than twenty tries before they learned what to do. In short, overmotivation — working under an excessive drive to succeed — actually gums up the works.

The human lesson in this may be that when each of us faces a serious problem and has been working at it earnestly for some time without getting anywhere, "sticking to it" may be just the wrong thing to do. Under excessive inner or outer pressure, the brain has developed something like what engineers call a "reverberating circuit" — the same thing goes around and around, allowing nothing new to break in. The best thing to do may be to leave the problem alone for a while and go fishing, listen to music, or chat with a friend; relaxation may give the mind time to clear its circuits and let the flow of imagination begin again.

The act of repression — the involuntary forgetting of something unpleasant, or productive of conflict within us — is also responsible for many mental blocks.* Consider the man who forgets his boss's name at a crucial moment — a small, but horrifying, block. Why does he? Psychiatrists have long known that the involuntary forgetting of things which are important to us often indicates anxiety, or hostility we don't

* See also "What Your Memory Reveals About You," page 86.

want to admit to ourselves. But comes the crucial moment, and the employee who unconsciously dislikes his boss is suddenly unable to recall his name — because the "forgotten" hostility deep down is doing its job of creating a short circuit.

The same is true of those people who forget appointments they were not looking forward to, or fail to drop letters on unpleasant business in the mailbox; and even perhaps of those people who hide or deposit money gotten illegally and then cannot remember where they put it. It may also be the reason some men can never find the right girl to marry — unconsciously, they may be afraid of marriage or women altogether. It is sometimes the reason a brilliant business executive fails to solve problems well within his powers — he may actually fear the prospect of promotion to a more demanding and responsible job. The cure for such mental blocks is not simple, but it starts with the crude self-examining question, "What's bothering me? — what am I afraid of facing?" For only when the repressed fears or angers are brought to light can the individual begin to handle them intelligently, evaluate them, redirect them, and so neutralize their effect on his mental powers.

As opposed to the mental blocks caused by emotion, there are many which have little to do with feelings but a great deal to do with the learning process and its effect on the inner connections of the brain. A major source of mental blocks, for instance, lies in preconceptions — prearrangements, so to speak, of the internal circuitry of the brain, which hinder it from using the data the senses furnish it. The late Professor John E. Arnold, who taught a course in creative thinking at Massachusetts Institute of Technology, had a favorite demonstration of this. "List all the red objects in this room," he would say to his students. After a minute or two he would put his hand over his necktie and ask if anyone knew what color it was. No one would. "The fact that you were looking for red things," he would explain, "provided a temporary 'mental set' that excluded every color but red from your perception. People see those things they want or expect to see, and scarcely notice those they aren't looking for."

If you have ever misplaced an important scrap of paper on a cluttered desk, you know the effects of mental set. You shuffle through everything again and again, but just can't find it. Then someone else comes in and spots it at once. The paper turns out to be a little larger or smaller, or different in color, from what you had thought; your preconception kept you from recognizing it.

Related to this is a powerful kind of mental block called "problem set." It's a ready-made notion about how to go about solving a problem at hand. In most cases, problem set is a useful thing; it enables one to get right to work, and helps filter out everything extraneous. But it may also blot out any way of approaching the problem except the one first thought of.

An old parlor trick, used by German psychologist Karl Duncker, demonstrates the workings of problem set perfectly. Laying six matches on a table before his subject, he would say, "Make four equal-sided triangles, with the sides of each the length of a match." Most of the subjects merely shuffled and reshuffled the matches on the surface of the table, gradually becoming convinced that the problem was insoluble. Finally, though, a few of them realized that Duncker had never said the matches must lie in the same plane, as they first appeared when the problem was presented. These few immediately put the matches together in the form of a tetrahedron, the three-dimensional figure that looks like a pyramid with three sides. The others remained frustrated; having first seen the matches on a plane surface, and having been fixed in that frame of reference, they could never solve the problem.

Problem set is often a part of everyday business life, where it masquerades under the name "experience." And as useful as experience may be in greatly facilitating work and the solutions of routine problems, the experiences of the past may get in the way of creative solutions to new kinds of problems. Charles H. Clark of the Ethyl Corporation has compiled a blacklist of "killer phrases" which put a blight on new ideas by invoking experience. Here are a few of them: "We've never done anything like that." "I'm against making a change now." "But our operation is unique." "Customers won't stand for it." "Everybody does it this way."

Ironically, it is success that often creates the most powerful kind of problem set, and causes stubborn persevering along one line of effort after the best ore has been mined out of it. Professor Harvey Lehman of Ohio University, who spent twenty years compiling data on the most productive periods in the lives of great men, found that chemists hit their peak between twenty-six and thirty, mathematicians between thirty and thirty-four, and so on. He concluded that although men of unusual ability work hard all their lives, they get most of their new ideas and make most of their significantly new contributions during their earlier years. Typically, a man makes a discovery at age thirty and spends the next forty years fussing with minor refinements of it. His early success with it gives him a problem set, and he remains relatively slow-moving from then on while the front ranks of discovery rush on past him.

Closely allied to problem set is the effect of pure habit. Habits are highly useful short cuts to action; without them we could scarcely get along. But while routine duties can be expeditiously handled through habit, problem-solving or creative thinking requires complete use of the brain's crammed files of information, rather than the slim selection habit offers. Some research organizations, including Bell Labs and Arthur D. Little, Inc., are so aware of the limitations caused by habit that they often build their research groups carefully so as to include on any given project at least one man who has no experience with the problem at hand. His maverick ideas, his fresh approach, his lack of a ready-made way to tackle the thing, not only produce new and better ideas, but shake up the thinking of the experts in the group. About the time he really gets to know the project, it's time to bring in someone else as the human catalyst.

What can the average person do about problem set and habit in his own thinking? First, he can make himself aware of them; just to suspect one's self of being in a rut due to past experience may be enough to start reorienting his thinking. But if he still finds himself saying, "There isn't any other way to do it," or "You don't go about it that way," he may need a catalyst. One is to ask himself, "How would a high-school kid try to do it? How would my wife do it? How would the brightest man I know do it? How would a man from outer space do it?" If such mental trickery doesn't help, it may be useful to go talk to friends and acquaintances — especially those whose training and education are remote from the problem being considered.

For the very process of education, curiously, is a potent source of mental blocks. Not that a man without an education can solve problems better than a man with one; but the educated man's advantage in creativity depends on whether he was trained to be flexible and uninhibited in drawing upon his knowledge, or was rigidly schooled in a "right" or textbook way to do things. And this is why that highly creative man, C. F. Kettering, once defined the successful inventor as "a fellow who doesn't take his education too seriously."

One example of the mental block produced by narrow or rigid training is known to psychologists as "functional fixedness." This means the tendency to attach only one "proper" value to an object or to expect that only one object can fill a given need. For example, some college students were once given the task of retrieving a ping pong ball from the bottom of a rusty pipe that had been bolted upright to the floor. In the room the students found a hammer, pliers, rulers, soda straws, strings, bent pins, and an old bucket of dirty wash water. After fishing around vainly with the objects, most (but not all) of the students saw that the solution lay in pouring the dirty water into the pipe and floating the ball to the top. Afterward the psychologist repeated the experiment with other students, but with one difference — he replaced the bucket of dirty wash water with a pitcher of ice water set on a crisp tablecloth and surrounded by gleaming goblets. Not one student solved the problem, because each one "knew" that the fresh ice water in the pitcher was for drinking, not for pouring into a rusty pipe to solve a problem.

Another experiment with the same kind of block was recently performed by two research psychologists at the City College of New York. They taught two groups of students how to build a simple electric circuit. The first group learned to connect a relay to open and close the circuit. The second group learned instead to use a simple switch. Then individuals of both groups were given a problem: two cords hang from the ceiling and are to be tied together. The distance between them is such that when the student takes hold of one, he cannot reach the other; yet they are long enough to meet midway. The student sees, after a while, that they must be set swinging, and caught in the middle. To make them swing, he looks around for weights to tie onto them. On a table nearby are two boxes of objects — one of relays, the other of switches. Almost without exception the switch-trained students choose relays for the pendulum weight, and relay-trained students choose switches. What does this mean? That whichever object they had come to attach a specific value to was, from then on, ruled out as having other merits and possibilities. A switch is a switch is a switch. It isn't a weight. Training and experience, in short, add to your knowledge in depth — at the risk of creating a mental block.

A quite different sort of experiment shows how specific skills taught to a person can likewise limit his vision, by providing him with a patterned response to a type of problem. Professor A. S. Luchins of McGill University used a problem analogous to certain parlor games. "Here are three jars," he would say. "They hold twenty-one, one hundred and twenty-seven, and three cubic centimeters respectively. Here is a pitcher full of water. Can you measure out one hundred cubic centimeters of water?"

After some fumbling, his subjects would work out this answer: fill the 127-cc. jar, pour off enough to fill the 21-cc. jar, then pour off enough more to fill the 3-cc. jar, dump it, and fill it again. This subtractive process (127 − 21 − 3 − 3) would leave exactly 100 cc. in the largest jar. Luchins then gave a series of similar problems, all involving the same routine of adding and subtracting with three jars. The subjects happily and deftly solved them all. Then came this one: measure out 20 cc. from three jars of 23, 49, and 3 cc. The great majority filled the 49 cc. jar, poured off 23 cc., and then poured off 3 twice to get 20, thus sticking to their routine. But the problem can be solved in half as many steps by filling the 23-cc. jar first, and simply pouring off 3 cc. once.

If training and education can produce such mental blocks, would we be better off without them? Of course not. The answer is not to avoid education, but to avoid rigid and overly routined education. If teachers and parents alike pound into a child's head the idea that there is a right and a wrong way to do everything, he will tend to be limited and stereotyped in his thinking. If they encourage him to work things out for himself, however, and develop in him the faith in his right to experiment, he will grow up far more flexible in his thinking. As an adult, whether he is trying to design a new automobile engine, resolve a quarrel with his wife, or write a report for his boss, he will not be limited to tried-and-true materials and methods, but will dare to think about new and possibly zany — but possibly valuable — answers to the problem.

Not only formal education, but the kind of discipline imposed on the child in the home, has a great deal to do with the ability to think freely versus the disability of thinking rigidly. This was demonstrated some years ago by an interesting experiment conducted by Dr. Else Frenkel-Brunswik of the Institute of Child Welfare, at the University of California. She showed children a series of pictures; the first was quite clearly a dog, but picture by picture it changed gradually into a cat. The children had to identify each picture. Some held onto the dog identification long after the cat qualities were becoming obvious; others willingly shifted their opinion as soon as the new features became evident. When Dr. Frenkel-Brunswik then studied the children's backgrounds, she found that the rigid ones came from homes where the parents were strict, harsh, and dictatorial. Such children are torn between loving and hating; what they want most in life is for things to be clearcut and certain. And therefore they tend to be rigid, and find it difficult to change their minds about a problem. But the children who could easily change their minds, as the pictures changed, came from warm, permissive, democratic homes, and had no desperate need to cling to something certain.

In reaching its true potential, the creative mind also has to overcome the cultural blocks caused by growing up in a given time and place, among people who do things in a certain way and frown on or ignore other ways. As a result, when we try to reach certain goals, we never consider — in fact can hardly conceive of — the many alternative ways of doing things accepted by other cultures.

In the year 1845, two stout, well-equipped sailing vessels set forth from England under the command of Sir John Franklin to find the Northwest Passage through the Arctic. Both ships became icebound in the Hudson Bay area. For long months, their crews suffered a slow deterioration of body and spirit as they fought scurvy and general starvation. At last, when it appeared impossible that they would ever free their ships from the ice, the enfeebled men struck out overland. Not one survived; 129 men died of starvation and exposure. Yet this happened in a region where Eskimos were living in perfect health, hunting effectively, and eating adequately in a fashion the European explorers could have copied. But the Englishmen were too "civilized." They could not believe that their own foods, in this new situation, could be inferior to the "disgusting" diet of the Eskimos, nor would they stoop to learn from "savages" how to hunt and fish successfully in an ice-locked environment. Not that they consciously rejected any ideas: rather, they were so serenely convinced of their own superiority as civilized men that they never thought to ask candidly what they might learn from "inferior" people.

In the fight against the unnecessary limitations imposed on our brain-power, an awareness of the kinds of mental blocking is, as already pointed out, an essential first step. Sometimes, psychotherapy may be needed to go beyond this, if the problems are deep and emotional in nature. But for the average healthy person, mental blocking can be partially broken down by the specific effort to shake loose of patterned thinking and to allow, or make, one's self "think wild." For the wild thinkers are the ones who draw upon the whole vast accumulation of data in their brains. Dr. J. P. Guilford of the University of Southern California has long used a little test which clearly shows the difference between narrow and wild thinking. He asks his students to spend five minutes writing down all the uses they can think of for a common brick. Almost everyone starts off with such items as "to build a house," or "to lay a pathway." Some branch off into less usual avenues such as "for a paperweight." A few come up with oddities such as "heat it and use it for a bedwarmer," or "grind it up and use the powder as a pigment in paint." To be sure, there are better ways to do these last two things — but they *are* possible uses for a brick. The point is that to think of them at all, one has to be capable of making remote associations and of putting into words ideas that seem different and possibly outlandish.

To fight the blocks that limit your imagination, you must make the effort to generate wild ideas and you must remain on guard against having too much "good sense." Thomas Edison allowed no preconceptions of good sense to get in his way when he was seeking the right substance for a light bulb filament. He tried six thousand different substances — including a piece of Limburger cheese — before finding the right answer. Writing to a friend about the creative capacity, the eighteenth-century German poet Friedrich Schiller explained, "It hinders the creative work of the mind if the intellect examines too closely the ideas already pouring in, as it were, at the gates. In the case of a creative mind the intellect has withdrawn its watchers from the gates, and the ideas rush in pell-mell, and only then does it review and inspect the multitude."

This often happens in sleep, when the critical judgment is not working. Jacques Hadamard, a French mathematician, had been working unsuccessfully on a difficult theoretical problem; one night a noise awakened him. "A solution long searched for appeared to me at once," he later wrote, "without the slightest instant of reflection on my part." Otto Loewi, who won a Nobel prize in 1936, had been working on the problem of proving the role of chemicals in nerve activity, without getting any but contradictory answers. One night, waking from a fitful sleep, he had an idea for a brilliant experiment that would clarify the matter, and scribbled it down. When he awoke in the morning, he could make nothing of his scrawl, and had no recollection of the idea. Happily, at 3 A.M. the next night he awoke with the same idea; this time he flung himself into his clothes and hurried to the lab — and a Nobel prize. The nineteenth-century German chemist Friedrich Kekulé solved the problem of the structure of the benzene molecule (a ring, rather than a chain, of carbon atoms) when, in a daydream, he saw a snake swallow its tail.

This isn't to say that all, or most, discoveries or solutions to problems are automatic. But such notable cases do prove the point that much important thinking goes on below the surface of the conscious mind far from the watchers at the gates. A simple yet effective way to catch them off duty is to carry a little notebook or pad, and jot down at once any passing thoughts about your job, budget, or other problem areas. Passing thoughts that pop up in reverie may be notions from the unconscious sneaking past the gates, but like dreams, they will quickly rush back and disappear into that hiding place. If you jot such a thought down, you have captured it; then later you can do as much conscious thinking about it as you like.

One of the most successful modern methods for countering mental blocks is the conference technique called "brainstorming." Most committees and conferences generate few fresh ideas, for within any sizable group of people there are usually enough mental blocks to stop almost every promising line of thought. "If you want to kill a good idea," so goes a modern axiom, "give it to a committee." Brainstorming does just the opposite. The rules are these: (1) anything goes, (2) the wilder the ideas, the better, and (3) nobody may criticize any idea. Someone records all the ideas and only afterwards do the brainstormers go over them critically and choose the useful ones.

It's a technique you can use in your own family or your social groups, when you have a problem to solve. You can even do it by yourself, according to some students of creative thinking. By sitting down to think freely, and jotting down ideas as they come into your mind, you can conduct a solo session of brainstorming. Remembering the rules against censorship, you can help yourself to associate freely, and by playing mental games, such as trying to imagine what different people would say in response to each new idea, you may find an ingenious way to solve your problem, no matter whether it is great or small, human or technological.

All these illustrations point to the fact that much important thinking goes on below the surface of the conscious mind. The relaxed man is more apt to enlist the aid of his unconscious mind than the man with stern judgment, a rigid outlook, a stubborn problem set, strong fears, or a too eager desire to succeed. So when you have a difficult problem to solve or a perplexing decision to make, relax. Back off and take a fresh look at it. Try to clear your mind of fear; shake yourself mentally. And be suspicious of your own training; it may be giving you the "old fogy" syndrome — the conviction that there is only one way to do things.

Finally, if mental blocks still prevent you from seeing the solution to a problem, you can sometimes break the log jam by simply starting — anywhere, but at once. Finding yourself in the middle of the consequences may so change your perspective on the problem that you can proceed towards a solution. A prominent writer I know told about the dreadful difficulty he used to have trying to get a good lead or beginning for an article; it always cost him days of wasted time. His solution: he starts anywhere, and gets going; then, when he's all through, he finds it easy to go back and get the right beginning. As he put it, it's like deciding whether or not to jump into cold water. Once you jump, the problem doesn't exist.

Marital Difficulties

One could fill a very large book with articles on psychological aspects of marital difficulties. I present only four pieces here, but the first three touch upon three of the most important and frequent sources of marital difficulty, while the fourth, an examination of the changing roles of husband and wife, is virtually a survey of the entire area.

Why They Fight About Money

I T WAS the expensive Duncan Phyfe coffee table that saved the marriage of a couple I will call Carl and Evelyn Williamson. It had been one of their more extravagant purchases, costing them $250 only two years ago. Now it lay upside down on the living-room floor, with one of its graceful mahogany legs snapped off, showing a raw, white, splintered stump.

There had been a quarrel. It started like all the others: tall brooding Carl, a twenty-seven-year-old bacteriologist, was adding up the month's bills, and began asking Evelyn to explain various items. She didn't remember certain of them at all; others seemed too high, but she couldn't recall the legitimate reasons why they had been so. Finally she grew flustered, then angry, and then weepy. Carl meanwhile progressed from icy to caustic to furious.

When she actually began crying, it came over him — a sudden hot, choking need to hit or smash something. Not her, of course; he would never do that. But he flung the checkbook across the room and knocked a lamp over; and when Evelyn stared at him speechless, he swept a batch of books onto the floor, threw his coffee cup into the fireplace, and kicked out blindly at the coffee table. His foot snapped one of its legs, and the table flipped over onto its back like a shot animal.

Carl stood there gazing at it, stupefied. He had banged books onto the table in some of their previous arguments; he had slammed doors; once he had even broken an ashtray accidentally. But now this —

"Something's the matter with me," he muttered after a long silence. "I'm sick. Sick in the head. I don't do things like this. I must be crazy."

So the broken table was the turning point: the next morning Carl telephoned the Community Service Society of New York, a leading non-sectarian family agency, and asked to see a social caseworker, to find out why he and his wife were breaking up over money troubles, and why fights about household finances were making him do idiotic and destructive things.

After the first hour's discussion, the caseworker suggested to Carl that Evelyn also come in for counseling. From both of them, two separate caseworkers pieced together the story, as Carl and Evelyn saw it. Evelyn was incompetent at handling money: she couldn't budget well, she overspent, she was often caught short without supplies on hand, she lost bills, she forgot to write out check stubs, she never seemed to put aside money for the long-term expenses. Carl grew so furious at her incompetence that he could not even discuss money with her logically; every discussion began softly enough, but soon turned into a violent quarrel, and ended with a tantrum and tears.

And yet this was not the real story after all. For by the third week of counseling sessions, both Carl and Evelyn separately had admitted there was another problem they didn't discuss with each other at all. Evelyn, to be plain about it, found the sex act distasteful. "Of course, a wife *has* to do it for her husband's sake," she told her caseworker. "But I guess I try to discourage him sometimes, though I'm as gentle and subtle about it as I can be. And I try to be a good wife in every other way. Is it very terrible of me not to like it? Is it really my fault?"

Carl's version was likewise calm and decent. "I can't blame Evie," he said. "Let's be broadminded; she must have deep-seated feelings about it that she can't control. I have to try to be understanding, even though it hurts me when she doesn't respond to me."

But little by little, in the course of counseling, Carl began to realize it wasn't that simple. Broadminded as he thought himself, he *did* resent the sexual trouble down deep; and in the area of money he had unconsciously discovered a way to punish her for her shortcomings. He had been giving her too little money all along, and refusing to plan with her how to spend and account for their income; then, since she could not help getting into trouble, he always had something to get furious about. The family budget became a weapon of revenge.

Evelyn's sexual problem, however, was not unsolvable. After two years of weekly visits to the caseworker, she gradually came to understand her own feelings and fought to change them little by little. And she *did* change them; even if sex still was not as exciting to her as to Carl, at least she no longer viewed it as disgusting, and was able to regard it as a natural expression of affection.

By that time, there were no more money quarrels in the Williamson home — yet no one had yet discussed budget techniques with the Williamsons. Evelyn did later spend an hour with Mrs. Luise Addiss, budget expert and consultant home economist of the Community Service Society. Surprisingly enough, Evelyn proved to have quite a bit of real information about buying and budgeting, but she needed organization in her thinking and planning. And now Carl was giving her a much more generous allowance and had begun planning their expenses with her quietly and amiably; he had no need to punish her any longer. The money problem had all but disappeared.

Like the Williamsons, a great many American husbands and wives fight about money. According to sociological surveys, money is just about the major subject of quarrels in nearly half of all marriages, and differences over money may be far harder for married couples to reconcile than differences over friendships, religion, in-laws or social activities.

Yet, like the Williamsons, they fight about money not because of real financial problems, but because of deep-seated, crucial emotional difficulties — conflicting attitudes towards living, towards loving, towards work and play. Such is the curious paradox about money quarrels: they actually haven't much to do with money.

Husbands and wives *think* they fight about money because "there isn't enough to go around," or because they differ on how and where it should be spent. They usually believe that if things were "somewhat better," or if they had, say, forty or fifty per cent more coming in, there would be no quarrels at all. They couldn't be more wrong. The additional income would solve nothing, for money quarrels are merely a disguise for more basic disagreements. If the Williamsons had been given only budget advice, or if Carl had gotten a better-paying job, nothing would have been solved for them. You can quarrel quite as bitterly over the price of filet mignon as over that of hamburger.

Money quarrels should be a warning sign, a red flag marked "Danger," a distress flare signaling that important emotional problems need to be solved. Husbands and wives who realize this will not endure their quarrels and unhappiness through long bitter years; they will recognize the fights over money as an unmistakable symptom of some hidden trouble, and will seek remedies to make not just their spending, but all the varied aspects of their daily life, richer and happier.

These, according to the Family Service Association of America, are the conclusions reached by social caseworkers and psychiatrists affiliated with the leading family service agencies and counseling services throughout the country. During the Depression, such agencies used to give a great deal of budget advice and home economics information to the hard-pressed and the unemployed. As time passed, the problem of how to survive dwindled, and the past decade of uninterrupted prosperity has greatly altered the circumstances of most of the families that seek out the agencies with their problems. Yet the number of them coming in with "money problems" has not decreased. What has changed is the emphasis. Nowadays the agencies, instead of seeing people who haven't money enough to get along, see people who can't get along *with* money.

Over the years, many of the ways in which money is misused as an expression of emotional difficulties have become as familiar to caseworkers as the symptoms of measles or grippe are to the physicians. There is, for instance, the prosperous and devoted husband who gives his wife furs, a new car, and plenty of cash, but spends his free time at the golf course and has never been able to say a tender word to her without great effort. To him, money is as good as love, and he pays off his wife in one way instead of the other.

There is the woman who foolishly and impulsively buys things beyond the family's means, or wastes her husband's income on treatments for vague lingering psychosomatic troubles. Often, such a woman resents something about her marriage and is getting even with her husband by means of money, without even realizing what she is doing.

There is the woman whose husband hates to hear about her extravagances for hats and permanents, but wouldn't complain if she just didn't tell him about them. Yet she insists on bringing up the matter every time she spends money for these things. Why does she knowingly start discussions that have to end in quarrels? Often it is because she is unsure of her power over her husband and wants to make him openly and outspokenly accept her and approve of everything she does.

And there is the man who always grabs the check for the whole dinner party, buys a new car every year, tips too much, and wastes his money in gambling. Often he proves to be someone who had ungenerous and unloving parents, and who now has to reassure himself continually that he is loved — even if only by himself, and even if only in terms of money.

The astonishing thing is that so often people believe money is the real problem, and fail to recognize that hiding behind it is something far more basic. Two years ago a young real estate salesman I will call Tom Milner came to the Counseling Service, a private family consultation group in the Bronx. A thickset, curly-haired, blond young man, his look of woe sat ill on his plump pink face. To casework therapist Louise Schiddel he blurted out, waving his hands wildly: "Miss Schiddel, my marriage is on the rocks. What do I do about it? Do I give it up or is there some way to fix it up?"

The caseworker asked him what the problem was.

"We fight all the time," he said. "Harriet and I have long, miserable, awful fights. And always about money, nothing but dirty rotten money. I like silk shirts; I like to play poker; I like to be a good sport when we're out with a gang of friends. But every time, there's an all-night fight about it afterwards. She's so stingy it embarrasses me. She doesn't know how to enjoy life. She works in a high-class lawyer's office, but she walks in there every day with sandwiches in a paper bag so she won't have to spend fifty cents in a drugstore."

Tom's tastes outran his income; he spent freely, yet not wildly. His wife, a dutiful, thrifty girl, was simply trying to keep the family from getting into debt. All they really needed was a little more income. That's the picture you'd see at first. And it would be a completely false one.

For shortly after Tom and Harriet began coming in to visit separate caseworkers at the Counseling Service in the hope of untangling their money troubles, Tom's father died and left him his building-contracting firm. Tom's income jumped overnight from $100 a week to about $400, and the budget problem vanished. Well — at least, for a month or so.

Then it reappeared in new and more elegant form. Instead of silk shirts, Tom splurged on a thirty-five-foot yawl; in place of poker he began to play the stock market. As for Harriet, she nagged him as strenuously as before, served even a stingier dinner, ruined his vacation by refusing to set foot aboard the boat, and infuriated him by sticking to her secretarial job — and to her paper bag of sandwiches.

The real problem, as caseworker Schiddel slowly pieced it together, was one of clashing personality patterns. Harriet was not especially attractive, felt unsure of herself, and hence was jealous and demanding; she needed more reassurance and devotion than most people can easily give. Tom was particularly ill equipped to fill the role; he was still a teen-ager at heart, interested in pleasing himself, and deeply ill at ease whenever he had to express a gentle or warm sentiment. The two patterns were disguised in terms of money: Harriet became miserly, and sought security in the form of savings, while Tom angrily spent money on himself, to demonstrate his independence.

The two Milners are working intensively on their problem right now. For months they have been talking over their feelings with their caseworkers, exploring their own hearts, puzzling about their own shortcomings. As they have begun to understand themselves, they have tried to start meeting each other halfway. Now it looks as though their marriage is going to prosper. They may even learn how to handle money intelligently; but it was not money that nearly broke them up. Money was merely the weapon with which they chose to duel.

A woman who will fight, like Harriet, for more love (or for money in place of it) is understandable. But what can you say of a woman who uses money quarrels to destroy her husband, or reduce his virility? Fantastic as that seems, it is not at all rare. Many a woman resents her husband's male superiority and wants to have freedom and importance and to "wear the pants" in the family. Money is a symbol of masculine success in our world; if she can win control of the family funds, or make her husband feel he isn't a good enough provider, she will have whittled him down. She will have — in a purely theoretical sense — "castrated" him, and made herself more nearly dominant.

But some wives who appear kind, loving and dedicated to the welfare of their husbands and homes do the same thing, in subtler ways. Frank and Marian Berger are a case in point. If they had been your neighbors, you'd have thought them a devoted, close-knit family, and you'd have said that Marian was a wonderful wife, and a fine mother to her three children. Only one thing: every so often, you would hear, coming across the lawn from the Berger house, the sounds of bitter quarreling in the living room. Then for days or weeks Frank Berger would mope around in the garden, his pale fat face wearing the sad look of a whipped spaniel.

And what were the fights about? Money. The Bergers, it seems, would drift along fine for a while, then suddenly find themselves deep in debt and being harassed by creditors. That's when they'd have a pitched battle, with the three children being called in and told all the family troubles, and scolded for their own extravagant tastes.

So dreadful did these recurrent crises and wrangles become that the Bergers finally went to the Jewish Family Service, another leading counseling agency in New York, to see why they couldn't keep their budget in hand. The curious fact appeared, at the very first conference, that Frank, part-owner of a men's store, made $13,000 a year — a reasonably good income and was at least $2000 more than most of his friends and neighbors earned. Yet over the years he had saved nothing and had been in and out of the hands of loan sharks. At each stormy war session the whole family would agree to cut down on everything, and for a while the Bergers would live frugally. Gradually the debts would be cleared away, and the Bergers would look cheery again. They would begin to treat themselves to a few things they long wanted — and soon blossom forth into free spending, and new trouble.

It was good, plump, graying little Marian who caused all this without ever buying herself one foolish Dior gown, or begging for a winter cruise. She spent money only "for the good of the family" — like sending all three children to the very finest camps in summer; like ordering the living-room furniture luxuriously redone when a special was offered by the department store; like talking Frank into buying a bigger, costlier new car to keep up his standing among the neighbors.

In one of her sessions with a caseworker, Marian reminisced about her father: "Dad was a regular patriarch," she mused, "worse than Father Day in *Life With Father*. He was the absolute dictator of the house, and he made every decision, without tolerating any back talk. Well, at least *my* husband isn't like that, thank goodness." Five months later, Marian had begun to see behind her own statement; she understood that her fear of having a husband who would domineer over her, as her father had, had led her to keep him continually in debt — thereby reducing his self-confidence and his manly status. She had — in a symbolic sense — unmanned him.

The Bergers had apparently had only budget trouble, but no budget written on paper could have survived the onslaught of an unconscious drive like Marian's. Now that she has brought her fears to light, Marian is trying to conquer them, and the Berger budget has been working tolerably well for nearly half a year. Frank, meanwhile, is not only relieved and feeling a lot happier, but is trying extra hard not to act like the boss of the household.

The reason money is so convenient a disguise for emotional troubles like those of Marian Berger is that in our society it is a symbol of so many different things. As little children, we first learn that it takes money to buy toys, vacations, and other good things. People who love us give us objects that cost money. Rich people and their children can do what they want to; poorer ones cannot. Parents can prevent children from going to the movies or buying things they want by holding back their allowance. And so on. So from our early days on, we tend to use money as a means to, and a symbol of, love and affection, of power and punishment, of security and self-gratification, and many other things.

Whether or not you use money sensibly and easily for some of these purposes, or whether it is a sickness with you and a substitute for real human emotions, depends on the nature of your own emotional machinery. Many people explain that they spend money foolishly because it was hard to come by when they were children, and they're simply making up now for hard times in the past. But others who had the same childhood problem turn out instead to be skinflints and hoarders. Still others have been untouched by a Depression childhood, and use money in a balanced, healthful way.

So you can't trace money troubles simply to an impoverished childhood. What really counts is not the size of Father's income, but the way he and Mother feel and act toward each other and towards their children in their everyday give-and-take, in all their little acts and deeds. A poor but smoothly functioning family may produce a child who handles money well when he grows up; a wealthy but antagonistic family may produce anything from a chronic gambler to a miser.

It isn't *what* a family does with its money, but *how* it does it, that is truly important. One man may dislike handling household bills and checks, and be delighted to have his wife look after things and take charge of the home. He may almost feel that she takes care of him as Mother used to do; and if she is a strong, protective woman, she may find that kind of set-up completely gratifying. But the same arrangement might work out miserably, if the wife thinks of the role of Mother as one who is stern and thrifty, rather than warm and generous.

A typical case, from the files of a Midwestern family counseling agency, is that of a charming and boyish auto salesman, who can spin out yards of facts and figures on the showroom floor, but at home hates to have to "worry about" the family funds and expenses. So he turns over his check to his wife, and then gets from her a weekly cash allowance. But often she holds back part of it, claiming he spends it foolishly, or nags him for an accounting of what he does with it. She herself was the last — and very much put-upon — child of a series of six, and from her own experiences this is her concept of a proper mother.

The result is pathetic. Her small-boy husband is driven to filching cash from the household purse; with it, he goes off on a drinking bout or gambling session, and comes back sick and sorry to ask forgiveness and beg for an advance against next week's allowance. Sometimes she tongue-lashes him until he threatens to cash his pay check himself and spend the whole thing, and goes slamming out of the house to spend the evening walking the downtown streets. Sometimes there is a tearful reconciliation, with promises and kisses, and vows and understandings. In either case, he and she wind up exhausted, sad, and one step nearer to gray disillusion.

Yet in many an American household, the wife is the chancellor of the exchequer, and everybody is happy. There is no single "right" way to handle the money within a family. In one, the man may earn and handle it entirely, giving his wife nothing but her own personal spending money. If she likes that arrangement, well and good. In another, the man may give his wife a personal, plus a household, allowance and let her pay the food and daily bills. If they both find that a comfortable pattern, so much the better. In a third, a man may simply bank his money to a joint account, from which both he and his wife draw as needed, or from which she pays all bills and hands out all cash. And if that pleases both, it is good likewise.

"It even suits some people," says Mrs. Frances L. Beatman, associate executive director of the Jewish Family Service of New York, "to get too small an allowance, run out of money once a week, and come asking for more. If both partners enjoy that, that's fine too."

None of this implies that well-adjusted husbands and wives have no disagreements about money. They do, just as they disagree from time to time about the children, the need for new furniture, or the wisdom of changing jobs. To handle money well takes technique, and most people need years to acquire it. But, in a happy and healthy home, the debates about money, even though they be heated, end in agreement and cooperation.

For the others — that very large segment of our married people who fight fiercely about money and to whom money management and budgeting are a constant torment — the picture is quite different. No amount of technique, no timely pay raise or promotion, no lucky inheritance, would erase their problems. For them, the money quarrels are a way to express their resentments, their dislikes, their desires to dominate and punish and hurt. Only a better understanding of themselves, and a genuine adjustment of their relationships to each other, will truly solve the fighting about money. But such an adjustment and such understanding will do a great deal more: they will turn the marriage from a painful and wearisome burden to a joyous fulfillment and a real reason for living.

Why Husbands Are—or Are Not—Faithful

A LARGE NUMBER of American husbands commit marital infidelities. This fact, underlined by studies in recent years, has made many people, particularly young wives, very uneasy.

Many experts have gone on to study the reasons for this infidelity. Why, they have asked, should so many men at some period in their married lives feel the need for extramarital relations? Their answers not only help explain why some men are unfaithful, but provide a basis for understanding the husband who is faithful to his wife and the kind of marriage relationship that helps him remain faithful.

The easiest way to explain sexual promiscuity is simply to attribute it to the natural biological inclination of the male animal. "The human male," concluded Dr. Alfred Kinsey, after studying thousands of men, "would be promiscuous in his choice of sexual partners throughout the whole of his life if there were no social restrictions." Psychologists have often pointed out that men are far more easily aroused than women, and by a far greater variety of stimuli. Major surveys of marriage have shown that most men desire intercourse more often than their wives, are refused more often, and think about extramarital intercourse more often. Not surprisingly, then, Dr. Kinsey found that about twice as many men as women are unfaithful.

In our society, morality and the law say that a man should limit himself sexually to one woman for life. Yet this precept runs counter to the experience of most of mankind throughout the ages. Only one-sixth of the societies on which anthropological data exist in the Yale Human Relations Area Files have tried to limit a man to a single mate, and few even of these have wholly disapproved of extramarital experience.

Some men have eased their own minds with the reflection that modern society is wrong in restricting their liberty. The great sex educator, Havelock Ellis, once wrote: "The sex act is of no more concern to the community than any other physiological act. It is an impertinence, if not an outrage, [for society] to seek to inquire into it."

Most unfaithful men are hardly so eloquent. Their reasoning tends to be less sophisticated and more personal, more an excuse than a statement of principle.

There is the man whose affairs are always the result of circumstances beyond his control. "I was in Detroit on a buying trip, and this girl and I happened to strike up a conversation in the restaurant. We had a few drinks, talked about a million things, and something just clicked. I couldn't stop it. It was like being on a toboggan."

There's the man who is torn between his wife and his mistress and can't make up his mind. "How can I explain it? Do you believe a person can love two women at the same time? Well, I can, and it's killing me. I can't give up either one."

There's the man who thinks of himself as a boiler, always about to explode. "When Mary is pregnant or sick, I just can't stand it. I have to have an outlet, and I head for the nearest bar to find some woman. But it's only a physical act; it doesn't change my feelings for Mary in the least."

And then, of course, there is the man who feels misunderstood. "I'm not going to break up our home, because I've got to think of the kids. But when a man finds he's married the wrong woman, he has to find love outside, or his soul just shrivels up."

In the opinion of most family experts, marriage counselors and psychiatrists who have studied infidelity, such explanations are generally self-deceptive. They are the rationalizations men create for themselves to conceal deeper urges which wear less pleasant colors. Granted that occasionally a faithful man may slip, when a series of circumstances catches him off guard; granted that an unhappy marriage can leave a man looking for love; granted that a man whose relations with his wife are unsatisfying may be tormented and frustrated to the point of seeking extramarital affairs; still such factors explain only a small part of infidelity in our time.

For infidelity, most marriage specialists agree, is generally a symptom of some kind of emotional disorder.

A man who has inferiority feelings may be unfaithful because he needs reassurance from many sources that he is attractive. But, being neurotic, he never stays reassured for long. He may fool himself by thinking his affairs are toboggan slides of passion down which he hurtles helplessly, but he himself climbs onto the toboggan, deliberately, every time, hoping for something to happen.

A man who harbors deep resentment against his wife may find a long-term outside affair satisfying because it is a way of punishing her — by cheating her, mocking her and giving part or all of his love to someone else. Not choosing between his wife and his mistress may be a further refinement of the torture, for he can thus keep his wife alternating between reconciliation and estrangement for years.

A man who is sexually inadequate may commit repeated infidelities in an attempt to convince himself that he is an extraordinarily passionate fellow and that it is actually his wife who is frigid. Many people still think of the Don Juan type as a supermale with superpowers, or as a romantic figure, tragically unable to find the perfect woman. On the psychoanalyst's couch, however, many a modern Don Juan has admitted that he is often impotent and that he more frequently arouses the motherly instinct in his women than wild passion.

The man who regards himself as a high pressure steam boiler is usually full of hot air.

Finally, a husband who is unfaithful to his wife because "she doesn't understand me" is, all too often, blaming her for his own shortcomings. He is "projecting," as the psychiatrists say, his own faults onto her. He does not love her unstintingly; he is insensitive to her needs and moods. And since he himself has never learned to *give*, he still thinks love consists of *taking*, wherever and whenever he can.

There is one underlying cause of all these types of infidelity — emotional immaturity. As a male child grows up, he must overcome a number of normal predictable crises in his emotional development. First, his capacity to love and to rise above pure infantile selfishness can grow only with loving relationships at home. Next, he faces the classic conflict of wanting all his mother's love, yet trying simultaneously to love his greatest rival, his father. He must synthesize these emotions and master his jealousy. Finally, since any infantile sexual interest in his mother is strictly ruled out, he separates sex and affection in his mind; then, in his adolescent years, he must try once again to weld them into the feeling we know as heterosexual love.

In any of these crises, if his mother is niggardly with her affection, if his parents are harsh, cold, or inconsistent toward each other, the child may be baffled, hurt and stunted in his growth toward emotional maturity. The capacity to love a woman in a positive way is lost; instead, love remains a childish emotion — demanding, selfish, insecure. Such men are still trying to obtain love from women, yet are never sure it is sincere; they, therefore, tend to search and to philander — shallowly, greedily, even cruelly.

At the famed Menninger Clinic in Topeka, Dr. Karl Menninger has found that the married man who carries on an outside affair is often one who never completely loves either woman, or any woman, because he fears, mistrusts, and even hates them — although he probably recognizes none of these things.

It would be extreme to say that all unfaithful men are neurotic, especially since the bulk of them, according to Kinsey's data, commit only one or a few random infidelities during a lifetime. But it does seem that those who are *regularly* or *frequently* unfaithful are very likely to be the immature, the self-centered, and the maladjusted.

Yet how can infidelity indicate emotional maladjustment if it has been so widely accepted throughout the history of mankind? This is a fair question, but the psychiatrists and marriage counselors are not speaking of mental health or sound marriage for first-century Romans, medieval courtiers, or Trobriand Islanders of fifty years ago. Their concepts apply to our own time and culture. Within that framework, a man must be abnormal to do certain things that were once normal.

What can the study of unfaithfulness tell us about the faithful husband? Why — in the context of our time and our country — do 50 per cent of American men remain faithful?

The most easily observed factor making for fidelity is social pressure and public opinion. But although Dr. Kinsey thought this was the *only* restraining force, most psychologists give it far less importance. The fear of hanging did not keep men from stealing; in sixteenth-century England, even while a pickpocket was being hanged as an example, his fellow pickpockets would be working diligently in the crowd.

So, too, with marital fidelity. By far the strongest guide is an inner one, a self-originated desire for control. Psychoanalyst Dr. Jean Munzer of the Institute of Group Psychotherapy in New York guesses that outside pressures are perhaps 20 per cent of what restrains men from infidelity; the other 80 per cent comes from inside.

A second and equally obvious factor would seem to be sexual satisfaction. An adequate outlet within the marriage is often thought to be the best insurance against infidelity. Marriage is popular, George Bernard Shaw once wrote, "because it combines the maximum of temptation with the maximum of opportunity." But this, too, is an easily overvalued answer. According to all the biological evidence, men are not innately more passionate than women in the first place; it is only custom and upbringing that make them think they are. And their belief that they do not have enough sex activity may often be more a mental assertion of manhood than any strongly felt need. Even among the happiest couples surveyed by psychologist Lewis Terman, in his famous study of more than 700 marriages, men generally wished for more intercourse with their wives — yet this did not seem to prompt them to do anything about it.

Even more to the point, most unfaithful husbands said that they *did* have fairly adequate sex relations with their wives. It appears, then, that although a very poor sexual relationship may drive some men outside of marriage for satisfaction, most unfaithful men are not really suffering from deprivation.

If the psychiatric point of view is correct, they are suffering from a lack of fusion between sex and love. Only within the past few decades has any large number of men and women begun to join the two; our era is seeing the emergence of a new pattern of marriage. It is a democratic, equalitarian joining together of two people of equal status, bound by love and common interest, rather than the purchase of a sort of indentured female servant and child bearer, chained to her master by total economic dependence.

In the new relationship, sex is no longer the prerogative of men, to be visited upon unresisting women when and as desired. It is, instead, enmeshed in the entire love relationship that involves affection, companionship, sharing and lifelong comradeship. And when sex is completely entangled with love, it cannot be practiced in a pure physical form out-side of marriage without disturbing the personality of the unfaithful partner and his relationship with his wife.

For modern marriage, as Clifford Kirkpatrick, Indiana University sociologist, puts it, is a "whole personality interaction" between a man and a woman. To each, the other becomes a part of his or her own per-sonality; each "owns" the other — not physically, but in the most inti-mate psychological sense. Harry Stack Sullivan, exponent of the inter-personal theory of psychiatry, said once, "When the satisfaction or the security of another person becomes as significant as one's own satisfaction or security, then the state of love exists."

If marriage involves love of this kind, the basic force that makes a man faithful becomes clear; his wife is the dearest part of himself, and he cannot endure to hurt that part, or to separate any segment of his being from it. Unshared experiences, secret affairs, emotions or moods that he must keep locked away all seem dangerous and even detestable because they mar the deeply satisfying identity that exists between his wife and himself.

"Anything less than fidelity," says Dr. Abraham Franzblau, "chips away at the security which both partners ardently desire and which is the necessary foundation for what they are striving to build." Dr. Abra-ham Stone says that, in his twenty-five years of marriage counseling, he has almost always found infidelity to be a disrupting force, even though carefully concealed from one's mate, for the guilt, fear of detection and need for excuses drive a wall between man and wife. One woman, talk-ing to a psychologist about her own infidelity, put it more intensely. "He still doesn't know what I did," she wept, "but it has destroyed what we used to have — a oneness of purpose."

Fidelity, therefore, really comes from a mature capacity to love com-pletely. Marriage clinics have files bulging with case records of unfaith-ful and promiscuous men who could not fulfill their need for sex and affection in one woman, but who, after consultations or psychotherapy, were able to do just this. What happened to them in therapy was, in effect, an accelerated growing-up process. Infidelity is a symptom which disappears as the disease of immaturity is cured.

Yet emotional maturity and a happy marriage are not sure guards against infidelity. Even the happiest of husbands is often surprised by his own uneasy feelings of desire for some inviting or beautiful woman he meets. The Terman survey showed that even the most happily married man occasionally desires extramarital relations. Is it inevitable that men must have such thoughts? Does it mean they are innately promiscuous?

In a sense, yes. But there is no need for alarm.

As a baby, a little boy wants to grab and keep everything he sees. He wants to play with messy and dirty objects without restraint. He wants to hit anyone who hinders or annoys him. But he soon learns to curb and disguise those feelings. The grown man may lust for the new custom-styled imported car, but he restrains himself because there are other things that will yield him a better balance of happiness. He may want to punch the fellow who has just jostled him, or crack his boss over the head with a paperweight, but he knows that such actions would frustrate his other and more important desires.

So, too, with his sexual instincts. Unbidden feelings are stirred up in him by a pretty face, a good figure or a mood-filled situation, and he begins to weave fantasies of conquest. But his inner voice — not blue-nosed and nagging, but fatherlike and kindly — reminds him that society would condemn him, that his children would suffer shame, that, above all, the precious union of personalities between him and his wife would be damaged and perhaps destroyed.

But if such considerations and feelings keep him faithful, they do not keep the yearnings from arising. Those are as much a part of his heritage from his four-legged ancestors as the hair on his chest. Indeed, some experts believe this urge to be so fundamental that they recommend allowing it some acceptable harmless outlet, rather than striving to repress it completely.

The childish impulse to grab and keep, for instance, is transmuted into the adult pattern of hard work, saving and investing. If a man still harbors a desire to be dirty and messy, he fulfills it by going off on a fishing trip with "the boys." If he has a lot of unpunched faces bothering him, he lets off steam by hunting or shouting himself hoarse at a boxing match.

And for his ancient ineradicable impulse towards sexual activity with any desirable partner he sees, he can, say some experts, substitute mild, socially accepted forms of flirtation — not the tense searching of the man consciously tracking down a woman at a cocktail party, but the healthy, frank appreciation by a civilized man of the attractiveness of the various women he meets. The intelligent wife does not scold her husband for his wandering eye or his playful gallantry. She tolerates it — in fact, she even prizes it, knowing it to be the controlled conduct of a well-matured male animal.

"Moral people," says Sylvanus M. Duvall, professor of social science and religion at George Williams College in Chicago, "will be unashamedly lusty and feel no sense of shame at sexual interest in those other than a marriage partner. They will refrain from sexual relationships outside of marriage for the same reason that they will refrain from smoking near a gasoline tank which is being filled. The dangers of disaster are too great."

Dr. Goodwin Watson, clinical psychologist of the Institute of Group Psychotherapy, adds, "Flirtation is a kind of acceptable substitute that many people can allow themselves. Generally it is harmless, and it can be helpful to the egos of all concerned." Instead of the effort totally to repress the thoughts that often arise — which, say some experts, only heightens desire and produces feelings of guilt — a purely social, good-natured kind of flirtation may make the faithful husband feel attractive and manly in the eyes of other women. It may also stimulate him to practice again with his own wife some of the delightful nonsense of courtship which he has almost forgotten.

And so even within faithful men there exists the daydream of sexual freedom. But to the man who is able to love bountifully, generously and in complete absorption with his beloved, that old primal instinct is no great danger and his fidelity is no deprivation. It is, simply, the sincerest tribute of his love.

How Husbands Really Feel About Pregnancy

ONE OF THE oldest jokes in the world is the one inflicted by maternity nurses and obstetricians on practically every young man in a hospital waiting room. "Now don't you worry," they tell him, "we've never lost a father yet!"

Everyone seems to regard the expectant father as a somewhat comic figure whose feelings are not to be taken seriously. Innumerable movies, television shows and stories repeat the stereotype: the childless American man is supposed to be ignorant of his wife's condition until she breaks the sweet news; at that point he leaps up, overjoyed, implores her to sit down, and stuffs a pillow behind her back. He is happy, fond and foolish, but never, absolutely *never,* dismayed or unenthusiastic.

The truth — known to sociologists, psychiatrists and social workers — is far different. Three separate surveys made by different teams of sociologists have shown that *before the birth of the first child, between one-quarter and one-third of all husbands are genuinely and deeply frightened at the thought of their wives' undergoing pregnancy and labor.*

Recently a team of doctors, social workers and other specialists, making a five-year study in a clinic of the Boston Lying-In Hospital under the auspices of the Harvard School of Public Health, found that only 40 per cent of first-time fathers were genuinely delighted by their wives' pregnancies. Another 20 per cent were at best resigned to it, and the remaining 40 per cent were distinctly unhappy or distressed. Most of the unenthusiastic fathers thought they felt that way because of the timing, but in interviews they revealed deep-seated worries about the effect of the coming child on marital adjustment and personal happiness.

At Mitchel Air Force Base on Long Island several years ago, medical officer Captain James Curtis studied a number of expectant fathers, some of whom were neurotic or immature and some of whom were normal. Most of the neurotic men reacted severely to the pregnancies of their wives, but even among the 24 normal men there was a curious outbreak of symptoms. Nine men showed up on sick call more often than usual, 11 suffered stomach and intestinal troubles, 3 began having headaches and dizzy spells, 5 took to alcohol or had a series of minor accidents. Only 7 of the 24 had none of these symptoms.

Other studies uncover the same well-kept secret — that some men actively resent or fear impending fatherhood, and that most men, however delighted or affirmative they seem, have a dark vein of doubt running through their happiness.

Many wives are hardly aware of their husbands' feelings. For that matter, the husbands themselves often fail to recognize the cause of their discomfort. Most of the normal men in the Air Force study, for instance, failed to connect their symptoms or their odd conduct with the situation at home; and many men deny having any but happy and positive emotions, despite the presence of clinical symptoms.

Dr. John Parks, of the obstetrical department of the George Washington University School of Medicine, says flatly that "psychoanalytic and hypnotic investigations have proved that many patients consciously express one attitude toward pregnancy while unconsciously they maintain an entirely different feeling."

Just what are the uncomfortable — and sometimes devastating — feelings so many men secretly have?

Most expectant fathers are openly concerned with a number of immediate, practical problems. When a pregnancy occurs, nearly all couples face the need to rearrange their living space or even to move. In an era when space is at a premium, a young couple can worry for weeks or months over the question of whether to seek another, more expensive place, expand the sleeping space in their present home or keep the baby in their own bedroom the first year.

When the wife begins to accumulate baby things, the prospective father's pleasure in seeing them is compounded with alarm at the cost. His alarm deepens when he finds out that the simple process of getting a baby born costs several hundred dollars. All these expenses come at the very time when the family income is reduced by the wife's retirement from her job. It dawns upon the father-to-be that the baby will be a luxury, displacing many other luxuries in his life. The average modern parent is out of pocket some $20,000 by the time his child is eighteen.

For many a father-to-be the baby may suddenly seem like an obstacle to his career. More than ever, American men are marrying before finishing their education and training, and the coming child often is thought of as a double handicap: interference with study and a block to attainment of a higher status in life.

Other practical problems may be less weighty but more immediately depressing. The day starts off discouragingly for a man whose wife has morning sickness, particularly if he himself cleans up the basin, then tries to make his own breakfast, and dashes off in the midst of it to get to work on time.

Many men, furthermore, find the entire discussion of the baby's delivery worrisome and fear-producing. Such words as "labor pains," "lacerations," "dilation," "rupture of the bag," still retain their old frightening connotations. The young husband who has prized his wife's body as an object of love may feel guilty at the prospect such words seem to imply. And indeed it is true that until recent years childbirth often did leave the birth canal lacerated and enlarged, with the result that for some women sexual relations after childbirth were unsatisfying. Though this outcome can be avoided, thanks to modern medicine, the fear of it still lives on.

The fetus itself is a source of concern to many fathers. The Reverend William H. Genné, formerly teacher-counselor at the Clara Elizabeth Fund for Maternal Health, in Flint, Michigan, says that in the parent-training classes given separately for fathers and mothers, the fathers-to-be expressed considerably more fear about possible abnormalities in the child than did the mothers-to-be.

For all these reasons the physical details of the birth process may come as something of a shock, particularly to a city-bred man who has never seen the birth of a calf or a puppy. In a parent-training class at a major New York hospital a few weeks ago, an obstetrician lectured to a group of fathers on the labor and delivery process, using colored slides and cutaway models. In the middle of the lecture a young man, looking gray and shiny of face, tiptoed out into the hallway; there he promptly fainted.

Most of the physical and economic worries, however, are entirely normal and can be eased without much effort. The Reverend Mr. Genné, now executive director of the Family Life Department of the National Council of Churches, says that the Flint classes relieved many of the serious concerns of expectant fathers remarkably fast; educators at hospitals and in other organizations have had the same experience. When a young man learns the medical facts, some of his fears are eased; when he learns about the many space-saving and money-saving techniques, he begins to think that some of his own pressing problems can be solved; and when he hears other men expressing some of his own doubts, he feels reassured that his troubles are entirely within the normal range.

A more important — but less easily discussed — group of worries stems from changing personal relationships. Mrs. Florence Cyr, research social worker on the study made by the Harvard School of Public Health, reported that among the husbands interviewed, emotional and personal problems outnumbered the practical problems at least two to one.

Some men were worried about their own adequacy for the new role. "I keep wondering," said a young insurance salesman, "if I'm really ready to be a father. Some days it just sweeps over me — the thought that I'm about to be really tied down for life, before I've done half the foolish, wonderful things I meant to do." Others, however, were apprehensive on behalf of their wives, and would hesitantly make remarks like: "I'm just not sure that my wife's mature enough yet to make a really good mother, or that she's ready to enjoy tackling it."

Others were worried about future in-law problems. "It took me a year to pry my wife loose from her family," said an earnest-looking draftsman. "Finally we became man and wife, two private people together. Now she's beginning to run off to spend the day with her mother, or having her come over here. I can just see how it's going to be when the baby's here."

These and similar worries also yield in considerable part to reassurance and information. But the deepest, most painful problems are the very ones most often avoided in conversation and discussion.

Professor Gerald Caplan, a Harvard School of Public Health psychiatrist who was a member of the team working at the Boston Lying-In

Hospital, says that the most significant disturbances of the expectant father arise because the unborn child interferes in the relationship between husband and wife. The expectant mother is sometimes touchy and moody and ready to burst into tears or snap at her husband rather than try to please him. At other times she is dreamy and contemplative, with an abstracted, inward-gazing look on her face where her husband used to see interest in himself and his needs. She frequently has other women visit her, and he feels something clanlike about their mood and their chatter of babies and baby things.

Month by month, as she moves toward motherhood, he is progressively displaced as lover. He may even find it hard to think of his wife as a sexually desirable person — not so much because of the changes in her body as because making love to a mother-to-be makes him feel uneasy and even guilty. Yet though his sexual appetite decreases all during her pregnancy, hers decreases more and faster. He hardly dares even speak to her about it, for fear of seeming selfish.

Several years ago, two young sociologists named Thomas and Shirley Poffenberger investigated the effect of pregnancy on sexual adjustment among 212 married couples at Michigan State College. One husband out of every four reported that pregnancy had had an unfavorable effect on sexual adjustment.

Fifty-eight per cent of the husbands thought there had been no effect, but when the Poffenbergers asked them why they eventually stopped having intercourse during pregnancy, their answers revealed a variety of reactions. Twenty-nine per cent of the husbands said they stopped for fear of hurting the baby and another 18 per cent said they stopped because it caused the wife pain; medically speaking, however, there is not very much justification for either answer. Ten per cent said they stopped because "it didn't seem right" or because they no longer enjoyed it, and an additional 10 per cent because their wives no longer enjoyed it.

Sexual difficulties are only one form (though very likely the most obvious) in which the husband senses the over-all change in his wife's relationship to him. Prior to her first pregnancy he has had her all to himself in her several roles — as his lover, his homemaker and his companion. Pregnancy cuts into all three.

In classes for expectant fathers given by many hospitals and by Red

Cross chapters in a number of cities, men often say things that reveal their concern about the changing relationship. "Why does she blow up at me?" is a frequently asked question. "Is she always going to be so wrapped up in herself?" is another. A nurse who does parent-training at a major Eastern hospital says that when a man asks, "How soon can my wife go out after the baby arrives?" he may really mean "— go out with me?" Another asks, "When she's nursing, can she leave the baby alone for a few hours at a time?" but may mean "— to pay some attention to me?" A third says, "She seems so different now — sometimes I don't seem to understand her moods at all," but in his eyes is the unasked question: "Will it ever be the same again with us as it used to be?"

And sometimes that sense of rivalry breaks through all barriers and comes out in words as plain as those of a jealous child. At a large Eastern hospital, during a fathers' discussion of breast feeding versus bottle feeding, one man suddenly burst out, "As far as I'm concerned, my wife's breasts belong to me, not the baby!" Another man told Dr. Caplan, of Harvard, that he disliked seeing and feeling the movements of the fetus within his wife's body, and ended by making a painfully honest little joke: "To tell you the truth, Doc," he said, "he's practically beginning to kick me out of bed at night."

Reactions of this sort, or physical and mental symptoms such as those mentioned earlier, occur in only a small per cent of fathers-to-be, but the mechanisms that cause them are also at work in most other expectant fathers. The difference is that the better-adjusted man channels his feelings into loving and constructive actions. He becomes more protective of his wife and does the heavier chores; he takes out a new insurance program; he personally paints the baby's room and assembles the crib; he begins to read infant-care books, and fondly imagines himself in the many situations where he expects to be the good pal, kindly teacher and voice of conscience to his children.

Wives may think that expectant fathers find loving emotions toward the baby welling up in them simply and spontaneously. But as anthropologist Weston La Barre, of Duke University, points out in his book *The Human Animal,* "The anatomy of paternal love is missing. . . . The human male has no instincts, no anatomy, and no physiology to teach him to love the child as such." A woman may or may not be delighted at finding herself pregnant, but as the creation within her grows, she is gradually suffused with pride, wonder and love. How could she not love it? It is part of her own living, feeling body, an extension of her very self. The man has none of this built-in guidance. He learns to feel paternal love by analogy: he pieces together some of his own protective feelings toward younger brothers or sisters or childhood playmates, his memory of his parents' feelings toward him, and his present observation of his wife's developing emotions. But first he must master and use constructively his negative feelings — his jealousy, his resentment of his wife's new importance and his own relegation to a secondary position in her life.

Among primitive peoples it is easier to see men doing this emotional work. The most common form is a custom known as the couvade. Shortly before his wife's confinement the expectant father takes to his bed, avoids his usual work, and abstains from most foods. At times he even groans and thrashes around in mock labor pain, while relatives and friends hover around and commiserate with him. Anthropologists explain that this behavior is the result of the father's unconscious resentment of the attention his wife is getting and his childlike jealousy of the coming baby. These hidden and even unrecognized feelings cause guilt, which is relieved by self-inflicted punishment; additionally, the man gains public respect and attention for sympathetically suffering along with his wife. In this way his resentment is conquered and his childish jealousy is transformed into a crude expression of love.

Civilized people are more subtle and more complicated, but basic behavior is much the same. The two Poffenbergers, in their study of Michigan State couples, specifically concluded: "There is evidence in this study to indicate that in a way, many husbands of today practice a psychological couvade during the wife's first pregnancy." Whereas the primitive man identified himself with his wife by pretending to be in labor, many of the men in the Michigan State study did so by becoming more attentive, settled, and gentle toward their wives.

The modern man often finds ways to remain in the area of attention, but his ways are more constructive than those of the primitive man. A growing proportion of first-time fathers read books on maternity and on infant care with their wives, and visit the gynecologist with them at least once or twice. Twenty per cent of the first-time fathers whose wives register at a typical leading New York hospital attend a series of classes offered by the hospital, and possibly as many more go to classes given by outside agencies. Throughout the country, attendance at similar courses given by the Maternity Center Association, the Red Cross, and by other hospitals has been increasing steadily for some years.

It is also becoming popular (though only a minority do it) for husbands to go into the labor room with their wives and remain there to comfort and support them. The director of parent education at one leading Eastern hospital says no one can be so reassuring to a woman in labor as her husband, but attendance in the labor room may be a painful duty for him. "The man who stays with his wife through labor is practically in labor himself," she says. "He's in real distress, and gets thoroughly wrung out by it. Nevertheless, more and more fathers want to do it, and nearly all of them are thrilled and happy once they've seen it through, or stuck with it most of the way. We're even beginning to get requests from some of them to be allowed into the delivery room to watch the actual birth."

Investigation suggests that the negative feelings about pregnancy secretly felt by a large proportion of first-time fathers are not only overcome but creatively used by most of them. According to a study made by the Milbank Fund not long ago, the very husbands who dread childbirth most before the arrival of the first child eventually have more children, on the average, than other men.

Miss Hazel Corbin, director of the Maternity Center Association, says, "Practically all the expectant fathers, by the time they come to us for training, *want* to grow and *want* to become good parents. They genuinely want to move onward to an important new status in life and in their marriages." A similar conclusion emerges from Mrs. Cyr's report of the Harvard School of Public Health study: although 60 per cent of the men in that study were either unhappy about or merely resigned to the pregnancies of their wives, every husband developed sufficient positive feelings by the time of delivery to be delighted at the actual birth, and almost all the men took an active, helpful part in the care of the new infant in the weeks immediately following birth.

The evidence indicates that at the very time when the body of woman is teaching her to love the coming child, man is still the same old selfish animal and must learn, without the aid of biological machinery, to hide his jealousies, master his selfishness and transmute his negative feelings into warm, protective devotion. Fortunately, the evidence also shows most new fathers learn to do this quickly and exceedingly well.

What Is a Husband? What Is a Wife?

RIDING ON A BUS one day, I heard a four-year-old girl solemnly instructing her grandfather on the difference between husbands and wives: "Daddies have big muscles and make money, and mommies take care of everybody and smell good."

This little girl's definition of the sex roles in marriage, I had to acknowledge, was admirably neat and clear. Unfortunately, in today's complex world nothing is quite that simple, least of all the true nature of the role of each sex in modern marriage. As the little girl grows up, she will discover that almost all the neat and clear distinctions on this matter — distinctions that have held good for most of the past several thousand years — are becoming blurred or have already vanished. The more she learns on the subject, in fact, the less she will know — and, perhaps, the less cheerful she will be. For — and this is not surprising — many wives today are failing to find the roles of the husband and wife in marriage as sharply defined as they had expected, and many of them feel a vague, aching dissatisfaction with themselves and sometimes with their husbands. They wonder, either consciously or unconsciously, "Am I really as much of a 'woman' as I should be, or am I sacrificing some of my womanliness by encroaching in areas that are rightfully my husband's?"

A woman may ask herself, "Is my husband, in failing to shoulder responsibilities that are traditionally a man's, being less manly than he should be? Have I married less than a 'real' man?"

Each year countless wives, confused about femininity and masculinity, appeal to doctors, ministers, marriage counselors, and others for help and clarification. Others wind up in divorce courts, alleging such reasons as the law allows but actually driven there by inner misery resulting from the part they found themselves playing in marriage, or the part their partners seemed to be trying to force them to play.

By far the largest number seek neither the medicine of counseling nor the surgery of divorce, but live with and suffer from the continuing pain of their uncertainties, their dissatisfaction, and their yearning to be more clearly effective and sure as women, as wives — and as people. More democratic, intimate, and equalitarian than it has ever been, marriage today has all but erased, for many husbands and wives, the traditional outlines of manliness and womanliness.

All this is quite a recent development. During most of Western history, the roles of husband and wife and the meanings of masculinity and femininity were clearly and firmly established in the pattern known as "patriarchalism." However unfair this may have been, one thing it did *not* cause women was confusion. The husband was the dominant partner.

In the past few generations, an immense change has taken place, with men and women becoming more nearly equal. If the fact that things are changing in their relationship could be easily accepted by husbands and wives, there would be less friction between them. Yet men, even more than women, are uneasy and defensive about the changing sex roles. Understanding this — and acting accordingly — can help a woman achieve a greater degree of tranquillity in her marriage. In this regard, a leading Boston marriage counselor tells about a patient of his — a professor of English literature who remained a bachelor until he was thirty-two, then married a pretty, shy young undergraduate. Though she had been timid and demure when he dated her, she began to flourish and to show her real abilities shortly after marriage. Half a year after moving into his bachelor apartment, she proceeded to redecorate it; later she found his checkbook in a mess, took over, and straightened out their financial affairs. She learned enough about university politics in a year or so to begin socially maneuvering for his promotion, and she even began to offer him pointed but excellent criticisms of his lectures. Then he began to drink heavily and quarrel over a hundred trifles; soon he lost almost all sexual interest in her.

As the marriage counselor explains the case, successful invasion by the professor's wife of what he had thought were manly and superior functions made the professor doubt his inherent manliness. Both the professor and his wife are now struggling, in counseling sessions, to re-define masculinity in a way they can live with; meanwhile his wife is trying not to undermine his belief in himself, and his symptoms are improving.

What happened to this young couple is happening to many couples over the nation, and the difficulty is almost always traceable to the in-ability of either one or both partners to recognize the simple basic truth: *because the social role of the partners does not seem to correspond with the old-time conceptions of what a man or a woman should be does not make either the man less manly or the woman less womanly in a bio-logical sense.* Nor, conversely, should the social roles of men and women necessarily be determined by biological relationships. There are very few things that must be the private province either of women or of men, as the comparatively recent advance of women into many fields formerly dominated by men has proved.

According to one school of thought, the reason many couples fail to differentiate between their biological and social roles, and to understand that one does not necessarily determine the other, can be traced in part to Sigmund Freud. The founder of psychoanalysis believed that woman's personality is inevitably shaped by her physical nature. According to Freud, every little girl sooner or later discovers that physically she is not like boys; and this, according to Freudian theories, supposedly makes her feel inferior or defective; she therefore becomes passive, dependent, weak, vain about her looks — by way of compensation for her "lack" — and willing to be dominated. Her role in life is neatly symbolized by her part in the sex act — in Freud's view, submissive, subordinate, and comfort-giving. Similar thinking is found even in contemporary writing. Dr. Helene Deutsch's two-volume *Psychology of Women* is built on the premise that normal women are inescapably passive and masochistic because they feel themselves defectively made, and because they cannot help viewing sex as submission.

In recent years students of human behavior have come to take sharp issue with such theories as these. Freud's theory of the female person-ality has been seriously questioned. Some psychologists have begun to suspect that a little girl's discovery of her "lack" is not necessarily as severe a blow to her ego as Freud had thought. The theory is that what Freud had seen in his female patients was possibly not an inevitable inferiority complex, but rather an effect of the Victorianism and prudery of his own time — a socially "learned" response which could be changed. This has been strikingly confirmed by the investigations of anthropologists like Margaret Mead, who showed that in many other societies women do not act in the least as Freud thought they all had to act. In various times and places, women have run the gamut from slavery to equality, from submissiveness to aggressiveness, from typically "feminine" interests to full participation in worldly activities.

Most of the confusion over the roles of each sex in modern marriage — and the resulting marital troubles — can be charged to the fact that these roles are very much in a state of change. This creates an ever-widening gap between the older conceptions of what roles a husband and wife are *supposed* to play and the roles they actually *are* playing in today's family and today's world. The wider this gap, the greater the confusion and the greater the conflict between the sexes.

This situation is pointed up by Dr. Elliot H. Drisko, Executive Director of the Family Service Society of Yonkers, New York. He says: "Our family life today, which is rapidly changing to suit modern needs, is still full of carry-over from the time of George Washington — or, for that matter, from the time of Christ, or Plato. Many of the problems we see in family service work — the struggles over career or money or control of the children, the domineering wives and the weak husbands, the suffering wives and the brutal husbands — are in considerable part the results of the confusion people feel because of the clash between their leftover concepts and realities of modern life."

This transition in the nature of the sex roles is far from complete, and in the normal give-and-take of married life it may seem that it will never be completed, but we can take comfort from the fact that although there are many harsh critics of the way things are developing, four out of five of the people who know most about what is going on in family relations — the sociologists and social psychologists who study marriage scientifically — find the changes generally beneficial and the emerging pattern better suited to modern life than the old one.

In past generations, for instance, a husband did not *need* so much from his wife, and therefore did not have to give so much back to her. For close friendship he turned to other men; he sought physical love with a mistress; but from his wife he wanted and demanded chiefly obedient service and housekeeping. All that has been overturned by industrialism and modern democracy. For most men today there is no close little fellowship of warriors or aristocrats to provide him with friendship, and a wife need not put up with infidelity; obtaining obedient service by comands and beatings has become impossible in a society which gives his wife equal legal rights.

Thus, as a wife you necessarily become to your husband all the things other people used to be to husbands of the past. At various times you may be his pal, his lover, his mother-substitute, his admirer and flatterer, his truest adviser, his playmate, his nurse, his friend. And likewise you need him to be all things to you: your pal, lover, father-substitute, admirer and flatterer, adviser, playmate, protector, and friend.

As marriage partners, you and your husband require all these qualities of each other, though not all at the same moment; but this multiplicity of roles — the very strength and glory of modern marriage — could not exist in the iron framework of the traditional patriarchal conception of marriage in which the man was the undisputed boss. The man or woman who tries to play the time-hallowed role, and that alone, is cheating himself or herself — and his or her mate — of many of the functions of modern marriage and may be endangering the foundation of the marriage itself.

Modern marriage involves not only many roles but great flexibility, allowing the partners to act and react differently in regard to each other at times of different need. One day your husband may unconsciously want to be pampered and treated as ruler; another day he may want you to be a sparkling, witty companion. One day you may need to be comforted and petted; another day you may enjoy caring for him as though he were a child.

The multiplicity of social roles and the freedom to vary them day by day has its biological parallel. The traditionalist views the sex act as necessarily involving active domination by the male and passive submission by the female. But almost all leading marriage counselors say that the modern husband and wife are capable of a wide range of sexual expression, paralleling or symbolizing at each point the varied roles they play for each other. It is not unusual for a wife to have a feeling of guilt when, although usually interested in satisfying her husband, she may, at times, play the selfish part and be intent on her own pleasure. Yet this guilt need not be. Love-making need not be a chore or a duty, with one's relief or fulfillment invariably relegated to second place; in modern marriage either mate may be the artful and unselfish lover one night, and self-seeking and demanding the next — and the other may accept and love both aspects.

Making love or performing any of the other aspects of married life with such flexibility and variation is bound to be a more complicated and subtle thing than it once was. "The present family," says Professor Mirra Komarovsky of Barnard College, "is a more severe test of adequacy of personality than the patriarchal family of the past. But it has possibilities of finer harmony and more complete satisfaction of personal emotional needs."

As men and women have become better accustomed to these new patterns, they will cease worrying about whether they are being mistaken for each other, and the conflict between them will be reduced. Men will participate in household and family life without fearing for their manliness, and wives will be less worried that careers will "unsex" them.

Men will not feel their maleness endangered if they must make love, in general, with due regard for their wives' satisfaction; but if, occasionally, they play the old-fashioned kind of male, their wives will not feel wronged or cheated. Women, indeed, will feel all the more female when they stop competing with the male and trying to match him in his experiences, when they are willing to enjoy their own kinds of experience in their own ways — ways men cannot ever quite know or understand.

IV

Some Major Emotional and Mental Problems

VI

Some Major
Emotional and
Mental Problems

Fears and Guilt Feelings

I have retained the original title of this article, although the article cannot and does not supply a simple, categorical answer — for herein is, perhaps, the most important thing to be learned from it. The human being is a marvelously complex creature, but he is forever seeking simple answers to the riddle of his own feelings. All too often, popular writing on psychological matters tries to give him the kind of answers he wants, though they are neither true nor good for him. Concerning the telling or suppression of one's fears, the honest answer is irritatingly complex: some fears, if told, spread contagion without relieving the one who tells them, while the telling of others does no harm to anyone else and yet prevents serious psychological damage to the one who unburdens himself. To know which fears to tell, when to tell them, and to whom to tell them is a complicated formula for mental health in this area; but I remind the reader of the wise words of Ovid, "Nothing worth while is without difficulty."

Should You Keep Your Fears a Secret?

IT IS a winter afternoon and I am sitting at my desk, intent on some work; faintly, from another room, I hear my wife teaching a song from *The King and I* to our five-year-old son. I stop working and smile at the sound of his piping treble repeating the song after her:

Whenever I feel afraid, I hold my head erect,
And whistle a happy tune, so no one will suspect
I'm afraid.

A charming and a wonderful song for a small boy to learn; a song to swell out his thin little chest and square his narrow shoulders. From the other room I hear his voice, high and bright and confident:

Make believe you're brave, and the trick will take you far,
You may be as brave as you make believe you are.

Without leaving my desk, I hear him strutting around the other room, probably looking absurdly manly, and fond, foolish tears suddenly well into my eyes.

But are the words of the song really valid? Is it such good advice to urge one to keep his fears secret and locked away inside himself? The temper of our times runs the other way; we tend to think, nowadays, that every inner torment needs to be ventilated and discussed with others — friends, ministers, spouses, therapists.

Yet this is the kind of oversimplification that does us harm. For in many circumstances, the very blurting out of fears robs us of the drive to find courage and to master our problems by ourselves. A friend of mine, faced with debts, a flare-up of his ulcer, and a wife on the point of a nervous breakdown, was grimly doing his job and carrying on, until his boss one day decided to sympathize with him, and urged my friend to tell him all about it. After an hour or so of pouring out all his dammed-up worries and fears, my friend was no longer the self-reliant fellow he'd been. For one thing, he came away tearful and filled with self-pity; for another thing, he had floated a loan from the boss and suddenly lost all his personal drive. For several months he hardly did any work, and on three different occasions cried again on the boss's shoulder and tried (in vain) to get further loans. Then, just in time, someone passed the word to him that he was about to be eased out; by a superhuman effort he pulled himself together, a mere week before he would have been fired, and got back into his normal pattern.

The same thing is actually happening on a massive scale everywhere; the spirit of our era tends to make us seek comfort and re-assurance for our troubles, and assume that we have an unquestionable right to lean upon others. Our Puritan and pioneering ancestors scorned to run to other people for comfort and reassurance; but we, living in the age of psychology, welfare agencies, compensation programs, and the like, believe that troubled persons should seek a friendly professional ear. We subscribe automatically to the idea that freedom from fear is as noble an ideal as freedom of speech, freedom of worship, and freedom from want, and therefore expect the government, the insurance companies, and our employers to take care of us from birth to death. We are not such people as dared to colonize this country, or to push off westward from St. Louis with all their possessions in a wagon. Ours is the era of social security, the paternalistic company (or union), the industrial psychologist, and the ready excuse for the lack of courage. Robert Louis Stevenson once said, "Keep your fears to yourself, but share your courage," but in our own day that sounds old-fashioned; instead, we applaud and reward those ex-celebrities who tell us, in maudlin books and television shows, all about the fears and insecurities that drove them to drink, drugs, and dissipation.

Stevenson may have been old-fashioned, but there *is* some contemporary scientific evidence to back up the viewpoint that courage can be shared, if fear is missing or kept hidden. In laboratories at Yale, psychologists have found that even rats that had been made fearful of a blinking light by shock-conditioning were less afraid of the light when a new, nonfearful rat was put among them, and similar experiments with cats at the University of Chicago had much the same result. During World War II, English children were known to survive bombings and even burial alive for days without much anxiety, as long as their mothers were with them and pretended to be calm and unworried.

History is full of evidence that men who have deliberately concealed their fears and shown courage have sustained their fellow men in times of trial. Pliny the Elder, during the eruption of Vesuvius that buried Pompeii, comforted his friends who were unable to escape by assuming an air of great cheefulness while dining with them and, when the house later began to shake dangerously, by lying down calmly on the beach to sleep, although stones were falling all about. Dr. Joseph Warren, strolling on the ramparts at Breed's Hill during the Battle of Bunker Hill like a gentleman out for his constitutional, did a great deal to keep the ragged Yankee rebels from bolting at the sight of the superior British forces preparing to storm the redoubt. Columbus, Washington, Lincoln were all men with misgivings and fears which they steeled themselves to conceal, and but for which concealment their men would have made a different and ignoble sort of history. Psychologist John Dollard of Yale interviewed three hundred combat infantrymen some years ago and found that practically all of them felt that in actual combat it helped them to see other men acting courageously; moreover, they even felt better when they themselves tried to set a good example of courage to the others.

Even in our private lives in peacetime, the show of courage can make the difference between life and death. The look of despair on the faces around a bedside may rob a critically ill person of the necessary will to live, and, via the autonomic nervous system, weaken his pulse and other functions just enough to kill him. A courageous look can have just the opposite effect. In *Portrait of a Family,* Eleanor Farjeon tells how Margaret Farjeon, the lovely young daughter of the great actor Joseph Jefferson, fell ill of an infection in her right lung. Outside her room, doctors met with her husband Ben, and told him she could not live. But Ben came into her room a few moments later looking so triumphant, and kept up so gay a barrage of smiles, laughter, and hummed tunes for weeks, that she never asked what they had said. She recovered, and lived another fifty years with one good lung. But a year after her illness, the specialist who had doomed her met her at a party, looked stunned, and said in awe, "Good God, Mrs. Farjeon, what are you doing here? You have no business to be alive at all!" She told him, and many others, that Ben had pulled her through. Even today, with all the improvements in modern medicine, many a doctor can tell similar stories.

Parents who betray their own fears to their children before the children are old enough to accept them can easily infect the youngsters with long-lasting anxieties. It is the overanxious mother who unwittingly makes her boy afraid of the water, the steep steps, or the rough-

and-tumble of the playground. Even tiny hints of fear can have a considerable effect. A correspondent writing in the *Christian Science Monitor* told not long ago how her own mother used to send her off to school each day with the warning, "Be careful!" This little repeated urging led the child to think of the journey to school as a dangerous trip, and of life in general as fraught with perils — a view it took her years to unlearn in adult life. Having unlearned it, she today hides her vague anxieties about her own son, and, as he leaves for school, calls out gaily not "Be careful!" but "Have fun!"

A celebrated opera singer I know was accompanied everywhere, for years, by her mother, who fussed endlessly about drafts and chills that might affect her daughter, kept a supply of herb tea and pills on hand, and protected her from all "dangers," including friends. The singer, not surprisingly, was a touchy, temperamental hypochondriac, and a kissless wonder. Then, by a lucky accident, she fell in love, got married, and left Mother behind; since then, over a number of years, she has slowly discovered that she is healthy as an ox, that she has a zestful appetite for living, and that people aren't her enemies. She is not only a far happier person nowadays, but a much better performer.

The disseminating of fear or frightening information is often justi-fied on the grounds that it leads to corrective action, but one can also argue, as does sociologist Robert K. Merton of Columbia University, that it sometimes produces the very thing it fears. Many of the bank runs of the Depression, for instance, were produced by the very people who talked too much about their fears of bank runs. And I person-ally wonder whether those high-minded organizations which constantly terrify us about the dangers of heart disease and cancer don't some-times negate their own purposes. My late father had heard so much about cancer that when he found himself suffering from certain in-testinal difficulties, he actually put off going to a doctor for fear of what he might learn; he could not allow himself to think of the possi-bility of finding out the worst. As a result, he let a critical half year go by before he did go in for examination; by then, it was too late. Had his level of induced fear been lower, he might be alive today. Nor is this just an unfounded supposition. In one recent experiment, psy-chologists gave different lectures to three groups of college students on the care of their teeth and the results of neglect. The group that got the most frightening lecture on the results of neglect nervously tried to pooh-pooh the whole thing, and in consequence followed the dental hygiene rules less faithfully than the groups that had heard milder, less frightening lectures.

Broadcasting fear may thus paralyze the listener, but sometimes it may even immobilize the broadcaster himself. Dr. Isidore Portnoy of the American Institute for Psychoanalysis characterizes courage as that response to threat in which the healthy organism musters its resources and takes suitable action. But talk is not always a real action; in many a situation, talking about one's fears only lets off steam for a short while, weakens the drive to do something about the problem, and leaves it unsolved. Every bartender can name a score of chronic complainers who tell him their fears and troubles, but never lift a finger to help themselves. Every doctor can cite a score of middle-aged female patients who visit him to complain and talk of their anxieties, but not to carry out his advice. Every minister can provide a roster of people who come in to whine and beg for sympathy, but who depart in a huff at the first suggestion that they take courageous action.

Yet all of this only means that there are some times and places when telling our fears either hurts us or hurts those to whom we tell them. It does not prove that keeping one's fears secret is *always* wise. Life is not so simple as to permit a piece of categorical advice to be good advice.

There *is* a fundamental reason for not always keeping our fears to ourselves and it lies in the basic chemistry of our bodies. Like the lower animals, we respond to threat or danger with a number of involuntary reactions — increased heartbeat, a shift of the blood to the large muscles of the body, the temporary shutdown of such organs as the kidneys, the release of cortical hormones into the blood stream, the increased discharge of stomach acids, and so on. Some of these reactions, which originated when we had four feet and lived in the jungle, were designed to help us fly from danger, or to do battle; others were not particularly useful, but merely were transitory by-products of the fight-or-flight preparations, and had no harmful results since the emergency lasted only a matter of minutes.*

* See also "The Wisdom of Tears," especially pages 17-18.

Civilized man often has reason to be grateful for these ancient mechanisms in his body. There is an old story of a boy who, pursued by a wild animal, leaped over a wall with inches to spare — and could never do so again until he was full grown. Anyone who has ever fought his way out of an overturned boat or wrecked car, or fled from a forest fire, knows the astonishing reserves of power he found within himself, but on which ordinarily he cannot draw.

But unlike the animals, man is most frequently threatened not by things from which he can run or with which he can immediately fight. For the most part, his fears come not from temporary threats, but from such enduring and unavoidable dangers as hard times, sickness, a nasty or sadistic boss, an enemy army, and so on. For these, the bodily mechanisms he inherited from the jungle animals are woefully inappropriate. "Man, feeling threatened," writes the renowned physiologist Dr. Harold Wolff, "may use for long-term purposes devices designed for short-term needs. . . . When so utilized, [they] may damage structures they were designed to protect." The ever-alarmed stomach gradually ulcerates due to excess acid; so does the colon; the overactive respiratory tract clogs up with allergies; the blood vessels and heart break down from overwork.

A friend of mine has been facing a critical fight with his partner for control of his shoe business for half a year; if the partner wins out, my friend may lose everything he owns. In a way, he has been living with fear as sharp as that of any antelope pursued by a lion — but this chase has gone on for six months. Three weeks ago, in a restaurant, he doubled over, fainted from pain, and was rushed to the hospital; there, doctors discovered that a quite unsuspected ulcer in his stomach had just broken through. They patched him up and put a lot of blood back in him, and now he is on vacation and mending — but if his business situation doesn't clear up, that patched-up stomach is sure to give way again.

Reliable observers and anthropologists have reported cases of voodoo deaths (deaths seemingly produced by witchcraft) in many primitive lands. The explanation of them is not, however, supernatural: a savage who genuinely believes in sorcery may be so panic-stricken when a curse is put on him that his body develops a chronic alarm reaction, and after a while his circulatory system and internal organs succumb to total exhaustion. We civilized men smile at the ignorant savages, but my friend the shoe manufacturer was hexed by his partner just as surely as if he wore a bone through his nose and believed in the malevolent power of incantations and effigies.

Since, however, civilized man cannot always run away or fight immediately with his foe, talking of his fears can be a real help. Dr. Jurgen Ruesch, professor of psychiatry at the University of California, says, "The process of talking, though not an act of great physical expenditure for the individual, will absorb the overflow of readiness [or] 'continuous alarm.'" For this fundamental reason, psychotherapy, counseling, religious confession, or even telling one's fears to a sympathetic listener, eases the pressure by getting rid of some of the unused readiness. The only problem here is to distinguish between talk as a legitimate safety valve for tension, and talk as a pure enjoyment in itself: as the priest asked the wicked old man, "Are you confessing these sins, or just bragging about them?"

A more important reason for talking about one's fears is that many of them, as Professor Dollard points out, are "shadow fears" based not on real threats but on imaginary ones, and originating in misconceptions or incorrect interpretations of the world around us. The fears of sexual enjoyment that make some men impotent and some women frigid are shadow fears; so are many people's fears of failure, of crowds, of childbirth, of foreigners, of germs, and so on. Such fears, resulting from misinformation or a lack of information, can be dissipated by an inflow of correct data. Sometimes this comes through direct experience (a child, afraid of the water, loses his fear after playing in the shallow part of the pool without harm), sometimes through educational programs (97 per cent of Professor Dollard's infantrymen felt that being given a real picture of the dangers of battle had helped them), and sometimes only through long and costly treatment (psychoanalysis, lasting years, is often the only way to unearth and replace the misinformation in the unconscious mind of a neurotic person).

The key factor in the process of repair is the *expressing* of fear by the fearful person. Dr. Ruesch, borrowing a term from communication theory, says that the conquest of unreasonable fears occurs in large part through "feedback" — the sending out of a signal, and the receiving of a response which either strengthens or weakens it. When a person with unreasonable shadow fears communicates them to a responsible outsider, the reply he gets fails to corroborate his fears; he receives instead a new piece of information, a new datum concerning reality, which enables him to begin the process of self-correction. Dr. Ruesch, in fact, says that mental illness can even be considered the failure to communicate and to obtain feedback — in short, the maintenance of erroneous ideas without any outside corrective.

It matters greatly, of course, to whom you transmit, for feedback can work both ways. A cry of fear by one person in a stalled subway car may produce a responding cry from others; the first person, restimulated, grows still more frantic and makes the others more so. The alarm level of the crowd thus rises, through feedback, to the point of panic and stampede. Precisely the opposite, however, happens when a frightened patient visits his doctor and is quietly given explanations, reassurances, and a treatment program for whatever is bothering him. Even a calm friend, listening to your fears and discussing them quietly, is in effect giving negative feedback — a reduction of the stimulus — that permits the lowering of the alarm level. Yet this beneficial process cannot take place unless there *is* communication from the fearful person to the outside; the child, for instance, is not apt to get over his fear of the dark unless he tells adults about it and so has a chance to learn that his fear is groundless.

Perhaps the most convincing proof of the value of talking about fears comes from the experience of our armed forces in World War II and in Korea. In Tunisia in 1943 a couple of Army psychiatrists inaugurated a new program of dealing with soldiers suffering from combat nerves. Instead of shipping them back to a rear hospital, where distance, delay, and comfort made the soldiers' fear of combat solidify and become permanent, the psychiatrists handled the men at a forward evacuation hospital. There, within hours of actual crack-up, they provided them with clean clothes, sedation, and an hour or two of talk with a psychiatrist. The men were encouraged to speak openly about their fears, free of any threat of disgrace or punishment. The resulting relief of tension, and the discovery that combat fear is normal and widespread, had a miraculous effect. Although only 5 per cent of the men sent to rear hospitals could ever return to their fighting units, half or more of those being given immediate front-line psychiatry were able to do so after four days.*

Even those soldiers who never become nervous casualties feel the same way. Professor Dollard's poll of combat veterans revealed that over four-fifths of the infantrymen he questioned felt that the discussion of fear is a good thing before a battle, and helps men avoid feelings of guilt; 70 per cent said that merely learning that other men were also afraid made them feel better and fight better. (As already pointed out, however, they felt that signs of fear should be hidden when the fight was actually on, and were strengthened by seeing other men act calmly.) It is, in a way, only proof of what Epictetus said nineteen centuries ago: "It is not death or hardship that is a fearful thing, but the fear of death or hardship."

All of this has direct implications for ordinary life. It is plain that prolonged exposure to severe fear may harm us physically; it is also clear that secrecy about our fears may deprive us of the chance to find out whether we are afraid of a mere shadow, or — if the fear is based on reality — to find out that fear itself is not wrong or sinful. Even though it is true that talking about our fears may sometimes weaken the drive to take action, at many other times it may be the safety valve that prevents our stomachs from being perforated or our psyches from collapsing into nervous breakdown.

For we cannot — despite President Roosevelt's brave words — soon or perhaps ever hope to know total freedom from fear. It is simply not in the nature of modern life to permit it. "No member of our generation who has a mature sense of reality and responsibility," says Bonaro Overstreet, "can experience a literal freedom from fear." That being so, our aim should be to minimize fears, when we can, by tackling the problems that cause them rather than by complaining; and when we cannot tackle them, by communicating our fears to those who can best help us face them or relieve them.

And so the conclusion is not a simple rule — neither "Keep your fears to yourself" nor "Talk about your fears" — but something more complex.

* This program, and later developments of it in both Korea and Germany, are reported in detail in "The Army Learns About First-Aid Psychiatry," page 279.

For the evidence on both sides is not contradictory, but complementary. Some secret fears ought to be told, and some ought not; some secrets should be told to some people, and not to others. Surveying the evidence, I believe the question rests in each case on two criteria:

First, what effect will the telling of a secret fear have on the one who tells it? Will he turn out to enjoy whining and complaining, robbing himself of incentive, and begging, in effect, for permission to be ineffective and dependent in life? Or will he be letting off some tensions about which he cannot, in the nature of things, do anything else? Is his fear one based on reality, and about which he could be taking action, or is it a distorted phantom fear which might be dispelled by comparing it to the opinions of informed outsiders?

Second, what effect will the telling of the secret fear have on the one to whom it is told? A man who tells his fears about flying, or sickness, or money problems to a young child who has no idea how to deal with the problems, is not helping the child to grapple with life, but only causing fright and the formation of lifelong anxieties. But a man who takes such fears to a psychotherapist, a doctor, a minister, or a specialist in the field of his problem, is not likely to harm or alarm his confidant, but to evoke a helpful and comforting reappraisal of the situation.

Being animals, we cannot get rid of the fear apparatus in our bodies, and being mortal, we are not likely soon to be without causes of fear. But through intelligence and good judgment we can learn to live with them. We can use some of our fears as valuable fuel for activity, and deal with their causes courageously; we can learn to minimize others in various ways, being careful not to spread their contagion to those who will be infected by them and return them to us augmented and doubly ominous. "Render therefore to all their dues," wrote Saint Paul, "tribute to whom tribute is due; custom to whom custom; fear to whom fear; honor to whom honor." If one interprets the part about fear in a modern psychological sense, there is hardly any better advice to be had.

Guilt Feelings — Our Most Confusing Emotions

A FRIEND OF MINE was taking care of his children recently while his wife was in the hospital. At one point — tired, worried and impatient with them — he angrily slapped both children several times and bundled them unceremoniously off to bed. That night he was sleepless and depressed. He continued to feel miserable all the next morning. Then, on an impulse, he went out and bought several expensive toys for the children — and he began to feel better.

Another friend, a young actress, left an unhappy home life and a domineering mother in Boston to seek happiness in New York. Popular and successful now, she lives in a lovely apartment, dresses beautifully and seems relatively happy. A few months ago at a party we fell to talking of our early lives. She jokingly contrasted what she called her parents' "shabby" way of life with the one she was now leading. Half an hour later she was stricken with a splitting headache and had to lie down in a darkened room. A few months later, at another party, the same thing happened to her. Coincidence? It's unlikely — she herself thinks there's a deeper reason.

Improbable as it may seem, many psychiatrists, psychologists and social workers would agree that a common reason underlies these two vastly different incidents. Both of my friends felt guilty — the father, for scolding his children; the actress, for attacking her parents' way of life. By buying toys the father could make up for his "sin." The actress, on the other hand, atoned through physical punishment. At the time neither of them knew why they felt uncomfortable. It was only later, when they examined their actions, that they became aware of what had been going on inside.

Most of us, when we think of guilt, refer to it in the legal sense —

the fact of having committed a crime or offense against the law. But when my two friends recognized their guilt feelings, they were thinking, not of an illegal act, but of a kind of inner crime. They had both, in different ways, violated one of their personal laws of moral and social behavior.

At one time or another we have all done things which we believe to be wrong. We feel guilty when we cheat on income tax, when we tell a social lie to get out of an unwanted invitation, when we hear of a friend's financial troubles and do not try to help him. Most of these situations are relatively simple and easy for us to deal with. We know clearly that we have acted contrary to some law or some inner belief and, when we feel troubled, we can pinpoint the source and, if we want, do something about correcting it. But for every situation of this sort, there are dozens in which we feel depressed or uncomfortable or even ill without fully knowing the reason. Often a feeling of guilt lies at the core. Indeed, Dr. Franz Alexander, former director of the famous Institute for Psychoanalysis in Chicago, expresses the view of most psychiatrists when he says that no other emotional reactions play so permanent and central a role in our being as do guilt feelings.

Everyone is familiar with some of the common expressions of guilt feelings. Many a man, for instance, puts in an occasional day or week of ferocious work when he drives himself and others like a madman. Many a housewife yields from time to time to a maniacal outburst of cleanliness; she attacks the house like an enemy and reduces herself by the end of the day to total collapse. Such bursts of work often come when one has been slackening on the job or letting the house go a bit. The wild burst of work isn't the most efficient way to catch up, but it is a release and a washing away of the guilt that we feel for not having worked conscientiously enough. It is no mere coincidence that many religions throughout the world have featured cleansing rites and purification rituals; the very act of cleaning ourselves physically seems to symbolize the washing away of guilt feelings.

One almost universally shared guilt feeling is that which follows an argument between husband and wife — we feel it is wrong to let ourselves hate someone we love, even momentarily. Most of us, too, have occasional daydreams of being married to a different husband or wife, or we have fantasies of extramarital love affairs with someone new and better looking; these thoughts may be followed by what seems like unaccountable gloom and pessimism about life in general.

Most of these feelings are normal and universal and our sense of guilt is only temporary. But guilt feelings can, and too often do, lead to serious marital problems. The guilt-ridden person, unable to accept the normality of his feelings, may try to salve his conscience by finding someone else to be at fault rather than himself.

Social workers in two leading family counseling agencies tell me that family budgets are a frequent source of trouble. In one typical case, a man flew into such rages when he went over his wife's monthly expense record that he would strike her and break furniture. He complained about his wife's extravagant food-buying habits and her failure to keep proper records of where their money had gone. Ordinarily he was a decent husband, and it didn't make sense for him to act so badly over minor matters. In counseling sessions the truth emerged. *He* was the real spendthrift — he had bought a too expensive house and he didn't want to admit his error. His continuing sense of guilt made him seek someone else to blame.

Guilt feelings need to be only a little more intense than normal to make us perform acts that are harmful and detrimental to our own search for happiness. A psychologist told me of one married couple that had a defective first-born child whom they institutionalized. They did so on perfectly logical, rational grounds. But the illogical and irrational parts of their minds said something like this: "You do not love children. . . . You are hardhearted." The result? Despite a moderate income, they have had six more children in seven years, trying to prove to their inner voices that they are overflowing with love for children.

When guilt is still stronger than this, it can be emotionally and physically crippling, particularly when it is unconscious guilt that the victim does not even struggle with directly. Psychiatrists have found such guilt to be a basic factor in such emotional disturbances as phobias, depressions, persecution complexes, and inferiority feelings; in such physical malfunctions as impotence, migraine headache, and arthritis; and in such unconscious efforts to punish one's self as alcoholism, inexplicable financial mistakes, wild and wasteful gambling, accidents, and suicides.

Severe guilt feelings are often, for example, the cause of digestive troubles. Dr. Erich Lindemann, an eminent psychiatrist of Harvard University, has studied grief and collected impressive evidence to show that it can be devastating when felt by a person who had a hidden hatred of the deceased and, incorrectly, feels somehow responsible for his death. Many of these guilt-laden people suffered from digestive troubles — loss of appetite, vomiting, diarrhea and sometimes even ulcerative colitis — which often cleared up only with psychiatric help.

Air Force psychiatrists at the Don Cesar Convalescent Hospital in St. Petersburg, Florida, studied hundreds of fliers who cracked up in combat in the last war. Many of these men collapsed shortly after the death in action of one of their crew members or bunk mates. But the breakdowns were rarely due to simple sorrow or to fear of death. In most cases, the surviving flier had disliked the dead crewman or been competing with him for a promotion or for a girl. And the unconscious mind was saying, "You're bad — you're glad to see him gone!" The overwhelming guilt they felt as a result caused them to panic, or even to lose control of their muscles.

Marriage counselors and social workers find that impotence in men and frigidity in women are generally caused by guilt feelings. We repeatedly tell children that sex play is improper, dirty, and evil; then, when they grow up, we expect them to find beauty in marital sex. A man who has been taught that sex play is vulgar and animallike may be unable to have sexual union with the wife for whom he has tender feelings. A woman who has grown up thinking it is wrong for a girl to feel desire may find it less painful to submit to sex without pleasure than to enjoy herself and feel vile afterward.

Where do guilt feelings come from — the normal guilt and the sick guilt, the conscious guilt and the unsuspected guilt? In a number of primitive and Eastern societies, people have little or no experience of guilt feelings; instead of being guided by a strong inner conscience, they control themselves, as adults, out of a sense of sympathy and solidarity with their tribe or out of fear of reprisal or social disgrace. These are all controls that come from outside.

But conscience and the guilt feelings that are tied up with conscience are an internal disgrace. When we feel conscience pangs, it is *we* who are displeased with ourselves — and we will do anything to still that disapproving voice, from buying toys to leaping off a high building. Most psychiatrists and many anthropologists believe that, by having a conscience inside ourselves, rather than outside (as in the primitive and Eastern cultures), we have been able to rise to greater heights of morality, social decency and creativity. But conscience has a price — guilt feelings.

How does conscience develop? Psychiatrists have often likened it to the voice of the parents, speaking from within the unconscious mind. The growing child hears thousands of dos and don'ts from his parents. He soon learns that good behavior wins him approval and love, but bad behavior brings him disapproval and punishment. Soon the child begins to feel anxiety when he misbehaves. He anticipates punishment, which will both pay off the debt of badness and restore love. When he feels guilty, he not only expects punishment, but sometimes wants it, to assure the return of parental affection.

A three-year-old girl I know was acting badly one day, but her mother was too preoccupied in reading the mail to stop her. The child played with forbidden things in the living room, threw ash trays on the floor, and finally climbed onto the piano and walked up and down on its polished surface. When even this drew no notice, she looked really distraught. At last she shouted, "Mommy! Mommy! Why don't you come spank me?"

Spanking is even cautiously prescribed as temporary therapy in some excellent hospitals where problem children are treated. An occasional child, filled with a sense of his own badness, can go to sleep only after he is gently and lovingly scolded, with a little play spanking thrown in to relieve his anxiety and make him feel his day's sins have been atoned for.

As a child grows, he begins to gain self-control and keeps in his head the mass of parental commands and directives. He struggles with the forbidden impulses and conquers most of them. When he fails to, he is haunted by his misdeeds and either tells on himself or manages to let them be discovered in order to have the cleansing ritual of punishment. He has, in other words, acquired a conscience — an inner voice that speaks for his parents and will come also to represent God, the law and the morals of society.

In order to become social, self-controlled, loving creatures, we have to learn to repress or redirect many of our basic impulses — anger, greed, selfishness, free-wheeling sexual interest and the like. We live, not according to impulse, but guided by a set of goals and precepts. But the old impulses are always within us; when they rise to the level of random thought or when they emerge unexpectedly in the form of some harsh word or cruel action, they put us in conflict with our conscience. Guilt feelings are the immediate result; they are the controlling factor that makes us restrain ourselves and try to heed our conscience.

The guilt-edged conscience is a sharp weapon, and cuts even the tough souls of most professional criminals. Many of them are caught because of clues they leave behind; but Dr. Franz Alexander and many police psychiatrists feel there is nothing accidental about most clues any more than there is about most slips of the tongue. Each reveals something a person unconsciously wants to say with his conscience, although his ego (conscious self) may have wanted to keep it quiet. Even lie detector tests rest on the effect of conscience. Be the criminal ever so composed and sure of his alibi, the key questions are apt to provoke a struggle in the interior of his personality, and his heart and blood vessels make the results visible.

It is a curious paradox that conscience and guilt, which have been so useful in the development of our civilization, are often the focal point of personal unhappiness. Their role should be to aid people in living a satisfactory life but many of us, leading decent lives, suffer from what seems like excessive guilt.

Some sociologists and anthropologists believe that the reason lies in the rapid growth of our culture. Dr. Margaret Mead, for instance, points out that we live in a period "when social change is taking place faster than can possibly be registered in the character structure of those who must live within the changing order." In most of previous history children were reared in almost the same world in which their parents had grown up. The ideals, the morals and the courtesies taught to them became a conscience that was entirely suitable to the life they led when they grew up. Today this is no longer true. Everything about us alters, proceeds, reverses or grows at bewildering speed. Our approach to child-rearing, for instance, has undergone several revolutions in the past thirty years. The shape and size of the family have been radically modified in fifty years. Dating and courting customs of today's teen-agers are baffling even to adults only ten years away from that time of life. In the modern suburbs, people have worked out a whole set of folkways and manners strange to city dwellers of the 1930's. The plane, the car, and the television set have totally reconstructed our habits of work, travel and play.

What this means is that today's young adults have implanted in their unconscious minds a set of beliefs and commandments that were right for the world of their parents a generation ago, but are in conflict with contemporary living patterns.

"Honor thy father and thy mother," we were taught in childhood. But the world of today believes the young married couple should live apart, should break away, should be independent and private. We do not want our parents to live with us, and United States Census Bureau data show that fewer do so today than ever before in American history. Thy father and thy mother wither and fade, having little that is use-ful to do; they exist longer, thanks to medicine, but often the longer life is only a prolongation of boredom. They grow cranky, fussy, and foolish; we shake our heads and make clucking sounds about them, but secretly we feel partly to blame.

Hard work, thrift, and saving for a rainy day — these were shining virtues fifty years ago. But we have come a long way, thanks to pros-perity, machines that make each man's work fabulously productive, and social security plans that reduce the uncertainties of life. Hard work has lost its nobility; work is an unwelcome interruption in the life we consider more important — the life of play and pleasure. Thrift is as dated as antimacassars: Federal Reserve data show that more money is currently out on loan in mortgages and installment-plan purchases than ever before in our history, and pension plans and retire-ment schemes have made the habit of saving seem unnatural and cow-ardly. Most of us prefer to "live a little." We spend billions annually on faster cars, liquor, sexy movies, and vacations, and we are assured by advertising a score of times every day that we owe ourselves the en-joyment of leisure, physical pleasures, comfort — *fun!*

But the still small voice is neither still nor small. The man with excess leisure is often bored and ill at ease; suicides, heart failures, and other disasters are especially common among newly retired men. The installment-plan customer has a foam-rubber bed in his new highly mortgaged house, but he sleeps badly at night and scolds his wife and children for their expensive tastes. The very man who enjoys the sexual stimuli of movies, novels, and newspaper stories is willing to let censors and snoopers attack publishers for printing so-called obscenity, and even in the midst of his daydreams of sleeping with Sophia Loren he is sternly critical of the way his neighbor's adolescent children carry on in parked cars.

The same clash of values affects many other phenomena of modern married life. We believe today — except for those whose religion forbids it — that men and women deserve happiness in marriage, and should be free to try again if they fail to find it. Yet most divorcees are still ashamed of, and even apologetic about, their divorces. Many of the rest of us avoid the breakup of marriage by choking back angry words or differences of opinion, but the unspoken anger makes us dream of revenge via outside love affairs — or actually seek them — and this in turn produces corroding inner guilt.

We hand over more and more of our duties as parents to teachers, playground directors, camp counselors, and even psychotherapists; we believe in the right of modern parents to enjoy their leisure and have their own vacations; but the old ways are embedded in our minds nevertheless, and we feel a gnawing sense of wrong at not personally seeing to the entertainment and the character development of our offspring. We go to PTA meetings, vote for higher school taxes, and spend money to give our children the things they want; cash has a way of buying off the conscience, at least temporarily.

It is no wonder that, under such circumstances, our consciences may often be instruments of trouble, rather than guides to satisfying social behavior. But, with some care and thought, the average person can learn to reduce those guilt feelings which are out of reasonable proportion to his actual deeds.

During World War II and the Korean conflict, Army psychiatrists were able to salvage the great bulk of men who collapsed of "combat neurosis." Most of them were able to go back to the front lines in fighting condition within a day or two. The method called for a few hours of talk and explanation. The soldier was reassured that it is normal to feel fear and the desire to retreat to safety. Most men can endure knowing they are imperfect, and obtain relief from crippling guilt feelings, by learning that imperfection is universal.*

In the same way, by bringing our guilt feelings to the surface and examining them, we can often become realistic about our conduct. Sometimes we may decide that our conscience was right and that we should change some part of the pattern of our lives. But often we will conclude that the automatic, unthinking voice of childhood is not always as good a guide as the rational intellect of maturity. An experience of mine several years ago made this forcefully clear to me.

One Monday I received a letter that summoned me to appear in Philadelphia to hear my father's will. While he was dying, the thought had come to me that I would soon inherit several thousand dollars, and I began to daydream about what I'd do with it; then, shocked at myself, I had violently banished the thoughts from my mind.

The morning after the letter arrived, I went to the station, bought my ticket and walked down to the train platform. Suddenly I was overwhelmed by pain and nausea. I made my way back to the waiting room and sank onto a bench, swallowing and gasping, too weak even to head for the washroom. I thought over what I'd eaten the night before, but could find no obvious reason for the attack.

Almost an hour later — two Philadelphia trains had gone, and I was no better — a startling idea occurred to me. It wasn't food that had turned my stomach, but hunger for my father's money. I was greedy to find out how much I would get, and my stomach was turning upside down with guilt and self-loathing.

The result was astonishing. As I realized these things and thought them out sanely, the nausea began to fade. Of *course*, I had loved my father. Of *course*, I felt greedy desire; any normal person would. Of *course*, Dad wanted me to have part of his money and to enjoy it. Yet I felt guilty because somewhere each of us holds the belief that, in wanting to inherit something, we must have wished also that its owner were dead.

* This program is described in greater detail in "The Army Learns About First-Aid Psychiatry," page 279.

I have learned since then that in our society we cannot avoid guilt feelings. But I have also learned that, by examining our guilt as I had done, we can help avoid feelings that are disproportionate to our thoughts and deeds. Most important of all, perhaps, I have come to know that parents can do much to shape a useful kind of conscience for their children.

A child whose parents are too stern, too demanding, too ready to shame him for every fault or failure or burst of temper can easily become an adult with a painfully overactive conscience. He never feels he is working hard enough. He is never satisfied for more than a day or so with any achievement or advancement. He is never sure that people really like him, and he thinks that most troubles that arise in his life must be his own fault. He feels the crushing weight of continual disapproval and supposes that it is the world that disapproves of him, but, of course, it is he himself. Hoping for acceptance, he may even actively seek punishment — although he doesn't realize that's what he is doing — by driving recklessly until he has an accident, or drinking too much at an important party and making a fool of himself.

Whatever we ourselves may be, our children are acquiring the basis for their future feelings of guilt right now. Their freedom from a crippling conscience depends on the extent to which we make them feel decent and loved, rather than naughty and nasty. Conscience is a useful thing — but a little of it goes a long way.

Malfunctioning Under Stress

In this section are three articles: the first describes experiments in inducing neuroses, or neurotic symptoms, in animals in a controlled laboratory setting; the second discusses very similar occurrences in men in combat or in a combat-ready zone, along with the preventive psychiatry that saves them from emotional ruin; and the third describes the malfunctioning and failure of many of today's college students under conditions of intense and prolonged stress.

I am particularly pleased to be able to reprint "Neurosis Factory," the first of these three. It was only the second or third article I had ever written in the field of psychology, but it was awarded the George Westinghouse—American Association for the Advancement of Science prize as the best science article in magazines for the year 1952. Though the article was printed a dozen years ago, the findings reported in it remain valid today; there is, moreover, a follow-up note at the end of the article bringing the story up to date.

Neurosis Factory

NUMBER 41 (that was all the name he had) was standing by the fence, looking unseeingly out over the rolling countryside, avoiding the others, when he saw the doctors walking across the grass. He started to run — a few steps one way, a few steps the other.

"All right, all right, now," said the gray-haired doctor. "Take it easy, old fellow." As they led him off toward the long building, his eyes rolled, his chest heaved, he felt his stomach contracting into a tight ball. By the time they had got him inside and put the straps and wires on him, it happened again: his head hung down, his eyes stared blankly at the floor, and his body went rigid. Number 41 was in the midst of a severe nervous breakdown.

Number 41 wasn't a combat-shocked veteran, a ruined businessman, or a bereaved father. He was a three-year-old Merino sheep. But like his millions of neurotic human cousins, poor 41 had the familiar symptoms. He avoided his companions; he slept poorly and jumped at sudden sounds; he breathed unevenly and sighed often; his heart was rapid and irregular.

In addition to the monotonous clocklike ticking of the metronome, there was now a tiny electric stimulus applied to 41's right front leg. But it was always preceded by a warning: either a buzzer buzzed for ten seconds, or the lights dimmed, or a tone came from a radio speaker. And since the warning always told him that the little annoying shock was coming, he would anticipate it tensely; about a thousand such accumulated waitings and tensions over the months had turned him into a nervous wreck. He acted and felt remarkably like a human being involved in, say, cold war diplomacy — always under tension, always exposed to new unpleasant jolts — who develops an ulcer, an anxiety neurosis, and a chronic state of exhaustion.

The man who did this to number 41 is no demon or torturer. He is Howard S. Liddell, a benign, plump, gray-haired professor of psychobiology at Cornell University in Ithaca, New York. Fatherly-looking Dr. Liddell feels kindly and sympathetic toward his animals, but he feels even more so toward the harried human race. For twenty-three years he has been turning happy, healthy sheep, goats, and pigs into analogues of suffering humanity, and thereby tremendously increasing medical understanding of how neurosis is caused and cured.

Also from his work has sprung a keen appreciation of the way in which human fears, worries, and dislikes can turn into skin rashes, heart trouble, high blood pressure, ulcers, and the like. "Our nervous sheep and goats," says a devoted admirer of Liddell's work, "are the real godfathers of modern psychosomatic medicine." (Liddell was himself one of the original editors of the official journal *Psychosomatic Medicine.*)

Dr. Liddell's work goes on in surprisingly modest surroundings. Two miles east of Ithaca, in upstate New York, a 20-acre farm sprawls across the top of a hill. A rutted dirt road leads up the hill to a long, low, cement building. Outside, in enclosures, some eighty-five sheep, goats, lambs, and kids are grazing and sleeping.

Inside are a large classroom, a workshop, an office, and a string of small, bare test cells with observers' control rooms adjoining them. The entire place seems a tangle of expensive equipment and relative junk. Tables are piled with radio amplifiers and tubes, stacks of heart and respiration graphs, clocks and relays. In another room a beautiful, expensive, new magnetic-recording-tape machine is running, to produce the regularly timed shock signals; next to it is a tin breadbox with knobs outside and radio tubes inside — a handmade cardiotachometer, which counts heartbeats better than some of the shiniest new ones on the market.

Dr. Liddell and his half-dozen assistants drift in and out, usually wearing overalls or ancient shapeless clothes. Liddell himself, now fifty-five, originally was a physiologist interested in ductless glands. His chief assistant, Dr. A. Ulric Moore, is an easygoing, blue-eyed man of forty-eight, who sports a mud-colored beret to cover his bald head; he has a Ph.D. in literature, used to teach drama, and has a genius for improvising new equipment. Others who have been with Liddell in the past include doctors, psychiatrists, a mechanical engineer, an electrical engineer, a merchant captain, and so on.

Out of this modest setup there come, every year, quietly revolutionary findings about anxiety, monotony, frustration, and tension. Though an animal's nervous breakdown isn't point for point identical with a man's, still the similarities are astonishing, and the basic facts learned from goats or sheep help doctors disentangle the workings of the complex human personality.

The way Liddell gets this basic information looks simple enough. He goes out to the pasture one day and leads in, for instance, a young ewe, who has never been inside before. In a testing cell he fastens a stimulus wire to her right foreleg; otherwise she is free to move about the room.

(In some experiments, other wires are used to record pulse, breathing, and so on.)

Suddenly, the lights go dim for ten seconds; then, as they go up again, a slight but startling shock prickles her leg. She jumps, bleats and runs around a bit. All is quiet again for a few minutes; then the cycle repeats. After ten or twenty stimuli, she begins to get the idea. Now she grows anxious when the lights go dim: she starts running about at once, breathing more heavily, and holding her head tensely erect.

But in later sessions, as the wearing process takes effect, she may give up running about. When the lights go dim, she backs tightly into a corner and crouches there, lifting her leg again and again as if to draw it away from the coming stimulus. Her breathing and pulse are getting faster; she trembles and twitches at outside sounds; you can hear her gritting her teeth. Like a soldier under mortar fire who hears the slow, awful sound of impending blows, she can only wait and hold tight.

Months later, after five hundred or a thousand shocks, she has probably passed over into a full-fledged nervous breakdown. She may jump and twitch and jerk continuously, no matter whether there are signals and shocks or not. Or she may become rigid as soon as she enters the test cell, with her test leg so stiff that it resists bending by the experimenter. Back in the pasture she avoids the flock — a truly astonishing thing in so gregarious an animal as the sheep. She sleeps poorly, and paces up and down at night. At the oat trough, in the morning, she is afraid to fight her way in with the rest and hangs back until they are finished. She is a very sick sheep. Like her human counterparts, she has acquired a full-fledged phobia. If dimming lights have been the pre-shock signal, any dimming now frightens her.

Professor Jules Masserman, formerly at Chicago University, once taught some cats to open a food box, after a light was flashed, and get a morsel of salmon. Later on, though, when they opened the box, they might instead get a startling jet of air across their noses. The conflict between the two desires — to get the food and to avoid the air blast — made nervous wrecks of them. Even a semistarved cat, seeing the food box brought near, would run to the far corner and huddle there, face to the wall, in cataleptic rigidity, not even daring to turn around and look at the box.

Sheep and cats have taught psychiatrists that some of the ills we think are due to our great human intelligences aren't so at all. An overwrought sheep, for instance, can behave as if he had a bona fide hallucination. Not long ago, a big ram was being tested in Liddell's laboratory. In the long quiet pauses between buzzer signals, he'd frequently jerk his leg upwards and jump, just as he did when he got a real stimulus. His straining nervous system must have "thought" it received stimuli, again and again. If he'd been a man, he might have been seeing snakes or ghosts, or talking to invisible companions.

Some types of behavior that we have thought of as typically human must be rooted deep in the basic mammalian body. Animals can become "perfectionists," for instance. A small brown goat learned that when he stood up on his hind legs, during a signal, he wouldn't get a stimulus (the controller in the next room would interrupt the circuit to give him this result whenever he lifted the leg or stood up). As time passed, he became very careful to do it in just such-and-such a manner, standing upright at exactly the same spot, and with careful attention to his posture. Professor Masserman had a neurotic dog who would eat his food only after circling the food box twice and then bowing on his forepaws in a far corner of the room before stealthily approaching the food box. These symptoms of neurosis aren't too different from the "compulsive" behavior of humans who must walk on every crack in the pavement, touch every tree they pass, or sterilize every object they use.

We often think of some human beings as "naturally aggressive" or "warlike by nature." If you ever manage to drop by Liddell's farm, you may change your mind. The accumulation of annoyances can turn even these most meek and mild of animals into aggressive beasts. Workers at the Behavior Farm have been butted, bitten, and kicked by sheep with frayed nerves.

By learning how basic such patterns of neurosis are, psychiatry can sweep out some of the medieval debris left around in its house. Psychiatry has long been in need of a large-sized injection of plain laboratory fact; and that's just what it is getting from the animal studies on Dr. Liddell's farm. Such well-known psychiatrists as Dr. Franz Alexander, Dr. Béla Mittelmann, and Dr. Carl Binger have publicly expressed their great indebtedness to neurotic animals for a better comprehension of neurotic humans. A number of techniques of cure tested on animals have been extensively used by the Armed Forces, and now are being adopted in civilian practice.

The first work on animal neuroses grew out of tests of what scientists called "difficult differentiations." Over thirty years ago, the great Russian physiologist, Ivan Pavlov, was teaching a dog to expect food wherever he saw a circle, but not when he saw an oval. Day by day Pavlov showed him ovals that were nearer and nearer to being perfect circles. One day the dog suddenly went wild — howling and showing what could only be called "neurotic" behavior. He had had a near nervous breakdown from trying to make too difficult a decision, just as human beings sometimes do.

Liddell's early work in this field involved similar "problem" situations. Tiny, a 435-pound pig, was taught to open a food box when she heard a certain tone on the loud-speaker. But a lower tone meant she'd get a shock if she opened it. Gradually, as the tones were brought closer and closer together, Tiny got badly upset; at last she gave up eating at all in the experiment room — a most unpiglike attitude.

Sheep were taught to lift a leg at the sound of the buzzer, to avoid a shock. At the same time, they learned that a different signal, such as a flashing light, was "safe" and didn't require the lifting of the leg. But after they'd learned this, the signals began to be switched. The light might be followed by a shock. Or maybe, when the buzzer was the signal, even the lifting of a leg wouldn't help. This inconsistency and uncertainty, like the difficult decisions, precipitated neurosis and breakdown.

Dr. Liddell cites, as a parallel human case, a girl who was undergoing treatment. Her troubles were shown to be due to the fact that her parents had been divorced years earlier, and as a child she had spent half her year with each one. Her easygoing, tolerant father would reward some kinds of conduct and punish others; her stern mother would reverse the rewards and punishments. The girl, in other words, was getting signals switched on her — and she wound up mentally sick.

More recently, Dr. Liddell has come to the radical conclusion that it doesn't necessarily take inconsistency, difficult decisions, and confusion to bring about a breakdown. All it requires is that commodity so richly available in our modern civilization — simply monotony. An animal, given a regular shock at regular intervals and after a regular amount of warning, will inevitably build up a complete state of neurosis. Even if he has been taught to avoid shock by lifting his leg or standing up, the tension built up during each warning signal is enough to do the damage. Anxiety and tension occurring at reasonably frequent and regular intervals will wear away the nervous system.

You can make your own applications of that discovery to human beings. Here's one: if your work involves unpleasant tension and monotony, and if you've been getting sleepless, irritable, and angry, you'd better take a fast look at yourself. You may be in for trouble. Buying a new suit, bowling with the gang at night, or joining a new church may not be enough to stop you from blowing up. Perhaps it's the situation itself that you ought to get away from — and permanently. It may take a change of job or a major change of a way of life to keep you on balance.

The Behavior Farm is also exploding some old notions as to what to do for the patient, once he has his neurosis. Possibly the most surprising discovery, as far as the general public is concerned, is that so-called rest cures don't always cure. A highly neurotic sheep was allowed to live in the pasture undisturbed for three whole years. His sleeplessness disappeared within months, his heart became nearly normal, his digestion improved, and he rejoined the flock. Outwardly he seemed quite normal. Then he was brought into the laboratory once again for more shock conditioning. Within two sessions, all his symptoms returned in full force — in one hundredth the time it had taken to create them originally. The rest cure had been a cure only while it continued; but the submicroscopic damage to the nervous system was still there, inside him, waiting for the old situation to touch off the old trouble.

It's pretty obvious, therefore, that trips to the mountains or the seashore may make an improvement in the worried wage earner or the harassed salesman, but the improvement may be neither deep nor permanent unless the basic cause of his neurosis — whether it be job, home life, sex life, or religious conflicts — is clearly determined and the difficult situation eased.

An even more surprising development is the recent notion, now being tested by Drs. Liddell and Moore, that the *tension* is more important than the actual *shock*. They can shock an animal without warning signals hundreds of times; he'll be startled, but he won't become neurotic. (In human terms, he doesn't "worry." Many Londoners in 1945 preferred the V–2s, which hit without warning, to the puttering, droning V–1s, which noisily announced their approach.) But the warning signal touches off an alarm reaction in the body. Adrenalin spurts into the blood, the heart speeds up, muscles get tense, blood pressure increases, the brain races madly — and the real damage is under way.

Even though a goat or sheep learns to avoid a shock by lifting his leg, he can become neurotic just from the repeated strain of the warning, tension, and waiting. He may look a lot quieter than a new animal just experiencing stimuli for the first time, who thrashes about excitedly, for he has learned that mere thrashing does no good and he imposes restraint on himself, tensely waiting for the shock or the end of the signal. But this quiet, restrained phase is the real sign, to Howard Liddell, that his animal is on the way to trouble.

Air Force psychiatrists had some firsthand experience of the value of releasing tension during the war. One of their methods of establishing contact with severely neurotic patients who were uncommunicative, rigid, or speechless was to inject sodium pentothal (the so-called "truth serum") and to tell the drugged patient that he was back in his airplane. In an electrifying fashion, the fliers would instantly begin to relive their most harrowing experiences, speaking to invisible buddies, cringing as the flak burst around them, firing madly at imagined fighter planes, and groaning from their wounds.

The purposes of this "narcosynthesis" were many. First, they helped the psychiatrist learn what experiences, hidden in the unconscious, had caused the collapse of the personality. Secondly, the flier himself would afterwards be able to remember the events and talk them over with the doctor.

But interestingly enough, the narcosynthesis often gave a temporary improvement by itself, because it released hidden tensions. Usually the improvement was quite brief, and it took many talks with the psychotherapist to do the real work. But occasionally the release of tension by itself effected a real cure.

One fighter pilot, for instance, had a typical mild neurosis that made him continually anxious, jumpy, sleepless, and without appetite. Under pentothal, he relived a strafing mission south of Rome. As the psychiatrist looked on, he described a low-level run on German trucks. Suddenly he was hit by flak; he pulled up to 6000 feet to bail out, but saw that his rip cord was shot in two.

The boy turned greenish, and sweat poured from him as he lay on the table. The doctor turned a fan on him. "That's much better," the boy said, thinking his plane's canopy was open. "I can feel the wind in my face." He "flew" back to his home field and made a crash landing. The psychotherapist told him he was making a splendid recovery from the crash, and that he would have plenty of time to recover before returning to duty. The narcosis was then ended. Several days later, the boy entered the office to tell the doctor that he'd been feeling fine and was anxious to return to flying duty.

Unfortunately, few cases are so astonishingly, and happily, concluded by the mere release of tension — or a good binge would cure anyone. Usually, the man who blows off steam by getting drunk and picking a fight gets rid of his tension only temporarily. Until the underlying causes of his trouble are ended, he'll keep on needing his liquor again and again.

Dr. Liddell is spending a lot of time trying to find new and more efficient ways of curing neuroses. Sheep are hard to cure, in that you can't reason with them. But they do perceive things slowly. If a sheep that has always had signals followed by shocks begins to get signals with no shocks, he slowly unlearns all his fears. This is called "deconditioning." It's comparable to what happens when a child from a hostile and unhappy home is adopted into a calm and affectionate one, and slowly learns that "father" doesn't always signify punishment, that "mother" doesn't mean scolding, that "children" don't mean fights.

Our Armed Forces, drawing directly on animal work, applied the theory of deconditioning during the war. In 1943 and 1944, Commander Uno Helgesson ran a Battle Noise School in the South Pacific. Here men who had become neurotic under shellfire and machine-gun fire were put through a training course in simulated combat. They were assured they'd be perfectly safe, and then they were made to lie in foxholes and trenches and listen to mock strafing, dive bombing, and carefully controlled fire of all sorts, knowing that these sounds meant no danger to them. Gradually they were able to listen without being terrified. It was a harsh and crude type of deconditioning, but it was effective enough at the time.

Somewhat closer to peacetime methods was the technique tried on Tiny, the pig who was afraid to open her food box for fear of a shock. In an effort to try psychotherapy, all further shocks were suspended, and a graduate student, who fed Tiny out in her pen (and whom she therefore liked), took her into the laboratory. He put a juicy bit of apple into her food box, but Tiny rigidly ignored it. "Why, what's the matter, Tiny?" he said, amiably scratching her back. "Why don't you eat your apple? Go ahead, try it." He pointed to it, and continued to talk soothingly. Tiny grunted in worried bewilderment, and after a while she tentatively tried it. Eveything was fine.

After a few such sessions, Tiny would eat if he were merely near by. Later she'd eat if anyone at all were near by. Finally, she'd try it under any circumstances. She had been deconditioned and cured.

Deconditioning is becoming a standard part of modern psychotherapy. When a patient who has suffered from a series of severely shocking incidents brings them forth under narcosynthesis, he is reliving his experiences — but in safe circumstances. Every time he and the doctor talk about it afterwards, they are desensitizing him to the stimulus. The more they go over and repeat this material in the sure, calm world of the doctor's office, the less terrible it seems.

But deconditioning is just one of many types of treatment Dr. Liddell and Dr. Moore and their associates have been working with. There may be far swifter methods of altering and reshaping the disturbed personality, methods hardly touched upon yet by the world of medical practice.

One clue is the profound relationship between the body's many hormones and the personality. Some years ago, Dr. Liddell found that removing the thyroid gland from a highly nervous sheep caused all the jumpiness, tension, and other neurotic behavior to vanish. So, alas, did a lot of other things, including normal metabolism, alertness, and so on, and the sheep died of its total lack of thyroid. But if thyroid removal is no answer to the neurotic and the psychopathic personality, it certainly hints that there may be an answer somewhere in the intimate tie-up between the body's interlocked glandular system and its nervous system.

Trying another tack, Liddell and Company tried adrenal cortical hormones some years ago. The hormone mixture Liddell used calmed a neurotic sheep down considerably, though not permanently. A doctor friend of Liddell's gave some adrenal hormone to a woman who had been bedridden by neurotic fatigue. The hormone alone was enough to get her out of bed for the first time in years.

Recently three New York doctors revealed that at the Creedmoor State Hospital in Queens, some forty psychotic patients had been given another type of hormone treatment, this time made up of sex hormones. Nearly a third of them were so much calmed that they could be released to their homes.

Brain operations are one technique where practice has run ahead of full information. Many hundreds of the operations known as lobotomies, lobectomies, and topectomies have been performed on human beings. They all involve what might be called a cutting of the short-circuited wires in the malfunctioning brain. This cutting eliminates a lot of static but it may also stop a lot of good information from getting through. Violent psychotics are calmed by such an operation; but often they become so apathetic, lackadaisical, and deficient in emotional qualities that they seem entirely lost to friends and family. Ulric Moore and Howard Liddell, along with many medical men, are beginning to question the wisdom of such operations except in the most hopeless cases. In the neuroses, unlike the more extreme psychoses, they may be tragically wasteful.

For that reason, the Behavior Farm set forth on a program of experimental lobectomies, to see just how much could be accomplished with a minimum of brain damage. One lobectomy completely cured a neurotic goat of her condition; but after the operation, said Ulric Moore, "she became a really terrible mother. You should see her butt her kid away from her and refuse to feed him."

Electric-shock therapy and insulin-shock therapy are also used on human beings, but they too have frequently destructive effects. Since thoroughgoing experimental human studies can't be made, for fear of causing deaths, sheep and goats are once again coming to the rescue, and a program of such shock therapies is now under way at the Behavior Farm.

At least one sort of major shock apparently won't turn out to be any kind of a cure. An ex-Air Force officer, working at the Behavior Farm in 1946, suggested that the Bikini atomic blasts then being planned might have a shock effect like nothing ever tried before. Liddell was unimpressed, but decided to gamble a few animals. In May, 1946, with official permission, three female goats and one castrated male goat, all neurotic, were crated and shipped off to the Pacific.

When their crates reached Bikini, the goats were duly stationed aboard a ship in the target area. Afterwards, they were kept by the Navy until they lost their radioactivity; then they came home. Their individual neuroses were completely undamaged and ready to operate at the very sight of the laboratory door.

One of Liddell's genuine regrets is that he never got to experiment on Aïda. Aïda was a two-year-old sheep who had been brought up as a house pet, along with several dogs, by a Cornell graduate student. She, too, seemed to think she was a dog; she would indulge in rough-house play, follow her master down the street, and try to chew bones. When he left Cornell, the student gave her to the Behavior Farm, and Liddell and Moore planned a course of experiments on her. But Aïda, in the pasture, studiously ignored the flock and refused to learn from them. She nearly starved, since she wouldn't eat grass. Moore finally bought her some dog biscuits, which she gratefully wolfed down. But, alas, two years of such unfitting diet had resulted in kidney stones from which she died before the experiments could be run.

"Great pity," says Moore, wistfully scratching his head through his beret and staring off across the fields. "Never can tell what we might have learned from her. A neurotic sheep who thinks she's a dog — why, it's just like a neurotic housewife who thinks she's got hidden talents better than Grable's. It would have been interesting."

The work of Howard Liddell and his associates at the Behavior Farm continued much as described until late 1962, when Liddell died. Since then, the farm has been renamed the Liddell Laboratory for Compara-

tive and Physiological Psychology; work now conducted there ranges broadly throughout animal psychology, rather than concentrating on experimental neuroses, and the sheep and goats have been replaced mostly by monkeys plus some rats. For in every area of scientific research there comes a time when the richest ore has been mined out of the vein, and one must move on.

But the findings and the significance of Dr. Liddell's work have entered the general body of psychological and psychiatric knowledge, and are there to remain. Many of the implications of his work spelled out in the article are now accepted parts of the theory and practice of psychosomatic medicine, preventive psychiatry, and psychotherapy. To be sure, Dr. Liddell considered his own psychological orientation to be Pavlovian, and he was doubtful as to the scientific validity of some of the Freudian explanations of the sources of neurosis; but the seeming conflict of the two theories has not prevented modern psychotherapists, most of whom are wedded to Freudian thought, from borrowing and applying some of Liddell's formulations. For in a very real sense, much of psychotherapy consists of eliminating intra-psychic conflict (the Freudian goal) by a kind of studious deconditioning (the Pavlovian aim); this is indicated in "Major and Minor Emotional Problems," page 102.

Two other points made in "Neurosis Factory" need updating. The comments on the possible value of hormones in relieving severe emotional disorders are now out of date: after some experiments in this direction, psychiatrists have generally given up hormone therapies because of the far greater effectiveness, and lesser side effects, of the tranquilizers, which had not yet appeared at the time I wrote this article. Dr. Liddell's suspicions that lobotomies were not going to be a major answer to severe psychosis have, however, been borne out; after a few years during which lobotomies were "popular" among mental hospital psychiatrists, the operation began falling into disfavor because the results were often disappointing and frequently included unwanted vegetative behavior in the patient; moreover, again, tranquilizers preempted the field.

Perhaps the most important outcome of the work at Behavior Farm is not any practical application, but rather a basic understanding of some of the connections between monotony, anxiety, difficult choices, frustration, and neurotic symptoms or behavior. The animal experiments laid down a bedrock of knowledge upon which human psychologists can build as they will.

The following two articles, though they do not show Pavlovian therapies being applied, do portray two quite different human situations in which stress, anticipation, anxiety, and monotony produce personal failure and breakdown; in that sense, both combat-ready soldiers and college students are brothers and sisters under the skin to the now-vanished sheep and goats of the former Behavior Farm at Cornell.

The Army Learns About First-Aid Psychiatry

SUPPOSE TWO ENTIRE 800-man infantry battalions guarding the West German frontier against Communist aggression were mysteriously to vanish for seven or eight months. What would be the United States reaction? You can guess: alarm, rage, and the demand for instant action.

Something like that is happening, but the Communists have nothing to do with it.* An enemy is effectively keeping United States fighting strength down, but the enemy's name is emotional and mental illness. Soldiers of our crack Seventh Army in Germany have been spending 60,000 man-days per year in Army hospitals due to psychiatric ailments. And for each man in the hospital, four or five others remain on duty with less severe symptoms — yet are no better capable of defending a border than men suffering from violent colic or raging fever.

Our nation has seldom occupied a foreign land so long, or kept a large peacetime army. So it came as a shock to our military leaders to find we could suffer so many psychiatric casualties during peace. After almost ten years of inaction, something is finally being done.

* All data in this article refer to the situation as it was in 1955. A note following the article brings it up to date.

This past year, in the critically important Seventh Army, a brand-new program of psychiatric first aid has been started to find and check emotional and mental illness before it gets serious. Only months old, the new program is already cutting sharply into the amount of lost manpower, and sparing thousands of young Americans anguish of soul and ruin of their personalities. It is doing even more: it is pointing a way for the civilian world to reduce its own staggering, and growing, burden of mental ills.

In the terrible stress of combat, nervous breakdown is understandable. During World War II, one out of every five sick men shipped back to the United States was an NP (neuropsychiatric) case. But nobody is shooting at our soldiers in Germany today. Why then do they get "nerves," psychosomatic diseases, and actual breakdowns so often? Why should peptic ulcer, a disease largely caused by emotional upset, be "the number one medical problem" among our soldiers in Germany, causing 10 per cent of all admissions to Army general hospitals, as a recent report to the Surgeon General showed? Why should the rate of NP illness among our soldiers be *almost as high* (more than 80 per cent) in peacetime Europe as it was among United States forces bitterly fighting the Reds in Korea in 1952?

In the five combat divisions strung out along the West German frontier, some 90,000 young Americans live a strange and uneasy life. A few miles from them are the powerful forces of a waiting enemy. All around them, the often hostile people they live among do not speak English with the familiar and beloved Yankee twang or Southern drawl, but mouth-filling, incomprehensible German. Home, careers, and girl friends are unthinkably remote, and painfully unreachable. Month after month, they train in the field under grueling conditions, always keyed up for an attack that never comes, always ready to fight but never fighting.

These are a few of the reasons you can find men there like a pfc I will call Joe Simkin. Joe is beefy and blond, and comes from a steel town in Pennsylvania. He used to be a swell guy, comical, noisy, funloving, acting the part of an amateur Jackie Gleason, yet often warmhearted and willing to talk about serious things. Then Joe began to change. He talked a lot about the "Krauts," claimed they would knife any GI they caught alone, were playing ball with the Reds, were always saying foul things to Americans in German. Then one night he got mad in a beer parlor at something he thought a German said about Americans, and started a free-for-all. On Monday morning he was missing, and turned up dead drunk in a local bordello, having beaten two girls black and blue. In the guardhouse, he cursed and beat his fist against the wall all day, thinking of how his mother would cry in shame if she knew.

Or you might find skinny, balding Edward Griffin, lying on a bunk in a barracks room reading the same page of a book unseeingly for the twentieth time, and hoping the fellows would leave him alone as they passed in and out. Ed is a married man with two children, but the boys call him "Ethel" because he's as fussy and gentle as an old lady. He washes his hands twenty times a day, and lives in terror of catching some unspeakable disease in the barracks. He hasn't been able to eat a decent meal for several months, and is looking gaunt and sickly. A bright and competent accountant at home, he has recently been messing up his clerical work at regimental headquarters until the captain personally bawled him out in front of the office force. Ed is thinking of suicide tonight; he also is wondering whether he could accidentally get in an auto crash or something, and be shipped off to the hospital in Munich, but he knows inwardly he'll never have the courage to do anything except lie there, with tears rolling out of the corners of his eyes.

Or you might find a tall young fellow from a good decent home in the midwest, proud of his three stripes and excellent record, suddenly going AWOL on a five-day alcoholic binge, and quite unable to understand, afterwards, why he did it. Or an intelligent, curly-headed lad of eighteen, who begins one evening to get the names of all his barracks mates mixed up; for a while he stares at them in deep wonderment as though they were strangers and enemies, then starts cursing and mumbling accusations that no one can understand.

These are a few of the men you could meet there — men like your own neighbors, friends, cousins, and sons, succumbing to prolonged anxiety, danger, loneliness, rigid discipline, loss of their own personal importance, and the absence of people who filled their own special needs. They are frustrated, bored, fearful and unhappy; and some of them get sick from it all.

Strangely and tragically, our Army had found an answer in two wars, yet overlooked it and neglected for years to apply it in peacetime Germany.

In the North African fighting of 1942, men with combat exhaustion — battlefield nervous breakdown — were arriving in large numbers at the medical clearing stations. They tottered in, haggard, filthy, glazed of eye; some twitched spasmodically, some mumbled to themselves, some wept or cursed softly, some suffered continual diarrhea or nausea. After a check-up, the doctors shipped them off hundreds of miles to the rear to base hospitals; here they lived in NP wards of the hospital, and began to get treatment. But the delay, the distance from the front, and the comfort of hospital life all caused their fears, their physical symptoms and their self-made excuses to jell into firm mental ailments. As a result, only a pitiful few — 5 per cent — ever got well enough to rejoin their own outfits up at the front.

In the spring of 1943 two army psychiatrists in Tunisia tried working at a forward evacuation hospital with newly arriving psychiatric casualties. The moment they arrived from the battlefield, the doctors prescribed four days of rest and sedation a few miles from the fighting, good food, clean clothes, and an hour or two of personal interview during which a psychiatrist explained that fear and guilt were normal human reactions to battle, and let the men talk out their shame and their gripes. Does it sound too simple? Perhaps; but the number who could shake off the gathering neurosis, pull together their shattered personalities, and rejoin their buddies at the front soared from 5 per cent to 50 per cent.

"With the passage of time," explains Colonel Frederick Hanson, who was then psychiatrist for the Mediterranean theater, "the process [of neurosis] tends to become stabilized and fixed, but early it is still amorphous, and can be easily dissipated." The use of front-line psychiatry spread throughout the Army, and in the last year of the war between 45 and 70 per cent of all men who "cracked up" under battle had their nervous disorder swiftly aborted, and returned to their outfits. This invaluable discovery was apparently forgotten afterwards, for when the Korean conflict broke out there was no provision for psychiatric first aid for our forces there. Through extraordinary efforts a program was set up, however, and operating within two months. A one-to-two-day rest at a clearing station — with sedation, a bath, and a reassuring interview — got fully half the men back to duty, and to health. The half whose disturbance was too severe to yield to this were sent further back to a field hospital where they were given five to ten days of rest, games, training and exercise, special treatment under narcosis in some cases, and rather deeper-searching sessions with the psychiatrists; they remained in uniform the whole time, and did not lead a hospitalized type of life. Over half of these, in turn, recovered under this treatment and went back to their units. The remainder had either to be reassigned to noncombat duties, or sent to special neuropsychiatric hospitals in Japan.

But a terrible danger lay in wait at the rear hospital — a thing the doctors call "secondary gain." A soldier fighting on the front cracks up, and finds himself after a while in a clean warm bed, hundreds of miles from battle. This is quite an improvement; failure has become a kind of success; and almost inevitably his physical and mental symptoms ossify into a stone-hard neurosis.

"By the time they get to the rear hospital," says Colonel Albert Glass, who set up and ran the program in Korea, "such patients may become resentful and hostile towards therapy. The success of the neurotic mechanism fosters a repetitive pattern." A man afraid of death becomes sick from his fear, the sickness saves him from death, and a pattern of neurotic escape from his problems may remain with him for life.

Colonel Glass is only one of many psychiatrists who point out that the factors that make men break down in combat are only exaggerations of similar pressures all of us feel, more or less, in peacetime life. When they get too strong or too numerous, some of us react with illness, and a kind of escape.

Many of the most painful sorts of pressures have been bearing upon our soldiers stationed in Germany for years, pressures keener and stronger than those at home; hence Seventh Army troops have been succumbing to psychiatric ailments 35 per cent more often than troops in the United States, and almost as often as soldiers actually fighting and living among death in Korea. Yet astonishingly enough, for years it did not seem to occur to anyone to try a program comparable to the World War II or Korean front-line psychiatric service.

In January, 1953, Major General Charles T. Lanham took command of the First Division, and as he pored over the medical records and troop strength reports in his new headquarters, he was dismayed at what he found.

In Kitzingen, some ten miles away, thirty-one-year-old Captain James Bell, the division psychiatrist, was startled and a bit alarmed to hear that the CG wanted to see him post haste. Bell's duties had been limited chiefly to sitting in a small musty office and initialing reports of problem soldiers up for discharge. He had had almost no chance to use the psychiatric knowledge he had gained as a civilian doctor in hospital service, or as an army officer on NP service in a military hospital in Munich.

"Bell," said General Lanham when the psychiatrist was shown in, "what are you doing over in Kitzingen anyhow?"

"Reviewing separation cases, sir," quavered Bell.

"Nonsense," snapped Lanham. "We can use you better than that. We need to stop men from getting ill and into trouble, not just ship them home after they're hopeless." Lanham wanted Bell to locate and treat the men who were starting to drink, fight, get the jitters, or fail in their duties. Newly integrated Negro non-coms, tensely competing with white non-coms, Korean vets trying to maintain their exalted status over green troops, adolescent kids, lonesome young husbands, weaklings, bullies, and just plain guys of all sorts who were showing the strain of a tense border-patrol life in a foreign land — all were to be in Bell's domain.

Bell practically stammered in his enthusiasm. But he was only one man, he pointed out, and additional psychiatrically trained doctors were all but impossible to get. He and Lanham talked it over for hours, and finally decided that the program would have to rely on the help of the company doctors, chaplains, and commanding officers.

"Okay," said Lanham. "It's all yours. You work out the details of a program, and we'll start to spread the word around." Any psychiatrist would have jumped at the chance; but perhaps James Bell was even more excited by the idea of helping people in emotional trouble, who were living under pressure. For he knows all too well what those things mean: he himself is a Negro.

At the next monthly command conference with his division staff officers, and regimental and battalion commanders, General Lanham lit into a vigorous sales talk about early psychiatric care. "I don't want the average lieutenant to become a doctor looking for symptoms," he explained. "I *do* want him to think of guys who begin to act strangely or hit the bottle or fail in their duties — not as goldbricks, but as men who need help quickly." Then he introduced Bell, who talked earnestly and fervently to the sixty-odd officers about the history of combat psychiatry, and how a peacetime equivalent might work.

Immediately after that first session, Bell began jeeping around the Bavarian countryside from one unit to another, seeking out and talking to company doctors, line officers, chaplains and even non-coms, until he felt that they all began to understand the program, and how they could be part of it. "I was amazed," he says, "to find that a lot of them had never even heard of preventive psychiatry. They thought a psychiatrist sees only 'crazy' people or horrible criminals. But a lot of them took to the new idea pretty well, except for some hard-bitten officers of the 'treat-them-tough' school." Instead of cracking down on a man who was acting out of line, Bell encouraged them to try to help the man directly, and if that failed, then to refer him to Bell himself for early treatment.

"Often just a sympathetic CO or kind chaplain is what's needed," Bell used to explain, "— someone higher up to whom the soldier can let off steam, someone reassuring and protective, who can make him see his problems sanely and without exaggeration." Within a matter of months, Bell had scores of unofficial psychiatric assistants throughout the division. In tents, on a fallen tree in the woods, in a recreation room of some *Kaserne*, in a company doctor's office, troubled young men halfway into the bewildering nightmare of nervous breakdown began to sit and talk out their troubles with newly sympathetic officers and doctors. In our own lives, each of us has known the warm relief of simply explaining all our irritations to someone who can hear us out, and who can then tell us how it seems from his outside perspective.

That is perhaps half of the job in simple psychotherapy, and that is what Bell got started in General Lanham's division. "We had the front-line stuff working so well," General Lanham says, "that for a guy to get back to Bell, he had to be a *real* problem."

Nevertheless, Bell was still the key man, and the only professionally qualified psychotherapist. As the officers and men of the division became aware that a psychiatrist wasn't there just to issue "Section Eights," but to help the average man with deeply personal worries, the number of men they referred to Bell for treatment zoomed up. From seven or eight a month, the case load swiftly grew to twenty, then thirty, then fifty. Instead of watching a soldier worsen until he had to be packed off to a general hospital, a CO would send him over by jeep or truck to see Bell for an hour, then have him hustle back to his outfit to resume his duties that same day until time for his next visit. It minimized his illness in his own mind, yet got him into medical treatment; indeed, it got him into treatment long before he would have sought it out for himself, had he been a civilian.

Dr. Benjamin Balser, an overseas psychiatric consultant to the Surgeon General of the Army, came through Wurzburg and Kitzingen on an inspection tour and was enthusiastic about what he saw. "Mental first aid," he says, "was proving almost as useful in a peacetime situation as I had seen it prove in the Korean fighting."

A typical case was that of a twenty-two-year-old private who had begun "riding the sick book" with headaches, backache, and a variety of vague but incapacitating pains. The company doctor could find no disease, and felt that the man was a neuropsychiatric case for Bell. The soldier was a sullen, unfriendly young man who had no pals in the outfit, and was often getting into scraps with the other men when they badgered him for being lazy, ill-tempered, and vain about his long, carefully brushed hair. Bell interviewed him, and recognized that this was an "immaturity reaction." The fellow had had a domineering mother who never let him grow up and learn responsibility. At heart he was still a selfish, rebellious small boy who wanted everything his own way. Life among his unsympathetic fellow soldiers was consequently so miserable that his only way out — not consciously taken, of course — was to feel sick enough to escape it all.

In the course of half a dozen visits to Bell, the soldier slowly came to put all this into words, under Bell's skillful guidance, and see himself, at least a little bit, as others did. He was angry, resentful, and yet impressed and thoughtful. One day he walked into Bell's office sporting a crewcut, and Bell was vastly encouraged. Clumsily and unconvincingly, the soldier started trying to play the role of a "good fellow" in the barracks, and he very distinctly improved in his job in the engine repair shop. Some weeks later he was actually invited along one night when a group of the men headed off for town. Two months later he won a promotion to corporal; by that time, he had stopped coming to Bell, and hadn't had a headache or unexplained pain for weeks. He isn't a charming and wonderful man even today; you might still find him often selfish, or unreasonable, or stubborn — but he functions well enough to be a member of his society, a good soldier, and at least a moderately healthy human being.

A quiet slender man from Salt Lake City was practically unable to carry on as staff sergeant of a company because of tormenting doubts about the faithfulness of his wife back home. The torment turned out to be mostly a result of his pinning on her his own secret guilt in cheating with German girls. The psychiatrist couldn't remake the man's character and reform his weekend habits, but at least got him to discard his irrational worry and go about his work again.

A husky, fresh-faced farm lad from Iowa was disobeying orders, picking fights with the platoon leader, and talking back to the lieutenant to the point of being almost ready for court martial. Bell pointed out to him he was reacting illogically to the Army as though it were his own unhappy home, and to the CO as though he were his own father. Grudgingly, the boy began to accept discipline, and has managed to stay out of trouble ever since.

So it went: migraine headaches, inability to keep food down, fights with broken bottles and switchblades, fear of weapons, trouble with the topkick and the CO, a loss of the sense of duty, a blind disregard for the penalty of disobeying orders — these were some of the symptoms that Bell attacked and dissolved, before they could become a permanent part of a man's way of life.

In June, 1953, as Bell's program was beginning to run smoothly, he was sent back to the United States on rotation; but General Lanham, who remained with the First Division another year, kept up his personal enthusiasm, and succeeding division psychiatrists had no difficulty keeping it going. The results have therefore been continuously excellent.

In 1952, before the program began, only a few score men in the division had gotten any personal attention from the psychiatrist. In 1953, Bell and his successor personally attended 378 men, and in 1954 more than 500. Many unrecorded hundreds of others were seen and helped by their company doctors and immediate superiors, and given encouragement, time off, reassignment, reassurance and friendly understanding.

The exact effects of all this are hard to measure. To a large extent, it has resulted in a better division, with higher morale and greater fighting strength; but in peacetime one can hardly prove these intangibles.

There are some revealing measurements, however. In 1953, the first year of the program, there was a 45 per cent drop in the number of men separated from the First Division for "unfitness," a type of discharge given to certain kinds of psychiatric cases. From February through June of 1954, the First Division lost 1683 man-days due to psychiatric illness; three other comparable infantry divisions lost 2213, 3024, and 3895. Between February and the end of August, 1954, the First Division had to ship back to the United States only fourteen of its men for NP reasons; the three other infantry divisions shipped back thirty-three, twenty-four, and thirty-two respectively.

In the far-off fastnesses of the Pentagon the top brass heard, was impressed, and finally acted. In early 1954 a new Army regulation called for "mental hygiene consultation services" to be set up in all divisions of the Seventh Army, and the divisions other than the First, which had had authorized openings for psychiatrists, but had never been able to get any sent out by Washington, now started getting their men. In May, 1954, the program became official and in force for the Seventh Army, little more than a year after "Buck" Lanham and James Bell first started trying it.

Today the division psychiatrists of the Seventh Army are seeing about

1500 men per year for treatment; and one can only guess how many hundreds or thousands more are being helped by their own psychiatrically alert company doctors and chaplains. It is still too early for any statistical results from the Seventh Army, but there is every reason to expect that the First Division success will be repeated.

What can such a program actually do for the men it treats? Colonel Glass says it won't often change the fundamental character of a man or remake him in a fine new mold. What it *will* do is arrest and dissipate an illness that arises when the personality he happens to have tangles with a temporarily difficult environment.

"If you put a man in the hospital to tackle his mental or emotional illness," says Colonel Glass, "he fixes his attention on his symptoms. They become his way of adjusting to the stresses he was under — by escaping them. That's what makes for a chronic neurotic. Remaining on duty and *handling* the problem is the adult way of acting. Psychiatrists can't make everybody happy all the time, but we *can* help get them geared to realistic and more healthful living."

Dr. Balser, one of the many prominent civilian psychiatrists who believe that preventive psychiatry is the hope of the future, feels that the Seventh Army program is showing the way for civilian medicine. "The soldiers get sent in early, whether they want to or not," he points out. "In civilian life, few people go to a psychiatrist or a clinic until they feel so terrible that they *have* to go — and then most of them don't go anyhow, not realizing what their trouble is. In any case, by that time treatment involves long hard work, and a cure isn't at all a sure thing."

There are 717,000 Americans in mental hospitals at this moment, and about 20,000,000 others not in hospitals who suffer less total, but nevertheless agonizing and hampering emotional and mental illnesses.[*] That means there is only about one psychiatrist for every 1500 people actually needing his help. Sometimes it seems hopeless. "But," Dr. Balser points out, "it was preventive medicine, not curative medicine, that has all but wiped out diseases like typhoid fever and diphtheria. I believe it can be the answer to mental disease as well — perhaps the only answer in the long run."

[*] These are 1964 figures.

Since the publication of the above article in 1955, Mental Hygiene Consultation Services have expanded and become part of the over-all pattern of Army psychiatry, and Colonel Glass, in a recent study of the subject, attributes to the Army psychiatric program a significant part in the "consistent decrease in noneffective personnel."

Brigadier General Conn L. Milburn, Jr., Acting Surgeon General, writes me as follows about the above article:

"Preventive psychiatry has continued to flourish in the Army military establishment, both in this country and overseas. The 3rd Infantry, 8th Infantry, 3rd Armored, 24th Infantry, and 4th Armored Divisions in Europe saw a total of 7350 different military personnel in the Division psychiatric facilities in 1962. [As for results], the Mental Hygiene Consultation Service of the 3rd Armored Division in 1961 saw 902 individual military patients, less than 4 per cent of whom were referred to hospitals. The Mental Hygiene Consultation Service of the 24th Infantry Division in 1961 saw 1186 individual military patients, and referred only 25 [2 per cent] to hospitals, [etc.]. The Division psychiatric facilities overseas have, in my estimation, all continued to operate within a preventive frame of reference. The Army's rates of discharge for psychiatric reasons and our incidence of hospitalization for psychiatric illness have continued to decline worldwide, since the time of your article in 1955, while the rates of outpatient psychiatric treatments have continued to rise."

Our Tormented College Kids

(Coauthor: RENA CORMAN)

THE SCENE is a fine old eastern men's college; the time is night; the action consists of a young man — dead drunk and loudly profane — walking around the coping on the fourth floor of his dormitory, while police, doctors, and friends hold their breath below.

The scene is a large university in the west; the time is 2 A.M.; the action consists of a young girl slipping softly out of her sorority house and hurrying to a car, in which a sweating young man is waiting to drive her to an abortionist in a city a hundred miles away.

The scene is a railroad track not far west of Philadelphia; the time is early morning; the action consists of the onrushing train, a startled engineer slamming on the brakes, and the wheels decapitating an eighteen-year-old coed from a fine prestige college, who had calmly lain down and put her neck on the rail a minute earlier.

The scene is almost any American college campus; the time is just about any time; the action consists of any of a thousand different deeds, some dreadful, some pitiful, some solitary, some violently public — all of them the result of overwhelming emotional distress.

A fine old American tradition says that the college years are a veritable Golden Age, the Best Years of Our Lives. Though there have always been some disturbed, wild, frightened or unhappy college kids, the prevailing mood on most campuses in the past was that college was an intoxicating time of carefree fun, flowering youth, intellectual stimulation, and intense, marvelous emotions. Almost unnoticed by anyone but deans and school psychiatrists — and college students themselves — that tradition has, for many, been changing radically. For a minority of the students — but a surprisingly large minority — the college years have become a time of confusion, misery, frustration, and failure. At the University of Pennsylvania, 20 per cent of the students require help from the mental health service during their college years. At Harvard, 25 per cent of the undergraduates sooner or later go to a psychiatrist or social worker. But these percentages reflect no discredit on Penn or Harvard; elsewhere, at scores of colleges which offer mental health services, the figures are comparable, or would be if students used the services as they should. A recent poll of six hundred college psychiatrists revealed that about 15 per cent of the students in their institutions seek psychiatric help — but that about 30 per cent ought to.

What is geniunely surprising is the extent to which this distress has been ignored, or left to the students themselves to handle. So far, only about 6 per cent of the two thousand institutions of higher learning in this country have established mental health clinics for their students. These schools know the emotional distress that underlies much of present-day college life; many of the others ignore it or conceal it behind familiar pedagogic labels such as "underachievement," "overcutting classes," "probation because of borderline averages," "unbecoming conduct," and "suspension because of violation of privileges." And, of course, "drop-out [or withdrawal] for academic reasons"; nearly half of the 1,100,000 hopeful young men and women who enter college this fall will join the shadowy ranks of those who never graduate, and who are perennially ashamed, defensive, or dishonest about what happened to them.

Behind the outmoded and inadequate labels is the truth of widespread emotional disorder among today's student population. Campus physicians and nurses often see it as headaches and nightmares, cramps or retching before examination time, fatigue, overweight, and forgetfulness. Campus disciplinarians frequently see worse symptoms: drinking and rioting, gambling, outbreaks of cheating on exams, sexual promiscuity. And the police and coroner occasionally see still worse things: the hypodermic syringe and the packet of "snow," the empty bottle marked "Poison," the open tenth-story window.

Is this the American Dream come true — the dream of a college education for everyone who could benefit from it? Where are the joy and zest that are supposed to go with intellectual discovery, and why have they so often been replaced with worry and strain? Why are the lighthearted undergraduates, who once got A's in canoe, dance floor, and parked car, a shrinking variety; and the earnest, weary, worried undergraduates a growing one? Problems and emotional upsets may always have been part of this time of life, but they used to seem rare, and even romantic: Yale men, for instance, have long sung, in charming melancholy, "We're poor little lambs who have lost our way: Baa, Baa, Baa . . ." Only it isn't so charming now: a study done at Yale showed suicide to be the second most common cause of student deaths at Yale (second only to accidents, though considerably lower), and studies at other colleges would probably show similar results. Nationally, among people of the same age group, suicide is the sixth most common cause of death.

What on earth is happening? It would be comforting to discover a single cause for the emotional troubles that afflict a quarter to a third of our college students — especially if it were one that could be easily overcome. But the fact is that there are many causes — none of them easy to overcome.

If there is no single cause, however, at least many of the separate causes named by authorities have a single origin — ironically enough, the American Dream itself. The idea of college for everyone, and the importance attached by our society to a college degree — especially the right degree from the right school — have created a whole set of unique new pressures on our young people, causing many of them to feel distress, and making others falter, thrash about wildly, flunk out, or even succumb to nervous breakdowns.

Since World War II, our society has become so explosively college-conscious that teen-agers start to worry years ahead of time whether there will be room for them in a good school. In the 1930's only a relative handful of high-school seniors took the grueling College Entrance Board Exams; today, although they are much tougher, about a million and a quarter seniors take them — plus several hundred thousand sweating and straining juniors, who suffer through them just for "practice." No wonder these youngsters, by seventeen, toss sleeplessly at night, develop nervous twitches, and scream at their brothers and sisters, while waiting for the letter of acceptance on which their whole life seems to hang.

A generation ago, a high-school student applied to college somewhere in the spring of his last year; today, admissions officers at the more desirable colleges get letters and applications from parents of seventh- and eighth-graders. Dr. John D. Black, director of the Counseling and Testing Center at Stanford University, says that in many cases the pressure to be accepted by a good college actually begins in elementary school.

But being admitted is not the end of the long years of stress; after a brief period of respite, things only get worse, since today there is no acceptable answer except successful graduation from college. "To quit school or to flunk out are no longer reasonable options as they were when most of us were in college," says Dr. Black. "They are as unacceptable as a dishonorable discharge from the service or a felony conviction. The result is more intense, self-serving competition, more temptation to succeed by hook or by crook, more hostility and anxiety."

One of the modern thumbscrews applying these damaging social pressures to the student is, all too often, his own well-meaning father or mother. Many a dad, from the time his boy is crawling on the floor in diapers, envisions him as, say, a Harvard man, and begins the propaganda. What the boy may prove to want or need is ignored; after all, what does a kid know? The Harvard roommate of a boy who had just flunked out described such a relationship bitterly. "Bob was a good kid. He'd have made out almost anywhere else, but no, his father had to have a Harvard man for his law firm. So now he's got a Harvard failure. I hope he's satisfied."

Ronald (as we will call him) was another case of misplaced parental ambition. Blond, crewcut, athletic and good-looking, he seemed perfectly typecast at a fine Ivy League college. But he didn't act it; he stayed alone in his room a great deal "to beat the books," as he said — though often he smelled not of the lamp but of whiskey. Besides, his grades weren't all that good, though he had an excellent high-school record. By sophomore year, he was cutting classes frequently, drinking much more, and teetering on the brink of academic failure. The night he punched his fist through a window and needed ten stitches, the physician was able to persuade him to see the college psychiatrist.

"I never wanted to come here, anyway," Ronald admitted to the psychiatrist. "But my father did. He was always bugging me to get another prize, or join another club, so I'd be sure to be accepted — to make up for him. And I did. I made the honors list all through high school. And I think half the people in the town where I come from knew me, I belonged to so darned many organizations. It's different here, though — all the guys must come from the same prep school, or something. They're just one big happy family, talking their own special language, and a fellow like me can't make it with them. When I used to try, they'd freeze up, and look at me down their noses, as if I smelled bad or something. So I started to drink. And then the guys liked me even less, and my grades got even worse. I didn't know what to do, so I took another drink."

Ronald talked over his problems searchingly with the psychiatrist for half a dozen hours, and then decided to transfer to a coed state college; there he was much more comfortable, and got along well. He was one of the lucky ones; thousands of others like him never get such help, and quietly sink from view. Others muddle through on their own, at the cost of lifelong psychic damage.

Parents also pass society's pressure on to their children via excessive emphasis on academic success. In their eagerness to believe they have a brilliant child, they may fail to hear their average child's cries of distress. Barbara, a petite dark-haired girl from Chicago, had been driven hard enough by her parents to get good grades in high school. At an excellent western university, however, she got C's and D's — and even then, only by dint of denying herself any time for fun and relaxation.

Feeling guilty and inadequate, she was ripe for trouble. It came in the form of Dan, a boy she fell in love with in her second year, but who only partly returned the feeling. At once her grades began to slip badly and unfinished assignments piled up. Deeply depressed and full of morbid thoughts, Barbara visited the university psychiatrist and, at his advice, wrote to her parents, asking them to let her take a leave of absence and reconsider her plans in life. They were horrified, and wrote directly to the psychiatrist.

"Our Barbara is a brilliant girl," they said, "but she has never even begun to achieve what she is capable of. Instead of leaving now — which would wreck all our plans for her — she should stay, give up that boy, and redouble her efforts to make the dean's list. That's *our* idea of psychotherapy!" Barbara, when she learned of this letter, spoke out more plainly — she gulped a dozen sleeping pills. Found in time, she was saved and sent home — a winner of the battle, a loser of the war.

A third, and very common, way in which parents put pressure on their children is in the matter of choice of career. Hundreds of thousands of unhappy young men and women have suffered through years of training in some field they dislike, because their parents are using them to achieve a vicarious glory. Social worker Bernard Neugeboren, formerly of Yale's Division of Student Mental Hygiene, describes one solution such students unconsciously find as "passive-resistive failure."

"They assert the right to decide about their lives," he says, "by quietly failing in the work they were forced to take."

Louis, a premedical student whose high-school record and entrance exams gave him a predicted college average of 89 at Yale, was actually averaging only 71, and sliding down towards expulsion. He himself had little idea why. "My professors are creeps," he would say one time; later he would say, "What's the use? — we're all going to be blown up soon, anyhow"; still later he'd admit, "I try but I can't seem to concentrate." In three hours of discussions with Neugeboren, however, he quickly managed to see that his near-failure was his way of protesting against a medical career; he thereupon asserted himself by boldly switching to economics and telling his family about it in unarguable terms. Within weeks, his average rose to the 80's.

Not all the pressures bearing down on today's students are passed on to them by their parents. Indeed, students themselves often feel that they generate a lot of their own tensions. "We tell each other again and again how many of us are likely to flunk out," said a senior at M.I.T. "We pass on all the rumors about how only the top guys get decent jobs. We work ourselves into a real lather and grind away at our books all night. No wonder we get stomach trouble or nightmares."

But students who talk like this are hardly to blame; they are merely reflecting the attitude of the society all around them. And of the college of their choice. For the colleges themselves bear a considerable share of the responsibility for this situation. Most of them — particularly the desired schools — have been raising their standards of admission, increasing the requirements for passing courses, dropping many students who would have sailed through easily in the 1930's, and encouraging an atmosphere of fierce competition — even though students suffer from it all.

Moreover, the increased academic competitiveness hurts not only the less capable students but many of the extremely bright ones as well. Former Dean Everett Hunt of Swarthmore has said that melancholia seems especially common among exceptionally able students, and Richard C. Carroll, associate dean of Yale College, candidly says, "Somehow, in striving for brighter students — and getting them — we have increased the incidence of emotional instability. Indeed, of those students who have academic difficulty at Yale and drop out, at least half have IQ's and abilities definitely above average for the school population." The most desired schools, accordingly, have tried to screen out applicants who show signs of emotional instability — and this, too, has failed. When Stanford, for instance, began to be swamped with applications a few years ago, the school was enabled to choose only well-adjusted students, but it made no difference. "We are now far more selective than ever," says Dr. Black — "and the demand for psychotherapy is heavier than ever."

How does this come about? For one thing, some gifted people cannot thrive — cannot even endure — in a highly competitive and regulated atmosphere; they need one that is more cooperative, or permissive, or intimate. For another thing, many a student who was outstanding in his local public school is shocked and depressed, on entering a fine, highly competitive college, to find that he has at best a middling sort of talent. "It nearly threw me," said a Cornell sophomore, "when I came here last year. I'd always had a straight A average, and suddenly I was making only C's. This was the Big Time, and I found out I was from Hicksville. I was so miserable I wanted to throw in the towel." Many bright young people lack the self-discipline to raise their grades, and let themselves slide into the discard heap. But others furiously goad themselves on, in a single-minded dedication that is also dangerous, or at the very least is productive of misery. This is how one of them, a girl at the University of Illinois, explained it to a dear friend in a letter: "You exist from one assignment to the next, one weekend to the next, living for the time the exam is over — only to start right in on the next one. The pace doesn't let you stop and take a look at *what* you're doing or *why*. You feel like you're on a something-or-other that keeps going and you can't get off. That's how I've managed to make the honors list — big deal! I don't even know why I care — or *if* I care."

So far, the people who know most about student emotional disorders show little agreement on the subject; each classifies them in his own way, each has his own idea which factors are most responsible. But many agree with Dean James H. Robertson of the University of Michigan that "far and away the chief cause is personal unreadiness or immaturity."

Teen-agers who have always had their parents on hand to guide and direct them are suddenly told that they are young men and women on their own. This has always been a problem with college freshmen, but today it is a much greater one, for now it is "the thing" to go to a college far from home, and utterly square to go to one within daily commuting distance. The modern stresses and strains of college life bear down particularly hard on the young man or woman whose immaturity is the result of parental overprotection. Formerly, many such young people delayed going to college or even avoided it altogether; today, in obedience to what society seems to expect, they plunge right in, often in a remarkable state of prolonged childhood. At Penn a social worker interviewed a fidgety, almost tearful young man who was suffering from heart palpitations and depression, and thinking of leaving school; at eighteen he was still so unused to relying on himself that he would call his parents long distance for permission to go out at night to a movie. At Yale, a distraught freshman came to the student mental health service and hesitantly explained that he couldn't study, had no love for his family, acted awkward and foolish on dates, and felt continually anxious. The psychiatrist found that he was still emotionally a small boy; his mother, in fact, sent him fried chicken once a week and cookies in between times, and visited him on campus in between the three-hundred-mile round trips he made home almost every weekend.

According to some college psychiatrists, the most common disorder they see is that kind of immaturity technically known as "personality disorder" or "character disorder." People with a character disorder are often irresponsible, impulsive, and lacking in conscience; they do what they please, without caring what society will think of them, even as does a small naughty child. Typically, they may get drunk, cheat on exams, cut classes, smoke "pot," act rude and vulgar, "sleep around," or build bonfires on the president's front lawn — all without feeling particularly uneasy or guilty. On some campuses, character disorders account for a substantial portion of suspensions and expulsions precisely because, of all students in trouble, these are the least likely to give a damn, or to respond to mental hygiene techniques.

And yet there is considerable hope for these people, for time is an effective medicine against immaturity. At Harvard, immature students who are misbehaving or verging on failure are urged to take leave of absence, rather than flunk out, and to return after one or more years; half who do so come back later, by which time most of them are ready to take themselves and their studies seriously. At Yale, the director of the student mental-health service, Dr. Robert L. Arnstein, said, "We encourage young men of this sort to delay entering college, or, if they have done so and run into trouble, to go on leave and put in their two years of military service. We once did a follow-up study of drop-outs and found that the majority of those with character disorders either came back and graduated, or finished college elsewhere, or were successfully at work. All in all, a very high proportion of them turned out relatively well."

On a far larger scale — though less serious, as an emotional disturbance — is the universal problem of growing up, which Erik Erikson, the eminent psychoanalyst and student of child development, has called "the identity crisis." Somewhere in the process of maturing, every young man and woman must figure out and assume his or her adult identity. Everyone, of course, has to cross this barrier, but it assumes a special difficulty for college students because they delay their final decisions for years, at the cost of facing a bewildering array of new possibilities. Though the delay may lead to a more satisfying choice in the end, it may also lead to illness; as psychologist Charles McArthur of Harvard says, "This overlong tentative state of mind is fertile soil for the growth of neuroses."

There are two special points on which the collegian's identity crisis fastens — choice of career, and sexual identity. Though many students find the freshman year bewildering and difficult, it is during the sophomore year that most students must decide on a major subject, keyed to their choice of career. The frequent result is "sophomore slump" — declining grades and deteriorating behavior, the by-product of indecision and perplexity. For the woman, however, this crisis occurs a second time, in stronger form, in the senior year, when her future is imminent, and seems to involve the dilemma of marriage or career. Each seems to have its penalty — the former, the abandonment of all her college interests and achievements, the latter, the risk of missing out on love.

marriage, and motherhood. All too often, says Miriam Shelden, dean of women at the University of Illinois, they succumb to "senior clutch" — a frantic grasping at whatever men are currently nearest to hand, with resulting marriages that create more problems than they solve.

Sex is the other aspect of the identity crisis which makes difficulties for many college students. "Am I really a man?" is a painful question for any youth — particularly when, being in college, he can only answer it by premarital experiences (which may be difficult and guilt-producing) or by early marriage (which may force him out of college altogether). Moreover, the college student, with his supposedly decent habits, regular studying, and cultivated tastes, is aware of the typically American prejudices that regard the "good boy" and the scholar as vaguely feminine. As a result, many a student comes to the college psychiatrist filled with needless fears of latent homosexuality. Some men refuse to go swimming nude with others in gym class; some try to avoid having a roommate; some desperately seek to prove their own manliness with any available girl — and fail precisely because they have no real interest in the girl.

Sex is a somewhat different problem for the girl. She wants to prove her desirability, but is well aware that intimacy is frowned upon more severely for women than men, and sanctioned neither by her parents, her church, her school, nor even many of her friends. She has the responsibility of setting limits on the relationship with any boy she dates or likes, and risking his deserting her for an easier, surer thing. In several recent surveys, the majority of college women admit that at times they have "gone farther" than they should have, and that they feel guilty about it; even if, because they are in love, they feel it is morally all right to pet, or "go all the way," they still sedulously conceal what they are doing from their families, and even from their roommates, and have to bear the burden of their secrets alone. As one college girl put it, "Freshman year, the problem girls talk about is what to do when a boy tries to unbutton your blouse; sophomore year, when he reaches up under your skirt; and after that, everybody shuts up."

One extremely grave emotional trauma that results from this secrecy is the unwanted pregnancy which the girl and her boy friend have to terminate by abortion. Just how many college girls get pregnant today is unknown. Startling rumors float around on certain campuses: a senior at a small, highly respectable girls' college said, "Why, half the girls on this campus are going to bed with their boy friends. I know three girls personally who've had to have abortions." But neither health officials nor deans know all the facts, since the vast majority of the girls never tell the truth about their one-week or two-week absence from classes, or their withdrawal from school "for reasons of health."

Sexual problems of all sorts have a special force in college because today so many young people are thrust suddenly into a sophisticated, open-minded environment for which nothing in their background has prepared them. But such difficulties are only part of the larger problem implicit in the broadening out of the college population from a small élite to people drawn from nearly all walks of life. "Two or three generations ago," says Dr. Carl M. Grip, dean of men at Temple University, "only 5 or 10 per cent of high-school students went on to college, and the undergraduate population was pretty much of a piece. The students came from homes with a college background and a good deal of sophistication. They all had relatively comparable standards and ideas of behavior. Today the picture is radically different. Nearly 60 per cent of our high-school graduates now enter college — and hundreds of thousands of them come from homes in which there was no preparedness for college life. People of all sorts of beliefs, manners, and attitudes are rushing into college and mingling with each other. In a way this is marvelous, but some of them are profoundly shocked and unsettled by their experiences, and many of them suffer keenly."

The great influx of students creates yet another hardship: at the larger state colleges and universities, school populations are so huge — total enrollments of 15,000 to 20,000 are becoming commonplace — that students are apt to feel lost and ignored. Some exist as virtual nonentities, wretchedly lonely for four years. Others redouble their exertions to make themselves known. A bright senior man at the University of Illinois explained it to us. "You get your ID card, and you're afraid all you'll be is just a six-digit number. So you sweat for good grades, you get into all sorts of activities, you poke your way in here and there and run yourself ragged — all to overcome that sense of obscurity and show up as a person." As a psychiatrist at one fine midwestern university says, "Life for students on our campus should be a calm, rich period of maturing and of intellectual activity. Instead, it's filled with all the insecurity, the striving, and the grasping at trivial, mundane things that one finds in the world outside."

Is college today really so much more trying than it has always been? Perhaps not for the majority of students — but it obviously is for a sizable and probably growing minority. Dr. Dana L. Farnsworth, psychiatrist and director of all of Harvard University health services, says: "The emotional problems of today's students certainly seem more severe than those of a generation ago," and Dr. John Black of Stanford is convinced that they are not only more severe, but far more common.

The very fact that there were not more than a dozen clinics or psychological services on American campuses before the war is a strong indication that student problems are genuinely different in kind and volume today. An estimated 125 colleges now have mental-health clinics, most of which have been set up only within the last fifteen years. About 80 other schools employ psychologists, over 150 have guidance and counseling services in which relatively simple emotional problems get at least some attention, and over 100 other schools refer students to easily available and reputable psychiatrists, if they ask for names.

In college after college, as soon as a service is established, the students quietly make their way to it in larger numbers than were expected. Indeed, on many a campus the experience has been that the more psychiatric facilities the school provides, the more students come in with problems they had tried to wrestle with on their own. Harvard inaugurated a Bureau of Study Counsel in 1947, in addition to its long-standing mental-health clinic; each year since then, though admissions standards have risen, the number of students using the bureau has grown. At the University of Pennsylvania, which opened its mental-health clinic on a full-time basis eight years ago, there was a 25 per cent increase each year in the number of students using it until a separate study-counseling service was established as well.

Many, to be sure, come with minor problems — temporary glooms, anxieties, and difficulties with roommates, sex, liquor, or study habits — and are helped in short order: these fleeting disturbances account for perhaps a third of the patients at most clinics. Youth is, after all, flexible and generally healthy, and hurts of all sorts can be healed rapidly if they get early attention.

Other students, with deeper-seated problems, need longer: they may come in once a week for a dozen or two dozen visits. Some schools set no time limits, but none provide deep psychotherapy of the daily-visit variety. Most schools with mental-health clinics offer the services free; a few make a nominal charge. Psychiatrists, psychologists, and social workers make up the staffs; the bulk of their work consists of confidential discussions with the students, utilizing a variety of psychotherapeutic techniques to help them uncover and resolve their problems. Clinic personnel can also test students where necessary, to uncover deeply hidden factors causing disturbance, and in the case of attempted suicide, or other symptoms of serious mental illness, a college psychiatrist can arrange for admission to a nearby hospital. Many colleges also use dormitory counselors — upperclassmen or graduate students who advise perplexed students, lend a sympathetic ear to their troubles, and steer the more seriously vexed ones to the mental-health clinic.

Professional psychological help for college students with emotional and mental disorders is undoubtedly valuable. Yet as of today, most parents and students will still not find this the answer, simply because so small a proportion of the schools have such facilities. What, then, can anyone do? What steps can a parent or his child take by himself? These seem fairly clear, in view of the origins of the problem.

First and foremost, parents should strive especially hard not to apply damaging pressures to their children — even though they may think they are doing so with the best of intent. Glamour schools, prestige careers, high grades — these and other glittering goals may be painful, or even genuinely hazardous, to the student, unless they are really right for him.

Then, parents and their children should pay particular attention, when choosing a college, to selecting one in which the pressures on the student will be minimized — unless he happens to thrive under pressure. The mediocre student should avoid the academically tough college, no matter how alluring or prestigious it is. The student who is unnerved by competition should seek a college with a relaxed and permissive atmosphere, no matter how bright he is. The shy or retiring student should probably avoid the vast impersonal school; and the gregarious, ambitious student might do well to avoid the small egghead liberal arts college, and so on.

Too, parents might prepare the incoming student for the fact that there may be difficulties in adjusting to college. As Dr. Arnstein says, "Stress the fact that initial difficulties do not mean that all is lost; indeed, that there are ways of dealing with them which benefit the student, in the long run."

Parents should also think about the suddenness of the leap into college, and try to minimize the change for the immature child. This might mean that, instead of going out of town his first year, he would go to a school in the vicinity of his home — and plan to transfer elsewhere his second or even third year. It might mean starting at a junior college, and stepping up to a larger, more demanding school for the last two years. It might even mean delaying entrance into college two or three years in order to work or travel, and become somewhat more independent and self-sufficient. Or, if he is already in college — and having trouble — it might mean voluntary withdrawal on leave for a couple of years.

Our sons and daughters may not be able to echo the words of the Yale graduate of 1928, who said as he strolled through the sun-drenched court of his former dormitory, "I can recall only one unhappy period when I was here. That was in May of my senior year, when one morning I suddenly thought, 'My God, it's nearly over — this best time of my life!' " But neither need today's young men and women reflect the sentiments of a bitter senior at M.I.T., who said, "It's a rat-race, a grind, a meaningless ride on a roller-coaster. I'm counting the days till it's over." With enlightened parents and students, and an administration prepared to cope with the problems which must and will arise, college may still offer a liberating, exciting, and inspiring experience. Indeed, perhaps the rising generation will regild the American Dream.

Suicide and Psychosis

The most drastic results of emotional or mental illness are a break-down in the ability to remain in touch with reality, or a violent flight from life itself. I have grouped in this section three articles: the first deals with suicide; the second illustrates five different forms of the breaking-off of contact with life — five different forms of severe mental illness — and the treatment the patients received in a modern mental hospital; and finally, as a kind of mild corrective to the psychodynamic explanations offered in the first two articles, the third article describes investigative work done by a psychiatrist who believes that heredity plays a very large part in mental illness.

The Killers Who Never Go to Jail

THE AIR IS CHILL, this March evening in 1948, but there is a promise of spring in it. A car drives around behind a large, handsome, brand-new home in the sleepy college town of Bloomington, Indiana. In the car is a good-looking young man upon whom fortune has showered blessings: he is physically healthy, happily married; his book is a best seller; he has just been paid $150,000 for movie rights to it; he is full of honors and acclaim. For this young man is Ross Lockridge, Jr., thirty-three, author of the novel *Raintree County*, and brilliantly successful.

But what is young Mr. Lockridge doing? He drives into his garage and locks the door, but he lets the engine continue to run; now he seats himself in the driver's seat, thinking such thoughts as only his Maker knows, while the motor continues to idle. After some minutes, he slumps inertly over the wheel. The harsh light shines down and the motor continues to murmur for hours, until midnight, when his terrified wife and neighbors break in the door and find him there, far beyond any help.

Why? What makes a person do such a thing? We human beings cling to life so tenaciously, despite our fears and burdens, that the act of suicide is a horror and a mystery. And in most cases, as in Lockridge's, the mystery is never really solved.

Yet an even greater mystery is the fact that our society does little or nothing about suicide. It is, after all, the killing of a human being. In 1952, 8270 people in the United States were murdered by other human beings, but 16,030 died by their own hands.* Actually the figure is probably much higher. Because of society's condemnation, a great many cases of suicide are concealed by the relatives. In addition, most psychiatrists believe that a number of the 39,000 annual auto deaths involve an unconscious impulse to self-destruction. At a conservative guess, therefore, between 25,000 and 50,000 Americans take their own lives each year, while as many as 100,000 others attempt suicide, but fail — often to try again. Yet, although we have extensive police departments and courts which try to prevent and solve murders, our coroners and medical examiners and public hospitals are able to give only the most perfunctory attention to preventing or explaining suicides.

Nor is suicide the kind of thing that never happens to you, but only to other people. A sociologist in Chicago and a psychiatrist in New York have separately sampled groups of healthy normal people and found that about 80 per cent of them admit to having thought about committing suicide. Thinking about it isn't the same as committing it, yet the figures seem to mean that nearly all of us harbor a

---

* Latest figures published by the Bureau of the Census (1961) are: homicides 8578; suicides 18,999.

mysterious urge to self-destruction — an urge most of us would, most of the time, violently deny having.

Psychiatrists the world over agree that the real reasons for any suicide are almost always hidden from outsiders, indeed from the victim himself. And because the real reasons are deeply buried in our unconscious minds, says Dr. Gregory Zilboorg, chairman of the now-inactive Committee for the Study of Suicide, Inc., "we grasp at any straw of external plausibility when faced with the discomfort of looking closer and deeper into the problem of life and death."

A case in point concerns a plump, balding, forty-nine-year-old hardware dealer. One Sunday afternoon last summer, he sealed the windows of his Brooklyn apartment with towels, ran a rubber hose from the stove to his own mouth, opened the jet and lay down on the linoleum floor to die. According to the newspaper accounts, a friend tried to call him, got no answer, became worried and finally called the police. A squad car arrived, broke down the door and found the dealer unconscious, but still alive. A suicide note stated that he was too ill to wish to continue living.

The explanation seems satisfactory. A man could reasonably want to kill himself if he were dying anyhow. But the hardware dealer wasn't that sick, and he isn't now. Back at work, he never discusses his "accident," and the friend who summoned help is a perplexed man.

"I never could buy that deal," he said recently. "He wasn't really very sick; just a little of this and that. And do you know why I called the police? Because he had called me on the phone. Sounded stinking drunk. He must have taken some gas already, then called me, then gone back for more. I guess some part of him didn't really want to die; he didn't have any good reasons I know of, and I know him pretty well. How do you figure it, anyhow?"

Detectives both of fact and and of fiction seldom accept the obvious clues to murders or the plausible alibis of the suspected. But they and the rest of us eagerly accept any plausible "reasons" for suicide, even though, like the hardware dealer's illness, these explanations often fail to stand up.

In Fort Worth, in 1952, thirty-one-year-old Air Force Captain Arthur Nelson shot himself to death in his bathroom; in a note, he said he was doing it so that his wife, incurably ill with multiple sclerosis, could collect his $10,000 insurance. Yet how could a man help such a woman less efficiently than by leaving her alone, helpless — and with only $10,000?

Ottmar Fischer, a twenty-five-year-old German baker, had just arrived in San Francisco last summer after a long wait on the quota list. The fog rolled into the harbor; Fischer paced the floor of his aunt's apartment hour by hour, and told her the foghorns reminded him of air-raid sirens. Finally he ran to the roof and leaped four stories to his death. That is all the police and coroner need to know, but who can be satisfied that a man could kill himself for such a reason when millions who lived through air raids feel no such urge?

The commonest of all explanations offered by would-be suicides, according to the National Save-A-Life League, a volunteer organization which tries to talk them out of it, is that they "are tired of life and find it intolerable," but Dr. Zilboorg, whose files include an exhaustive analysis of about 1000 suicides, says that "actually, this has proven to be the least frequent of the valid explanations. If the difficulty of living could, by itself, cause suicide, there would be a thousand times as many as there now are." Whatever a suicide may or may not have known about life, he almost certainly did not know the real reasons for his own final bitter deed. And, for the most part, neither does anyone else.

Yet, although mysteries ordinarily intrigue us, and violent crime moves us to strenuous efforts at investigation and punishment, suicide remains largely ignored or is dealt with in the most superficial manner by the law and the public-health agencies of the nation. In the average city, for instance, when the body of a suicide is found an inspector from the medical examiner's or coroner's office goes along with police to have a look. If the circumstances or the existence of witnesses makes it clearly a case of suicide, the body is quickly released to the relatives' undertaker and the victim becomes a simple statistic. We know whose hand murdered him, but why that hand so acted we have no true idea. "We don't even try to look for the real motives," says an official of the New York City chief medical examiner's office. "All we're concerned with is, are they real suicides or not?"

Cases which are not clear-cut remain at the morgue and are autopsied in the effort to prove the manner of death. If even then the situation remains unclear, the D.A. gets the case and investigates the possibilities of homicide.

Even this limited amount of investigation — cold, frigid, dehumanized — is in large part due to the complications of insurance law. Most companies do not pay benefits if suicide occurs in less than one year, or sometimes two, after the policy took force; and all companies refuse to pay a double-indemnity accident benefit to the beneficiary of a suicide. As a result of these rules, relatives quite often bring suit against the insurance companies, and juries have been known to show more sympathy for a widow than respect for the chief medical examiner's testimony.

One recent case involved a man who was killed by a subway train a hundred yards down the track from the station, where he had no possible reason to be walking. His coat had been left behind, neatly folded, at the edge of the platform — a typical last act of many jumpers and self-hangers. But his widow sued the insurance company for double-indemnity accident benefits, and since there was no other evidence, such as poison in the stomach, she won.

Such is the extent of society's interest in those who have died by their own hand. Its interest in those who wish to die, but are not yet dead, is somewhat keener — or at least more dramatically expressed. The job of foiling suicide attempts falls to the police department. In New York City, for instance, a special section known as the Emergency Service Division handles this assignment, along with many others.

When a call comes in about a jumper poised on some window ledge or gas seeping out from behind some locked door, radio patrol cars of the Emergency Service Division rush to the scene, as does a specially equipped truck which carries antijumper nets, inhalators, and other first-aid equipment. If the police successfully talk the jumper in or revive the gassed victim, they send him in an ambulance to Bellevue Psychiatric or some other city hospital.

Here the staff psychiatrists and other workers make a "case workup," which consists of interviews, tests and a certain amount of therapy in the form of discussions with the psychiatrist and possibly some shock treatments. At the end of the work-up, which takes between one and two weeks, about two-thirds of the cases are considered out of "immediate danger" and they are released to relatives or in their own custody. The others are committed to state or private hospitals for further treatment.

City funds permit nothing more to be done for the two-thirds who are released. Yet the brief work-up has performed no miracles; it scarcely ever uncovers the hidden factors that caused the wild act, and certainly it has little chance of making permanent changes in the patient's personality or pattern of life.

Of course, the search for the real causes of suicide has not been entirely ignored. For over half a century, sociologists, statisticians and others have been examining the death rates from suicide in various ways, and have made a number of surprising discoveries.

An Italian named Morselli found long ago, for instance, that suicide rates in England and Scandinavia were higher than those in Italy. The former are foggy and gloomy, Italy is sunny and cheerful. *Ergo,* said Morselli, bad weather causes suicide. In the United States, Seattle — which has more rain than almost any other major city — has two and a half times as many suicides per 100,000 people as the rest of the country. But actuary Walter G. Bowerman recently spoiled this "explanation" by showing that the five rainiest states in the United States are all far down the list in suicide rates, while the five driest average out quite high.

The clichés of literature hold wintertime, the lonely weekend and the dark of night to be the most likely times for suicide. All three clichés are wrong, according to doctors of the Harvard School of Public Health who surveyed all available data and found that springtime, Monday and Tuesday, and morning are the most likely times.

Some scholars have maintained that religion plays a major part, and point right back to Morselli's figures. Italy is Catholic, Scandinavia Protestant. The Catholic Church takes a sterner view of suicide than the Protestant churches. Hence, the rates are low. Ireland's rate is about one-tenth that of Denmark; Prussia's rate is much higher than that of Catholic Bavaria. But a recent survey in Toronto clouded this picture by producing evidence of a higher suicide ratio for Catholics than for Protestants in that city, and Catholic Austria has one of the highest rates in Europe today.

There does seem to be good evidence that there is less suicide among parents of large families than among the childless — but does it mean that children are a kind of prophylactic or that potentially suicidal personalities don't choose to have children? For half a century suicide rates in the United States have been higher in cities than in the country, and the larger the city the higher the rate. Does this mean that the lack of belonging to small social groups is to blame or that people with an X-factor in their personalities tend to migrate into cities, where they later commit suicide and make the rates high?

Hard times are commonly thought to cause more suicide, and 1932 marked the high point of recent American suicide history. But oddly enough, the rate had been rising from 1923 on, all through the years of the big boom. It is the richer states that have the higher rates, and within each state it is not the poor classes that are most suicide-prone, but the middle class and the rich.

Age apparently has something important to do with suicide. There are few suicides below the age of fifteen. Then the rates rise steadily, getting larger for each later decade of life, although beyond the seventies the figures are too small to be reliable. This has the sound of an understandable concept — the less life there is ahead, the less one wants to hold onto it. But to turn this digestible idea into a lump of stone, you need only separate the male statistics from the female. It is true that a larger proportion of men commit suicide in each older age group, but suicide among women levels off at about the change of life and never goes higher. Again, a mystery.

But while the statistical approach has, in general, proved disappointing, some encouraging sparks of light have been struck recently by a group of investigators digging from another direction altogether — the psychiatrists. They have, to be sure, come up with no single dramatic revelation, no beautifully simple wonder-drug solution. But from the intimate study of tens of thousands of cases, a fairly consistent theory has begun to emerge over the last fifteen or twenty years.

Take the case of a lady whom I shall call Mrs. Sally Collins. On a Friday morning about six months ago, she stood at the kitchen sink of her pleasant suburban home outside Boston. She was trying to wash the dishes, but her hands were shaking. They had been shaking for months, more and more. Mrs. Collins, a little, plain-looking, graying woman of forty-five, had been under a strain for many years, what with her husband's business deep in debt, a daughter chronically ill of a glandular disease, and a son critically wounded in Korea.

But a year ago things had taken a turn for the better: Collins's business got a big, steady, new account; the boy came home on the mend; and the daughter's illness began to yield to a new hormone treatment. That made Mrs. Collins's condition all the more peculiar, for it was only since these happy events that she had begun to feel increasingly gloomy. She felt old; she seemed not to think clearly any more; her children were grown and ready to leave home; the very sight of her careworn face and lumpy body in the mirror offended her.

As she washed dishes that morning a terrible thing happened to Mrs. Collins. "All of a sudden I felt my mind split right apart," she says. "Then a piece of it stood up on end and toppled over. I wanted to scream out, but I said to myself, 'That was your unconscious mind that fell over. Get hold of yourself. Think your way out of it.'"

The rest of the dishes went unwashed while she sat down and thought. Weeks went by, and she still sat around and thought all day. She was confused, incoherent, totally unable to attend to her housework; even to lift the phone and order groceries seemed an immense task. One day she finally found an answer. "I'm losing my mind," she figured. "I'm going insane. There's nothing ahead but misery and sickness; I'll be a burden on my husband, a shame to my children. There is one intelligent choice — death. That's logical, reasonable. That's the best possible answer for me."

Mrs. Collins thereupon poured out a glass of milk and with it chased down eighty-five aspirin tablets. Several hours later she was discovered gasping and in a coma by her daughter. In the hospital her stomach was washed out, and by the next day she was recovering from the drug. Since then she has spent half a year in a leading mental hospital in the East, making an excellent beginning toward complete recovery from her nervous breakdown.

But had Mrs. Collins died, what reasons would have been given?

Exhausted from overwork? Despondent because of ill health? The facts belie either answer; she should have been happier and less likely to desire death than at any other time in nearly twenty-five years. The causes of her suicide lay deeply hidden in her unconscious, and only the most persistent psychiatric detective work could ferret them out.

For despite the theoretical and technical differences among the many contemporary schools in psychiatry, they almost all agree on one thing: our conscious motives do not adequately explain human behavior, especially pathological behavior. Much or most of what we do and think is shaped by the unconscious, and by desires and experiences that have been forcibly "forgotten."

This was the crux of Sigmund Freud's original work, which centered in the basic sex drive. Freud claimed that the sex drive existed even in infants, and that it was responsible for much of our unconscious motivation, our character formation, and — when misdirected — our neurotic tendencies.

But Freud and other psychiatrists kept finding so many aspects of human behavior which did not relate to this drive that in his later life he reformulated his thinking into a dual-instinct theory. There are two basic conflicting instincts, he said: love (sex, creativity, self-preservation) and hate (destruction, aggression and the drive toward death). Dr. Karl Menninger, who, with his brother, Dr. William Menninger, developed the world-famous clinic, foundation, and school that bears their name in Topeka, Kansas, is one of the psychiatrists who have developed and applied this dual-instinct theory, especially in trying to solve the mystery of suicide. Not all psychiatrists agree with it, but even those who don't are nowadays stressing the role that aggression and destructive wishes play in human conduct; as a result, most of them use similar and strikingly effective techniques of treatment for suicidal patients.

From a child's earliest days, explains Dr. Menninger, he displays both love and hate. At first, both emotions are directed toward himself, for his own body is the source of both good and bad sensations. Later he begins to see that these feelings are the results of outside forces and people, and he begins to transfer his emotions outward. Every parental restraint and command frustrates him to some extent, and the instinctive reaction is rage or hate, directed at the parent. Happily, the same parents are also the source of so much love and satisfaction that his own love overrides and cancels out the hate.

Toward nearly everything in the world, all of us mingle love and hate in various proportions, according to the dual-instinct theory. If our personalities have developed healthfully, the love is far stronger than the hate toward those people who are important to us.

We learn, the psychiatrists say, to redirect our basic feelings of hate or aggression toward hitting a golf ball, digging the garden, earning a living or fighting our real enemies and the imperfections of the world.

But suppose aggressive drives aren't channeled into legitimate, useful activities? Suppose they remain directed toward one's parents, or friends, or wife and children, barely controlled by an inadequate flow of love, but inhibited by agonizing feelings of guilt and remorse? Then you have a personality which is like a boiler building up steam with no escape valve. At some point the pressure has to be used — and it sometimes succeeds by blowing up the boiler itself.

That is why a leading psychiatrist named Dr. Paul Federn concluded, twenty years ago, that suicide is the result of aggression turned back upon oneself. Dr. Wilhelm Stekel went even further, and said that "no one kills himself who did not wish to kill another or who, at least, does not wish the death of another." The wish is generally not a conscious one. Dr. Zilboorg and Dr. Menninger, as well as such recognized authorities as Dr. Franz Alexander, Dr. Erich Lindemann, and Dr. Karen Horney, have concurred in this concept of suicide, and have based successful therapy on it.

And just this kind of explanation would solve the mystery of Mrs. Sally Collins's suicide attempt. Brought up by her grandparents when her father ran off and her mother, an actress of sorts, took to the road with touring shows, she felt rejected at an early age. Still worse, her grandparents were stern, puritanical, and unloving. Again and again they made her feel guilty and sinful. At the age of nine she was the butt of schoolroom humor when her classmates found out about her parents; and when her grandmother started having heart attacks, she felt that even those were in some way her fault.

Sally grew up, married and embarked upon an adult life that most people would agree held little joy and much sorrow. But only when all her difficulties seemed on the point of disappearing did she go into her suicidal depression. Why? Because, says the chief psychiatrist at Mrs. Collins's hospital, "the buried feelings of rage against her parents and grandparents, and the terrible sense of guilt at having such rage, had been transformed into similar feelings about herself. But they had been assuaged all her life by hard work and worry — the equivalent of punishment or expiation. When suddenly there was no punishment in daily life to allay the guilt and no hard work to use up the excess rage, she turned these emotions inward and all but destroyed herself."

"Today I understand all this," she says, "because of the psychiatric help I've had. The incredible thing is how I thought that suicide was simply the most logical, intelligent thing to do. I'll never think that again — it's only an illusion." Next month Mrs. Collins goes home, and she'll come in once a week for continuing psychotherapy. Her major trouble is probably over for good.

From his clinical experience with hundreds of suicidal patients in the Menninger Clinic, the Winter VA Hospital and the Topeka State Hospital, Dr. Karl Menninger has also concluded — as he first theorized fifteen years ago in *Man Against Himself* — that there generally are three distinct elements in a suicide attempt: a wish to kill someone else (aggression), a wish to be killed (that is, to be punished), and a wish to die (the death instinct). When only one or two of these are present, the attempt is generally a failure, and deliberately so.

Some weeks ago, for instance, a twenty-one-year-old girl crawled onto a window sill of a five-story building in Oakland, California, and screamed that she was going to jump. She spat on the crowd below, tore shreds off her clothing and shrieked out a stream of threats. A priest finally talked her in, after friends and police had failed, but even then it took several burly officers to restrain her from further violence. Her wish to "end it all," interpreted in the light of the Menninger theory, was really a seething hatred of others turned against the only nonresisting person at hand — herself. Yet in a way, the girl was making a plea: Someone please love me, help me to love; this hate is hurting me. For had she really wished to die, she could easily have jumped.

The psychoanalytic explanation of suicide also throws some light on a number of heretofore-baffling statistical studies. For example, it is fairly certain that the national suicide rate decreases during wartime — just when things are often worst. But, according to the aggression-turned-within theory, this is perfectly natural. In wartime the blind, bottled-up aggressions which a man is ashamed to vent on his family and friends, and not skillful enough to sublimate in his work or play, are given an outside focus and sanction. He hates the enemy. To that extent, he hates himself — or the internalized equivalents of other people — that much less. It is a tragic paradox.

Another statistical puzzler has been the odd inverse relationship between suicide and murder. It seemed, from various early studies, that there was less murder where there was more suicide, and vice versa. Yet why should not both acts of violence be high in a violent society, and both be low in a calm and orderly society?

Sociologist Austin Porterfield, of Texas Christian University, recently made some careful analyses of this very point, taking a number of American cities and states. The early studies proved to have had some truth in them; Porterfield found that Alabama, for instance, had only half as high a suicide rate as the entire nation, but two and a half times as high a murder rate. Vermont had a higher suicide rate than the nation, but only one-fifth the murder rate. Murders exceeded suicides in most of the Southern cities, but suicides exceeded murders in most of the Northern cities.

Porterfield's study lends excellent support to the psychiatric theory, for it seems to indicate that murder and suicide are opposite types of adjustment to a basic built-in aggressive drive in human beings. Our various classes and cultures condition us to express anger in different ways — either by acting it out against other people or things, or by turning it in upon ourselves.

Still other puzzling facts about suicide no longer seem so mysterious to the psychiatrists. The family man is less likely to commit suicide, they say, because he has more external objects for his love instinct — and sometimes, alas, for his hate instinct. There is more suicide among the wealthier and the better educated, not because wealth and education are harmful, but because such people are curbed and made more "proper" in their aggressive desires by a different culture pattern. And how about the most mysterious of all suicides — those committed by people who have just reached a pinnacle of success in something they have been striving for, as was the case with Ross Lockridge? To some people with keen aggressive drives that were originally directed against a father or brother, according to Dr. Menninger, the overactive conscience says, "success means you are robbing or displacing someone, or usurping the position once held by your envied baby brother or someone else in the family." When good luck or hard work brings success to such a person, "the conscience reacts with a prohibition, and the wish to be killed develops in response to it."

Out of such current theorizing there has emerged some very practical therapeutic help for the suicidal. At the huge Winter VA Hospital where Dr. Menninger is chief consultant, doctors on the maximum-security ward have for the last few years used a new technique with deeply depressed suicidal patients. Instead of kindness and love, the doctors treat them with firmness and a degree of severity, almost unfriendliness. At the same time, they prescribe long hours of such dull chores as floor scrubbing or sanding down of furniture.

This kind of work symbolizes punishment and so relieves the guilt-ridden patients of the need to punish themselves by suicide. It also makes them thoroughly mad at the doctor. "And when the patient blows off and curses the doctor," says Dr. Herbert Klemmer, chief of the Closed Active Intensive Treatment Section at the hospital, "his suicidal depression flies out the window and we have an enraged person on our hands instead. We've had patients paint a doctor's face on the punching bag on the porch, beat the stuffings out of it, and be vastly improved afterward."

As the patient begins to talk out his anger, he becomes amenable to psychotherapy or psychoanalysis, which may help him unravel the sources of his discontent. Through such psychotherapy, the patient learns to re-evaluate himself, the people around him, and the meaning of his own feelings. Along with this most important process of gaining insight go some specific physical activities. From the mop, the sandpaper block and the punching bag, he graduates to games — volley ball, baseball, even bridge — and learns to release aggressions in an acceptable way.

Finally the patient is encouraged to divert his aggressive activity away from his loved ones altogether and channel it into useful work. It may be anything from carpentry to playwriting, but it represents the culmination of the healthful development of man's aggression as well as his love instinct.

Doctors at Winter VA Hospital, the Menninger Clinic and the Topeka State Hospital also make generous use of medical methods, including insulin and electroshock therapy. In the past few years these have revolutionized the treatment of about 25 per cent of suicidal patients. Why they magically dissolve certain kinds of psychotic depressions in less than a week no one knows. Perhaps they disrupt troublesome memories, perhaps they serve as symbolic punishment, relieving guilt. No one really knows, but shock treatment does work wonderfully in a number of cases.

Yet, despite the progress that has been made in treating it, suicide is still largely an enigma. Dr. Menninger believes that one step toward gaining more knowledge about it would be to make suicide a "reportable" disease — one which the law requires, under penalty, to be reported by physicians to state boards of health and to be accurately recorded. He would also like to see researchers or public health workers assigned to the job of tracing the life histories of every suicide case and suicide attempter. "That would cost plenty of money," he admits. "But if the public wants protection, it will have to be spent."

Research into suicide could follow a score of different lines of endeavor, if someone were willing to pay for it. One fertile field would be a study of ways to spot the presuicidal personality, for there still is not one reliable medical or psychological test that will pick out such persons. Even richer rewards might come from the point-by-point mapping out of those mistakes in child-rearing and family life which stunt the outward development of love and the normal channeling of aggression into valuable activity.

Of the many external factors which seem to bear a predictable relation to suicide — the size of a city, the size of a family, the level of income, and so on — some, surely, must be significant rather than accidental. If any of these are truly meaningful, perhaps they, too, will show us unsuspected ways of reducing the rate of self-destruction through social planning.

Suicide is not only a matter of up to 50,000 lost lives each year. Many leading psychiatrists believe that the self-destructive impulse is also involved in at least half of our 9,400,000 annual nonfatal accidents; that it plays a part in much of our psychosomatic disease, in cases of self-sacrifice to foolish or ignoble causes, and in the unaccountable errors and forgetfulness that make so many people fail where others, no more intelligent, succeed. Like it or not, in short, suicide is more or less a part of the daily life of nearly every one of us.

There has been no significant change in the psychiatric theory of suicide since this article was published, but it is worth noting that in addition to the shock treatments mentioned, suicidal patients have been considerably helped in recent years by the several classes of new drugs that have come into wide use — the tranquilizers, of course, and even more notably the psychic energizers and antidepressant drugs (a large number of suicide attempts occur during a period of severe depression). To be sure, these drugs do not of themselves eliminate the internal sources of the suicide attempt, but they tide the patient over, past the critical point, and make him amenable to psychotherapy; moreover, merely by permitting him time and relief from inner pressure, they enable him, in many cases, to re-establish his own ego defenses — which may not be strong, but were at least strong enough to get him through life for a number of years.

So much for the changes in the pharmacological treatment of suicide. As for the psychodynamics of it — the internal processes which cause it — I have received the following comment from Dr. Karl Menninger.

Ten years ago when Mr. Hunt wrote the above article I told him, and I said publicly, that it was the best article on suicide that I had ever seen. I still think it is.

Mr. Hunt has asked me to help him bring this article "up to date."

But it is quite up to date as it stands. We are still losing some of our best fellow citizens at the rate of a hundred or more a day in this country under the clear banner of suicide, to say nothing of the much larger number, perhaps ten times that many, who accomplish self-destruction in other disguised ways.

In the first place, Mr. Hunt faced the reader squarely with the paradox of the suicidal act, the unbelievable, inacceptable, unimaginable piece of behavior. It can't happen but it does, all the time, every day. There is no sense to it but here it is, all around us. We feel helpless, and we act as if we were. Individually and collectively we do very little about preventing other suicides, and this too is a mystery!

Mr. Hunt brought out clearly the fact that suicide is not done for the dramatic reasons usually offered as explanation, but that on the other hand there are reasons beneath the surface which even the individual himself usually does not know. It is hard for the general public to quite believe this. They think they know why Romeo killed himself; he had had hard breaks — he thought he had lost Juliet. But he hadn't lost Juliet. He just thought he had. Shall we say, then, that he committed suicide because he was mistaken, or because he was stupid? He committed suicide as a logical step in the extension of his lifelong affliction — his disease if you want to call it that. This disease was a rash, aggressive, destructive impulsivity which had already cost him his best friend, his citizenship, and his family's peace. Romeo's suicide begins in the first act of the play, not the last. And so it is with many suicides — as with many murders. People all about us are headed in that direction. Suicide is far more important than murder. It occurs more frequently. It occurs, on the average, to better-equipped and more useful people.

There are even more suicidal gestures than successful suicides, which has led numerous psychiatric authorities to emphasize the communicative nature of the suicidal "attempt." It is the most poignant, desperate cry for help that some sufferers can utter. Twenty-six years ago I was so impressed by the tendency to ignore this cry, in relatives, spouses, friends and even doctors, that I wrote a book, Man Against Himself, which attempted to analyze the reasons it was uttered and the reasons it was often disregarded. I developed Freud's point that man is driven and *sometimes pilloried by self-destructive drives. A book was promptly issued by a sociologist entitled* Man for Himself, *which implied that this was absurd.*

But as the years have passed I have come to feel that far from being absurd, the self-destructive drive is the most terrible and at the same time most persistent element in all human "misbehavior."

From many examples I cite only one, fresh from today's headlines. The United States Public Health Service (and incidentally many other investigators) after prolonged studies has come out with the announcement that cigarette smoking is dangerous to health and to life. What happens? In magazines, in bars, in drawing rooms one hears declarations like this: "Well, I'd rather smoke here than hereafter." "I'm going to smoke if I want to. Nobody is going to tell me what I can do." "I shall continue to smoke and continue to enjoy it." And so forth. In England, after a temporary diminution in the cigarette consumption, the preannouncement rate was resumed and even exceeded. Everyone who smokes a cigarette knows that it is just what it was one time called — a coffin nail — but he does it anyway. Why?

The only change I have made in my notions about suicide in human behavior since Mr. Hunt's article appeared is to advance it to the pinnacle of personality pathology. As we have explained at some length in our new book, The Vital Balance, *suicide is the most extreme perversion of the life instinct, the most antithetical, the most irrational, the most ego-paralyzed kind of behavior.* When the almost unquenchable spark of life flickers out in despair and the hate that has been controlled at such great cost turns upon the defenseless body of the individual — when all hope, need and effort give way to futile, self-directed sabotage, demoralization has been reached of a degree beyond which we cannot imagine anything.

Admittedly the suicidal process is always tinctured with elements of attempted salvation, of reintegrative efforts to live and be loved; no suicide is ever completely wholehearted. Most of what is called mental illness represents a struggle against this extremity but if self-destructive forces clearly gain the upper hand, the die is cast. And like Samson, all suicides bring down some wreckage around them, and this final self-directed aggression may be at the same time the most cruel and devastating blow the individual ever dealt his friends and foes. The pity is that however justified such a blow may once have been, the passage of time and space makes it likely that its victims will not be the ones who originally engendered the uncontrolled hate.

Where is the proper point, and when the appropriate moment for preventive intervention? How and when do I, my brother's keeper, answer his desperate cry and stay his irrevocable act? There is no easy answer to this most pertinent question. What are the clues to imminent critical self-destructive acts, and what clues indicate a preponderance of dramatization, appeal for help, or reproach? Shneidman and Farberow, among others, have worked assiduously in the past decade in search for answers to these questions.

One can report with some satisfaction that there is more scientific interest in suicide than ten years ago. But the masked forms of self-destruction, for example by means of accidents, are still regarded as "just carelessness," "too much speed," "drunken driving," etc. Mr. Hunt's appeal to a greater public concern is thus as fresh and important as the day it was written.

KARL MENNINGER, M.D.

Five Who Broke Down

The following article is a somewhat condensed version of one part of a two-part series on Pilgrim State Hospital which originally appeared in 1961 in The New Yorker. In presenting it here, I have excerpted primarily the portions relating to the five case histories followed in the original, for they represent the five major diagnostic categories of patients arriving at New York state mental hospitals in recent years. In contrast to this emphasis on the patients themselves, another portion of the series, focusing upon the hospital personnel and the treatments they *provide, is in the next section under the title "Revolution in the Mental Hospital."*

O N AN AVERAGE DAY, eighty-two residents of New York City do something, or fail to do something, that forces the persons around them to suspect the presence of a mental disease and to take steps to get them to a public hospital for observation and possible treatment. (Fifteen or twenty more go each day to private hospitals for the same reason.) The moment of crisis and decision takes many forms. On a muggy Wednesday morning last spring, for instance, a plump, rather plain college girl I shall call Miriam Hirsch (all the names of patients and their relatives in this report are fictitious) went into a precinct station near Prospect Park and blurted out to the desk sergeant, "I want my father arrested! The bastard! He smacked me — me, a grownup. He wants to wreck me; he doesn't care. He makes me go to a psychiatric clinic, and now I'm staring into space. They've ruined my mind. People stare at me. It's all his fault. I want him arrested!"

"Take it easy, now," said the sergeant. After jotting down some information, he asked her to wait in another room, and in the next few minutes he telephoned first her father and then the psychiatric clinic. Finally, he called her father back to advise him to come at once by cab and take her to Kings County Hospital.

Later that same morning, a telephone, trailing a length of wire, burst through a third-floor window of an apartment house on the Grand Concourse, in the Bronx, and crashed to the pavement, narrowly missing the superintendent, who was lounging near the front door. In the living room of Apartment 3-D, Arnold Peterson, a stringy radio engineer of about forty, giggled, took a long pull at a bottle of bourbon, and, lurching around, hoarsely continued an incoherent but exuberant monologue about his talents and his plans for the future — a monologue that the ringing of the telephone had interrupted. The superintendent stormed upstairs and rang the bell of 3-D, where he was received by Mrs. Peterson. She was in a state of terror but managed to tell him the story. It seemed that her husband, who of late had been sometimes dreadfully moody and sometimes boisterously gay, had been on a nonstop bender for four days, and was so wound up that, except for a few cat naps, he had been talking continuously all that time. The superintendent said there was nothing for it but to call Bellevue.

At noon that same day, in a sparsely furnished but immaculate apartment in Jamaica, Mrs. Thomas Pfeiffer was fixing lunch for herself and her aged mother, Mrs. Olga Janaczek. The previous Friday, Mrs. Janaczek had gone for a walk alone and become completely confused about where she lived. Then, on Tuesday, she had flooded the bathroom, and at 3 A.M. on Wednesday she had made her way into the kitchen and partly opened a gas burner; the pilot light finally ignited it with a whump that rattled every window in the apartment. At lunchtime, Mrs. Pfeiffer put some soup and sandwiches on the table and went to get her mother. The old woman was standing near a living-room window, mumbling to herself; at her feet, on a small Oriental rug, a pool of water was spreading.

"Mama, not *again!*" shouted Mrs. Pfeiffer.

The old lady turned and snapped, "Don't yell at *me,* Marie."

"Mama, I'm not Marie," said Mrs. Pfeiffer. "Marie is dead twenty years. I'm Millie. Now come right to the bathroom and clean yourself up."

"You leave me alone," said Mrs. Janaczek. "I know who you are. Don't come near me." She began to grit her teeth and shake all over.

Mrs. Pfeiffer ran to the bedroom telephone, dialed her husband's number, and told him she couldn't stand it another minute. Mr. Pfeiffer tried to soothe her, but he finally said he would come right home with the car and take them on the short trip to City Hospital at Elmhurst.

When school let out that afternoon, a seventeen-year-old Negro named Joseph Freeman, ambling homeward along West Ninety-second Street, saw a smaller boy, whom he knew slightly, turn the corner at Amsterdam Avenue and walk toward him, on the opposite side of the street. Although no one was near Freeman at the moment, he heard several voices echoing in his head: "He's one of *them.* Go punch him in the mouth! Let him have it!" He crossed the street, walked casually up to the boy, and hit him full in the mouth and nose. The boy collapsed, screaming and bleeding; Freeman kicked him once in the stomach and ran off. When he got to the building where he lived, sharing a cold-water flat with his sister and brother-in-law (his mother was dead and his father was an alcoholic drifter), he raced up the stairs and told his sister he was going to wait for his brother-in-law and have it out with him. "No wonder I got trouble at school," Joesph said. "No wonder the cops beat up on me last month. *He's* been fixing things, and I'm going to kill the son of a bitch. You wanna watch?" His sister ran into the kitchen and came back holding a long knife awkwardly in her right hand. Joseph began to quiver; then he stiffened and fell heavily to the floor, jerking spasmodically, his eyes rolling up, and foam appearing in the corners of his mouth. An hour later, he was transferred by ambulance from the precinct station to Bellevue.

At about the same time, in downtown Brooklyn, a thin, tired-looking barber named Edward Palladino hung up his white coat, locked his shop, and walked slowly home. He and his wife lived alone; they had three children, but all had grown up, married, and left home. For the past several months, Mrs. Palladino had been sleepless, nervous, endlessly complaining and nagging, and full of worries about pains in her breast, abdomen, and head; she felt sure that she was about to die, and she wandered around the apartment for hours in the middle of the night. She had had a thorough medical examination, which showed no disease, but this had not made the least difference. She refused to set foot outside the house, and whenever Palladino tried to find out why, she either snapped at him or merely sighed and said, "What's the use? What's the use?" That evening, when Palladino arrived home, he called out a greeting, but there was no reply. Going into the bedroom, he found his wife on the bed, waxen-faced, openmouthed, and gasping. A large, empty aspirin bottle stood on the night table, along with a water pitcher. Palladino ran to the telephone.

Every day, throughout the nation, there are hundreds of similar cases, each of them a variation on one of the basic themes of mental illness — inability to take care of oneself, or behavior that frightens or harms others, or a deep feeling of suffering on the part of the patient himself. In past centuries, the suffering rarely could get help, the incompetent were sent to almshouses, and the aggressive were put in jail; now, ordinarily, the suffering and the incompetent and (if there is any possibility that they are mentally ill) the aggressive, too, wind up in mental hospitals. At the moment, more than half a million Americans are resident patients in mental hospitals or psychiatric wards — more than are in hospitals for all physical ailments combined.

The great bulk of these patients are housed in state mental hospitals, which run the gamut from very bad to quite good. By coincidence, the world's largest mental institution — Pilgrim State Hospital, near Brentwood, Long Island, fifty-one miles east of midtown Manhattan — is one of the outstanding state mental hospitals in the country. Most of its patients arrive after having been briefly examined and evaluated elsewhere, often at city hospitals, as was the case with Miriam Hirsch, Arnold Peterson, and the others. If the patients' condition is not a passing episode, they are transferred to one of a number of New York state hospitals; as it happens, all five of the cases detailed in this report were sent to Pilgrim. Nearly fourteen thousand mental patients are now living at Pilgrim, making it as large a community as Beacon, Rensselaer, or Rye, and larger by far than Amityville, Haverstraw, Patchogue, or Nyack.

Life at Pilgrim is not nearly as unlike life in these towns as it was half a dozen years ago. In and prior to 1955, when the newly discovered tranquilizing drugs were first put to use in mental hospitals on a large scale, almost every window at Pilgrim was barred; patients clung to the bars and stared out like forgotten political prisoners. The broad, grassy grounds were nearly deserted except when special groups were herded along by attendants to visit the dining rooms, the library, the chapel, or the recreation field. Most patients wore shapeless gray and brown wool or cotton clothes, bought from the Department of Correction; though these were wretchedly ugly, they were highly practical, for in the throes of severe illness many psychotics would tear or soil their clothing. From the wards for the most deeply disturbed persons, one could always hear a babble of voices punctuated by the screams, enraged shouts, and long-drawn-out moans that had been part of the classic *mise en scène* of every madhouse since the fifteenth century.

Long before 1955, doctors realized that quite a few patients in mental hospitals grew markedly worse after admission. The prisonlike atmosphere and the tedium of the hospitals had almost certainly driven many patients further into violence or infantilism or whatever their ailments or symptoms were, and had permitted their psychoses to proliferate and sink deep roots. Mental treatment of mental illness being difficult and slow, doctors had long sought physical means of banishing psychoses. The principal physical attacks on disturbed behavior at Pilgrim for several years after it opened, in 1931, were the strait jacket (or "camisole," as it was and is euphemistically called), the tub, and the pack. A wild patient would be jammed into a camisole or kept in solitary confinement for a while — with a walloping dose of barbiturates, for good measure. A still wilder patient might be subjected for hours at a time to the sedative pack; inside a cocoon of wet sheets with blankets on top, the psychotic slowly grew warmer and more relaxed, steaming himself into virtual insensibility. Totally depressed patients, on the other hand, might be subjected to a tonic in the form of a "Scotch douche" — alternating forceful warm and cold sprays.

Starting in 1937, injections of insulin, which produced coma and in some kinds of cases, as a result, lessened violence and the force of delusions, became a regular method of treatment at Pilgrim, and in 1938 the injection of a drug called Metrazol was added to the list of therapies; it caused convulsions instead of coma but otherwise had somewhat the same effects as insulin and was especially helpful in cases of depression. In 1940, the new technique of electric shock — relatively quick, neat, and easy — began replacing Metrazol. Each of these therapies, however, was successful only in part in some cases and not at all in the rest, and Pilgrim's medical staff next took to the drastic new device of prefrontal lobotomy. Between 1945 and 1955, holes were drilled in the skulls of sixteen hundred intractably ill patients, in each of whom certain bundles of frontal brain fibers were severed. One out of four patients so treated was later able to leave the hospital, though the operation rendered a small percentage of the discharged men and women doltish. The rest had to remain, but a third of them behaved considerably better than they had previously.

Then, late in 1954, the state mental hospitals began testing chlorpromazine and reserpine, the first of the tranquilizing drugs, and found them remarkably effective in many cases. In 1955, the drugs started to be used widely, and the effect was immediate. That year, the state-wide mental-hospital population topped off at 93,314, and the next year it receded to 92,862. The decrease has continued every year since then, despite continually increasing admissions. Tranquilizers have made such a large proportion of recent patients feel and behave better, by eliminating or moderating fears, rages, and phantom voices, that most of the other physical therapies have become curiosa of medical history.

The new manageability of so many of the difficult patients made possible a rapid increase in the use of the so-called adjunctive therapies, which involve both work and recreation. The most typical hospital scene was once the large, drab locked dayroom filled with human carcasses either slumped on benches or aimlessly standing and staring; today it is the workshop, the playing field, and the "open ward," with television, ping-pong, and a great deal of easy conversation. The patients wear a variety of ordinary clothes, instead of the drab institutional dress. Bright paint and curtains have appeared in dayrooms where they had never appeared before.

All in all, Pilgrim's major function has changed from keeping patients in custody to providing them with a total environment of activities and human contacts that are helpful to recovery. Until a few years ago, a new patient was observed for many weeks before diagnosis was determined and treatment of sorts was begun, and by that time he was often far worse than when he arrived. In the past fifteen years, the view has been gaining ground that a brand-new psychosis is a semiplastic, semi-soluble sort of thing; if it is let alone, it hardens into a stony growth, but if it is instantly and energetically attacked, it can be far more easily washed away, and the damaged ego allowed to repair itself. In most state hospitals, this theory of immediate "total push," or intensive treatment, was just a piously accepted ideal until the tranquilizers arrived; then, suddenly, it was as if the new theory had been made for the drugs, and they for it.

Patients arriving at Pilgrim are not likely at first to be aware of the normal aspects of this abnormal community. Most of the wards in the two new-admissions buildings — there is one for men and one for women — are still barred, and, all in all, life in a mental hospital is apt to be full of sights and sounds bewildering to new arrivals, most of whom are quite capable of recognizing how peculiar some of the things about them look. A hospital dayroom is something like a waiting room, but it is never certain what anyone is waiting for. Many of the patients are lying on benches asleep, or sitting around with a glazed look, for tranquilizers cause sleepiness during the first week or two they are taken. Other patients stand in the middle of the floor, staring, for hours; still others rock ceaselessly in rocking chairs. Occasionally, one may talk softly to himself, an odd private glee lighting up his face; another may rush around asking if anyone has seen his briefcase (he had no briefcase); a third may sit at an old upright piano and hit a single note every couple of minutes.

In various ways, new patients experience a sharp transition into a new and separate world. When Miriam Hirsch, for instance, arrived at Pilgrim, two weeks after her visit to the precinct station, her eyeglasses and a small manicure kit in her pocketbook were taken away from her, because at Kings County, and on the bus, she had clawed and scratched — rather feebly — at the attendants. Arnold Peterson, the wildly talkative engineer, had his false teeth taken out and locked up, since in his moments of high euphoria he might lose or break them. The valuables of both the newcomers were also taken away and stored, and they themselves were quickly given a complete physical examination. Afterward, like all new patients, they were interviewed privately and briefly by the supervising psychiatrist of the appropriate new-admissions building. But with most psychotics, the distortions of thought and feeling are so gross that they appear plainly to doctors in response to even the most unsubtle and briefest questioning.

The doctor who interviewed Miriam Hirsch upon her arrival started off by asking her, "Do you know where you are?"

She replied correctly.

"Can you tell me why you had to come here to the hospital?" he asked.

"I'm hard of hearing sometimes," the girl said, staring fixedly at him. "That's my whole trouble." Her hearing had already been tested; organically, there was nothing wrong with it. "My parents are getting old and they don't understand me. . . . There's nothing wrong with me. . . . I ran away from home."

"What was the trouble?" asked the doctor.

"They thought I was a flop, socially," said Miss Hirsch. "And I studied too hard. I was too fat. That's my whole trouble. People would stare at me and talk about me in the street. So they sent me to a psychiatrist and he ruined me."

"What do you mean, 'ruined you'?"

"He cleaned out my mind!" she said, stridently. "So I cracked up! I don't ever want to see another psychiatrist. . . . Well, maybe I *did* need one for a while, but I'm all right now. I want to get a job. There's nothing wrong with me."

Arnold Peterson, upon being interviewed by a doctor in the men's admissions building, laughed boisterously at every question, talked grandiosely about his brilliance as a radio engineer and about the extent of his sexual appetite, and then darkly confided that his thoughts and moods could be controlled at long range by his father-in-law, who used a modified diathermy machine for the purpose. Peterson added that he had told his wife he might have to shoot her father if this continued.

As for the young Joseph Freeman, in response to a few plain questions about his life and habits, he spilled out loathing of his alcoholic father, dark suspicion and hatred of his brother-in-law, and a candid statement about the voices he heard urging him to hit people. Ten minutes after the interview, he stiffened and fell to the floor of the ward in what looked like a *grand-mal* seizure.

Old Mrs. Janaczek, interviewed in a special geriatrics building at the rear of the hospital, couldn't get it straight where she was, and acted grumpy for the first few minutes; then, for no apparent reason, she began to ramble on about household problems that she had been concerned about forty years earlier and now wanted to attend to at once.

Mrs. Palladino was in so deep a depression that she neither looked at the interviewing doctor nor spoke to him. Head sunk on chest, body as limp as a deflated balloon, she ignored all questions. Physically, too, she had been found to be in bad shape. Severely emaciated and dehydrated, she had refused almost all food and drink ever since her suicide attempt, and was in imminent danger of physical collapse. Within an hour, Mrs. Palladino had been wheeled into a small room on a stretcher, electrodes had been placed at her temples, and a hundred and twenty volts of current had flicked through her brain for three-tenths of a second. Instantly unconscious, she writhed in a convulsion for the next half a minute or so, then sank back in a stupor, and awoke ten minutes later dazed and bewildered, but vaguely cheerful. Half an hour after that, she was eating ravenously. (Her depression, the doctors knew, would probably return in a matter of days, and might require ten or twenty more shock treatments before being thoroughly dispelled, unless "psychic energizers" — another group of new drugs — served the purpose.)

On the basis of the initial interview, the doctor has a rough idea of what is wrong with the patient, and starts him on whichever drug is likely to be most effective, although a month or more passes before the patient is finally diagnosed. This may seem strange to the layman, but Dr. Holt explains it by saying, "Precise diagnosis isn't so important during the first steps, given the preceding screening. The agitated ones get tranquilizers of one sort or another, the depressed ones get energizers, and some get combinations of the two. Emergency cases or patients who don't respond to the drugs may get electric shock. The syphilitics or other diseased ones get special medication. And then, of course, everyone in admissions is on 'intensive treatment' right from the beginning."

"Intensive treatment" consists of a variety of influences — some large and some, perhaps, small — any or all of which may be brought to bear by prescription of the doctor, according to the patient's condition. A psychiatric social worker visits nearly every patient early in his stay, explains the hospital procedures to him, and assures him that his affairs in the outside world will be watched over. Some few patients, hand-picked as likely candidates, meet several times a week with psychologists or social workers for group-therapy talks. Pilgrim's recreation department plies all but the worst patients with exercise and entertainment. The Occupational Therapy Department operates twenty-seven "workshops," in which a good many Pilgrim patients build model boats, weave baskets and cane seat bottoms, print hospital stationery, paint in oils, take a refresher course in typing, make simple curtains, or do something else of the sort. The value of listening to barbershop quartets or tearing rags into strips for making braided rugs has never been put to any controlled scientific tests, but everyone in mental-hospital work feels certain that such things do help.

Each week, Dr. Leo Horn, an assistant director of Pilgrim who is in charge of the new-admissions service, holds a "diagnostic staff" — a conference in which he meets the patients who are now ready for formal diagnosis. Not long ago, one such was Miriam Hirsch, who had been in Pilgrim six weeks. As Dr. Horn skimmed her dossier before having her called to his desk, he noted that at first Miriam had had a few hair-pulling fights with other patients, and had been inclined to disobey or ignore the nurses and attendants. When her parents visited her, she cried a good deal and begged them to take her home. After several weeks under the influence of a tranquilizer called Thorazine, she was behaving somewhat better, and had been allowed to visit a typing class and the library. When Dr. Horn got around to talking with her, she seemed perfectly lucid until she got on the subject of her hearing, her weight, and her former psychiatrist at the private clinic.

"I can't seem to stop thinking about my hearing and my weight," she said, and burst into tears, blaming the psychiatrist, herself, and her parents, one after another, for her troubles.

When she had calmed down, Dr. Horn asked her whether people still stared at her and talked about her.

"Oh, that was just crazy," the girl said. "That was just stupid of me."

"Are you feeling better?" Dr. Horn asked.

"Yes," she said. "I'm fine now. I don't want to take any more pills. I just want to go home and get a job."

"The pills are helping you," said Dr. Horn.

"But they're making me fat!" she wailed. "And when I'm fat I get upset and I get sicker! . . . What's the *matter* with me, anyhow?"

Dr. Horn dismissed her after about ten minutes, and dictated a finding that read, in part, "No hallucinations can be elicited at present. Behavior much improved, though still somewhat hostile and cries easily. Has confused ideas about her illness, and little insight. Diagnosis: schizophrenia, paranoid type."

One of the residents asked Dr. Horn if Miss Hirsch hadn't made remarkable progress.

"Some," Dr. Horn said, "but she's still a pretty confused girl, and I don't think she'll regain control very soon. Personally, I think the private clinic she previously attended did a very poor thing if it really did throw her into analytic therapy. These incipient schizophrenics can't stand the probing; it can precipitate psychotic episodes. I think you can do more for this kind of patient chemically than you can analytically. Thorazine and intensive treatment will probably get her out of here, but it may take many months."

Mrs. Palladino came up at the same session. Her papers showed that her doctor had decided after her first shock treatment to put her on Tofranil, a psychic energizer, rather than continue shock. She had been something of a trial to her ward ever since. "Very disagreeable and complaining all the time," read one attendant's note. "Has diarrhea and spends half the night in the toilet, flushing and flushing. Keeps the whole ward disturbed and losing sleep," read another. She had ignored her husband during his first two visits, and had scolded him during most of the next two. Yet recently she had been doing a little sewing in the ward, and chatting a bit with other women. In the interview with Dr. Horn, she confirmed the impressions he had gained from the notes by complaining a good deal but asking when she might be sent home. "It's very dull here," she said, "and I'm not taking care of my husband the way I should. I'm not crazy, I just got a little too depressed for a while." Dr. Horn assured her that she would be sent home as soon as possible, and put her down as a standard case of involutional psychosis, melancholic type, to be continued in the new-admissions ward; prognosis, very good.

Joseph Freeman came to diagnostic staff under a handicap. He had been uncooperative and tough in the ward. Nothing had interested him, and when his sister and brother-in-law came out to see him, he had hardly spoken to either of them. Drugs had seemed to do him little good. From time to time, he had had a seizure, yet an electro-encephalogram had shown his brain waves to be normal. Laconically but without embarrassment, he had told his doctor about his voices (they had become faint since a brief scuffle in his first week), and about his brother-in-law's plots against him. Then, the day before diagnostic staff, another patient had accidentally nudged him, and Freeman had suddenly gone berserk; he had leaped onto a table, yanked out his belt, and started flailing at everyone around with the buckle. The next day, when he appeared for diagnosis, he was much sobered by a long stay in a camisole, but his manner to Dr. Horn was sullen and hostile. He would stare at the psychiatrist without replying to questions, or would say that since everyone was against him, there wasn't any point in saying anything anyhow. Dr. Horn diagnosed him as a schizophrenic, mixed type, with psychoneurosis and pseudoepileptic fits, and ordered him transferred to maximum security in a building for deeply disturbed and dangerous cases.

Old Mrs. Janaczek, naturally, presented a totally different kind of problem. Having no hallucinations but only mild delusions — primarily, a sign of a decreasing competence in the use of her brain, perhaps owing to general aging, perhaps to hardening of the cerebral blood vessels — she was classified as a case of senile dementia. In the six weeks between admission and diagnosis, she had shown no particular change except that she had grown accustomed to being taken to the bathroom at regular intervals; like an infant, she had become almost continent on this regime. Television, an occasional movie, and a simple round of daily activities suited her well enough, but in rare moments she would see things clearly and cry bitterly at having been "put away." At other times, she seemed to think she was in a hotel for people needing a rest cure, and thought it must cost quite a lot. Her prognosis, known by the doctors but not stated in so many words, was that of a terminal case; barring some unforeseen development, she would pass her remaining years here in her private world.

As for Arnold Peterson, he did not come up for diagnosis at the set time — he was later diagnosed as a textbook manic-depressive, manic type — because he was not in the hospital at all. Under Thorazine, he had come along well from the start, although the attendants made many a note like this one: "Never stops bragging, talks big, butts into every conversation, knows all about it. Loud, noisy, a wise guy." He had been agreeable and obedient enough to gain permission to wander around the hospital grounds, and had taken enthusiastically to oil painting — something he had never tried before. To his doctor he confided that his ideas about his father-in-law's diathermy machine were "goofy," and he claimed that his threats to kill his father-in-law had never been serious. He greeted his wife warmly on her visits — too warmly, perhaps, for when she came to see him two days before his diagnostic staff, he got in the car with her unnoticed, drove off the grounds, and talked his wife into taking him home to the Bronx. The hospital put his disappearance down as a "leave without consent" (in which a freely moving patient vanishes) as opposed to an escape (in which confinement is breached) and telephoned the apartment; Mrs. Peterson denied that he was there. For several weeks, Peterson puttered around, and even started one part-time job, but, being without Thorazine, he was talking and behaving a little more phrenetically every day. One evening, while he was out driving with his wife, they began arguing about some trifle, whereupon he jammed on the brakes and, laughing wildly, ordered her to get out and walk home; then all at once he grew sober and said he thought she ought to take him back to the hospital at once.

The hospital was originally designed for total custodial control of the patients. Every door was to be locked and every window barred. Nowadays, the open-door policy makes escape and leave without consent so easy that three hundred and sixty-five patients — almost none of them dangerous — slipped off last year by simply walking down a side road. (Seventy-seven of those departures were considered escapes, and the rest leaves without consent.) As soon as a patient is missed, ward attendants phone the police force, which sends prowl cars out to cruise around the hospital's three square miles of territory and the roads leading to the neighboring towns. Often, the patient is found walking down a road or lounging about in the center of a town; he is nearly always docile about returning. Other escapees make it all the way to the city, but the great majority of them are brought back to Pilgrim after a while by the same behavior that excluded them from society the first time. A few, marginally well enough to stay in society, never reappear.

Regrettable as such escapes are, they are a sign that the boundary line between the outer world and the hospital world is far easier to cross than it used to be. In the year 1941, when most cases were chronic, about thirteen hundred patients got out of Pilgrim — half of them by dying. A handful of others escaped or were transferred elsewhere. Only about a third of those who left Pilgrim one way or another were released as "improved or recovered." All this has greatly changed. Death is still a frequent way out of Pilgrim, since so many patients are old or long-term cases who, in the nature of things, cannot get well. By far the greatest number, however, now leave the hospital through the preferred means of direct discharge or convalescent leave; last year three thousand patients — roughly two-thirds of all those who left Pilgrim — were released in this fashion.

"Direct discharge" means just what it implies. The patient needs no further immediate care, as far as the hospital is concerned. On the other hand, a patient released on convalescent leave is obliged to make regular visits to one of the state's After-Care Clinics, where he receives drugs or some psychotherapy or both. At the discretion of the doctors running the After-Care Clinics, patients may eventually either be sent back to the hospital or be given a full release. In either type of release from Pilgrim — discharge or leave — the outgoing traffic passes through the checkpoint of another staff conference.

When the patient takes his seat across the table, the psychiatrist looks only for gross and unmistakable signs of emotional maturity, rather than for subtleties. Are the voices gone? What about the ideas of poison, or secret messages in the radio static, or the staring eyes? Does the patient cry, bluster, boast, make threats? (Some students of mental hospitals have pointed out that patients catch on to these things, and say in "home staff" what they know will be pleasing; hospital psychiatrists answer that this is, in itself, a sign of sanity and recognition of reality.) Most important of all, the patient must display "insight." "Don't misunderstand that word," Dr. Joseph Clifford, one of the psychiatrists, cautioned a group of residents recently. "It's not the kind of insight your neurotic tries to achieve in psychoanalysis. The kind of insight we want is basically little more than a recognition of the symptoms that brought the patient in. If he says, 'I came here because I kept thinking my neighbor was trying to poison me,' he's got insight. If he says, 'I came here because my neighbor was trying to poison me, and you should be treating *him* instead of me,' he's still sick." Similarly, Clifford added, the patient with insight knows that he was overworking, or trying to hold a job he wasn't fitted for, or living in a neighborhood where he was discriminated against. Whatever the unconscious factors involved, all that the hospital psychiatrist asks is to have the patient understand the external pressures and try to reduce them; insight need go no farther than this.

Of the five New Yorkers with whom this report began, the one who had most disliked her life was, as it happened, the first one ready to return to it. In early August, Mrs. Palladino's dossier showed that her diarrhea and sleeplessness had consistently diminished. Week by week she had grown less grouchy, and for some time now she had even shown a kind of gruff motherliness toward some of the younger patients. She had turned more and more to sewing for something to keep her busy, but recently it had only bored her; she wanted nothing in the world but to go home and start taking care of her husband, who, she said, was looking worn out and badly in need of her cooking.

Dr. Mary Holt, who was in charge of home staff that day, asked her what she thought had been her trouble.

"I don't know *what* got into me," said Mrs. Palladino. "I was never like that in my life. Maybe something about my time of life? It was all like a nightmare, those ideas."

Two days later, she received convalescent leave and went home to Brooklyn with her husband. Of the complicated reweaving of two lives that ensued, with its hesitancies, its faint alarms, its doubts, its rediscoveries of enjoyment, nothing shows in the record. One must read it all into the brief notations of Mrs. Palladino's weekly visits to the Brooklyn After-Care Clinic, at 490 Fulton Street. Here she would chat with the psychiatrist on duty; here she would receive her continuing ration of pills. There is a scattering of minor complaints; then comes a series of brief, satisfactory conferences; and then Edward Palladino is noted as coming in by himself to say that he is delighted with her condition and thinks she needs no further care. Finally, the case is closed.

Arnold Peterson, upon his return from his leave without consent, was sent to a closed ward to prevent further incidents of the sort. Instead of reacting to this with rage, he took it calmly, and, back on Thorazine, improved so rapidly that three weeks later he was approved for convalescent leave, though he was ordered to remain on drugs until final discharge. A note made at the Bronx After-Care Clinic shortly after his release reads, "Reported here today; in excellent contact, very pleasant, polite, coherent. Says he understands his 'true problems' about in-laws and own tendencies. No delusions. Has a satisfactory job. Wife very happy." The dossier is still active, however. Peterson, who now is supposed to visit the clinic twice a month, may be formally discharged within the next year.

Joseph Freeman, having been sent to a disturbed ward after his belt-buckle attack, seemed to get worse. He was in minor scrapes three or four times a week, and he rejected all attempts that his doctor and other personnel made to befriend him. His doctor finally prescribed a course of electric-shock treatments, which for a time made Joseph somewhat foggy and forgetful but turned him into a relatively docile and cheerful lad, without seizures or voices. After the final treatment, he was given a tranquilizer called Compazine to maintain the gains made by electric shock, and his doctor put him into group therapy. In the last few weeks, Joseph not only has gone for long periods without overt aggressiveness but has been described as "anxious to help out and to find something to do." Recently, he was moved to an open ward, given a job in the kitchen, which he found dull, and then reassigned to the post of recreation assistant, which he finds very much to his taste. His doctor hopes that after several months of this, he may be ready to try outside life again, in a supervised home, not far from Pilgrim.

Mrs. Janaczek has not come up for staff since her diagnosis. Although some senile psychotics respond in part to intensive treatment, most do not. Mrs. Janaczek still gets confused about the time of day, and cannot easily find her own bed again when she wanders about. She lives partly in dreams and partly in a vague, reminiscing kind of contact with several of her fellow patients. She is a discarded human being, whose mind is outworn and whose mental problem the hospital cannot solve.

Miriam Hirsch came up for leave only a few weeks ago. A month earlier, because she complained of severe headaches, she had been shifted from Thorazine to a less potent tranquilizer called Sparine, and she had been thriving on large doses of this. Reports of her activities in the ward indicated cheerfulness and friendliness. Owing to the drugs, she was a good fifteen pounds heavier than she had been on her arrival, but her manner was almost jolly. When she spoke about her breakdown, however, she smiled wanly as she said, "I guess I went crazy." As for her weight, she laughed ruefully about her recent gain. In the course of an interview with Dr. Holt, she voiced nearly every schizophrenic notion she had had earlier, but without either anger or tears. The doctor, a little surprised at her improvement, approved a weekend home visit for her, but put down on the record, "Prognosis: guarded." Her future was far from clear; unlike many a spell of mental illness that comes and goes rapidly, hers was a long-standing condition, and she might continue to be a borderline case for years.

Summing up present treatment of those who come to Pilgrim, its director, Dr. Henry Brill, comments, "What gratifies all of us is the fact that, of the patients under sixty-five being admitted today, four-fifths will be back in normal society in less than a year — and most of them in less than six months. Of course, some authorities, on psycho-analytic grounds, claim that all we're doing is suppressing the symptoms with drugs and shoving the patients back into the same old world with their same old inner weaknesses. That isn't the whole story, though; they've also got their same inner strengths, which supported them for most of their lives, and which have been renewed during their stay in the hospital until they outweigh or compensate for those weaknesses."

Dr. Henry Brill, director of Pilgrim State Hospital, has written me, bringing up to date both the above article and the one entitled "Revolution in the Mental Hospital." His comments will be found on page 411, following that article.

Dr. Kallmann's Seven Thousand Twins

IF HE WERE an easy man to discourage, Dr. Franz Josef Kallmann would probably have given up long ago. Most of his professional life has been spent in swimming against the tide of orthodox opinion on the subject of mental illness, and he still hasn't gained a really firm foothold on shore. Even his position as head of the Medical Genetics Department at the New York State Psychiatric Institute attests more to his personal stature as a researcher than to any turning of the tide.

Yet the fact that he hasn't given up may prove to be among the best breaks mental patients have ever had. Franz Kallmann's long swim has helped indicate that some day chemical treatment may cure hundreds of thousands of cases who are helped pitifully little by presently available methods.

A heavy-paunched, gray-haired, throaty-voiced professor of fifty-seven, Kallmann dissents sharply from the prevailing opinion among psychiatrists, psychologists, social reformers and others, that mental illness stems from environmental pressures — from an unhappy childhood, say, or from early sex experiences or overstrict toilet training. This kind of thinking, he feels, "explains beautifully why certain people are harmed mentally by certain circumstances. But it never explains why others who live in those same circumstances or worse are not harmed. There must be some more basic reasons."

The search for these more basic reasons, a quest he embarked upon some twenty-six years ago, has led him straight to the center of what is possibly the classic riddle of mankind's history: To what extent are we products of our environments and to what extent of inborn strengths and weaknesses?

Few questions have been argued more hotly or at greater length than this Nature vs. Nurture controversy, and few less conclusively. Speculation on the subject is easy, laboratory proof is not. Where mice are concerned, it is simple to collect evidence. If you want to find out, say, whether exercise (an environmental factor) can promote health — in mice, anyhow — you breed brother and sister mice generation after generation until you get a "pure" strain. All purebred mice are identical as to inherited characteristics. Whatever differences appear must be the results of different environmental forces.

You split them up into two groups, give one group regular exercise and prevent the others from having any. Then you inoculate all of them with the same amount of germs and see which group has more survivors. If there is a significant difference, it measures the power of the one environmental factor being tested.

Human beings are less tractable. They don't approve of inbreeding, and there are no perfectly "pure" strains of men. As a result, no two ordinary human beings can be scientifically compared as to the effects of environment upon them, for no one knows just what heredity factors each one has, influencing his reactions to the outside forces.

There is, however, one special class of human beings which corresponds, in usefulness, with the purebred mice. This class is made up of identical twins — pairs of individuals who inherit an absolute identity of genes, the elements which transmit heredity characteristics.

One out of about every eighty-seven live births in this country is a birth of twins. Roughly two out of every three sets are fraternal twins, created when two different eggs descend into the womb instead of the usual one, and are fertilized by two different sperm cells. The resulting twins are as alike or as unlike as any two brothers or sisters. But once in a while a single egg, fertilized by a single sperm cell, falters in its growth for no clearly known reason and splits into duplicate embryos, after which each resumes the normal growth process. Both embryos thus have an absolute likeness of genes, and the twins produced furnish the only perfect, or near-perfect, human laboratory experiment. The most striking proof of their absolute likeness lies not even in their facial and body similarities, but in their unique ability to swap skin grafts. Such grafts between any two ordinary mortals live a couple of weeks and then slough off. But an identical twin can give to, or accept from, his co-twin a skin graft and have it "take."

There is, of course, no more mental illness among twins as such than among people in general. But if you hunt up 100 mentally ill persons who have twin brothers or sisters, and if heredity really plays a part in mental illness, then you should find an unusually large amount of such illness among those twin brothers and sisters.

For this reason, Dr. Kallmann and various of his fifteen assistants spend many months every year making trips by automobile through-out the state, visiting psychiatric, tuberculosis and veterans' hospitals, homes for the aged, and schools, scores of which have been enticed into the Kallmann network and routinely let him know as soon as a new twin enters their orbits. Research teams visit each new twin, take fingerprints, interview him, get a medical record and then go out to check on the second twin, wherever he may be. They may find him in the same classroom, or across the state, or dead, or simply missing.

Since Kallmann works with many elderly twins, and with families of twins where one or both have succumbed to mental illness, his job is anything but easy. Despite his massive dignity and professional manner, he has had hundreds of doors slammed in his somber face. He has, on occasion, beat inelegant retreats from farmhouses where his questions were met with shotguns. And once he spent many weary hours over a five-year period tracking down one missing twin, only to find her in the same mental hospital as the sister with whom his search had started — but one floor up and registered under a different name. He interviews sexual perverts in sordid hideaways, and considers it a fine summer vacation to drive 1500 miles in order to interview several scores of cranky old ladies and suspicious neurotics.

He and his staff sometimes spend months painstakingly checking the status of twins, as to whether they are fraternal or identical, by physical measurements, mental tests, blood samplings and fingerprint analysis. Although the fingerprints of identicals are not identical, the number of ridge lines they show are much more similar than those of less closely related persons. Finally, Kallmann and his assistants also visit the family doctor, the schoolteacher and relatives, trying to fill in the evidence.

The results of all this work have led Kallmann to become the chief proponent in this country of a highly unpopular point of view — namely, that severe mental illness is far more a hereditary matter than an environmental one.

Because this genetic theory of mental illness, in considerably cruder form, was the old attitude of a century or more ago, Kallmann has often been accused of promoting a backward, medieval, racist and even fascistic theory. By the dogged accumulation of facts, however, he has succeeded in gaining a measure of recognition for his unpopular concepts. His work is now financially supported by New York State, the Scottish-Rite Masons — through the National Association for Mental Health — and the United States Public Health Service. Even more important, a number of biologists are finding that the body chemistry of the mentally ill is out of balance, and are beginning to believe, along with Kallmann, that chemical treatment may be the solution.

Actual scientific use of twins as research subjects began on a small scale in the last century. A little over a generation ago comparative twin studies began to pop up in half a dozen different European countries and the United States, and in recent years they have multiplied rapidly in number. Many of these studies have been in the area of purely physical diseases. Tuberculosis, for instance, seems like an environmentally caused disease — we know the organisms and how they attack; we know that poor diet, insanitary conditions and underweight all lower the body's chance of resistance. Where, then, is there any room for a hereditary side to this disease?

Dr. Kallmann and an associate once went over the records of numerous tuberculosis hospitals, finding 78 tuberculous patients who possessed identical twins and 230 who possessed fraternal twins. Now, whether fraternal or identical, twins normally have approximately equal exposure to infection and equal living conditions until adulthood. If environmental factors were all that counted in tuberculosis, there should be as much sickness among the twins of the hospitalized fraternals as among the twins of the hospitalized identicals.

After years of tracking down all these twins, the investigators found the facts quite otherwise. Seventy-four per cent of the twins of the hospitalized fraternals had remained free of tuberculosis themselves; but only 13 per cent of the twins of the hospitalized identicals had remained free of it. The only reasonable answer, Kallmann concludes, is that the hereditary difference is the factor to blame. A case of tuberculosis may require the presence of a germ and a host for it to lodge in, but whether that host gets sick or not evidently rests, to a great extent, upon his hereditary resistance.

Twin studies by a number of doctors have also revealed that there are hereditary elements in some kinds of blindness and deafness, in diabetes, epilepsy, polio and many other ailments. Generally speaking, these studies and their findings have been accepted as valuable additions to the sum of medical knowledge. Genetic research in the field of psychology and psychiatry, however, always seems to get people riled up. It offends the average man to think he is not captain of his own soul; the very suggestion that mental ability is largely, and personality partly, determined by inheritance — despite the best efforts of upbringing — seems like dour pessimism.

The ideal way to study the relative effects of heredity and environment occurred to several scientists about twenty years ago: find a pair of identical twins who have been reared apart; then any differences in them can be ascribed entirely to the differences in rearing. A Midwestern zoologist named Dr. Horatio H. Newman spent ten years scouting out twenty pairs of identical twins who had lived apart since childhood. Actually, of the twenty pairs only four pairs had had environments that differed to a major extent, but Newman picked up some valuable clues from those four pairs.

One such pair, for instance, were thirty-six-year-old women whom Newman called Gladys and Helen. They had been born in an Ohio town and separated by adoption at eighteen months. Helen had been well educated and had become a schoolteacher, city-bred, cultured, socially gracious. Gladys had been taken out of school after third grade, when her foster father became ill and moved to a remote region; later she went to work as a teen-ager and wound up being a hardheaded businesswoman, blunt and forthright. They still looked enough alike to confuse anyone, but on IQ tests Helen scored twenty-four points better than Gladys — a very wide spread and apparently due almost entirely to the ten extra years of schooling. Still, many people with a full high-school education score below even Gladys's medium IQ figure. Newman's conclusion was that Nature draws a set of outside limits for any given person, and Nurture selects a specific site within those limits.

The late well-known psychologist Dr. Barbara Burks managed to find a few sets of identical twins reared apart, and probed deeply into their psychology. Though her sample was very small, her results, too, hinted that it was not environment alone that made a type of personality; rather, environment worked upon a built-in tendency and either minimized or accentuated it.

One case was particularly instructive. Clara and Doris were identical-twin daughters of an illiterate midwestern logger. He deserted his wife, and the twins were given out for adoption when still infants. Clara grew up in a small town as the spoiled, loved, only child of an easy-going couple; Doris grew up in a large eastern city as one of four children in a strife-torn religious family, where all pleasures were considered sinful. Despite these differences, both girls were dull pupils in school and suffered from the same physical ailments, including some that were clearly of a nervous origin.

Clara married an older man who protected her and loved her; with him she led a comfortable, secure life. Nevertheless, she was always easily upset by trifles, unsure of herself and apt to have crying jags over the slightest problems. Doris married a neurotic war veteran who made her life a horror. By the age of thirty-nine, she had developed all the fantastic fears and the hallucinations of a full-blown mental illness and had to be committed to a mental hospital.

If any conclusion can be drawn from this one case, it might be that heredity had given both girls a feeble nervous structure; Clara, thanks to a warm, protected environment, remained on the borderline of normality, while Doris was pushed over into complete mental illness by painful experiences.

And therein lies the heart of the problem. Why is the cure rate for severe mental illness still so low, in spite of all that modern psychiatry can do? Can it be that for the hopeless or difficult cases science ought to look not so much at the environmental stresses as at the hereditary structure?

Fully half the hospital beds in America today are occupied by some 720,000 mental patients, but that statistic doesn't begin to tell the story. Fewer than half of those who enter a mental hospital for the first time recover enough to leave it within five years.* And the average hospitalized schizophrenic has been there for eleven years. Yet if one

* With the advent of tranquilizers in 1955, the figures became more encouraging.

could show that life experiences do not so much cause as simply trigger these severe illnesses, a great new impetus might be given to research into chemical and physical treatment of the susceptible nervous systems.

This was exactly what Franz Josef Kallmann set himself the task of doing in 1928, when, as a young psychiatrist in a Berlin hospital, he first became uncomfortably aware of the frequency with which schizophrenia appeared among the relatives of the cases he was treating. For a while, Kallmann tried to disprove any hereditary basis of schizophrenia by taking careful family histories and gathering copious statistics on all the relatives of his patients. The longer he worked, the more his data disproved his own disproof, until he finally accepted the fact that schizophrenia seemed to have some familial tendency.

He then began a new direction in research, becoming one of the world's few psychiatrist-geneticists — perhaps the only one. By 1935 he found Hitlerian theories so obnoxious that he and his wife came to New York to work in a free atmosphere. The New York State Psychiatric Institute, a unit of the Medical School of Columbia University, presently made him a one-man department of medical genetics. Over the years Kallmann's department has grown, until today it has a large full-time staff, a network of thousands of doctors and twins who correspond with Kallmann from all parts of New York State, and a case-history file of more than 7000 twins, identical and fraternal, plus data on their families.

Instead of hunting for rare cases of identical twins reared apart, Kallmann took a completely new tack. Unlike many orthodox psychoanalysts, he maintains that identical twins reared together have approximately the same environments, that their minor rivalries don't really make much difference. So, both genetically and environmentally, they are the same.

Fraternal twins reared together likewise have overwhelmingly similar environments, but they resemble each other only half as much, on the average, in the genes they inherit. Ordinary brothers and sisters represent much the same situation as fraternal twins, except for their different ages; genetically they are just as close. Half brothers and half sisters, however, have as similar an environment as full brothers and sisters, but far less of a blood relationship. And stepbrothers and sisters, while they share the same environment, have no blood relationship at all.

Here, then, is a kind of laboratory experiment going on throughout the country, just waiting to be noticed. The environments for all these classes of people are fundamentally alike, yet their biological relationship varies from 100 per cent identity to no blood ties at all. If mental disease has any hereditary basis, that fact should show up more and more as the blood ties become closer all the way up the line. This entire approach, Kallmann's invention, is called the "twin-family" method of study.

The biggest such study Kallmann has ever made, and the most controversial, deals with schizophrenia, the major serious mental illness. He has collected cases of about 1000 schizophrenic twins over the years, and with agonizing persistence tracked down all their available co-twins, brothers and sisters, and half and stepbrothers and sisters.

While the chance of the average person's ever succumbing to schizophrenia is about 1 per cent, stepbrothers of his schizophrenic cases, he found, had a less than 2 per cent chance of also developing the disease. But a half brother, having some of the same genes from one parent in the nucleus of every cell of his body, has a 7 per cent chance of also being schizophrenic, and a full brother — who shares genes from both parents — has a 14 per cent chance. A fraternal twin of a schizophrenic — no closer in blood ties, but a lot closer in daily experiences, than the ordinary brother — has a 14.5 per cent chance.

But what of the identical twin of a schizophrenic — the human being who started as the same fertilized egg, and who has 50,000 genes in his every cell identical with those in every cell of his twin? For him, Kallmann found, the odds are an incredible 86.2 per cent that he, too, will be schizophrenic. Furthermore, in each genetic grouping there are additional borderline persons who never fully develop the disease, but show minor symptoms of it. Kallmann concludes from all this that the basis of schizophrenia is some specific defective gene which remains mostly hidden unless inherited from both sides of the family, and is worked on by an aggravating environment.

It might be supposed that the genetic view of mental illness would lead Kallmann to pessimism, but he doesn't see it that way. Quite the reverse. For if the defense against schizophrenia is built into our bodies by the right kind of genes and by their actions within the cells, then those defense processes, he says, "can be identified and somehow duplicated biochemically." Though no one has yet found a chemical that will cure schizophrenia, Kallmann firmly believes that someone will someday.

Another prevalent form of severe mental illness is the familiar type which involves wide swings of mood from wild excitement to blackest gloom; this is known as manic-depressive psychosis. Somewhat less than one half of 1 per cent of Americans develop this kind of illness at some time or other during their lives. In contrast to this figure, Kallmann found, through his twin-hunting methods, that fraternal twins of patients with this disease also suffer from it in 26.3 per cent of the cases.

But when Kallmann and his staff totted up their figures on identical twins of the manic-depressives, they did a scientific double-take and rechecked everything — for 95.7 per cent of those twins were also victims of the same mental illness, with the few remaining twins being borderline types.

Analyzing these and other data, Kallmann believes that this mental illness is quite distinct from schizophrenia, and that when a child inherits the particular faulty gene responsible from even one parent, it will be enough to produce the disease in him almost every time. On the other hand, it also means that a person who never develops the disease does not carry a hidden taint in himself, and therefore has not passed it along to his own children and grandchildren.

Kallmann has studied not only mentally ill twins but also many hundreds of normal pairs. As much in the well as in the sick, he feels, personality has some physical basis — not that environment doesn't play a part in shaping it, but that it is the product of an interaction between an environment and a given nervous or physical structure.

In many cases, he finds, the strength of the genes seems to override even the most powerful environmental differences. A pair of identical-twin brothers who are now in college were rudely set apart by fate when one of them suffered birth damage to part of his brain; he has always been a spastic-paralytic whose walk, stance, speech and manual skills are severely affected. If anything should affect a man's personality, that should, especially as Ralph, the spastic brother, always sees in his twin, Norman, the image of what he himself might have been.

Yet, when studied by Kallmann's staff, both boys proved to have superior IQ's, similar grades in college, friendly natures, similar control of their emotions and a high degree of sociability. The differences are minor; Ralph has, if anything, a keener sense of humor.

A pair of identical-twin sisters were separated at about eighteen, one marrying a farmer, the other beginning a course in Bible school and later going to the Orient as a spinster missionary. At the age of sixty-five she came home and rejoined her twin sister, who was by then a widow. They had been completely separated for forty-seven years, living in totally different cultures and climates, and having grossly different personal relations with their intimates; yet the twins are still absolute look-alikes, equally gray, with the same kindly lines etched in their round, cheerful faces; both are serene, placid and good-natured. "Even by means of a long and repeated series of psychometric tests," Kallmann says, "it was difficult for me to tell them apart."

None of his studies have been more startling than those on homosexuality. For many years, almost no doctors have accepted the once-popular theory that male homosexuals are lacking in proper sex-hormone adjustment and are an "in-between" kind of creature. The generally accepted view today is that homosexuality stems from such causes as the lack of a father from whom to copy the ways of manliness, or too close ties with a protective mother. Yet oddly enough, it is a condition which psychiatrists seldom "cure"; usually they must be content to adjust the homosexual to his oddity, helping him live with himself and society as painlessly as possible.

Kallmann had no end of trouble trying to gather his data. Homosexuals, he found, are uncommonly adept at disappearing without trace, at changing their names and occupations, and at refusing to answer questions even when finally found. After years of such difficulties, however, he has rounded up the histories of forty pairs of identical twins and forty-five pairs of fraternal twins in each pair of which homosexuality is involved.

Among the fraternals, only 11.5 per cent of the twin brothers of homosexuals were also homosexual — an extremely low figure, if family and parental influences are really the major causes. But the identical-twin cases show a shockingly different picture — in thirty-nine out of forty pairs, both identical brothers were homosexual. Kallmann concludes from this sharp contrast that the purely Freudian explanations are inadequate, to say the least.

Such are some of the general findings that have come out of Kallmann's years of twin research. Even if they hold forth the hope of future biochemical treatment of mental ills, many psychiatrists either doubt the validity of his techniques and findings or regard them as a counsel of despair.

"It's fine to talk about biochemical methods of attacking mental illness," says a spokesman for the American Psychiatric Association, "but while looking for them, we can't abandon the only ways we now have of actually curing the sick." Practicing psychiatrists, he points out, do cure or improve many of the psychotic by working on environmentalist suppositions — and without denying that there must be a hidden physical weakness also. What they do, in essence, is to surround the patient with a new and less hostile or, rather, less frightening world than the one he came from, until he can renew his own inner defenses. Some of the better state mental hospitals have recently been curing as many as half of their schizophrenics and discharging as cured or "improved" up to four-fifths of all first-admission cases.

Yet within the past few years some fascinating evidence has begun to appear that seems to tie in with the conclusions Kallmann has drawn from his twin studies. The National Institute of Mental Health, for example, has recently sponsored research on a drug called lysergic acid, which has been found to cause a kind of temporary schizophrenia when given in minute doses. Overdoses of ACTH often cause a temporary state of severe depression. Pentothal sodium, on the other hand, will make a schizophrenic briefly capable of talking intelligently. Dr. Winifred Ashby, of Washington, D. C., has found greater amounts of an enzyme called carbonic anhydrase in the brains of normal persons than in the brains of schizophrenics. At Boston's Peter Bent Brigham Hospital some of a group of alcoholics who were fed great doses of basic vitamins changed into moderate drinkers; when dummy capsules were substituted they relapsed.

None of these experiments has yielded any proved cures of any-thing. But they do hint strongly that mental illness is, in fact, linked with biochemical errors of our bodies, and that the nearly hopeless cases of mental illness with which psychiatry has had only limited suc-cess may in the near future be fruitfully attacked through drugs and medications.

The late Dean James S. Simmons, of Harvard University's School of Public Health, once summarized the new attitude: "We are spend-ing too much time, energy and money trying to clean up the cesspools of the mind," he said. "We could more profitably try to discover and remove the specific biological causes of the mental diseases."

Meanwhile, the major impact of twin studies may even lie else-where than in medicine. "The future of the human race," says Mr. Frederick Osborn, of the American Eugenics Society, "can be impor-tantly benefited when individuals begin to use genetic knowledge con-structively, and voluntarily limit their own reproduction if they carry major susceptibilities to mental illness."

Heredity clinics in which the advice and prediction of experts can be obtained already operate in seven universities, mostly in the Middle West, and the geneticists of several dozen other universities and hospi-tals frequently render analyses in special cases.

But mankind probably won't take the long-range view of eugenics, Dr. Kallmann feels, for many years to come. Long accustomed to sit be-low the salt at the table of psychiatry, he is quite resigned to seeing humanity fail to make full use of his findings until he himself has long been absent from the feast. Yet, like mankind's genes, both good and bad, he expects his theories to live on after him.

Dr. Kallmann informs me that since the publication of the above article, in 1954, the work of his department has undergone considerable change, due to the impact of recent breakthroughs in the field of ge-netics. The area of those breakthroughs was that of the beginning of the deciphering of the "genetic code" — that is, the identification of the molecular structure of the chromosomes that govern body chemis-

*try and, thereby, our inherited characteristics. This advance has per-
mitted Dr. Kallmann and his colleagues to concentrate upon the effort
to identify specific genetic factors — at the biochemical level — which
are connected with individual mental disorders. The twin studies
described above were, essentially, the first step in showing that there
was some genetic underlay to various types of mental illness, but the
connection was shown mainly in an over-all statistical fashion. Now
the effort has shifted to a much more detailed and concrete study of the
biochemistry involved. And this is already proving to have practical
applications: certain inherited enzyme deficiencies, for example, are
now known to produce certain kinds of mental retardation — and with
this knowledge, the enzyme deficiencies can be controlled and the retardation avoided or minimized. Hopefully, the future will bring a
host of other individual biogenetic discoveries of the same nature, adding a series of new weapons to the armamentarium of therapies with
which to combat emotional and mental illness.*

V

The
Mind-Healers

Throughout this book there have been many brief glimpses of, and statements by, the people who treat the emotionally and mentally ill. For a closer look at what some of them do and how they feel about it, I have grouped four articles in this final part of the book. The first illustrates the daily work and methods of a social worker dealing with school children; the second shows preventive psychiatry being practiced in a community mental-health center, in which several different kinds of staff specialists deal with the clients; the third is a discussion of one of the focal aspects of the psychoanalyst's working life, namely the feelings his patients have about him and, even more to the point, the feelings he has about them; and finally, the fourth is a series of walks and talks with staff members of a major mental hospital, in order to see what they do and learn what they think about it.

In the Schools

The Truant Officer Learns to Smile

EVERYBODY KNOWS what a truant officer is like. He's a pinch-nosed, thin-lipped killjoy who conceals a shiny badge under the lapel of his seedy plain-clothes disguise. He skulks about in the woods near Catfish Pond, and when some apple-cheeked lad, seduced away from school by the glory of a May morning, baits his hook with a fresh worm, the heartless fellow bounds out of the underbrush. He collars the boy and hauls him off to justice and a thrashing. The truant officer, in short, is mean and sneaky.

Such, at least, is the portrait of him painted in American folklore and cartoons over the past half century. To give him his due, his captives have not all been good boys following a rare wayward impulse; many were, and are, misfits, delinquents, or neurotics. But the picture is accurate enough in one respect: the truant officer has generally been a private policeman whose job it was to catch the runaway and drag him back to the hated classroom.

Now let's look in on a curious scene in an elementary school just outside Evanston, Illinois. Here, as in a number of other schools in the United States, the truant officer has recently undergone a transformation. Just off the front hallway of the College Hall School is a quiet secluded office with tables, chairs and toys in a bookcase. At one table a young man is playing checkers with a fidgety boy of ten. The young man is built like a gym teacher, but he wears scholarly-looking, horn-rimmed glasses and his manner is slow and gentle.

"O.K.," he says, "your move."

The boy sees something on the board and excitedly reaches out; then he draws back his hand and looks up in alarm. He hesitates.

"Can — should I ——" he falters. "Is it all right — your king, should I jump him?"

The young man looks surprised. "Why, of course," he says. "Why not? You've got me, haven't you?"

The boy looks worried, but he finally jumps the king and the game goes on.

This is a truant officer? Well, yes and no. Properly speaking, he's the lineal descendant of the truant officer of yore. In Evanston, as in many other urban United States communities, the attitude toward truants has been changing. Principals and teachers no longer regard them as willful miscreants, but as unhappy children whose emotional problems make school so painful an experience that they try, however foolishly, to escape.

Instead of using cops-and-robbers methods, such schools use social workers who employ techniques adapted from psychiatry to discover what the problems are, help the children to solve them, and thereby make them willing to return to school.

The young man is John Alderson, thirty years old, blue-eyed, healthy-looking, and possessed of a folksy Midwestern accent. He is one of eleven case workers employed by the public schools in Evanston. They are called visiting counselors. The boy, whom we shall arbitrarily call Billy, is crop-headed, jug-eared, and scared. Billy had first started playing hooky about a month earlier, when he missed school several days within a two-week period. On one of these occasions he was brought home by a janitor who found him playing in an apartment-house cellar. Two other times he simply wandered in the streets, and when the school nurse phoned home about him, he told his mother that "two big mean boys" had ordered him to stay away from school.

Formerly the school might have sent an officer to Billy's parents or had the boy haled into court after his next absence. Instead, the principal phoned Billy's mother and persuaded her to have the boy talk things over with the counselor.

Before the boy came to see him, Alderson had begun to collect information about him. From the fourth-grade teacher he learned that Billy, though only a little below average in intelligence, was far below average in achievement. The other children teased him, and Billy, unable to muster defenses against them, suffered passively. He seldom did his classwork and could not seem to concentrate on anything for more than a few minutes.

One morning Billy appeared for his first appointment at the door of Alderson's office.

"Hi, Billy," said the counselor. "I'm Mr. Alderson. Come on in and look around."

The boy ambled in and scuffled around the room, staring at the toys and kicking absent-mindedly at the legs of the chair.

"What do I do here?" he asked. "I didn't bring my books or anything."

"That's all right," said Alderson. "This isn't a schoolwork period. It's just a talking period. I'm interested in finding out what children like and dislike, and what makes them happy or unhappy."

Billy whirled about. "I'm unhappy most of the time," he blurted out. Then he flushed and turned away, and for quite a while he didn't want to talk. That's when the checker game started.

The meaning of his feeling about Alderson's king appeared in the second session, when Alderson learned that the boy was mortally afraid of his father. Billy had recently lost a new schoolbag and been whaled for it. Billy feared and hated his father, yet wanted desperately to please him and to be loved by him. Alderson was a grown man, like his dad, and jumping Alderson's king was like doing something awful to dad.

In later sessions, Billy modeled with clay, played with tin soldiers and finger-painted, unaware that he was talking freely to Alderson and answering his unobtrusive, softly put questions. Sometimes, though, Billy would stop and ask Alderson what he thought about something. Then Alderson might do a little direct steering or be reassuring or comforting. The effects were visible within a few weeks, as Billy began to show signs of improvement. Perhaps having a place to air his gripes was helping him. Perhaps having a grown man be kind and friendly toward him was helping him even more. And perhaps best of all was finding that Alderson considered him a nice and likable youngster. Indeed, giving affection to an unliked and unlikable child has perhaps more good effect than anything else. It isn't easy, though.

A neighbor once asked Alderson, who, grease-smeared and sweaty, was happily tinkering with his car, "You mean you have to like them? But what about when you get a real mean brat in the office?"

Alderson laid down his tools, looking a bit self-conscious. "It's the professional approach," he explained carefully. "Partly I make myself look for the likable side of the child. And partly I search through my own personality for the things that are making me react badly to him. Maybe this sounds strange, but if I think things through, I can conquer my inability to like him."

The neighbor edged away uneasily. "Yeah," he said. "Yeah, I see."

After the initial conferences with Billy, Alderson saw the boy's parents and pieced together what was essentially a rather simple story. Billy's father, a big, beefy, hearty salesman, had been both a good student and a fine athlete in school. He always tried to be best in everything he did, and the gangling Billy, neither good at sports nor particularly bright, was an embarrassment to him. The father goaded the boy and whipped him, out of a feeling of having been cheated by him. And Billy, whose school performance was one reason for his father's anger, got worse and worse, until finally he tried to avoid the whole thing by just not going.

In two long interviews, Alderson got the father to see that he had been punishing the boy out of his own desire to remain superior. After admitting it with some agitation and bluster, the salesman agreed to ease up on the child and to try to accept him for what he was.

Six months after Billy began seeing Alderson for half an hour each week, he was getting along with the other children, defending himself fairly well, and paying much more attention in class. He had even caught up on his reading, and his IQ showed an apparent rise of nine points. His father was holding himself in check and seemed to be learning to get along with Billy better at home. After considering all these things, Alderson closed the case at the end of the school year, and let Billy go it on his own, a child saved from a probable downward course of truancy, academic failure, and either delinquency or mental disorder.

Truancy, in short, is thought of now in Evanston as an indication of emotional pain, needing adjustment by professional treatment. Sometimes playing hooky is an attempt to escape from a place where one is a failure. Sometimes it is a means of getting back at one's parents. Sometimes it is part of a need to act tough or break the rules. Whatever the cause, it is only a symptom, and a late-blooming one.

Others can be spotted earlier in the classroom. Some children do poorly in their work, despite normal intelligence. Others are lost in reverie; others throw temper tantrums or pick fights; still others cannot play or work without getting into trouble with their classmates. These and similar symptoms indicate the many childhood emotional disorders that, according to the Mid-Century White House Conference on Children and Youth, affect 8 to 12 per cent of children seriously enough to make them needful of counseling services — the services of the new-style truant officer.

You would not, for instance, classify Gino as a truant. Gino, a dark-haired, handsome child of seven, came to class every day. But he was as absent as any runaway. He stared out the window and daydreamed hour after hour, until his teacher felt she could see the first awful foreshadowings of schizophrenia. Gino was chronically unable to get things done on time in class, and when the teacher tried to make him complete his work, he was apt to burst into tears or be doubled over with stomach cramps.

Gino took an immediate liking to John Alderson. He could talk with the counselor or play with clay, and Alderson never told him to hurry up or get finished. Nor did Alderson ever get angry with him when he experimentally spilled the checkers on the floor. At home he refused to tell about his meetings with Alderson.

"I just don't know what goes on there," the boy's mother said to her husband querulously. "I think Mr. Alderson lets him play and asks him questions. Gino won't tell me anything. But he loves going and wouldn't miss a visit for anything."

What was going on? Play, talk — and a lot more. Take one key item from Alderson's notebooks as an example: "January 23. Eleventh session. Today, while he was modeling a dinner table, I got Gino to recognize and verbalize the fact that his crying fits and stomach cramps in school are a direct transfer of his problems at home and his feelings of inadequacy at not being allowed to dress or feed himself at his own rate of speed."

Alderson called on the mother. He found her a voluble, excitable little woman, whose home, like her clothes, was immaculate and fresh. When he complimented her on her home, she told him that any kind of sloppiness made her almost ill. Indeed, she went on, the trouble between her and Gino seemed to be mostly over dressing and eating. His slowness and clumsiness so irritated her that she had been spoon-feeding him until a few months ago, and was still bathing and dressing him completely. "I can't tolerate his poking along," she said. "It takes forever. He's such a baby for his age. I don't know what to do with him."

Much later in the discussion, as she spoke about these things, it seemed to occur to her that all this was window dressing — that she really liked keeping Gino a baby by controlling everything he did. Perhaps, she said, the thing to do was to permit him to try on his own, no matter what a mess he made of things.

"It was like the thought came from nowhere," she told her husband later. "But now that I think about it, I believe Mr. Alderson drew me out and made me think of it. Funny thing. All the while, he just seemed to be sitting there, a quiet young fellow, listening and nodding and asking me a few questions, not saying much. I didn't think he was doing anything. Now, I'm not sure. I guess maybe he knew what he was doing."

Alderson had not only drawn her out, as she realized, but had slipped in some specific prescriptions. He advised her to let Gino dress himself and to ignore the time problem completely. "I'll explain to the school," he said, "that he'll be late because we're trying something with him." He also advised her to let the boy feed himself and not to inter-fere by so much as a syllable.

The first day she paced the living room, watching the clock as Gino fooled away the time in his own room. When he finally got to the breakfast table, the sight of his toying with his food and daydreaming so irritated her that she had to leave the room, to avoid snatching the spoon away from him.

The effect on Gino was astonishing. After being late to school three mornings, he began to dress himself in time, and he started to eat better and to arrive at school on time. In his talks with Alderson he was learning to take pride in his own achievements and growth. Several months later his teacher reported to Alderson that he was no longer an educational problem.

A boy who felt he wasn't any good, and a boy who wasn't allowed to grow up — these are typical "clients" of the counselor. So, too, were a big girl of twelve who bullied her classmates into a state of frenzy; an eight-year-old girl who became rigid with terror during outside play or exercise sessions; and a ten-year-old boy with a genius-level IQ who was obsessed by thoughts of guns, knives, and macabre scenes of torture. These are a few of the 190 children who have talked and played with the amiable, gentle young man in the past four and a half years. Most of them have come away healthier and happier.

Such a man is clearly a far cry from the truant officer of tradition. Yet counselors like John Alderson are a direct outgrowth of truancy work. After the Civil War the various states, one by one, passed compulsory-education laws and child-labor laws; to enforce them, schools hired truant officers who hunted for missing children, and spoke sternly to fractious or ignorant parents who preferred their children to be more gainfully occupied than they were in school. By the 1920's, compulsory education was well accepted and the truant officers' job was chiefly one of finding and catching kids who were staying out on their own initiative.

At that same time, some educators first became aware that skills other than those of the gumshoe might be needed to handle such children. The Commonwealth Fund paid the cost of putting thirty "visiting teachers" — another alias of the school social worker — into thirty different communities for a major five-year test. The experiment produced a bumper crop of hopeful reports. Educators were impressed. The movement began to grow. Better than one-fourth of all cities over 10,000 in population, scattered from coast to coast, have by now adopted the new concept.

At least, they say they have. In actuality, the movement is so new that the picture is spotty. In many cities the social workers work side by side with old-style truant officers. In some others they are the truant officers, stuck with the job of padding about town, hunting for absentees — and then trying to treat them in case work afterward. In one state, some counselors do not even have a high-school diploma; in others, they all have a master's degree in social work.

In Evanston, although state law called for the appointment of truant officers, the school administrators had found it simpler in the past to use the police department. Two cops in civilian garb who patrolled the department stores were always on the lookout for children during school hours, and when a call came in from the school about some absentee, the cops on the movie beats were also alerted. Kids nabbed by them were brought to headquarters and turned over to officers of the juvenile division, who interrogated them and then delivered them to the school or to their parents.

In 1948 the change began. Dr. Oscar Chute, superintendent of the grade schools, took advantage of a 1945 amendment to an old Illinois law concerning truant, incorrigible and delinquent children. The new amendment made state funds available to any school which provided preventive treatment to children who were in danger of becoming truant, incorrigible or delinquent. As an experiment, Doctor Chute hired a professionally trained social worker. Within a year, the demand for her time had grown so much that he had to add two more. He now has eight counselors serving the grade schools. Three others serve the Evanston high schools. All in all, some six hundred children were handled by the counselors last year.

In the beginning, many parents were hesitant about the new counselors. Some expected them to do home tutoring of backward children, and were annoyed on learning that they would not. Others thought they were psychiatrists, who would probe for "Freudian" secrets. Psychiatrists deal with unconscious conflicts, but social workers limit themselves to those at the conscious and "preconscious" levels.

Some, however, accepted them readily. One nervous mother said to Alderson, trying to reassure herself at her first interview, "This doesn't bother me a bit — I've been watching these things on TV and I feel right at home." And a smart-aleck kid of eleven told Alderson, at his first session, "I'll tell you what's wrong with me. It's very simple. I have an inferiority complex."

Teachers, too, were unsure about this interloper in their midst. When Alderson first arrived, not one teacher referred a problem child to him for a month. During that month he ambled around the halls, meeting and chatting with the teachers, eating lunch with them, asking them about new teaching techniques and revealing a little about himself.

They found him totally unlike Dr. Freud. Alderson looks like nothing so much as the happy young father in the typical life-insurance ad. His face is square, smooth, and boyish; he wears a broad smile much of the time; his hair, combed neatly sideways, usually has a small tuft defiantly upright at the crown; and his nose bears the traces of football scrimmage. How could one feel nervous about a thirty-year-old fellow who, as Alderson does, adjusts the valves and spark plugs on his own car? Or who lifts weights, teaches swimming in summer and goes camping with his wife? Or who has a baby son, a suburban house in a large development, and reads best-selling novels?

What makes him a good counselor is his professional training at the University of Illinois, plus the fact that beneath his muscular physique and suburbanite tastes there is a sensitive and sympathetic soul.

A friend once asked him what it takes to make a good social worker. Alderson rubbed his chin. "Golly," he said. "Well, let me see how to put it." He smiled uncomfortably. "I guess," he said finally, "one thing is that you have to have had a surplus of affection in your own background — more than you need, so that you can give affectionate understanding to your clients." He scratched his ear. "I suppose that sounds kind of odd," he added, "but I think it's true, all the same."

His grandfather had been, and his father still is, a doctor in central Illinois. Though medicine itself did not appeal to young Alderson, the doctoring spirit did. After studying psychology in college, he spent two years of postgraduate training in social work. Alderson spent one summer working in a mental hospital, and after what he saw there, preventive mental-health work seemed more important than ever. Of the many areas in which social work is now practiced, he felt, the schools offer the best chance to practice preventive techniques. He came to Evanston in 1952, fresh from his field-work training, and has been there ever since.

Seen from the outside, Alderson's professional life seems to consist of nothing but interminable talk — his own and other people's. It begins at 8:30 A.M., when he arrives at one of the two grade schools between which he shuttles. At once he begins talking with teachers, both those who have pupils in counseling and those who have children they think need it. At 9 A.M. or soon after, the first child arrives at his office. Six to eight of them come in each day, and return to class afterward. Between these sessions, he talks on the phone with parents or with a family doctor, a minister, a juvenile officer at the police department, a social worker at the Evanston Hospital, the schools' consulting psychiatrist or the Family Service of Evanston. He even talks on the phone while eating a lunch of sandwiches which he carries in a paper bag. In the afternoon he talks to more teachers and parents or calls on parents at their homes.

Only on the surface is this all like ordinary conversation. By far the larger part of it involves the artful handling of distraught children and parents, sensitively feeling for information, guiding their thinking into the open, absorbing the brunt of outbursts, tears, fears and hatreds, and listening intently for the truth hiding within a dense forest of words. By late afternoon, his tongue is leathery, his mind is battered numb and he feels "all used up." Alderson slumps wearily over a cup of tea, before beginning his final chores of the day.

He feels there are rich rewards in his work, though it pays only about as well as school teaching. But it brings the satisfaction of being a healer of the mind and spirit, and the gratifying belief that many of his cases might, except for his help, become anything from psychotics to criminals. On a day when a child who was a really tough case can have his interviews discontinued, Alderson is apt to go home in a holiday mood, and whirl his wife off to dinner and a movie by way of celebration.

That kind of feeling comes fairly often. Alderson has about thirty-five cases on hand at a time, and three-quarters of them show distinct improvement within the school year. Of the remaining quarter, he finds some too deeply harmed or warped for social-work techniques, and he tries to get the parents to take the child to a psychiatric clinic. In others, he suspects basic intellectual shortcomings, and asks the school system's psychologist to test the child to see if he belongs in a special training program. A few others just don't react well to case work or to Alderson as a person; these give him his gloomier hours.

Throughout all of the Evanston schools the ratio is the same — about 75 per cent of the troubled children make an adequate adjustment through counseling. "It's become invaluable to us," says Mrs. Grace Frey, principal of the College Hill School. "We have children who just can't be taught or who hold others back. The teacher can't do everything. It takes a social worker to clear up the emotional difficulties."

Superintendent Chute, speaking for all grade schools in Evanston, says, "Since we introduced counseling, we have been able to cut suspensions in half. Truancy has become a rarity."

Perhaps an even better judge of the results is assistant police chief Fred B. Wynn, who has been an Evanston cop for thirty-two years and spent part of them in the juvenile division.

"The way I understand it," he says, "the counselors get at the trouble before it hardens up. You can do 90 per cent more with a child of eight than one of sixteen. Before counseling came here, these children didn't come to our attention until the pattern was well formed. We like the counseling service just fine."

The cost of the new-style truant officers is reasonable enough. One counselor can easily handle as many disturbed children as there are in a school population of 1000 or so. Five dollars per child per year — about 2 per cent of the annual cost of each child's education — will install preventive mental-health service in a school. And, of course, the value received in human misery avoided cannot be expressed in terms of dollars. It is incalculable.

In the eight years since the above article appeared, school social work has continued to grow in size and importance in Evanston: the eight social workers in the elementary schools are now thirteen, the three in the high school are now five, and the number of children seen has increased proportionately. Treatment methods and administration tech-

niques have not changed. A note from John Alderson says that a study of school social work in Evanston, which he made in 1958-59, indicated that the teachers felt that three-quarters of the students getting case-work service during that year had improved as a result; this substantiates some of the optimistic estimates made in my article as to how many problem children could be helped by casework. Mr. Alderson, incidentally, has moved onward and upward: he is now an assistant professor at the University of Illinois Jane Addams Graduate School of Social Work, and is a field-work instructor for social work students getting their field training in the Evanston schools.

As for the over-all picture of the growth in school social work, Miss Barbara Moore, assistant director of the Department of Social Work Practice, National Association of Social Workers, makes the following comment:

"The growth of social work in the schools has been continuous ever since World War II. While there are no accurate national statistics on the matter, the number of school social workers who are now members of NASW is 1500 — nearly double the number there were within NASW in 1955. A further indication is to be found in Illinois — one state which does have detailed information: in 1949, 72 school districts in 25 counties had social workers, while today (1964) the number has jumped to 164 districts in the same 25 counties. In the same period of time, the number of social workers employed in these schools has gone from 98 to 252." While Miss Moore does not imply that this rate of growth applies to the nation as a whole, it is at least indicative of the direction of change.

In the Community

The Wellesley Experiment

AN UNPRETENTIOUS three-story white frame house stands at 162 Washington Street, Wellesley Hills, Massachusetts. Inside are a number of plainly furnished offices filled with piles of books and journals, a couple of untidy playrooms, and very little else. In these unglamorous surroundings a handful of people are conducting an experiment perhaps as important as any being performed in any laboratory in this country. It is the first major attempt to apply psychiatry to a whole community in a preventive, rather than curative, fashion.

Nearly everyone is aware of the remarkable results of preventive medicine in the physical-sickness field during the last half-century. In 1912, for example, 81.8 out of every 100,000 persons in the United States caught typhoid fever, and 139 out of 100,000 caught diphtheria. In 1949, thanks to sanitary measures, immunization, and isolation of cases, the number had dropped to fewer than 3 per 100,000 for typhoid, fewer than 6 for diphtheria. Pneumonia, influenza, and tuberculosis have had similar, if slightly less striking, histories. But there has been no corresponding drop in the field of mental illness. During World War II, 38 per cent of the men turned down for military service were rejected for neuropsychiatric reasons; a huge proportion of common ailments like asthma, ulcers, and arthritis, which are on the increase, are now generally considered to be psychosomatic in origin; and half of all hospital patients in America are confined because of mental sickness. Suicide ranks about eleventh in causes of deaths in the United States, far exceeding polio.

Many psychiatrists and clinics recognize that simple neuroses treated early can be stopped from becoming serious mental breakdowns later. But without organized attempts to apply preventive techniques on a wide scale, the psychiatrist of today is like the doctor of 1900 who used to spend his time treating hundreds of cases of smallpox and diphtheria.

Broadly speaking, a theory of preventive psychiatry rests on a few generally accepted assumptions: the Freudian assumption that most of the adult's mental ills are the results of weaknesses built into his personality during childhood; the theory that people are apt to break down when they have to live or work with other people who impinge on them in a distressing way; and the hypothesis that at certain important change-over periods in the individual's life there is a maximum danger of damage. The Wellesley experiment works on all these assumptions.

Wellesley, which includes Wellesley Hills, is a well-to-do suburb of Boston, scarcely the place one would choose to study as the breeding ground of disease, mental or other. But Wellesley in a sense chose itself. Some years ago progressive elements in the town set up, with the assistance of the Friendly Aid Society, a citizens' committee on mental hygiene to give psychiatric help to problem children. The chairman was Dr. William Rice, minister of the Unitarian Church in Wellesley Hills, and the committee received $1000 a year from the Boston Community Fund Drive. The members soon discovered that the money was nowhere near enough and also that it was all going to patch up disturbed children after they had got into trouble instead of trying to head off their disturbances. In 1948 they suggested to Dr. Rice that he call his friend Dr. Erich Lindemann of the Massachusetts General Hospital and get his ideas on a larger program for the whole community.

Dr. Lindemann, a plump, pink-cheeked, German-trained physician and psychoanalyst who came to this country in 1927, had for ten years headed the psychiatric out-patient clinic of Massachusetts General and had been interested in making psychiatry available to more people. In the course of interviewing and treating numbers of widely varied patients, he had investigated and written papers on such problems as the emotional complications of major surgery, the effects and treatment of profound grief, and the social analysis of suicide; he had come to believe that predictable crises in the lives of most people could cause emotional disturbances which might be circumvented or greatly reduced by preventive techniques applied in advance. Dr. Rice's telephone call gave him an opportunity to put his theories to the test and he agreed to head a town-wide program for Wellesley.

The first problem was funds. Dr. Lindemann rushed off to New York and returned with five-year backing from the W. T. Grant Foundation, the annual allowances from which have ranged as high as $69,000. The second problem was harder. The mental-hygiene committee wanted to be sure Wellesley citizens wouldn't be guinea pigs in any rash experiment and that no embarrassing secrets would be bared in any fashion. Neighborhood resistance to psychiatry in general expressed itself in the difficulty the project had in finding headquarters. It took almost a year to smooth this out, but by early 1949 the project was innocuously entitled the Wellesley Human Relations Service and set up in the former home of a recently dead, much-loved local doctor, under the control of an executive committee of leading Wellesley citizens and a steering committee representing several graduate schools of Harvard University. The Harvard School of Public Health handled the project administratively and almost all of the actual work was under the direction of Dr. Lindemann.

He assembled his staff from various fields. There are, or have been, social case workers, psychologists, sociologists, anthropologists, and psychiatrists. The full-time staff usually consists of from eight to ten people with another dozen or more doing part-time special research and consultation. By midsummer of 1949, a small but growing stream of Wellesley citizens were dropping in at 162 Washington Street; by the end of 1952, some 2000 people had been reached directly or indirectly by the practitioners of this newest form of medicine. What has Wellesley's Human Relations Service proved or learned about psychiatric immunization techniques during this time?

First and foremost, HRS has focused its work on children, their environment, and the crises in their lives. One such inevitable crisis is going to school. For several hours each day the child is cut off from his home and forced to live in another society. Children who are unprepared for this have trouble in their first year or two — and most of them continue to have trouble because of their bad start. Predicting which children will not adjust well to school is like diagnosing an illness in its first stages: it gives the doctor a chance to get to work before serious trouble sets in.

Sigmund Gruber, a husky young clinical psychologist, has tried to work out a preschool diagnosis in HRS. The spring before children are scheduled to enter the Wellesley kindergarten, their mothers meet with school officials for a briefing and the children get various health tests. The first year HRS was in operation Gruber asked these mothers if they would be willing to have their children take a school-adjustment test. Most of them were curious and agreed.

Gruber examined fifty children. He let them play and smear paint, he talked to them and their mothers, and he introduced them to a special doll house, his own modification of a familiar type of "play therapy." The dolls for his house — of all ages, both sexes, and various hair and skin colors — were in a box and Gruber handed them out only as the child asked for them. The choice of dolls, the things the child did with them, the extent to which he could concentrate on playing a game or telling a story, and other factors were all indicative of what Gruber called "task-orientation," or, in plain language, whether the child could start something and stay with it. If he could, he should be ready for school and society. If he merely banged the dolls about, had no idea of family life in the doll house, got bored quickly, hated the mother doll, wanted the psychiatrist to go away, and so on, he was probably not ready. At least, this is what Gruber hoped his test proved.

Of the first fifty children he tested, thirteen seemed fine, thirteen definitely unready, and the rest were somewhere in the middle. The next year, Gruber sent observers into the kindergarten to follow up on the children. From a series of complicated observations they reported back that almost all the unready children were, in fact, having trouble in one way or another; six were even referred by the school to the HRS clinic for special psychiatric help. Almost none of the children given an adequate rating by the doll-house test presented any serious problems.

The doll-house test, which locates an important weakness or predisposition in children, takes only an hour of the child's time and costs HRS — for the services of three staff members and follow-up observations a year later — about $35 per child. If future funds make it possible, the test could locate many "unready" children in time to allow simple case-work procedures, consultations, and other techniques to ease family tensions and fit the child for his coming plunge into the outside world.

On the applied, clinical side, HRS works closely with the public-school administration. Its staff members take part in the week-long fall workshop for teachers just before school opens; during the year they confer with individual teachers who want to know what makes a specific child "bad" and what to do about him; and they are always available to parents of children with problems whose teachers may suggest they consult the Service.

Sometimes what appear to be disciplinary problems are easily solved by very elementary applied psychology. One second-grade teacher came to the service to ask for advice about a restless, aggressive boy who had created a permanent state of wildness in her class. The class, an HRS sociologist discovered, was one of two into which a very large first grade had been split. The split had cut across the school "gangs" who had been together the previous year. Why not, the sociologist suggested, ask each child to write down which classmates he'd like to sit next to, giving three choices? This would enable the teacher to reseat the class and put friends together. It would also give the children a chance to let off classroom tensions by the mere act of choosing, of ventilating their feelings, and of expressing their likes and dislikes. A week later the teacher called back on the phone. "It's unbelievable," she said. "The problem has vanished."

Obviously most problems are not so easily corrected. A child who has real difficulty learning, paying attention, or getting on with other children needs more extensive help, and so does his whole family. For the child's personality is, after all, largely the result of the total pattern of emotions, command, loyalty, and affection in his family. "We have one boy, for instance," explains Dr. Suzanne van Amerongen, HRS staff psychiatrist, "who was a disruptive smart aleck in class, but outside class was unable to defend himself and was the butt of all the children's jokes and fights. Here in the office we can help him work ut his blocked aggressions and give him a sense of being respected and wanted. But when he goes home at night he is still forbidden to do anything naughty or rude or noisy; he is still ignored and rejected. Without a change in his family pattern we can do him only limited good."

So HRS psychiatrists and social workers try to speak to the parents of such children and gradually get *them* into the routine of coming to the office about *their* emotional problems. They do not attempt anything like a psychoanalysis of these parents: that is not part of a preventive psychiatry program. But they can, for example, make a too strict mother see that she is merely repeating a pattern that she learned — and detested — when she was a child. And having seen this she can begin to shed the pattern with their help. Nor do staff members need to probe deeply to awaken parents to the fact that the reason their "problem" child, the oldest, is unable to learn to read is that he misses the love and attention they are now thoughtlessly giving almost exclusively to the younger children or a new baby.

Preventive psychiatry cannot get anywhere near the root of a compulsively neat mother's basic neurosis, but it can, by teaching her the bad effects of early toilet training, get her to ease up in her demands on her child. And a relatively few hours of discussion with a trained staff member can show a father that his own deep anxieties about making a good impression in the neighborhood are contagious and are making his children tense and hostile in school. A harder problem, but one that still does not necessarily require deep analysis, is to lead a mother who unconsciously resents her child to realize that the child knows it is not wanted. Once she recognizes this, she may want to understand the reasons for her own hostility, and then perhaps begin to temper or change it. In some cases, HRS has persuaded a seriously troubled parent that psychoanalysis is a good investment and referred him or her to an analyst.

Occasionally, HRS staff members actually rearrange a family situation. In one family, a woman with a strong aggressive drive vented her excess energy on one child to such an extent that he developed chronic stomach trouble and became sickly and mentally retarded. When the Service began to work on the mother and child, the woman switched her surplus energy and aggressiveness to her husband in the form of frequent fights and nagging. It was obvious that her trouble was too deep to yield to short-term methods, so for the sake of the family as a whole, the staff psychiatrist got her interested in the idea of work outside the home and helped her find a job as foreman in a small factory — a job that called for strong, positive traits and let her blow off her surplus emotional steam.

As a result of its experience, the HRS staff believes that the greatest hope for preventive psychiatry lies in very gentle tinkering with the over-all family situations: a little reduction of tension here, a modification of a habit there, a bit of additional self-understanding, a small infusion of reassurance and confidence. These things can change a tense, potentially neurotic family into a reasonably well-adjusted organism. Using this kind of limited, short-term therapy, HRS has seen an estimated 75 per cent of the nearly four hundred families it has treated show improvement or even complete "cure."

The Human Relations Service has spread its lines of communication through Wellesley. All of the town's eight Protestant ministers are enthusiastic about its work and refer to it the family problems in their congregations that they think need psychiatric attention. So do several Catholic priests; and Monsignor Lord, pastor of St. Paul's Catholic Church, while he feels the Church itself has a highly important role in preventive work, agrees that the clinic has given fine remedial service to people already in real distress. Twenty town doctors have referred patients they suspected of suffering from psychosomatic complaints to the Service; and the Friendly Aid Society, the Department of Public Welfare, the Salvation Army, the Junior Service League, the Visiting Nurse Association, and a score of private clubs and associations try to steer cases of severe emotional disorder they come in contact with to the clinic.

HRS has also entered the field of direct education, as another means of forestalling incipient emotional troubles. It has sent its members to speak at PTA meetings, men's clubs, neighborhood societies, and professional organizations, spreading the gospel of prevention and the facts about the referral clinic, and breaking down the prejudice against seeking help for mental disorders.

One of the staff psychologists, Dr. Pearl Rosenberg, has inaugurated a series of parents' group meetings. These began when HRS ran a small ad in the Wellesley Townsman inviting parents to a free child-study group. The response was so great that seven groups representing about 125 families were set up, meeting two hours a week for three months. At first Dr. Rosenberg and her assistants lectured briefly on such subjects as aggression, dependence and independence, curiosity and learning, and so on. Gradually they let the groups themselves take over under their direction. The women became wonderfully adept at seeing little faults in one another and enormously resourceful in suggesting solutions to one another's problems. One mother was troubled by "disobedience" — her little girl refused to wear slacks. "Why should she?" asked another woman. "You wear frilly things all the time. She wants to be as feminine as you. That's not disobedience." At the next meeting the first mother appeared in slacks. "No more problem," she reported briefly.

The subjects under discussion became more complicated as the course progressed and the women and the psychologists took up the fatherless family, mothers-in-law, the role of women in the modern home, sibling rivalry, sex education. When the series was over, half a dozen mothers had decided on their own to come to the clinic for more thorough help. Nearly half the rest (an unusually high proportion for a direct mail query) answered a mailed questionnaire sent out by HRS, and every response said the discussions had been immensely helpful.

Dr. Rosenberg herself, after studying the questionnaires, concluded, "We taught them some elements of mental hygiene. But they taught themselves a great deal more. In any case I believe there definitely was a considerable over-all lowering of the tension levels in the families concerned."

Dr. Rosenberg applied the same technique to the first-year student nurses at the Newton-Wellesley Hospital. Throughout the nation about one-third of all new nursing students leave within a few months because of the severe discipline and emotional problems involved in nurses' training. Dr. Rosenberg led the girls in group discussions about being away from home, the reasons for strictness in the hospital, petting and necking, the causes of psychosomatic complaints, the psychological motives behind fighting with their families during weekend leaves, and any other topics that came up. The class proved surprisingly good when they got onto ward duty, with a minimum of giggling fits, faintings, and nausea. Even more important, all the girls except two stayed, when ordinarily about fifteen would have been expected to quit. An unexpected twist, however, is that half the class began flunking its studies — apparently the level of nervous tension was so lowered that the girls stopped worrying about grades. The hospital in return stopped worrying about them and decided they'd catch up later when they got deeper into the routine and the habit of study. By the end of the first semester the girls had begun to do so, and in one subject, chemistry, had bettered the national average.

All of these efforts come under the heading of applied clinical work and account for about two-fifths of HRS's time and money so far. The other three-fifths has gone into research. Preventive psychiatry cannot take the pulse of an abnormal family until it knows what the pulse of a normal family is, and Dr. Lindemann rapidly discovered that very little has been written about normal families: how often they fight, who is boss of which department, who punishes the children, who handles the finances, and so on. Two of HRS's staff sociologists have spent the major part of their time trying to find the answers to these questions and to map out the normal family — at least the normal, slightly-lower-than-upper-middle-class Wellesley family.

Their findings indicate that average "normal" fathers tend to expect too much of their sons, to magnify small faults, and to overlook genuine symptoms of distress. Mothers and fathers alike suffer from too little knowledge of child psychology, plus a high degree of worrisomeness about their own function as parents.

A rather startling impression, gained during more than four years of experience in Wellesley, is that better than one-third of the *supposedly normal* families actually harbor major emotional disturbances and mental problems, many of them serious enough to limit efficiency, happiness, and full functioning. This does not mean that Wellesley is a seething inferno of neurosis; as far as anyone knows, its rate of mental illness is neither higher nor lower than that of the average American community. The point is that behind the over-all external appearance of health throughout our nation, there is a hidden reservoir of maladjustment from which flows the tremendous stream of neurosis, psychosis, and psychosomatic sickness.

Frederick Richardson, a lean, austere-looking HRS anthropologist, has been doing another piece of research. By his laborious attempts to devise a way to analyze people and their physical surroundings, he hopes to correlate the rate of mental illness with such factors as the size of the family, the density of population, how long the family has been in one neighborhood, how good a house it lives in, and its racial and cultural background. He may then be able to discern from among these many interwoven elements which ones seem to be most closely connected with a high rate of mental sickness.

Another anthropologist, Dr. Beatrice Whiting, is doing a theoretical study of "affiliation needs." Children all want to belong. But no one knows how much it damages a child not to belong. If it were exceedingly dangerous, parents might think longer before moving from one town to another. Dr. Whiting is trying to find out how much the child's need for affiliation and his resulting dependence on his parents are affected by moving from place to place or from one social group to another.

Dr. Kasper Naegele, one of the two sociologists who investigated "normal" Wellesley homes, is now studying the fundamental nature of childhood isolation in school. How many friends does a child have? How many does he think he has? How many of those he thinks of as friends do not think of themselves as his friends? And how well do these facts correlate with actual observations on how well a child gets along in school? In the Wellesley High School, Dr. Naegele found that 15 per cent of the boys are not selected by any other boy in the school as a friend. He is trying to determine whether these boys are the most maladjusted, or whether it is the boys who *think* they have friends which they really don't have.

Dr. Lindemann himself is interested in learning to identify what he calls "pathogenic personalities" — people who do not themselves feel mentally ill but who tend to make others neurotic. One, for instance, is the mother who enjoys having a small dependent child and therefore tries to keep him from developing self-reliance. Another is the inwardly rebellious Milquetoast who has never himself dared to fight but is unwittingly encouraging his sons to be bullies. The domineering woman and the domineered man, both of whom may themselves enjoy their roles in marriage, are liable to raise children who will find it difficult to adjust to normal sex roles in adult life.

"Eventually," says Dr. Lindemann, "preventive psychiatrists will have to spot and treat pathogenic persons as public health officials now spot and treat 'carriers' at the outbreak of a contagious disease."

Wellesley's Human Relations Service is a real first. There has been an active mental-hygiene movement in this country for half a century, but there has never been as thorough an attempt to offer preventive psychiatry to a whole community. Several projects in other parts of the country have developed one or more features of the Wellesley service, but none has approached its integration. How well then has it succeeded?

The difficulty is that no categorical answer can be given. There is no way to compare Wellesley's mental health against that of any other community. No two communities are the same, and besides no one knows in detail the real incidence of mental disorder in Wellesley or any other American town.* There are some facts and figures, however. In a little more than four years, HRS has clinically handled 386 families, thereby affecting some 1500 persons. In roughly three-quarters of these families, there has been improvement of emotional problems; about 1100 persons have thereby been benefited.

What the mental health of these families means to the community can be guessed, in part, by the sources which referred them to the clinic. Of 257 children, 101 were sent by the schools, 45 by private physicians, 48 by their families, and 63 by various other sources. Adult

* Several surveys published since this article was written make this statement inaccurate — and yet it is true that the details of the incidence of mental disorder are unknown for almost every American community.

referrals came almost equally from physicians, clergymen, and the patient's family or friends. In addition, 125 families representing, say, 500 persons participated in Dr. Rosenberg's group discussions and so did 50 student nurses. Adding in the schoolteachers who had their own anxieties lessened and various and sundry friends and business contacts of all the patients, perhaps 2000 human beings living in Wellesley, which adds up to 10 per cent of the total population, have had their lives touched by HRS.

Wellesley itself by and large approves the program. Superintendent of Schools Lyman Owen says his program of cooperation with HRS has been mutually helpful, and all of the teachers with whom I spoke were unanimous in their praise. Dr. John Brines, speaking for Wellesley doctors, says the medical profession is grateful for the presence of HRS. Dr. Rice, the Unitarian minister, seconded by most of the other clergymen in town, told me, "A man who is in charge of a congregation can see the multitude of good results the Service has had." And the townspeople themselves are beginning to be aware of what HRS means. Because the Grant Foundation funds will shortly run out, a citizen's committee has been making a survey to see whether Wellesley would spend $25,000 a year of its own money to keep the clinical end of HRS going. Thus far the reaction has been extremely favorable. It looks as if the Wellesley project would be in operation for some years yet.

What is far more important, however, than the continuance of this particular project is the fact that, from HRS's accomplishments, a working hypothesis has moved toward becoming an acceptable theory. It is now reasonable to suppose that techniques of prevention can do in the field of mental illness much of what they have done in the physical-sickness field. The experiment in the white clapboard house on Washington Street may be the forerunner of a major advance in mental health.

Despite many changes in personnel over the years, the Wellesley Human Relations Service continues to operate much as it did when the above article was published. Its pioneering demonstration of preventive psychiatry, however, has spread out from Wellesley and been embodied in a number of other community mental-health services. Dr. Lindemann, writing me in March, 1964, has this to say:

"The Human Relations Service still exists and is now supported by the community as a private agency incorporated under state law. The responsibility for its support is in the hands of a board of citizens. Income is derived partly from the United Community Fund and partly from the taxpayers of Wellesley and Weston in consideration of services to their school systems and, finally, to a small extent from individual fees.

"The basic operations combine preventive services throughout the community with continued research on human relations issues contributing to emotional and mental disturbances. To this has been added an intensive training program for psychiatrists, psychologists, and social workers, as well as for social scientists interested in mental-health issues. This program is supported by the National Institute of Mental Health.

"The approach to mental-health problems in terms of emotional and situational crises has been widely accepted and has led to the development of similar institutions, particularly in Massachusetts and California. The new program for Community Mental Health Centers signed into law by the late President Kennedy is designed to facilitate many of the ideas and operations first demonstrated in Wellesley."

In the Office

How the Analyst Stays Sane —
Despite His Patients

MEN SEEM COMPELLED to find fault, or at least to suspect it, in the very people they most want to trust. It is tragically reassuring to us to find sin in the righteous, cowardice among generals, ignorance in professors — and madness in psychoanalysts. The psychoanalyst is therefore generally pictured as a suspiciously bizarre type: bearded, scribbling, thick-lensed, and distinctly peculiar in his manner. A demigod? Ah, no; an idol, suitably clay-footed.

Unfortunately, this stereotype has a certain factual basis. Freud and some of his early followers wore beards, and the analyst of modern caricature remains bewhiskered in an era when beards can seem malevolent. Many analysts formerly scribbled notes; few do nowadays but the pad and pencil remain standard equipment for them in cartoons. European analysts are sometimes thick-lensed from reading too much German printing, but the lenses are somehow symbolic of oddity. Lastly, some of Freud's brightest pupils did go strangely awry: Otto Rank showed manic-depressive symptoms, Sandor Ferenczi developed a severe psychosis, and Wilhelm Reich worked out his own "orgone energy" theory, explaining cancer, gravity and atomic energy as aspects of invisible sex radiation.

All this may make the mad analyst of fiction seem plausible. Mickey

Spillane has an evil blonde lady psychoanalyst shooting from the hip; the doctors in *The Shrike* are all sicker than the patient; and a novel, *The Horizontal Hour,* features a suave, high-priced analyst who first strips a pretty patient, then marries her, comes to suspect her of plotting against him, and winds up in a padded cell.

But neither the historical beard nor contemporary fiction explains the power of popular suspicions about analysts, for the suspicions stem from a deep emotional reaction to the analyst's kind of work — work that should, one thinks, make anyone lose his wits, or at least become thoroughly neurotic. For eight or nine hours every day the analyst must sit alone in a room with mother's boys, masochists, frigid women, homosexuals, suicidal depressives and the like, listening to an outpouring of bizarre fantasies, sickly fears, and nightmarish dreams.

Merely to be cooped up with such persons is strain enough. Freud himself said he couldn't endure having his patients stare at him all day, and hence worked out the traditional analytic position in which the therapist is seated behind the patient, out of sight. But not out of earshot. All day long he is assaulted by strangled, explosive talk, angry shouting, painful confessions, or, most baffling of all, hostile silences. Yet it cannot be helped; disturbed sessions are often the most useful ones. Progress toward emotional health comes through what analysts call "the working-through of conflicts" — a sort of refighting of old emotional battles, with the analyst serving as a punching bag that cannot hit back.

But patients, and laymen in general, often imagine that the analyst must want to hit back and, being denied that satisfaction, suffers acutely. At certain stages in analysis, for instance, patients make determined efforts to harass and upset the analyst (to see, among other things, if he will punish them, like other people in their lives).

A patient of one analyst once raged at him and accused him of brutality because a potted plant in the office had been moved from its usual place; a patient of another was reduced to tears because the analyst recrossed his legs while she was talking; a patient of a third artfully remembered long, interesting dreams just at the end of each hour, too late to tell them properly, too late for the analyst to analyze and interpret them.

Patients accuse analysts of boredom and indifference if they listen quietly, and of being dictatorial if they offer interpretation or give directions. Patients arrive late, and then complain bitterly of the high fees and the short time allotted them; they arrive early, and are sullen and furious because they are kept waiting. A member of the American Psychoanalytic Association says: "It has been likened to being indoors on a long rainy day with your own kids plus a swarm of the neighbors' kids."

The difference is that patients don't throw toys — they throw words, which can hurt much worse. In the *International Journal of Psycho-Analysis* a San Francisco practitioner recently published the sample diatribe of a typical patient on one of her bad days. Somewhat abridged, it goes about as follows:

"I'm fed up. A whole year I've been at this — a mixed-up, miserable, wasted year. And for what? Nothing. Not a goddam thing. You say I seem hostile today? God almighty, I don't need *you* to tell me that. I'm not hostile — I'm a mad bitch tiger, that's all. One of these days I'm going to find the guts to walk out on you and not come back. Why should I come back? You do nothing for me, nothing. Year after year, you just listen. How many years do you want? Who the hell do you think you are? How can you do it? — changing no one, curing no one, raking in the money and spending your week-ends in Bermuda, too gutless to admit that you're selling false merchandise. There's more humanity in my garbage man than in you."

And then there are equally painful pleas for love and affection: "I *know* you like me. *Please* don't tell me this is just something every patient feels. I find myself thinking of you all the time, though I know you're married. I can't help it. Whenever I see a blue car, I think it may be you and my heart leaps — and when it is you, I don't know whether to wave or pretend I haven't seen you. What am I going to do?"

Such a speech may end with an agonized plea for some physical sign of affection. If the patient is a pretty woman and the analyst a normal, healthy man, one imagines there must be a strain on him at this point; if she is ugly, the strain might be different, but worse; and if the patient is a homosexual, it could be terrible.

And even when the patient is not aiming his feelings directly at the analyst, doesn't his emotional illness have a contagious effect? Everyone knows that a jittery or panicky person can make those around him feel the same. What, then, of the analyst, listening to anxious, abusive, guilt-ridden, perverse, or seductive people all day, and able neither to escape from them, shout them down, nor shut his ears? Can such a man keep his balance? The practice of such a profession would seem bound to unhinge him finally, or at least turn him into the ailing counterpart of his patients.

Yet, according to leading practitioners and teachers of analysis, this is illusion and projection; this is only the patient's and layman's supposition of how he would feel if he sat in the analyst's chair. But the layman doesn't. A psychoanalyst does, and to him the hate and the love, the childish anger and dependency, the whining panic and admiration, are all clinically interesting and all useful. He listens to them searchingly, seeing them as clues to understanding, and steps toward recovery. But it is not merely objectivity that insulates him from harm; it is the knowledge that none of the hot emotion is truly meant for him.

For the emotions are all part of the patient's *transference* — a vital aspect of psychoanalysis. Although the patient originally comes to the analyst rationally thinking of him as a specialist capable of treating an ailment, he soon begins to transfer to the analyst a host of feelings that have nothing to do with a doctor-patient relationship but are replicas of the patient's feelings toward people who have been important in his life. This is made all the easier because the analyst guards and hides his own personality; his very mysteriousness is, really, essential to the process.

The feelings the patient begins to have toward the analyst are emotions he has been afraid of, and made sick by, in real life; but, in the protection of the analytic situation, he dares to feel them and to talk about them. "Accordingly," says Dr. Karl Menninger, "he may be as petulant as he was with his mother, as rebellious as he felt toward his father, as erotic as he would like to have been toward his sister or cousin. He can be this way, feel this way, and even *speak* it out because it is understood, not censored but interpreted to him."

In the early days of psychoanalysis, the usefulness of transference was not clearly seen. At first Freud used hypnosis, and later the technique of free association, to dig out the patient's unconscious feelings and repressed memories; it was thought that merely recollecting a traumatic experience, or having the analyst explain it, would solve everything; the patient would cry, "Aha!" and be cured. But many patients cried, "Aha!" a hundred times and improved but little. Something more was needed; intellectual insight alone was not enough. A higher rate of cure required a technique of strenuous reconditioning of the feelings.

Transference repeats the earlier feelings and disease-making relationships of the patient's life — but in a diluted, mild, controlled form; it thus gives both analyst and patient the chance to observe and to reshape his reactions to a host of stimuli. Whether the patient's mood is angry or suppliant, abusive or seductive, boastful or defeated, the analyst helps him study the situation and reconstruct his reactions to the analyst's supposed kindness or cruelty. The patient in effect lives a synthetic childhood in the office, but since the analyst reacts as a trained therapist, and not as the real parent did, the second childhood hopefully comes off better than the first.

All this explains why the analyst does not feel himself personally overwhelmed by the torrents of emotion. The analyst is only an actor, an animate dummy on whose vague form the patient can superimpose any set of qualities he likes. (He doesn't *deliberately* do it, of course.) Even a young analyst can seem parentlike to a middle-aged man; even a bald, fat, aging analyst can seem sexually irresistible to a young female. But however real all this may sound in his office, the analyst knows that the love and hate are meant for other people, people he is only a stand-in for.

This knowledge is the central fact of his technique — and the suit of armor that keeps him unwounded in the midst of emotional battle. It is almost a paradox: the very things the layman imagines would drive the analyst mad are the very things he seeks to elicit and analyze. When the patient snarls at him, or flatters him, he is neither wounded nor delighted; he wants to know which of his alter egos the patient was talking to, and why.

Yet psychoanalysts are not gods; they can be angered or flattered or led into harmful pity despite their intellectual understanding of the process. For it certainly *sounds* as though the patients are talking to them, at them, and about them. Analysts do react to their patients with a variety of feelings, and, according to one eminent New York practitioner, "Ninety-nine times out of a hundred the mood the analyst feels after the patient leaves is precisely what the patient wanted him to feel."

But there are a few minutes even during the treatment sessions and between them when the analyst is able to analyze his own feelings toward the patient — a set of emotions he calls his *countertransference*. He regards his own moods as additional laboratory data bearing on the experiment at hand. As one analyst explained it: "I consider myself a 'participant observer' — during the session I shift continually from empathy to withdrawal in order to observe. My own reactions are, in effect, a series of extra clues to my patient's problems."

Having used his reactions in this fashion, the analyst is free of them. The frustration wanes, the exasperation dwindles, and the erotic excitement fades. And this, therefore, is a second level of professional technique and a second layer of armor.

The ability to do this is gained, in large part, from the psychoanalyst's own "training analysis" — the three hundred or more hours he spends on the couch while completing his own studies, and for which he pays a handsome hourly rate. Without such analysis he is far less capable of understanding the unconscious meanings of things his patient says and does, but what is worse, he may not understand his own reactions.

In a recent report the Group for the Advancement of Psychiatry, in Topeka, Kansas, described the problems young psychiatric residents have before they gain this self-awareness. Some are driven by excessive sympathy to spend altogether too much time with patients (it isn't even good for the patients). Some are controlled and led by the nose by tearful or clinging-vine patients. Some become dictatorial, exerting a long-desired power over other people. Some fall into foolish despondencies, rages or moods of optimism. And some believe themselves as wise, as good, and as attractive as their patients say they are, an illusion from which the awakening is always painful.

Later on these same tyros learn how to handle and dissect such moods within moments of sensing them in the office. But this is only true of the analyst's professional life. "There is a complete dichotomy," explains Dr. Jean Munzer of the Institute of Group Psychotherapy, "between professional and personal relationships. Tension in a patient, for instance, produces no comparable similar effect in me. But tension in my husband is contagious. The wise analyst knows this, and does analysis only in the office; it's the beginner who tries to analyze his wife and friends — and he learns quickly that it gets him in trouble."

It is especially important for the analyst to use his professional defenses against erotic or tender feelings in the office. "Naturally he doesn't pooh-pooh the patient's statements of love," one analyst explains. "That would only be harmful. He listens, acceptingly, and then uses those feelings to examine the patient's problems."

But if the analyst himself is lonely, loveless, or insecure, he may be trapped into believing in the patient's love and returning it. This leads to a hopeless dilemma. If he actually becomes the patient's lover, the professional relationship is harmed, and the patient may never go further toward recovery. If, however, the analyst does his work successfully and cures her, she will eventually have to belittle his role, as she becomes self-sufficient, and her transference love will dissipate and vanish as she approaches the completion of analysis. Being a good analyst, in short, has the same disadvantage as being a good parent: the children desert one as they grow up. The analyst who fulfills his need for affection through his patients lets himself in for continual desertion and continual heartbreak.

A homely sixty-year-old analyst told of a beautiful young actress he is now treating, who swears she is madly in love with him. "If I believed it and let it become important to me," he says, "where would I be when I had brought her to a condition of health? I would be an ugly old man, abandoned and desolate. I don't deny that sometimes a pleasant feeling steals over me when she tells me how wonderful I am, but before the hour is over I have handled the feeling, thereby helping her, and protecting myself."

Despite the fiction writers, therefore, marriages between qualified psychoanalysts and their patients are extremely rare. The trouble is that the term "psychoanalyst" is loosely used, and not controlled by law in any of the states.

In this country there are only about one thousand medical analysts (psychoanalysts who are M.D.'s), plus anywhere from a thousand to several thousand lay analysts who have had no medical education, but who have been given thorough psychological and psychoanalytical training in any one of a number of first-rate institutes. But in addition there are a number of thousands — some estimates run as high as 25,-000 — half-trained, or untrained, or fad-oriented consultants who call themselves "psychoanalysts," and who are easily able to get their patients and themselves into deeper troubles than they started with by such dubious techniques as dianetics auditing, Reichian vegetotherapy, love-making, and the like.

The qualified psychoanalyst, according to Dr. Allen Roos of the New York Psychoanalytic Society, guards against letting his work be an avenue of sexual and social satisfaction. A primary condition for professional success, as a number of analysts told me, is a complete and satisfying emotional life outside the office. The analyst whose sexual and emotional needs are thoroughly and happily filled in his private life is much less likely to have his technique fail him in the office, permitting him to slip into dangerous involvement with his patients. Analysts sometimes fall into a joking mood about the problems of their profession. One of them said to me with a laugh: "Our real problem is a mechanical one. An analyst has to sit confined in the same chair all day long, hardly even moving. Can't squirm, can't get up and pace the floor, can't even scratch his ear. Now *that's* enough to drive a man crazy."

In the Hospital

Revolution in the Mental Hospital

The following article, like "Five Who Broke Down" which appears earlier in this book, is a somewhat abridged version of one part of a two-part series on Pilgrim State Hospital which appeared originally in 1961 in The New Yorker. *This article deals primarily with the personnel in a good state mental hospital, and with their activities and their attitudes toward their patients.*

AMONG THE STATE HOSPITALS caring for the mentally ill of New York City and its environs is the world's largest mental institution — Pilgrim State Hospital, a community with a population of close to fourteen thousand patients, situated fifty-one miles from Times Square, near the Long Island town of Brentwood. Over the last few years, I had read and heard a great deal about the drastic changes in mental hospitals that had been brought about by the new drugs known as tranquilizers, and Pilgrim State seemed to me to be an ideal place to observe such changes, for everything there obviously happens on a larger scale than in any other mental institution, anywhere. As I drove out to Pilgrim State for the first time, I found myself almost as deeply interested in the director as in the institution. What sort of man, I wondered, would be in charge of so many tormented or damaged souls — a saint, perhaps, or a martinet? All I knew so far was that Dr.

Henry Brill was the epitome of the Civil Service hospital psychiatrist — a very different breed from the highly paid New York practitioner, concentrating on his handful of neurotics. Dr. Brill was born in 1906 in Bridgeport, Connecticut, where his father was a small-time real estate dealer, and worked his way through Yale College and Yale Medical School. In the summer of 1932, he came straight to Pilgrim State with his brand-new M.D.; he stayed there, in various jobs, for eighteen years; in 1950, he left to head a state mental hospital in Sonyea, in upstate New York; in 1952, without relinquishing that post, he became assistant commissioner of the Department of Mental Hygiene; in 1958, he returned to Pilgrim State as its director; and, finally, in 1959, he was promoted to the office of deputy commissioner of the Department of Mental Hygiene, without giving up his post at Pilgrim. In spite of all his administrative duties, I gathered, he had acquired a considerable reputation as a practicing hospital psychiatrist, accustomed to handling patients by the thousands.

Eventually, I came to a side road that led to the hospital, and, swinging off the highway, I caught sight of a great expanse of red brick buildings, laid out on a vast grassy plain, which was crisscrossed by perfectly straight streets. This city had a building that looked like a church, a power plant belching smoke, and one or two modest skyscrapers — nine floors high — and, to my surprise, I entered it without passing through fence, wall, or gate. Driving down a narrow concrete road flanked by lawns and shrubbery, I came to the administration building — a red brick structure about half the length of a city block — where Dr. Brill, I had been told, made his headquarters.

Dr. Brill's office, on the second floor, turned out to be a fairly large room, furnished with a desk, a few chairs, and some bookcases, and Dr. Brill himself turned out to be a stocky, bald man with rimless glasses, thick features, and an amiable smile. He wore a brown business suit, and, meeting him in other circumstances, I might have taken him for a businessman. Seated beside him at his desk was a beaky-nosed, tweedy man in his fifties. "Meet Dr. Hyman Barahal, my acting director," Dr. Brill said as he waved me to a chair. "I spend four days a week in Albany, you know, and Barry runs things when I'm away. He and I were just talking about something pretty exciting." On Dr. Brill's desk was a small, unpainted wooden box, about the size of a medicine cabinet, and Dr. Brill tapped it. "Look intriguing to you? Probably not, but it does to us, because it's one more indication of the reform — or maybe I should say revolution — in mental-hospital practice that we're living through. We're thinking about making up a cabinet like this for every patient, to be hung over his bed. He'd keep his own things locked up in it and take care of them himself. Thanks to the tranquilizers, we suddenly gained a lot more control over behavior, and we can begin to restore the patient's lost dignity and identity."

Dr. Brill was interrupted by a ragged trumpet fanfare and the thumping of a bass drum. "Ah!" he said, looking pleased. "Something's going on. Let's see what it is." We hurried to a window at the rear of the building, and there we saw, marching down a road, an eighteen-piece band followed by a homemade pioneer wagon, a fire truck, and a group of straggling Indians. "A rehearsal for a holiday parade," Dr. Brill told me. "They're all patients, and events like this are part of their total treatment program." I looked more closely now, and thought I could distinguish some queerly fixed expressions among the marchers, but, parades being what they are, it was hard to be sure. The marchers had no obvious characteristics in common; they wore various sorts of civilian clothing, not the drab cotton uniforms I had expected to see, and they seemed to make up a random sample of the racial types of New York City and even of the ages of its people, except that there were no children.

When the parade had passed by, Dr. Brill and I set off to make the rounds. "We'll start in Building 23," he said, leading the way to the building in the center of the cluster. "This is our acute medical and surgical service." We went down to the basement, where Dr. Brill stopped off in the pharmaceutical supply room; ranged on long shelves were an enormous quantity of pills, powders, and liquids, in large cartons and gallon jugs. "Lots of medicines, for every human ailment," said Dr. Brill, "and half of everything in this room is tranquilizers." He turned to the head pharmacist and launched into a complicated discussion of a recently adopted procedure for unloading and receiving incoming shipments. As we left, Dr. Brill said, "You might wonder why I should be preoccupied with such prosaic details. But a director has to care about these details in order to run his hospital well. I have to think not only about therapy but about mobile radios for our police force, a new boiler for our power plant, the proper storage of towels for fourteen thousand patients, the problems of dealing with the employee unions, the obsolescence of machinery on our farm, and so on and on. You'll see, as you continue to look about Pilgrim, that we have most of the ingredients of a normal society — police, a power plant, religious services, road maintenance, and all that. In the end, everything affects the patients. The more efficiently everything is run, and the better satisfied the employees are with their jobs, the more therapeutic is the whole atmosphere in which the patients live."

On the second floor, he pulled out a large iron key, unlocked a door to a ward, and locked the door behind us. The ward looked like an ordinary hospital ward, and Dr. Brill and I walked between rows of beds in which women of all ages were reading, sleeping, or just staring. Here and there, other women, wearing robes and carpet slippers, were sitting or standing about. Almost all of them watched us guardedly as we approached, and in a bright, cheery voice Dr. Brill strewed greetings like a political candidate. "Hello, there!" he said. "How are ya? . . . Hello! . . . Morning! . . . How're *you* today?"

"Dr. Brill," a dried-up little woman said in a quaking voice, "I don't *like* it here. It's no good for me. I want to get back to my ward, where my own doctor is."

"Now, just don't you worry," said Dr. Brill, putting an arm about her thin shoulders. "Soon as we get you over this operation, you'll be going back there. Trust us, will you? We're trying to take good care of you." He smiled at her, and she looked pleased.

Leaving the ward, we went to a nearby X-ray room. A fat red-haired woman of perhaps forty was lying on the table whimpering while a nurse and a technician were getting ready for an X-ray of her abdomen.

"Hello," Dr. Brill said gently to the patient. "What's the matter — are you scared? Why?"

"The lights," she whispered, staring wide-eyed at the ceiling.

Dr. Brill looked up. "Why, we have fluorescent lights like that all over the hospital," he said. "They don't do anything to you, they just make the room bright. What's your name?"

"Hannah," she said.

"Now, Hannah," said Dr. Brill, holding her hand, "there's absolutely nothing to be afraid of. They're just going to take a picture. You won't mind it a bit. Don't be afraid of a thing."

"All right," she whispered. "If you say so."

As we headed back for the elevator, I noticed that several patients were strolling along the corridor, apparently going about their own business, and that some of the wards we were passing were locked while the doors of others stood open. Dr. Brill explained that patients who were badly upset were kept in locked, or closed, wards for their own good as well as everyone else's, but that more than half the wards in the hospital were no longer locked. In the old days, he said, practically all were locked; now many patients could live in open wards, being neither dangerous nor bent on escape. The doors of the locked wards bore a red dot and the doors of the open ones a green dot, as a reminder to anyone on the staff to lock them or not, as the case might be. The dot system had been adopted just a year ago, Dr. Brill said, and not until he and his staff had given it considerable thought. "I often have to stop and justify to myself my involvement in all these little things," he went on. "It isn't sufficient just to think grand thoughts; the job of governing any institution consists in coordinating a great many trifles toward one significant purpose."

Dr. Brill suggested that we look at the new-admissions building next. Because some of the patients in the new-admissions buildings are an unknown quantity and some are plainly disturbed — in traditional terms, maniacal — half of the wards are locked. We visited one of these. Fifty or sixty men of various ages occupied a large bleak dayroom at the entrance, beyond which I could see dormitory and lavatory facilities. Many of the men in the dayrooms were sitting limply on benches or chairs, groggy from tranquilizers; others were standing around idly, or watching television; several were working on one large jigsaw puzzle. Three attendants were on hand — husky men in black slacks and white shirts, who seemed friendly toward the patients, and not at all like the sadistic jailers described in some of the literature about mental hospitals in recent years. "These new patients are on heavy doses of the drugs," Dr. Brill said, "and what with their mental condition and the drowsiness, there isn't much constructive activity they can manage at this point. Still, the whole look of this room is revolutionary. Only seven years ago you'd have seen many of the patients pacing around like caged animals, and you'd undoubtedly have heard shouting and screaming. Some of our young doctors used to turn pale when they first tried to face it."

I asked Dr. Brill if he had been one of those who turned pale.

He smiled. "I was lucky," he said. "I never had any visceral reaction to psychotic behavior — I don't know quite why."

As we strolled about the ward, a wiry little man came up and said, in a thick Slavic accent, "Please, I want to change my doctor. He not help me at all. No good."

"Give him a little time," said Dr. Brill gently. "You've only been here a few weeks, haven't you? I know your doctor. He's very good. Besides, he can speak your language. Give him a little time. Will you do that for me?"

Dr. Brill patted the man's arm, and we moved on.

A curly-haired youth whose face was so tense that the skin seemed to be drawn taut over the bones walked over to us. "I'm gonna bust," he said. "I'm all cooped up and I need to move around more. Can't you get me some privileges?"

"Boy," said Dr. Brill, putting an arm around his shoulders, "boy, I'll try. But I heard you were acting kind of rough the other day. Don't work against yourself like that. Try it my way and you'll see."

The young man stared intently at Dr. Brill, as though trying to comprehend, and then slouched away.

When we were out of earshot of the patients, I asked Dr. Brill about the effect of discussing them in their presence, as he had been doing. "It never hurts if it's positive talk," he said, "and sometimes it helps. A few years ago, I was making rounds with a young doctor when we came upon a man standing absent-mindedly in a puddle of his own urine. The young doctor said scornfully, 'Look what they send me these days!' I said, 'I'll bet you five dollars this man will be home in six months, taking care of himself.' Some time later, a big, hearty fellow in a loud sports shirt met me one day in the administration building and asked if I'd collected my five dollars. Turned out he was the former patient, back for a routine checkup. My bet had got through to him, despite his blank appearance. By the way, he was a professional race-track tout."

In the women's admissions building, Dr. Brill again showed me a locked ward; the open wards looked about the same, he said, but were apt to be less interesting. A tall, wild-haired woman in her thirties instantly ran over to us, shouting, "Doctor! Doctor! Do you want to see a crazy woman? A really crazy woman? *Me!* Look at me! Aren't I a real nut?"

Dr. Brill regarded her with detached friendliness. "Hello," he said. "What's your name?"

"What's my name?" she repeated, laughing harshly. "That's the whole trouble! People tell me my name, but I don't think it's mine. I feel like somebody else, like I'm vacant. It doesn't do me any good to tell me my name. I'm no one."

"Have you been taking your medication?" Dr. Brill asked.

"Yes," she said. "Pills, pills, pills."

"Good," said Dr. Brill cheerfully. "Give it a chance. In a few days these ideas aren't going to bother you nearly so much. I can promise you that."

A pretty little dark-haired woman pulled at his sleeve. "My nose is broken," she said pathetically. "Won't you *please* do something about it? The ward doctor just keeps saying it isn't."

Dr. Brill peered at her. "I don't see anything wrong," he said, "but I couldn't be sure without making a proper examination. I'd trust the doctor if I were you."

"Examination!" she said, her face turning red with sudden fury. "What the hell's the matter with you? Don't you have eyes in your head? Just look at it. . . . Oh, my God!" She stalked away in a rage.

"A bit livelier than the male side," Dr. Brill remarked as we wandered among the patients. "Of course, it's nothing to what it used to be. Even back in the old days, I was lucky enough never to be hit by a male patient, but a number of women have punched me, bitten me, torn my shirt off, and thrown things at me. The women here are more volatile than the men. Actually, patients generally won't assault someone they know, if he's been friendly."

We went outside, got into Dr. Brill's car, and started off for a drive through the grounds. Around the buildings I had previously glimpsed were broad green lawns and trees, and a number of people were walking about, while others were sitting or sprawling on benches or sleeping on the grass. "Honor-card patients," Dr. Brill said, and went on to explain. "When a patient seems sufficiently advanced, he gets a card that gives him the right to come and go about the place freely, except when he has prescribed appointments. Just think — until half a dozen years ago, only a couple of hundred patients were allowed out in the fresh air by themselves. Now over seven thousand are. It's the most exciting thing I've seen in my professional life."

We stopped off briefly to visit a couple of "re-treatment" buildings, for relapsed patients, and "continued-treatment" buildings, for stubborn cases. The re-treatment patients lived in private rooms in long two-story structures, and Dr. Brill told me proudly that the patients are allowed to decorate their rooms for themselves, though he said that it was "just an architectural accident" that they had private rooms. In the continued-treatment buildings, which contained wards much like those I had already seen, he gazed with unconcealed delight at fresh pastel paint on the walls, flowered curtains at the windows, and a fake fireplace in a visitors' sitting area. "The more homelike we can make it, the less chance there is of severe retreat and complete withdrawal by the patients," he said. "We've always known that, of course, but there just wasn't any way to do anything about it until the tranquilizers came along. Some of them would have destroyed any refinements such as these."

As we were about to go back to the car, a soft-voiced, motherly-looking woman came over, and Dr. Brill introduced her to me as Dr. Mary Holt, one of his chief assistants. Dr. Brill mentioned what he had been telling me. "Oh, absolutely," she said. "Some years ago, before the drugs came along, I was in charge of two buildings of regressed women here at Pilgrim; they were so wild that I just couldn't keep them decent. They'd soil themselves, tear their clothes off, smash the windows, and gouge the plaster out of the walls. One of them would even rip radiators right off the wall. We'd sometimes have to surround them with mattresses in order to give them sedative injections, and these would help for a while, but then they'd get addicted to the sedative and we'd have to take them off it. I don't think anyone could have made a success of modern treatment without tranquilizers."

At lunch, I asked Dr. Brill when the tranquilizers had come on the scene.

"About 1952," he said, "a French scientist accidentally found that chlorpromazine, a new derivative of an old antimalarial drug of the phenothiazine family, had a remarkably calming effect on people, and, by an astonishing coincidence, an American cardiologist working on blood-pressure problems almost at the same time found that reserpine, an alkaloid extract of the Indian snakeroot plant *Rauwolfia serpentina*, had much the same effect, though it has no chemical similarity to chlorpromazine. We in New York State were the first to test them on a large scale, in 1954, and by the end of the year the growth of our hospital population had stopped. During 1955, we had the first significant decline since records were kept. Thereafter, tranquilizers swept the country, and the revolution was here. Now the combination of the drugs and the various other therapies — like recreation, occupational therapy, and so on, which had been used before but could now be stepped up — have produced still further gains."

Just how, I asked, do the tranquilizers work?

Dr. Brill smiled wryly. "The truth is that we simply don't know," he said. "Some say it's a biochemical action, but actually we have only the vaguest idea at what point the molecules of the drug invade the chemical traffic in the brain cells. In fact, it may not even happen there at all; they may do their work elsewhere, for all we know. But our ignorance is no ground for criticism of the tranquilizers; after all, we still don't know just how aspirin helps a headache. Most medical therapies are used empirically, without our having ultimate knowledge of the mechanisms involved.

"Still, ignorant as we are at the cellular level, I like to think I have a more general way to explain what they do. The body has natural healing processes that tend to repair every wound and to combat every infection, unless, of course, the wound or infection is overpowering. If you provide the support of antibiotics or wound dressings, and so tip the balance, the body may take over again and healing will begin. I believe that the mind, too, has its own natural healing process. Many people suffer minor attacks of nerves or the blues and get better on their own without being hospitalized. But for others an attack may be too strong, and they can't fight it off without artificial support. I think the tranquilizers probably provide just such support, decreasing the intensity of the hallucinations, the delusions, and the fears, and enabling the natural healing tendency of the mind to take over."

When I visited Pilgrim again, to see some of those therapies that succeed on an empirical basis, it happened that Dr. Brill was up in Albany, and Dr. Barahal was waiting for me instead. "I've arranged for you to start off by seeing the second most important somatic therapy, after the drugs," he said. "That's E.C.T. — electro-convulsive therapy, or, more simply, electric shock. I'd better tell you a little about it first. It's not particularly pleasant to watch, and you might get the idea that the patient is suffering horribly. The actual fact is that the passage of the current through the brain causes instant loss of consciousness; the patients don't even recall the event itself. They feel nothing and cannot remember the shock or convulsion afterward.

"It's perfectly true that a series of electric-shock treatments does cause temporary vagueness and forgetfulness, which bother some patients considerably, but all the studies I know of indicate a complete return of memory and thought within weeks or, at most, months. There is no evidence of any permanent damage. And it really relieves distress. You'll get a restless, agitated, deeply depressed woman in here, for instance, who feels that her husband mistreats her, her children have grown up and forgotten her, her health is failing, her looks are ruined, and her life is without any joy or sweetness. She's really in pain. Tranquilizers often fail with such a patient, and the anti-depressants — the so-called psychic energizers — may be no help, either. But put such a woman through shock in the morning, and ask her that afternoon how things are, and she'll tell you everything's fine — she's perfectly satisfied with her husband, children, and life, and her problems are minor and not worth making a fuss about."

I asked what it is that shock actually does to work such wonders, and Dr. Barahal smiled in a faintly embarrassed manner that I was getting to recognize. He said that at least fifty theories have been put forward but that none has been incontestably proved, and none generally accepted. Some doctors have maintained that electric shock works physical changes in the brain cells, others that it merely interrupts harassing repetitious stimuli in the neuron circuits of the brain, and still others that it provides a symbolic death and rebirth. "For myself," Dr. Barahal said, "I teach my students merely the demonstrable truths. Shock treatment, first of all, causes spotty amnesia that usually persists, at least in part, for a few days, and in traces for a month or two. Whatever the ultimate reason, the amnesia enables the patient temporarily to forget not his problems but the intensity of his feelings about them. As long as that relief lasts, he can do some rebuilding of his personal defenses. However, it may take ten or twenty treatments, spaced out at three a week, to do the job."

On the third floor of Building 24, I found Dr. Frederick M. Rosen, a large, pear-shaped man in his forties, in the treatment room, a small cubicle in which there was nothing but a table, with a sheaf of medical records on it, and a plain black box, less than a foot square, that was fitted with two dials, a voltmeter, and a button. "This is the whole apparatus," Dr. Rosen said. "It's a Medcraft E.C.T. Unit, adjustable for intensity and duration of shock. We give shock in the classic fashion here, aiming for a *grand-mal* type of seizure, so I'll be using a hundred and twenty to a hundred and fifty volts for three-tenths to four-tenths of a second, depending on the patient's convulsive threshold."

The head nurse opened the door, and two attendants wheeled in a moon-faced young Negro woman on a rolling stretcher.

Dr. Rosen glanced at her chart. "Good morning, Mary," he said. "This will be your fifth treatment. How have you been feeling?"

"Hi, Dr. Rosen," she said, in a tense, husky voice. "I'm doin' better. Things don' look so bad, and I din' hear no voices long while now. But I'm still skeered of that machine."

"You needn't be," said Dr. Rosen. "Everything's going to be all right."

The nurses tucked a drawsheet around Mary and stationed themselves at her feet, head, and left side. "Bite on this mouthpiece," one of them told Mary, handing her a rubber bit. The nurse at the patient's head took up two pencillike electrodes with flat, flanged bases and smeared contact jelly on them; she and Dr. Rosen then pressed the electrodes against Mary's temples. Dr. Rosen set the dials quickly and pushed the button. At once, Mary grunted deeply, and her head jerked back. "She's totally unconscious," Dr. Rosen told me. Her eyes were clenched shut, and her face was drawn into a tight, distorted mask. Her legs rose stiffly in the air, and spasms then spread through her body. All three nurses kept hold of her, "riding," as Dr. Rosen said, with her motions. As far as I could tell, she stopped breathing. At last, after forty-five seconds — a very long forty-five seconds, it seemed to me — the convulsion subsided, a long gargling sound came from her throat, and, as she sank down, her breathing began again.

The attendants immediately wheeled her into the recovery room, and other nurses stationed there lifted her into a bed. The women were treated at the rate of about one every three minutes — there were only minor differences in their reactions — and long before the last one was done, the first ones were awake, either lying sleepily still or sitting up with dazed expressions. Dr. Rosen and I went to see them.

"How do you feel, Mary?" he asked the first of the day's crop.

"Fine," she said.

"Do you know me?" Dr. Rosen asked.

"Yeah . . . yeah," she said, smiling with vague embarrassment, "but . . . can' think of your name."

"Have you had your treatment yet today?" he asked.

"Um . . . no," she said, after some thought. "Not yet. Soon, I guess."

We talked to several of the others, and not one knew she had been treated. "Later in the day they'll remember being wheeled in," Dr. Rosen said, "but they'll never remember the convulsion. A number of these women were pretty difficult or depressed last night, but by this afternoon they'll be acting and thinking well enough for some of them to go off on weekend visits home. Monday, before they can slip too far back, they'll be getting the next treatment."

I thanked Dr. Rosen and returned to Dr. Barahal's office, where I met my next guide, a small, gray-haired, snub-nosed woman named Helen Hedges, who is the supervisor of Pilgrim's Occupational Therapy Department, or O.T. "I hardly know where to take you first," she said. "We have eleven clinics for men and sixteen for women, and you wouldn't want to see them all. Let's just have a look first at Building 23." On the second floor of that building, we visited a woodworking shop for newly admitted male patients. About fifteen men of various ages were busy at benches — some of them equipped with potentially dangerous tools — and lamps, magazine racks, cigarette boxes, and other artifacts were ranged on display shelves. Miss Hedges introduced me to Fred Roll, the instructor in charge; he was a slim, athletic-looking man of about forty, who had been ambling around the room giving help first to one, then to another, of the patients. "I read the case history after the patient's been in the hospital a couple of weeks," he said, "and I don't take on any that I think I might not be able to handle. Still, with most of them being on drugs or shock, even a very hostile patient is likely to work out all right these days. If a man *is* marked down on his prescription card as suicidal or assaultive, though, I won't have him work with a chisel or knife; instead, I'll give him a coping saw or sandpaper. I haven't had one serious accident in four years."

One patient was rigging a model sailboat; another was sandpapering a roughhewn three-legged stool; still another was whittling a statuette of an Indian; and a fourth was painting plywood fish for use in a mobile.

I remarked that the whole scene was quite peaceful and normal.

"They *are* very well behaved, aren't they?" Roll said. "Not that I let them bang away aimlessly. I always try to give them goals, and help them fix up their mistakes so they can finish a job instead of giving up on it. I find that sometimes it's much better to be critical of them than just accepting."

We stopped at a bench where a blond, nearsighted young man was whittling one end of a brace for a model-boat hull.

"I think you'd better check your dimensions before cutting that down any more," Roll said.

The man looked up — rather resentfully, it seemed to me. "Yeah," he said, and took another swipe at the piece with his knife.

"Better measure it first," said Roll firmly. "It'll be easier than trying to patch it up afterwards."

The patient stared at him for a minute, and then took a blueprint out of a drawer and checked his work.

"He's coming along," Roll said to me after we had passed out of earshot. "A week ago, he couldn't take criticism at all, and wasn't doing anything constructive — just spoiling wood."

Miss Hedges and I left the workshop and proceeded to visit a typing class, a small printing plant, a ceramic shop, and several sewing rooms. The range of skills was considerable. At one extreme, we saw two businesslike young women editing copy for a hospital newspaper called, perhaps inevitably, *Pilgrim's Progress*; at the other, we saw an old, foolishly smiling woman slowly unraveling worn-out socks and rolling up the yarn. "Even this is useful," Miss Hedges said. "She might otherwise be sitting in the dayroom doing nothing and just atrophying. Partly, O.T. is a job of maintenance — preventing further regression. But there's a lot more to it, too. We don't have any major scientific studies of O.T. with control groups and all that apparatus, so we haven't any strict or absolute kind of proof. But we see and feel the good it does. And the patients often tell us about it themselves. Forty-five hundred of them are doing all sorts of things, and we feel that in many cases O.T. itself has been the major factor in cures. We can't prove it, but we O.T. people believe it."

It was time for lunch. Miss Hedges drove me to the staff house, where she introduced me to Miss Mary Jane Preston, a thickset, tousle-headed woman, who supervises the Recreation Department. Miss Preston told me that her work, like that of the Occupational Therapy Department, has never been subjected to controlled scientific study or rigorous evaluation. "But we know beyond any doubt that it does good," she said firmly. "We run dances and picnics and games of all sorts for patients who otherwise wouldn't attend any kind of social event and would forget how to talk or act in a social situation. Even taking them to a live play, or getting them to shoot pool or play cards, is bound to help keep them from deteriorating. And it does more than that. In many cases, it helps get the patient out of his shell. We get a withdrawn patient and put a basketball in his hands, and he just stands there; we have to take his arms and push them to get him to throw it. Then, after a while, he'll throw it by himself. Finally, if he gets it in the basket, we can see in his face that he's made some progress. Get them moving! Get them doing!"

After lunch, Miss Preston took me on a tour of her facilities. We first visited the Assembly Hall, a multi-purpose building with a peaked roof — the building that I had taken for a church. It had an auditorium that did, in fact, serve as a church as well as a theater and a concert hall, and it had a library, a cafeteria, and a commissary, where honor-card patients, some perfectly normal-looking and others with abstracted expressions on their faces or a stiff way of holding themselves, came and went freely. In the main auditorium, a seven-man dance band, composed of patients, was rehearsing for that night's honor-card dance. A young man in a sweater sang "Moonglow" in a flat voice whose lack of expression might have indicated schizophrenia or merely a lack of talent. We moved on to a small movie theater in the basement of one of the geriatrics buildings. Aged men and women were being herded in to watch a Western by attendants who had to push and steer them as though they were sheep. Once seated, a few of the old patients stared at their laps or at each other, but most watched the screen; whether they were amused or interested by the shooting and riding was not easy to tell, nor could I judge whether what they were watching was actually preventing regression and withdrawal. I could only hope so.

Afterward, we went through card rooms, game rooms, and gymnasiums. They seemed to thrill Miss Preston. "In the old days, we could never have had things like this," she said. "The patients would have ruined them, or else just couldn't have used them. We thought it was a big deal when we made up beanbags and got the attendants to toss them to the patients in the day rooms."

The pièce de résistance of the afternoon was a trip to Miss Preston's greatest thrill of all — the recreation field. At the rear of the hospital, it is a fenced-in area of thirty-five acres, with softball fields; courts for tennis, volleyball, badminton, handball, and basketball; a boccie alley; a roller-skating rink; and a miniature golf course. Here and there were shade trees, shrubbery, and benches. Hundreds of patients had come to the area on their own or been escorted by attendants, and were now scattered about doing whatever they wished. Some had gone off to sit alone under a tree or lie down on the grass; others were walking around or sitting on the benches and chatting; still others were roller-skating or playing, with varying degrees of skill or ineptitude, one or another of the games. At a quick glance, one could have taken it for a typical summer-afternoon scene in a public park, except for the lack of children; only after a minute or so did a faint tinge of oddness seep through. Among the strolling people, for instance, was one man whose right arm, at every second step, swung up smartly and touched his chest; another who walked bent sidewise, a gaping grin fixed on his face; and another who moved with a stiffness of body that might have been either catatonia or the result of heavy medication.

A few weeks later, I returned to Pilgrim for another talk with Dr. Brill. I pointed out that so far almost all I had seen concerned actively treated patients for whom there was hope; now I wanted to see those patients of whom I had heard so much — the hopeless ones living in what are commonly called snake pits.

"All right," he said agreeably. "I'll show you some things that we're not especially proud of, but they are certainly part of the total picture." As we drove toward the rear of the hospital area, he explained that the new drugs, much as they accomplish for new patients, do far less good with deteriorated patients who have been psychotic and hospitalized for many years. "The tranquilizers will greatly reduce the rages of the worst ones," he said, "but sixty to seventy per cent of these patients remain just as psychotic as ever."

We stopped and got out in front of Building 1. Dr. Brill opened the door of an upstairs ward with a key; the scene in the dayroom just within made me recall what I had read of debtor's prisons and dungeons — not that it was dark and cobwebby but that the mood conveyed was a total abandonment of hope and a slow decay of essential humanity. The walls were of rough, dingy plaster that had never been painted, and the dayroom was furnished with heavy, dark wooden benches and rockers, on which were slumped inert, shapeless male bodies. The men sat immobile, their faces so devoid of expression as to seem featureless. They were of different ages and sizes, but were all thoroughly rumpled, useless, and wrecked. A few shambled around aimlessly, and a handful sat near a television set, but paid little attention to it.

"This is what it used to be like in much of the hospital, but far noisier and less clean," Dr. Brill said. "Nowadays, we have only a few wards like this left. Most of these men have been here twenty or thirty years, and they got this way because we had no adequate techniques for coping with their particular diseases then. Nothing we do so far has seemed to help them much in a positive sense, but the tranquilizers have made a tremendous change in a negative sense — controlling aggressive and destructive behavior. Still, as you see, the advances made elsewhere in the hospital have not yet caught up here."

From Building 1, we drove to Building 25, a nine-story structure, which towers above the rest like an apartment house in a suburb. "This is our geriatrics and chronic infirmary, where we have all our bedfast cases," Dr. Brill said. "Once again, it represents an area in which we can do little curative psychiatry." We walked in and out of several wards, in which large numbers of patients, mostly elderly, were lying abed or were seated in wheelchairs in the day rooms. "We have twelve hundred and fifty of these feeble cases here — all people who are getting what amounts to nursing care," Dr. Brill went on. "You might suppose a mental hospital should be required to treat only mental illness, but these days, as society changes the traditional distribution of responsibilities between the individual and the state, we're being asked to care for patients with all sorts of additional problems. In previous generations, many of these people — almost all of whom are quite feeble, and not dangerous — would have been kept at home or cared for in old people's homes or nursing homes. Now we get them."

At lunch, Dr. Brill continued to dwell on the newer functions of mental hospitals. Even though mental illness had not been well understood in the past, he said, society had drawn a rather well-defined boundary between insanity and sanity. "Sane human beings had been held accountable for their actions. Our own society, however, having learned a good deal more about the familial and social determinants of behavior, has been explaining more and more antisocial conduct in terms of mental or emotional disturbance, rather than evil character or disobedience of the law. The very difficult question, of course, is this: Just where *should* society draw the line between responsibility for one's own acts, on the one hand, and mental or emotional disorder, on the other? As psychiatrists, we have to try to distinguish between bad conduct due to emotional or mental disorders and bad conduct due to cultural patterns and other causes. Somewhere in between lies a border line — vague and poorly marked, and changing year by year. Where it will end up is far from clear."

After suggesting that I have a talk about these new problems with one of his assistants, Dr. Brill drove me back to the administration building, took me to a small office just down the hall from his own, and introduced me to Dr. Joseph Clifford, a brisk, youthful man with an open, genial face and a rural accent that, he said, identified him as "an apple-knocker from upstate." "Right in that borderline area Dr. Brill was talking about," Dr. Clifford said, "is the type of individual who isn't crazy in the traditional meaning of the word, or psychotic in our meaning of the word, but who just doesn't act in a socially acceptable or responsible way. The individual who fights authority, for instance, or is chronically irresponsible, or — to cite two other kinds of problem — the promiscuous person or the homosexual. We refer to these types of behavior as signs of 'character disorders' or 'psychopathic personality,' and are they tough cases! Tranquilizers aren't much good with this kind of faulty character. What these people need is to have their personalities thoroughly reshaped and matured, but that's extremely difficult after they've reached the age of thirteen or fourteen, especially with the limited time we can give each individual. We do use some psychoanalytically oriented group therapy, hoping to get them to recognize their hidden needs and handle them less destructively. But just when you think you've worked wonders, and optimistically release them, some of them go out and do the same unfortunate things all over again. I had a church-going college boy in here for a few months who had been booked for making homosexual advances in the movies. He came along wonderfully well, and left here a couple of weeks ago all straightened out. Yesterday, I heard he'd just been picked up by the police in a park in Queens, trying to approach little colored boys. It's disheartening, to say the least.

"Where it gets even tougher is when the Nassau County Court sends us prisoners under the Code of Criminal Procedure — we call such cases C.C.P.s — and asks us to determine whether they should be treated or tried. We have up to sixty days to observe such a patient and give him psychological tests; then we have to decide. If we find outright psychosis, it's easy, but if we don't, where should we draw the line between conduct for which he should be punished and conduct for which he wasn't really responsible?"

Dr. Clifford told me that he and Dr. Holt were going to interview one of those borderline cases in a few minutes, and that I could listen in if I liked. The prisoner — she was not, strictly speaking, a patient — was May-Belle Collins (as I shall call her). She was a thirty-year-old Negro woman sent in by the Nassau County Court, where she was up on a charge of first-degree manslaughter. Six weeks earlier, Mrs. Collins, who had been employed as a housemaid in Long Beach, had hit a man on the head, and after several weeks in a coma he had died. The court had sent her to Pilgrim to see whether she should stand trial. So far, a battery of tests, including the Thematic Apperception Test and the Rorschach, had indicated that she suffered from feelings of inadequacy and aloneness. And no wonder — in her childhood she had seen her mother slain by her father; she had been married and separated at seventeen; and she had an IQ of sixty-eight, making her, technically, a moron.

We went over to Building 24, where we met Dr. Holt and settled ourselves in a small cell-like room furnished with a table and four chairs.

"I hear May-Belle got into real trouble yesterday," said Dr. Holt.

"Yes," said Dr. Clifford. "She walloped a patient, and when the nurse tried to give her a sedative, she went into a tantrum. It took several male attendants to restrain her for an injection. But I understand she's being a very good girl today." Nevertheless, two male attendants, I gathered, were going to stand by in the hall outside during her interview with the psychiatrists.

In a moment, Mrs. Collins, a plump, smiling, fresh-faced woman, came in and sat down.

"May-Belle, do you know where you are?" Dr. Clifford asked.

"Yeah," she said. "Pilgrim State Jail!" She laughed at her little joke.

"What was all that fuss about yesterday?" Dr. Clifford asked. "Why were you so excited?"

"Well, they tell me to take some medicine," said Mrs. Collins. "That nurse, if she *axe* me to take it, I'd take it, but she *tole* me. Then she wanna gimme a needle, and I'm scared of the needle. Wha'd I need it for? I smack a girl because she scratch me, but what I'm suppose to do, *let* her scratch me?"

"Well, what about your ripping the picture off the wall and throwing it at someone?" asked Dr. Clifford.

Mrs. Collins smiled good-naturedly. "All those men comin' at me," she said, "try to tie me up. That wasn't fair, one girl and all those men."

Dr. Holt asked her about the manslaughter case. Mrs. Collins said she had been in a bar, and a man had asked her for a date; when she refused, he shoved her around and called her names, and she walked out. But he confronted her on the street, his hand in his pocket. "I din' know what he had in the pocket," she said, "but I better do suthin', and I pull my shoe off and hit him side of the head with my heel. He stumblet and I run away. Tha's all."

Dr. Holt and Dr. Clifford questioned her about the incident several times, but neither in retelling it nor in answering other questions did Mrs. Collins get confused, refer to voices, allude to persecutions, or hint at any other psychotic symptoms; she was not bright, but she was perfectly clear about everything. At last, they dismissed her.

"You see what I mean?" Dr. Clifford said to me. "There are obvious factors in this girl's life to explain why she is impulsive and easily enraged, and why she acted as she did. But are they sufficient to warrant treatment, rather than punishment? And if they are, can we really do anything for her?"

"She may be primitive," Dr. Holt added, "but I don't think we can call her psychotic. I don't think we can certify her as mentally ill."

Dr. Clifford nodded, but looked unhappy. Eventually, he and Dr. Holt agreed on a finding. It read, in part:

The examiners do not believe that this patient has a psychosis but that she is a defective individual who becomes excited when frustrated. She was not found to be in such a state of idiocy, insanity, or imbecility as to be incapable of understanding the charges against her or the proceedings or of making her defense.

As it turned out, Mrs. Collins was shipped back to county jail, and a court-appointed lawyer advised her to plead guilty to both first- and second-degree assault; she was thereupon given a five-year suspended sentence on the first charge, and a six-month sentence on the second, which she is serving in the Nassau County Jail.

It was getting near evening, and I had a final appointment with Dr. Brill. I found him in his office, talking to a tiny gray-haired woman in a nurse's uniform. He introduced her as Mrs. Katherine Elliott, chief supervising nurse of the female services at Pilgrim. "Mrs. Elliott has been with us longer than anyone else now on the staff," Dr. Brill said. "She got here before I did."

"I came here in April, 1932 — just a few months after the first building was opened up," said Mrs. Elliott. "Only a few buildings were open, and we were just beginning to receive patients. They were transfers of long-term hopeless cases from King's Park, a state hospital seven miles north of Pilgrim, and other hospitals. Pilgrim was the dumping ground for all their worst cases. We'd get the patients in by bus, a great many of them tied up in camisoles. We'd march them into the ward, lock the door, write their names on their backs in gentian violet, and then turn them loose. What screaming! What wildness! It was enough to make all of us back off and look at each other."

"Of course," Dr. Brill put in hastily, "Pilgrim wasn't planned as a dump heap for the worst patients. It was built simply as a large new facility to relieve overcrowding of the state system. Still, even when we started accepting patients directly, instead of only getting transfers, fewer than one in three got out within the first year. Nowadays, if you leave out the geriatric cases, our newly admitted patients have a four-out-of-five chance of getting out sooner or later, and most of them leave here in less than half a year."

I remarked that the figures sounded as though there had been a real breakthrough in the field of psychiatry.

Dr. Brill looked thoughtful. "Some people think so, but others pooh-pooh it," he said. "The late Albert Deutsch, a writer on mental health, said that it wasn't a breakthrough — just something of a dent. Others talk as though it were only a matter of time before drugs and other intensive treatment emptied the mental hospitals altogether. I myself take a position between these two extremes. We *have* been undergoing a gradual shrinkage since 1955, and life in the hospital *is* very different, but we're handling far larger numbers of new admissions than ever before and we're taking on all sorts of new chores for society. I don't think we're seeing a general solution of the problem — a solution that will wipe out mental illness and depopulate the hospitals the way the tuberculosis hospitals have been depopulated in recent years. But there is no doubt in my mind that we're seeing a revolutionary transformation of hospital treatment of the mentally ill."

Dr. Henry Brill, director of Pilgrim State Hospital, and First Deputy Commissioner of the New York Department of Mental Hygiene, recently reviewed both the above article and the one appearing earlier in this book, entitled "Five Who Broke Down," which in lengthier form were originally a two-part series in The New Yorker. *His comments, as to the development or changes since the articles appeared in the fall of 1961, are as follows:*

Within the hospital there have been only small changes in externals: the roads now have road signs, there are more parking areas, several of the buildings have been rehabilitated, and a fine new patients' library has been opened. With respect to patient care, the gains have been held and some new ones made. You would be interested to see the patient government [i.e., self-government], of which Dr. Barahal is justly proud; he supported its development and keeps in close touch with duly elected patient representatives, who thus have a direct influence on hospital management.

The news of greatest general interest was the opening in January, 1963, of a narcotic unit of 105 beds, soon to become 165 beds — the upshot of years of study and preparation, and the first time the State and the Department of Mental Hygiene are assuming responsibilities in this area.

During the last two years we carried out a scientific evaluation of intensified treatment of long-term schizophrenic patients — the "backward" patients, as you called them — and our findings indicate that we can look forward to better future treatment results even with present methods. Of new treatment methods, however, there is nothing spectacular to report.

Finally, for several years we have been moving toward a closer integration of all types of psychiatric services in the state . . . seeking to draw all psychiatric hospitals, clinics, and agencies, as well as all psychiatric practice, into a smoothly working and actively cooperating system. I am sure that Pilgrim's place in this new order of things will be an important one.

HENRY BRILL, M.D.

Index